Turing's Legacy
A history of computing at the
National Physical Laboratory 1945–1995

Turing's Legacy

A history of computing at the
National Physical Laboratory 1945–1995

David M Yates

Science Museum

Published 1997

All rights reserved

British Library Cataloguing-in-Publication Data
A catalogue record for this publication is available from the British Library.

Typeset by AMA Graphics Ltd, Preston, UK
Printed by Hobbs the Printers, Southampton, UK

© David M Yates 1997

ISBN 0 901805 94 7

Science Museum, Exhibition Road, London SW7 2DD, UK

Contents

1 **Introduction** 7

2 **The classical era: 1945–1956** 11
2.1 Background 11
2.2 The establishment of Mathematics Division 18
2.3 Early plans for ACE: Turing's work at NPL 19
2.4 Pilot ACE 31
2.5 Other early work in Mathematics Division 46
2.6 Other early work in Control Mechanisms and Electronics 51

3 **The Uttley era: 1957–1966** 57
3.1 Outline of developments 57
3.2 ACE 66
3.3 Adaptive control 72
3.4 Pattern recognition 80
3.5 Biology and psychology related to recognition and control 85
3.6 Machine translation 93
3.7 Information retrieval 100
3.8 Cryotrons 103
3.9 Computing aspects of the work of Mathematics Division 107

4 **The Davies era: 1966–1978** 117
4.1 Outline of developments 117
4.2 Data communications 126
4.3 Information systems 147
4.4 Palantype transcription 160
4.5 Pattern recognition 165
4.6 Man–machine interaction 175
4.7 Mathematics and computing services 183

5 **The Albasiny era: 1978–1987** 199
5.1 Outline of developments 199
5.2 Protocol standards 203
5.3 Data security 210
5.4 Multiprocessors 216
5.5 Software engineering standards 219
5.6 Mathematical software 227
5.7 Human–computer interaction 232
5.8 Vision systems 239
5.9 Telerobotics 240
5.10 Computing services 242

6 Agency status and detachment from Government: 1987–1995   247

6.1 Outline of developments   247
6.2 Protocol standards   250
6.3 Data security   254
6.4 Mathematical software   260
6.5 Software engineering   268
6.6 Parallel processing   273
6.7 Human–computer interaction   275
6.8 Computing services   281

7 Retrospective postscript   285

Annex A: People   289

Annex B: Patents   319

Acronyms and abbreviations   323

List of illustrations   326

References and bibliography   329

Index   341

1 Introduction

In 1949 it was confidently predicted by one of the leading experts of the day that Britain's computing needs could be met by four machines[1]. Yet computers are now used everywhere from designing drugs to games for three-year-olds: in composing music, in enhancing pictures of Mars, and in tracking albatrosses, as well as in the more traditional areas of banking, insurance, weather forecasting, newspaper production and so on. And you may well have one at home: by 1992 more packaged software was sold per day in the United States ($63.5m) than books ($47m).

In fact in the last fifty years computers have revolutionised, directly or indirectly, nearly every working activity in the developed world, and many leisure pursuits as well. This headlong 'progress' shows no signs of slowing down. Far-reaching developments are still under way, in particular those popularly labelled the Information Superhighway. Used wisely, this technology is capable of transforming the present availability of information, and so the quality of many human decisions, both major and minor. Few revolutions could be of more lasting significance. The National Physical Laboratory at Teddington in south-west London is one of the places where all this started.

Scope

The aim of this book is to outline how and why NPL became involved in computing at the end of the Second World War, and what has happened since. It covers the vital contribution of the enigmatic figure of Alan Turing, the Pilot ACE computer developed from his plans, and the pioneering work on computer networks led by Donald Davies. More recent years could hardly be quite as dramatic, but they make an instructive story of continuing tension between professional (engineering and scientific) motivation on the one hand and political and commercial forces on the other which continues to unfold unpredictably to this day.

The aim is to be factual and not, in general, to make value judgements. Particularly in more recent years, only an outline can be given if the account is to keep within reasonable bounds. This means that no specialist knowledge is required of the reader. Readers who do have special knowledge in any area will therefore not find their pet subject covered in detail, but should find guidance for further reading if they want to know in more detail what went on.

---

[1] Professor D R Hartree, quoted by Hendry ref. 64 p.51; see also Halsbury ref. 60 p.155 and Lavington ref. 83 p.104.

Introduction

Demarcation is a necessary but difficult requirement in any historical survey. In this case my main concern is with the line of development starting with the foundation of Mathematics Division NPL in 1945, the subsequent computer development work, the establishment of the Control Mechanisms and Electronics Division in 1954 and its subsequent transformations leading to the work of the present Centre for Information Systems Engineering. Also arising directly from the start of Mathematics Division, as is shown in fig. 1, there are two other threads which can be clearly traced through to the present day: work on numerical analysis and on computing services. These are also covered, but more briefly than the computing research area. This does not imply any value judgement—it is simply that these areas deserve their own more specialist histories which are not for me to compile, and indeed in the case of the mathematical work considerable material has been prepared by Ernie Albasiny based on earlier work by Jack Michel (ref. 1).

Care is needed not to judge past work by present criteria, or for that matter present work by past criteria. NPL has evolved considerably in 50 years and in the early years of the period the 'pure research' motivation was strong. I have tried to avoid both the rosy glow in which it is easy to bathe the past and the taking of sides in old controversies.

Structure

The division into eras shown in the contents list is a natural one because the changes of Superintendent brought with them major shifts in the programme of work. However, these chronological divisions have not been rigorously adhered to, projects which belong chiefly in one era being described there in full to avoid artificial breaks in the account.

Balance

If some work has been given particularly short shrift, this may be for one of two reasons: either it needs specialist knowledge to follow more than a brief description, for example control systems theory; or detailed records of the work have not survived. This latter point is particularly significant: it has been common practice for detailed files of correspondence to be destroyed a few years after an item of work has been completed. But some old files have survived because of personal interest, which add considerable background to the purely technical published reports, and this leads to some imbalance in the summaries of projects given here. As with any historical account, it has to be highly selective and therefore reflects the compiler's personal view however much he may try to remain impartial.

Introduction

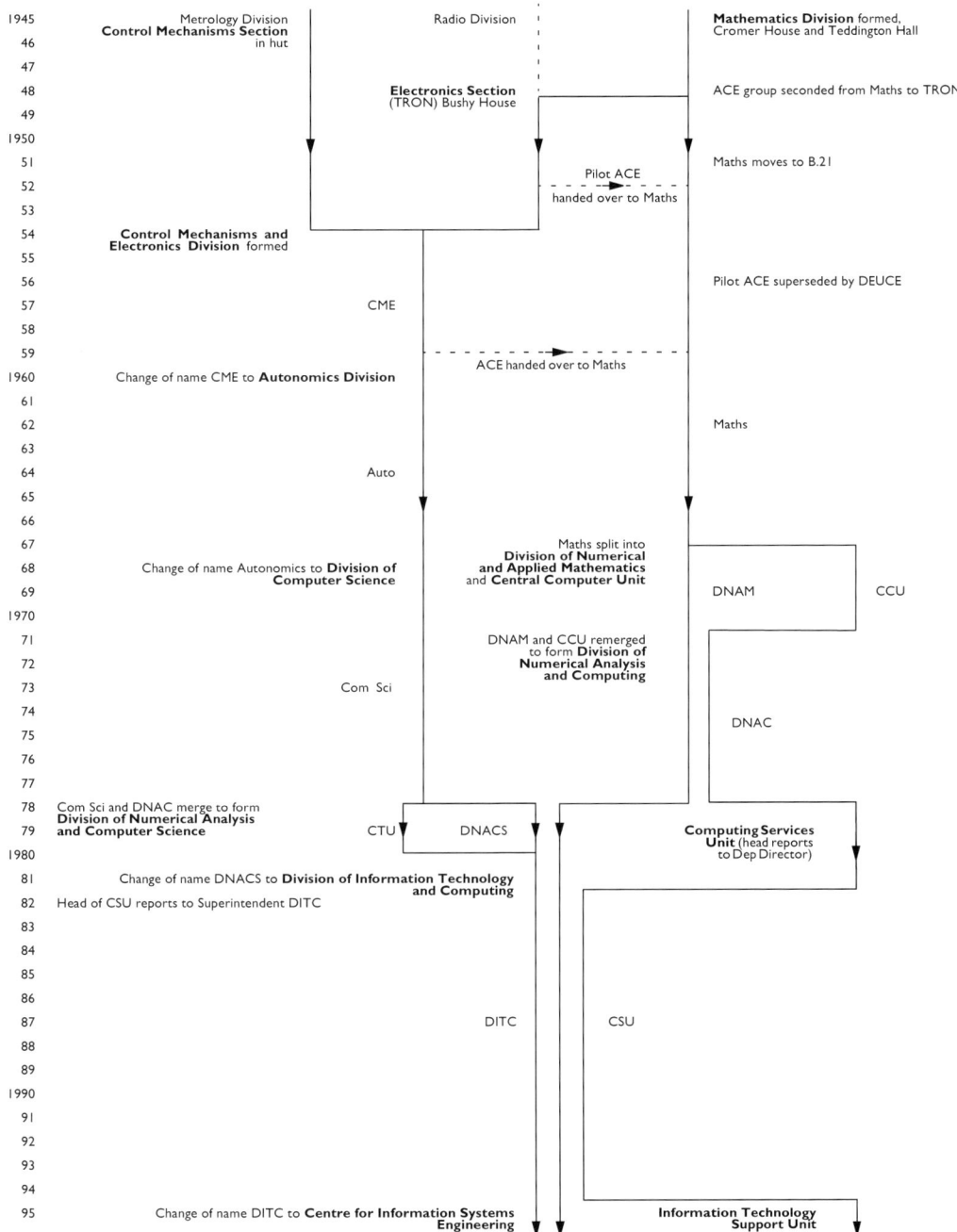

Figure 1. Organisational history of computing at NPL.

Sources, references and bibliography

The major sources are the NPL Annual Reports (ref. 99), the series of Divisional reports on individual items of work, other technical publications by staff, the NPL Executive Committee minutes (ref. 98), and the Woodger archive in the Science Museum (ref. 180); *NPL News* (ref. 102) and the sets of Open Day handouts (ref. 114) have also been very useful.

Introduction

In several areas detailed historical work has already been done, and I am happy to acknowledge my debt to Dr Mary Croarken for her scholarly study of early scientific computing in Britain (ref. 25) which gives particular attention to NPL; to Andrew Hodges for his most impressive and sympathetic biography of Alan Turing (ref. 66); to the late Ted Pyatt for his work on the history of NPL as a whole (ref. 126); and to Dr Martin Campbell-Kelly for three excellent papers, two on early programming (refs 15, 16) and one on NPL's pioneering work on data communications (ref. 17).

The references section (p.329) aims to list major sources, books written by members of staff, and all significant early papers (pre-1957). Documents with no author's name issued by institutions, including NPL, are listed under the name of the institution. Most individual sections in the book include a list of relevant publications by members of NPL staff; in several cases a complete list would be prohibitively long, and a selection has been made.

Acknowledgements

I am very grateful to all the following: Dr Peter Clapham, then Director and Chief Executive of NPL, and Dr Andrew Wallard, Deputy Director, for their permission to use NPL resources in the compilation; NPL Management Ltd for continuing this arrangement when they took over the management of the Laboratory in October 1995; Adrian Marks, Head of the then Division of Information Technology and Computing, for constant co-operation; Keith Dennis, Bill Bunce, Jackie Goodwin and NPL Personnel Section staff; Sue Osborne and NPL Library staff; Photographic Section NPL; the Laboratory's then Marketing and Information Services Unit, represented by Hilary Fuller, for permission to use pictures which are Crown Copyright, and for providing copies of photographs; Robin Barker, for preparing a PostScript® description of the floor tiling pattern on which the cover design is based (see p.59 for details); and the following for very kindly reading and commenting on sections in draft: Derek Barber, Keith Bartlett, Donald Bell, Mike Bevan, Nigel Bevan, Dickie Bird, Frank Blake, Bernard Chorley, David Clayden, John Cooper, Maurice Cox, Donald Davies, Clive Hall, Percy Hammond, Susan Hodson, Celia Kirkby, Tony Mansfield, Jack Michel, Graeme Parkin, John Parks, Wyn Price, Dave Rayner, David Schofield, Michael Stevens, Peter Stuart, George Symm, Peter Vaswani, Tom Vickers, Andrew Wallard, Bob Watson, Brian Wichmann, Peter Wilkinson, Fiona Williams, Mike Woodger and Michael Wright. I am also most grateful to Doron Swade, Senior Curator of Computing at the Science Museum, and Anna Hodson, then Publications Manager, for their endorsement of the book, and to Giskin Day of the Museum's Publications Department for all her work in preparing it for the printers.

2 The classical era: 1945–1956

2.1 Background

The curtain rises on the history of computing at NPL one morning in May 1945, to reveal Mr J R Womersley, the Superintendent of Mathematics Division, alone in his office; it is his first working day at NPL, and he is alone because the Division is newly created and he has as yet no staff. He has just returned from a thought-provoking visit to the USA, and his task now is to build a Division to carry out research into new computing methods and machines, and to provide mathematical and computational services; as early priorities he must recruit staff, organise training and buy equipment. For the moment we will leave him pondering on where to start, and look briefly at how he came to be there and what independent influences were contributing to the momentous events which were soon to follow.

NPL and its need for computation

Since its foundation in 1900, the National Physical Laboratory had been providing services to the UK in practical matters relating to physics. Then as now, the fundamental national need in this area was for consistent standards of physical measurement, and the Laboratory was responsible for realising the internationally agreed standards and enabling their dissemination in the UK through instrument testing, certification and calibration services. It also provided advice and help to industrial organisations faced with problems beyond their own capabilities. This meant that there was a flavour of engineering about much of the programme of work: aerodynamics, metallurgy, ship research and radio were amongst the major topics. Research into new techniques in all these areas was important to ensure that UK practice was kept up to date, but the emphasis was on services and the research element did not dominate even though the programme was guided by a General Board and Executive Committee appointed by the Royal Society. (From the foundation of the Department of Scientific and Industrial Research (DSIR) in 1918, the Laboratory was brought under its aegis, but this was a light hand on the tiller; the work programme remained firmly in the hands of the Executive Committee.) The Laboratory was conscious of its unique national role and proud of its reputation for the highest standards of work. The Second World War changed the nature of many of the day-to-day problems and their urgency, but the Laboratory's fundamental role remained the same; its diverse wartime tasks, most spectacularly the use of ship tanks to test the bounce of the Dambusters' bombs, simply reflected the new national priorities.

Since the laws of physics are mathematical, and the immediate result of any measurement is a number, NPL was from its foundation much concerned with numerical calculations. In the earliest days many of these were carried out with pen and paper using printed tables of logarithms, or with slide rules where these gave enough accuracy, but mechanical desktop calculating machines, which had been widely used in commerce in the second half of the nineteenth century, were rapidly gaining ground in the scientific community. The word computer was in common use; it meant a person employed to do calculations.

The influence of wartime computing services

At the start of the Second World War, the armed services had two particular needs for large-scale calculations: navigation and ballistics (the computation of the trajectories of missiles). The publication of astronomical tables for navigation was the responsibility of the Nautical Almanac Office (NAO) in the Admiralty, and ballistics work was carried out by the External Ballistics Board of the Ministry of Supply (which served both the Army and the Royal Air Force). Both these bodies employed mathematicians to specify the tedious computational work involved. Both soon found that they were being asked to solve mathematical problems sent to them by other areas of their ministries and in some cases from outside. This was particularly true of the NAO, and early in 1943 an Admiralty Computing Service was established, using the resources of the NAO at Bath, to meet this widening demand. Amongst its staff were E T Goodwin (previously with the Ministry of Supply at the Cambridge Mathematical Laboratory which they had leased), F W J Olver and L Fox. Amongst those employed by the Ministry of Supply at this time were J G Hayes, J G L Michel, T Vickers, J H Wilkinson, J R Womersley and M Woodger. All those named were later to join Mathematics Division NPL, and indeed this list includes most of the Division's senior staff in its early years.

Those responsible for the Admiralty Computing Service soon felt that the process of centralisation of services had not gone far enough; what was needed was a national computing organisation which would have the best resources in staff and equipment and make them available to all departments and their contractors. They prepared a *Memorandum on the Centralization of Computation in a National Mathematical Laboratory* (see Croarken (1990), ref. 25 pp.75–77), which was sent to the secretary of the Department of Scientific and Industrial Research probably in the autumn of 1943[1]. This remarkably comprehensive document covered the gains in efficiency and economy foreseen from the centralisation, the proposal that the new laboratory should carry out research into both machines and numerical techniques in addition to its prime role of providing mathematical and computational services, and explicitly recommended that it should 'act generally in the sphere of (numerical) mathematics and computation in a way similar to that in which the National Physical Laboratory acts in the sphere of physics'. Their vision went well beyond the current wartime needs and was clearly recommending a new permanent establishment.

This suggestion fitted in well with a wide perception that the existing fragmentation of computing services was inefficient. The Director of NPL, Sir Charles Darwin, had said to the Advisory Council of DSIR at their meeting on 10 March 1943 that 'he was inclining more and more to the opinion that a Mathematical Department should be established at the National Physical Laboratory' (ref. 40, minute 61), and he had amplified his ideas in a paper to the NPL Executive Committee (ref. 26) in about October 1943. In response to these recommendations DSIR established an Interdepartmental Technical Committee to 'examine the question of whether it is desirable to establish under Government control a Central Mathematical Station, and, if so, to make recommendations on the form it should take'. The committee was chaired by Sir Charles Darwin and included senior staff from the Admiralty Computing Service and the Ministry of Supply, notably D R Hartree, Professor of Applied Mathematics at Manchester, member of the NPL Executive Committee, and an influential figure throughout all these deliberations. The Committee's report (ref. 27), presented to the DSIR Advisory Council on 10 May 1944, recommended that a Central Mathematical Station should be established, with a role similar to that proposed in the Admiralty memorandum but with a significant change of emphasis, research being given much greater prominence. In the words of the report, the station was to:

(1) Undertake research into new computing methods and machines.
(2) Encourage the development of new computing methods and instruments and the dissemination of knowledge of them and of existing methods.
(3) Deal with problems arising from statistical science, in particular by assisting in the application of statistical methods to research, development and production problems in industry and to problems arising in the physical sciences and engineering, and by research into new statistical techniques. It would in general exclude economic, sociological and biological statistics from its purview.

---

[1] In her reference to this undated document Croarken (ref. 25) describes it as 'probably written . . . in 1944', but the DSIR Advisory Council covering note for the subsequent Interdepartmental Committee Report (ref. 27) says '. . . in the Autumn of 1943, the Admiralty suggested to the Department [DSIR] that consideration should be given to the provision of a computational service for Government Departments by an appropriate central authority', and this probably refers to the same Admiralty initiative.

(4) Advise on the need for new mathematical tables, and, if necessary, prepare them.
(5) Provide computing services for Government Departments, industry and Universities.
(6) Act as consultant on mathematical and statistical techniques to Departments, industry and Universities.

The report estimated that the station would need 25 scientific staff, 50 supporting staff, and a comprehensive set of equipment including the largest differential analyser in Britain, and recommended that it should 'constitute, at least in the first instance, a Division of the National Physical Laboratory'. This recommendation was accepted by the Advisory Council, subject to the agreement of the NPL Executive Committee and Treasury approval. Six days later, on 16 May, the NPL Committee gave its agreement, and at its next meeting on 20 June set up a subcommittee to interview candidates for the post of Superintendent of the new Division. The interviews were delayed briefly waiting for Treasury approval. Two candidates were eventually interviewed on 27 September, both of whom had been members of the DSIR Interdepartmental Committee. One, D H Sadler, was Superintendent of the Nautical Almanac Office and as such must have had a strong case, but the subcommittee unanimously recommended that the post should be offered to the other candidate, J R Womersley of the Ministry of Supply Advisory Service on Statistical Methods. This offer was agreed by the Executive Committee on 24 October. Womersley accepted, and on 21 November the Committee agreed that the Superintendent-elect should be invited to address their next meeting.

Sticking closely to the recommendations of the Interdepartmental Committee, Womersley duly prepared plans for his new Division (ref. 173), which he presented to the Executive Committee on 19 December 1944. The proposal included computing services, consultancy, numerical research, the design and construction of new types of computing machinery, and the establishment of a specialist library, but did not expand on the users of the services, the staff required or the necessary equipment. In February 1945 Womersley started an extensive tour of relevant establishments in the United States. At the University of Pennsylvania he saw ENIAC (a then-secret and still incomplete versatile electronic calculator intended for ballistic computations, not quite a computer in the modern sense because its program was not stored internally). Also, and crucially, he was told about their plans for its successor EDVAC, which was to be a true electronic stored-program computer.

Further details of the wartime computing services and the events leading up to the establishment of Mathematics Division are given by Mary Croarken (ref. 25 pp.61–88).

The work of Alan Turing up to 1945

The last element in the background to the formation of Mathematics Division is the work of Alan Turing before he joined NPL in October 1945. An outline of his career is given later (p.310); here we will cover the two major items up to 1945.

In 1928, following the work of Russell and others on the provision of a reliable formal basis for mathematics, Hilbert had proposed three remaining fundamental questions: was mathematics *complete*, in the sense that every well-formed statement could be either proved or disproved; was it *consistent*, in the sense that no contradictory statements could be deduced from its axioms; and was it *decidable*, in the sense that there existed a method for determining whether a given statement was true or false[2]. Two years later, Gödel startled everyone by giving an account of his proof that systems which include ordinary arithmetic cannot be both complete and consistent, thus effectively disposing of Hilbert's first question.

In 1937, then a Fellow of King's College Cambridge, Alan Turing published his paper on computable numbers (ref. 137), which forms one of the main foundations of the science and technology of computers. The paper does two things. Its conclusion is to answer Hilbert's third question (the *Entscheidungsproblem*) by showing that mathematics is not decidable. Although this was a very significant result, unfortunately for Turing it had in fact been arrived at independently and published slightly earlier by Alonzo Church. But to reach his conclusion Turing first built up a whole new conceptual framework: a hypothetical logical machine equipped with an indefinitely long tape which it could move in either direction and on which it could read, write and erase symbols. The machine, later to be known as a Turing Machine, had a finite number of internal states and a fixed *configuration table* which showed, for each internal state and symbol read, (1) the symbol to be written if any, (2) whether the tape was to be moved and if so which way, and (3) the number of the next state. Thus the sequence of states was entirely determined by the configuration table and the initial state and position of the tape. The sequence of states might terminate after a finite number of steps, or it might go on for ever. Turing then described a particular machine, now called a Universal Turing Machine, which could produce the same result as any other machine if the configuration table of that machine was written in advance in a suitable form on the tape. This Universal Machine has all the essential properties of a programmable computer. The numbers which it could calculate Turing called *computable numbers*. He

---

[2] It may appear that completeness and decidability are the same, but this is not so, because it might be possible to show that all statements were either provable or disprovable without showing how to prove or disprove any particular statement.

showed that not all numbers are computable, and his argument applies without significant change to all modern computers. He was not proposing the Universal Turing Machine as a practical device, and indeed although one could be made, or simulated on a computer, the task would be complex and ultimately unrewarding because any work for the machine other than the most trivial would be extraordinarily tedious to specify. But the intellectual stride he had made was enormous, and provided in advance a clear theoretical foundation for the practical machines which were eventually to be built, for their limitations and for their unprecedented versatility.

We turn now to a very different topic: the rumour of war, and the critical importance in war of deciphering messages in code sent by the enemy. In 1938, with hostilities looking increasingly likely, the British security authorities were making provisional plans to take on 60 more cryptanalysts. They were seeking 'men of the Professor type' who could fight the intellectual battle of cryptanalysis with imagination, logic and persistence. Amongst those considered was Alan Turing, who went on a course at the so-called Government Code and Cypher School in the summer of 1938. As soon as war was declared he joined the 'School', by then evacuated from London to Bletchley Park in Buckinghamshire. He was amongst the first of the new recruits to arrive; numbers built up gradually over the next year.

To encrypt military messages, the Germans used an electro-mechanical machine, the Enigma. The basic principles of this machine were well known (it had been exhibited publicly in 1923), but it later underwent several successive enhancements and the conventions for using it were also changed. Before the war, the Polish security authorities had had a remarkable degree of success in deciphering messages sent using this system, using purpose-built electromechanical devices called *Bombas*[3]. When the details of this work were passed to the British and French authorities in July 1939, the Poles had become unable to read the German traffic because of the latest improvement to the Enigma. This was still the position when Turing arrived at Bletchley Park. With Gordon Welchman, he devised a British 'Bombe' using relay technology, whose task was to generate automatically a long sequence of patterns, corresponding to possible settings of parts of the Enigma, and to stop automatically when certain criteria were met. This machine was completed and first used in mid-1940. Supplemented by vital instructions captured from German ships, it greatly improved the ability of the team to decrypt traffic in bulk. Even more importantly, it reduced the time taken for

---

[3] It has been suggested that Bombas were given this name because they ticked, but Donald Davies tells me he has heard, and considers more likely, an alternative explanation: that it was chosen because they were similar in shape to a popular ice-cream called a Bomba.

decryption, so that by June 1941 direct operational advantage could be taken of the deciphered naval messages (Luftwaffe messages used a somewhat simpler Enigma system and had been routinely broken from May 1940). The success with naval traffic resulted in a mass of material which the organisation took some time to learn to digest. Staffing was inadequate, and in October 1941 Turing and three colleagues wrote directly to Winston Churchill to persuade him to provide the resources they needed, with startling results. The balance in the vital U-boat war, the Battle of the Atlantic, swung in favour of Britain and her allies as a direct result of Turing and Welchman's success.

In February 1942 a new Enigma system was introduced for ocean-going U-boats and their messages could no longer be routinely decrypted. It was not until December, and then only because of carelessness by those in charge of the German use of the system, that the position was partially restored, and it was June 1943 before the balance was finally settled in favour of the Allies.

In the early years Turing had been in charge of the team responsible for the naval Enigma, but as the operation grew in scale it needed organisational skills he did not possess and his position was eventually taken over by C H O'D Alexander. His personal contribution to the war effort was of the very greatest significance because of the seriousness of the U-boat threat to Britain's convoy lifeline.

In 1943 Colossus, an electronic apparatus to help with decryption, was designed at Bletchley Park and built for them by the Post Office Research Station at Dollis Hill. The first Colossus, installed and working by December 1943, was followed by several more. Because it was programmable and electronic this system was an important step in the pre-history of computer technology, and indeed was two years ahead of its nearest American counterpart, the ENIAC. However, Colossus was not general-purpose and neither it nor ENIAC used internally stored programs, so they could not be called computers in the modern sense. Turing took little if any part in the development of Colossus or its predecessors the Robinsons, being by then somewhat shunted off from the mainstream of cryptanalytic work developing a system of speech encryption (Delilah). Although this never got beyond the prototype stage, it gave him a working if somewhat amateurish familiarity with practical electronics which was to prove useful background to his later work.

Further details of Alan Turing's work, both on computable numbers and on cryptanalysis, are given in Andrew Hodges' excellent biography (ref. 66).

2.2 The establishment of Mathematics Division

We can now return to Mr Womersley whom we left in May 1945 pondering on his responsibility for the foundation of Mathematics Division. His first priority was recruitment, and the main sources of professional staff were clearly the Admiralty Computing Service and the Ministry of Supply, where staff taken on for the duration of the war were looking for new peacetime careers, and where an important part of the impetus for the new Division had originated. The contacts and perhaps informal understandings that Womersley already had with many of those named above (p.12) had to be followed up, and formal Civil Service transfer procedures initiated. One key appointment which seems to have been very much his own work was that of Alan Turing. He knew of the pre-war paper on computable numbers, understood that the EDVAC which he had heard about on his US visit was to be a practical embodiment of the principles of the abstract machines Turing had invented, and decided he would be a useful recruit. In June 1945 he arranged to meet Turing, persuaded him to join NPL, organised the necessary interview, and made sure the NPL authorities realised that he would be a valuable acquisition (these key actions were recorded by Womersley in a later historical summary, ref. 175). The formal offer (of a post as Temporary Senior Scientific Officer) was duly made, and Turing accepted.

As a result of these efforts by Womersley, staff began to join the infant Division, which was accommodated in Cromer House at the north end of the NPL site (see map, fig. 31 p.126). Goodwin and Olver were amongst the first to arrive, on 16 September; Turing and Fox both joined on 1 October; and junior staff were found through NPL's normal recruitment procedures. By 23 October the Director was able to report to the Executive Committee that the Division was now functioning, with a staff of 22; by the end of 1945 this had risen to 27, and before long the Division expanded into the next-door building, Teddington Hall.

Desktop calculators, some 'liberated' from Germany, and punched-card equipment were acquired, and, on 1 December 1945, the differential analyser at Manchester University was taken over from the Ministry of Supply which had run it during the war. Differential analysers were devices for solving certain classes of differential equations; their operation and history at NPL is described briefly below (pp.47–49). J G L Michel, who had used the Manchester machine during the war, joined NPL staff on 1 January 1946, though until 1948 he remained in Manchester with the machine.

By the end of 1945 Mathematics Division had four sections: general computing, punched-card equipment, mathematical statistics and the differential analyser. They had undertaken various computational tasks for the Admiralty and had made 'a preliminary study of the possibility of constructing an automatic electronic computing engine'. These modest words in the 1940–45 report describe what was with hindsight one of the most important pieces of work in the history of the Laboratory, Turing's plans for the ACE computer. Because of their significance, these plans, and the subsequent early history of the ACE project, are described next in sections 2.3 and 2.4; remaining work in the early years of Mathematics Division is outlined in section 2.5.

2.3   Early plans for ACE: Turing's work at NPL

At least from June 1945 when he knew he would be joining NPL, Turing had been working on the design of an electronic digital stored-program computing machine. From his knowledge of his own abstract machines, the EDVAC plans and (it seems reasonable to assume) Colossus, coupled with his personal experience of electronics, he was confident that such a machine could be built and would be capable of carrying out any procedure that could be defined for it, subject only to the limitations of its finite memory size and finite speed of calculation. Although spending most of his time in late 1945 on the design of the machine and on experimental programming for it, his underlying interest was broader. Even in the Bletchley Park days, he had had vigorous discussions with his colleagues on the mechanisation of thought processes (as remembered by Michie, see Randell ref. 127 p.6). Later, probably in 1946, he was to write revealingly to Professor Ross Ashby: 'In working on the ACE I am more interested in the possibility of producing models of the action of the brain than in the practical applications to computing' (there is a copy of this letter in the Woodger Papers, ref. 180, folder M11). True to his genius, he had his eye on the evolutionary potential of what he was doing as well as on the immediate task.

The plans he produced were written up as a detailed report (ref. 138) for the NPL Executive Committee. In fact the report went into far more detail than the Committee could be expected to absorb, and Womersley wrote a supportive 'executive summary' paper (ref. 174) to introduce it. The two documents, which both used for the first time the acronym ACE (Automatic Computing Engine) devised by Womersley, were available to the Committee at its meeting on 19 February 1946, though they were not presented or discussed until the next meeting on 19 March; the Committee then 'resolved unanimously to support the proposal with enthusiasm'. As a result of Turing's work as detailed in this report, NPL can claim to have been, throughout 1946, at least joint world leaders in the development of computers[4]. Their only rivals were American groups, particularly those at Princeton led by von Neumann and the Moore School, though many others were developing an active interest. The report, which is summarised below, was an outstanding achievement, and ranks with *Computable Numbers* and cryptanalysis to form the triple crown of Turing's tragically short career.

Turing's 1945 design for ACE

Turing's report is divided into two parts: a 'Descriptive Account', mainly very readable, followed by detailed and sometimes obscure 'Technical Proposals'. Programming techniques are covered as well as hardware. The two key factors in the design are the decision to keep the number of valves to a minimum because of their unreliability, and the related choice of acoustic delay lines[5] as the main data-storage medium. As far as possible, complexity was to be left to program libraries rather than incorporated in the hardware.

The word length was provisionally fixed at 32 bits, and an instruction, including source and destination addresses, occupied one word (the paper is believed to be the first to use 'word' in this sense). The proposed memory consisted of 'between 50 and 500 mercury tanks with a capacity of about 1000 [binary] digits each' and 'quick reference temporary storage units (TS) probably numbering about 50 and each with a capacity of say 32 binary digits'; in total between 6.5 and 65 Kbytes in modern terms. The large tanks were designed to circulate in 1.024 msec, equivalent to one bit per microsecond; this clock rate of 1 MHz governed all the detailed functions of the machine. There was no single accumulator; an instruction called for one of:

(a) a transfer from one storage to another;
(b) an arithmetic operation (add, subtract, or multiply) on two fixed TS, with the result in another TS; there was provision for a double-length result;
(c) a bitwise logical operation (A & B; A ∨ B (inclusive); ~ A; or A ≡ B) again on two fixed TS with result in another fixed TS;
(d) a transfer from memory to cards or vice versa;
(e) an unconditional jump to a specified next instruction instead of taking the next in sequence as usual.

---

[4] For example, Carpenter and Doran (ref. 18 p.269), comparing the maturity of Turing's proposal with von Neumann's Draft Report on the EDVAC, say 'Turing's proposal is quite possibly the first complete design of a stored program computer architecture'. As late as January 1947, in Hodges' view (ref. 66 p.355) 'the Americans were no further ahead in constructing an electronic computer than was the NPL, and had run into parallel problems', in particular the cultural frontier between mathematics and engineering.

[5] An *acoustic delay line* is a memory device in which a string of binary digits is represented as a sequence of pulses of sound waves travelling down a long object, usually a liquid-filled tube. When a pulse gets to the end of the tube it is converted temporarily back to electrical form, amplified and reshaped as necessary, and then sent off from the beginning of the tube again. The technology had been used in radar systems during the war though it needed considerable refinement for computer use.

Conditional branching was done by programming in the sense that an instruction could be formed by calculation, planted, and then jumped to. Subroutine calls likewise had to be programmed by storing the return address. Turing was very clear about the importance of the ability to nest subroutines, and describes (p.12) what would now be called a stack for handling the return addresses. This meant that the processes of subroutine call ('BURY') and return ('UNBURY') were sufficiently complex to need library routines of their own.

Probably the first ever exhortation to good practice in the documentation of software is given in the report (p.29). Each 'instruction table' (program) is to have its own 'General Description' and there is a neat definition of its properties in the normal case where one program calls on others: 'It is intended that when we are trying to understand a table all the information that is needed about the subsidiaries to it should be obtainable from their general descriptions.'

The importance of checking performance is emphasised: built-in checks, both hardware and software, and program testing are all mentioned. 'In order to inspire confidence the checking must have some visible manifestations . . . there could be a facility whereby this was laid on temporarily at moments of shaken confidence.'

On the art of programming (p.18): 'Instruction tables will have to be made up by mathematicians with computing experience and perhaps a certain puzzle-solving ability. There will probably be a great deal of work of this kind to be done . . . This process of constructing instruction tables should be very fascinating. There is no real danger of it ever becoming a drudge, for any processes that are quite mechanical may be turned over to the machine itself.'

The need to link-edit library routines into a new program is addressed (pp.13–14), though Turing recommends that this should be done off-line on the program cards 'by a straightforward sorting and collating process'.

To illustrate the scope of the machine, Turing gives an interesting list of ten tasks:

> Problem 1. Construction of range tables. The complete process of range-table construction could be carried out as a single job. This would involve calculation of trajectories by small arcs . . .
>
> Problem 2. To find the potential distribution outside a charged conducting cube. This is a problem which could easily be tackled by the machine by a method of successive approximations . . .
>
> Problem 3. The solution of simultaneous linear equations . . . If we have a storage capacity of 6400 numbers we cannot expect to be able to solve equations in more than about 50 unknowns. In practice, however, the majority of problems have very degenerate matrices and we do not need to store anything like as much . . .

Problem 4. To calculate the radiation from the open end of a rectangular wave-guide . . .

Problem 5. Given two matrices of degree less than 30 whose coefficients are polynomials of degree less than 10, the machine could multiply the matrices together, giving a result which is another matrix also having polynomial coefficients. This has important applications in the design of optical instruments.

Problem 6. Given a complicated electrical circuit and the characteristics of its components, the response to given input signals could be calculated. A standard code for the description of the components could easily be devised for this purpose, and also a code for describing connections. There is no need for the characteristics to be linear.

Problem 7. It would not be possible for the machine to integrate the area under a curve, as the machine will have no appropriate input.

Problem 8. To count the number of butchers due to be demobilised in June 1946 from cards prepared from the army records. The machine would be quite capable of doing this, but it would not be a suitable job for it. The speed at which it could be done would be limited by the rate at which cards can be read, and the high speed and other valuable characteristics of the calculator would never be brought into play. Such a job can and should be done with standard Hollerith [i.e. punched-card] equipment.

Problem 9. A jig-saw puzzle is made up by cutting up a halma-board into pieces each consisting of a number of whole squares. The calculator could be made to find a solution of the jig-saw, and, if they were not too numerous, to list all the solutions.

This particular problem is of no great importance, but it is typical of a very large class of non-numerical problems that can be treated by the calculator. Some of these have great military importance [presumably an oblique reference to cryptanalysis], and others are of immense interest to mathematicians.

Problem 10. Given a position in chess the machine could be made to list all the 'winning combinations' to a depth of about three moves on either side. This is not unlike the previous problem, but raises the question 'can the machine play chess?' It could fairly easily be made to play a rather bad game. It would be bad because chess requires intelligence. We stated at the beginning of this section that the machine should be treated as entirely without intelligence. There are indications however that it is possible to make the machine display intelligence at the risk of its making occasional serious mistakes. By following up this aspect the machine could probably be made to play very good chess.

Input and output were to be by punched cards (pp.3, 12–14). It is interesting that in spite of the fact that fast paper-tape readers were used on Colossus, Turing does not mention the possibility of their being used on ACE.

The report also considers briefly the accommodation needed for the machine and its cost (£11,200, though Womersley in the accompanying paper prudently increases this estimate to £50,000–£60,000). A long section goes into great detail about the theory of the delay lines, calculating that their stability and freedom from error should be satisfactory on the basis of the known properties of the piezoelectric crystals and the liquid medium, and determining design details including the temperature-control requirements.

One might expect some reference to *Computable Numbers,* but this does not appear; von Neumann's draft report on the EDVAC (ref. 150) is however explicitly recommended as parallel reading. The report has many trivial errors; Turing was notoriously careless of such matters.

In summary: though the architecture of Turing's machine differs in many respects from von Neumann's, the broad concepts are the same; the hardware plans are much more complete than von Neumann's, more attention being given to input/output arrangements and to the central control circuits; and much more detailed and perceptive consideration is given to software. In particular Turing shows that he understands the importance and great power of the concept we would now call a procedure: 'Once we have written down how an operation is to be done we can use it as a subsidiary to any other operation,' (p.11) and 'The majority of actual instruction tables will consist almost entirely of the initiation of subsidiary operations and transfers of material' (p.29). Turing sees the computer as a liberator, opening up new possibilities, whereas von Neumann describes it in narrower terms, as a tool for carrying out numerical calculations faster than previously possible.

What happened to Turing's proposals in 1946–48

Unfortunately for the UK, the talents needed to take Turing's ideas and turn them into a detailed practical design and then into hardware were simply not available at NPL in 1946. This was not Bletchley Park, with the Prime Minister's personal backing, a staff of many thousands, and the electronic development skills of the Post Office giving their requests top priority. The authorities saw ACE as deserving the highest priority among the larger projects in Mathematics Division (ref. 98, 19.3.46, p.8), but at that time no one but Turing was working on it because Womersley had no appropriate resources and no clear means of getting them.

Some steps were however taken to improve the position. As explained above, acoustic delay lines were an important feature of Turing's design, and in June 1946 agreement was reached with the Post Office that they would undertake the development work these required. Probably there was an understanding that the Post Office was to undertake all construction work on ACE, with this as a first step, but this is not certain. Also, and in the long term very significantly for the future of computing at NPL, two

> ❑ SIDELINE ❑ DETOUR ❑ DIGRESSION ❑ BYWAY ❑ SCENIC ROUTE ❑
>
> **Glimpses of Turing**
>
> An informal look back over the first ten years of Mathematics Division in NPL News for August 1955 (ref. 57 p.3) includes two brief impressions of Turing. In Cromer House: '... Turing worked at his typewriter, behind closed doors which not even the Superintendent dared penetrate, tapping out ideas which culminated in the Pilot ACE...'; and later, in Teddington Hall: '... we were able to catch glimpses of Turing, on the ground floor and in the basement, sitting with legs off ground, gingerly probing a mass of wires, and fiddling about with drain pipes.' The 'drain pipes' were presumably experimental delay lines.

assistants were recruited for Turing. J H Wilkinson, a mathematician who before his wartime work in the Ministry of Supply had had a glittering undergraduate career at Cambridge, joined on 1 May 1946, followed by Mike Woodger on 20 May.

During 1946 the logical design of ACE went through many modifications, and considerable work was expended in testing the programming system. Pioneering library routines were written for division, square root, exponentiation, sine, cosine, logarithm, multiplication of complex numbers, scalar product of vectors, matrix products, and the solution of sets of linear equations; yet no one was doing anything effective about the critical need for detailed electronic design and construction. On 22 October Darwin reported to the Executive Committee that the assistance from the Post Office was not as great as expected. In spite of the fact that the use of delay lines was central to Turing's design, discussions were held with Dr F C Williams of the Telecommunications Research Establishment (TRE) at Malvern, who was developing an alternative memory technology using spots of charge on the inside of cathode-ray tubes. Discussions were also held with M V Wilkes of Cambridge with a view to possible collaboration, but he too had his own ideas about which Turing was critical, understandably in view of the investment in his own design. Williams shortly left TRE to go to Manchester University, and before long all four groups, Cambridge, Manchester, TRE, and NPL, were engaged in rival computer development projects. Meanwhile D R Hartree, as chairman of the Executive Committee's Mathematics Division panel, wrote to the Director in November 1946 describing the manpower available for ACE (two full-time and one half-time at NPL and one full-time at Dollis Hill) as inadequate and comparing it unfavourably with the scale of the US computer projects.

On 4 January 1947 Harry D Huskey, who had worked on ENIAC, joined Turing's small group at Hartree's recommendation for a one-year temporary appointment. He was a go-getter, who soon decided that some practical action was called for. He recalls (ref. 68 p.360): 'In view of no hardware effort at NPL and no prospect of related work elsewhere, our group suggested to Womersley that we build a prototype. Although I suspect that Turing was more interested in the full-sized ACE, our proposal was approved, and work started on a much simpler ACE that came to be called the ACE Test Assembly. To others outside the immediate project it was supposed to prove the feasibility of the ideas—however we intended to be able to do actual computation.' Jim Wilkinson (ref. 171 p.106) says of the Test Assembly: 'the objective was to build the smallest computer that could successfully demonstrate the feasibility of Turing's grand project.'

The grand project was described in a series of ten lectures given by Turing and Wilkinson to an invited audience at the Adelphi offices of the Ministry of Supply in central London in December 1946 – February 1947. A detailed record of these lectures (ref. 5) was prepared and circulated by one of those attending. The project was summarised in a further lecture, given by Turing to the London Mathematical Society on 20 February 1947 (ref. 139). After describing the ACE proposals (and this time comparing them explicitly with the Universal Machine of *Computable Numbers*), he launches in typical Turing style into a stimulating series of glimpses of the future:

> It will be seen that the possibilities as to what one may do are immense. One of our difficulties will be the maintenance of an appropriate discipline, so that we do not lose track of what we are doing. We shall need a number of efficient librarian types to keep us in order. (p.120)

> It would be quite possible to arrange to control a distant computer by means of a telephone line. (p.120)

> The masters [programmers] are liable to get replaced because as soon as any technique becomes at all stereotyped it becomes possible to devise a system of instruction tables which will enable the electronic computer to do it for itself . . . They may be unwilling to let their jobs be stolen from them in this way. In that case they would surround the whole of their work with mystery and make excuses, couched in well chosen gibberish, whenever any dangerous suggestions were made. (p.121)

> One could communicate with these machines in any language provided it was an exact language . . . This would mean that there will be much more practical scope for logical systems than there has been in the past. Some attempts will probably be made to get the machine to do actual manipulations of mathematical formulae . . . This system should resemble normal mathematical procedure closely, but at the same time should be as unambiguous as possible. (p.122)

> Let us suppose that we have set up a machine with certain initial instruction tables, so constructed that these tables might on occasion, if good reason arose, modify those tables. One can imagine that after the machine has been operating for some time, the instructions would have altered out of all recognition, but nevertheless still be

> such that one would have to admit that the machine was still doing very worthwhile calculations . . . It would be like a pupil who had learnt much from his master, but had added much more by his own work. When this happens I feel one is obliged to regard the machine as showing intelligence. (pp.122–123)

On the subject of chess:
> What we want is a machine that can learn from experience. The possibility of letting the machine alter its own instructions provides the mechanism for this, but this of course does not get us very far. (p.123)

Remarkable words, considering that this paper was written more than a year before the world's first computer ran its first program.

On 18 March 1947 the Director reported to the Executive Committee that he had had a meeting with the staff concerned with ACE and had decided that Dr H A Thomas of Radio Division should be put in charge of getting a prototype ACE made by a suitable firm, and that a pre-prototype model should be built in NPL's workshops. Shortly afterwards, the Post Office contract was cancelled[6]. The Mathematics Division group were displeased, but with hindsight one might say that, since they evidently did not have the staff to follow up their work on logical design with construction on a reasonable timescale, it was high time for some other approach to be tried. Probably their concern was that they knew Thomas was not the ideal man for the job either. He was an experienced radio engineer (having joined NPL in 1922 and been a founder member of the then Radio Department in 1933), with a particular interest in industrial electronics, but he had no knowledge of the pulse techniques needed for digital circuits. His ACE development plan (ref. 135) outlined a minimum of 16 months' work by 13 NPL staff on the prototype, followed by 20 months for the full machine; the plan made clear the primary importance of adequate pulse techniques. Fortunately Thomas seems to have recognised NPL's lack of skills in this field at an early stage, for one of his first actions was to do what in an ideal world Womersley and Turing would have done long before: to recruit someone who did have this special experience.

E A (Ted) Newman had worked during the war for EMI Ltd on airborne radar with the legendary electronic engineer A D Blumlein[7]. When Blumlein was killed in an air crash in 1942, Newman took over a major part of their current project, known as H_2S. David Clayden also worked for EMI during the war, and

---

[6] T H Flowers of the Post Office, who during the war had led the construction of Colossus with such great success, said (as quoted by Lavington ref. 83 p.25): 'Unfortunately the pressure of telephone reconstruction after the war left so little time for other projects that eventually the commitment [to build a computer] had to be withdrawn. Some mercury delay lines were completed but little else.' It is surprising that in spite of this collapse the Post Office seem to have eventually used the ACE plans as the basis for the MOSAIC computer they built for the Ministry of Supply (see below p.41).

knew Newman. Both had a thorough knowledge of the successful pulse techniques pioneered by Blumlein. Thomas recruited Newman, who arrived at NPL on 4 September 1947. Clayden followed at his own initiative on 22 September, and succeeded in persuading the Superintendent, Dr Smith-Rose, that he should work for Newman rather than going to the Falkland Islands to help with radio experiments as Smith-Rose intended. Newman and Clayden were sent immediately to Dollis Hill to find out about the Post Office's prototype delay line, which had proved too unreliable for use in ACE as it stood, and found that its circuitry could be much improved using Blumlein's techniques.

The small Electronics Section in Radio Division which they had joined[8] was soon to have its status enhanced, because the parent Division was being hived off from NPL to form a separate Radio Research Station (reversing a merger in 1933). In April 1948 Electronics Section was established as a separate unit in NPL, known universally as TRON, and led by F M Colebrook, who took an immediate and positive interest in ACE. The Executive Committee minutes for 16 March 1948 record: 'Director reported that he has now appointed Mr F M Colebrook as officer in charge of the sections dealing with the development of the ACE project (now under Dr Aughtie)[9] and the work on industrial electronics (for which Dr Thomas is responsible).' David Clayden remembers that he could talk electronics to Colebrook but not to Aughtie or Thomas. However he also says that Thomas was a good organiser who has been given more than his fair share of criticism for the long series of delays in the detailed design and construction of ACE; and Wilkinson, although disagreeing with the priority Thomas gave to industrial electronics, says (ref. 171 p.106) that this position was not unreasonable at that time.

My impression is that Hodges is too disparaging about both Womersley and Thomas (ref. 66 pp.317 and 366 respectively). Womersley, though not in the FRS class for mathematical ability like several of his staff, did a solid job in his prime task of establishing Mathematics Division, and can hardly be blamed for

---

[7] For an account of Blumlein's work, see: R W Burns. A D Blumlein—engineer extraordinary. *Engineering Science and Education Journal*, 1, February 1992, pp.19–33.

[8] The Thomas group had commenced operations on 18 August 1947. The Woodger Papers (ref. 180 folder M11) include transfer notices for F Aughtie, M A Wright, W Wilson, A F Brown and A I Williams from other NPL Divisions to Radio Division on that day.

[9] It is not clear how soon Aughtie took over responsibility for the ACE work from Thomas after his transfer from Engineering Division to Radio Division on 18 August 1947. The note of the inaugural meeting of the group on that day refers to him as Thomas's deputy (ref. 100), and he attended a meeting at the Royal Society with Wilkinson on 4 March 1948 (ref. 6) where he described the card input/output facilities proposed for ACE, but I have not found any other record of his involvement; he returned to Engineering Division in 1949.

not having the experience of electronics which would have enabled him to manage the ACE work more effectively. Thomas, although not the right man to lead the construction of ACE, at least quickly recognised which technical skills were needed and successfully set about recruiting the right person. Like an artist judiciously darkening part of a picture to emphasise the brightness of an adjacent highlight, Hodges may have inadvertently blackened Womersley and Thomas the better to show off the undoubted brilliance of his hero Turing.

In the meantime the ACE group in Mathematics Division gained two further recruits: G G Alway on 18 August 1947 and D W Davies on 1 September. But at about the same time it was decided, presumably by Darwin, that the work on the Test Assembly, which had been continuing regardless of the formation of the Thomas group, should cease[10]. By now Turing was evidently getting frustrated by the lack of progress, and he departed at the end of September for a year's sabbatical at Cambridge on half pay, no doubt hoping that by the time he returned the building of ACE would have been put on a more satisfactory footing.

Huskey says 'morale in the Mathematics Division collapsed' (ref. 68 p.361). Although it must have appeared wasted at the time, the work on the Test Assembly was to prove useful in two ways: it had stimulated the interest of the Mathematics group in digital electronics, and the design of the Test Assembly later contributed a good deal to Pilot ACE. In the early months of 1948, Jim Wilkinson, in charge of the ACE group in Turing's absence, organised the production of a major report on the current state of the ACE plans (ref. 157), but the group was by now thoroughly disillusioned.

Part way through his year at Cambridge, Turing decided to accept a position at Manchester University, where the world's first working computer was to run its first program on 21 June 1948. NPL did not take kindly to this breaking of the understanding that paid sabbatical leave involves an obligation to return[11]. Hodges says he resigned on 28 May (ref. 66 p.376); his mother's

---

[10] There is some doubt about the timing of this decision. A note in NPL file MA 26/02 (see list p.40), probably written in 1949, refers to it as having been made in November 1947. On the other hand, two documents in the Woodger Papers (ref. 180, folder M11) indicate action being taken in September. First there is a note telling Womersley to lend Wilkinson, Gill and Wise to the Thomas group for six months from 1 September 1947 (Wilkinson ref. 171 does not mention this, and it seems that nothing effective happened on these lines until the following year). More significantly, there is an apparently aggrieved note from Fieller in Mathematics Division, writing on behalf of Womersley, to the Superintendent of Radio Division, dated 17 September: 'During Dr Turing and Dr Huskey's absence on leave most of the apparatus in our laboratory in Teddington Hall has I believe been removed to your Division . . .' (the bizarre vision of a successful raid by the Thomas group on the rival camp in Teddington Hall, though tempting, must surely be unjustified?).

biography says he 'sent in his resignation . . . it was something of a shock to find himself summarily dismissed; quite probably he had completely forgotten the terms of his contract' (ref. 145 p.89); the NPL Executive Committee minutes for 28 September 1948 say that his 'pay was stopped as soon as his acceptance of the Manchester post was notified'; and NPL's personnel records simply say 'left 31.5.48', when 'resigned' would have been their more usual term.

As regards its effect on ACE development, Turing's departure was not the serious blow one might expect from the fact that the project was entirely his brainchild. In fact his combination of dominance of the project with a lack of ability to collaborate, and a lack of interest in the organisation needed to get practical development moving, must have constituted a significant factor in the delay in implementing his plans. He was generous enough himself to say that the later developments were much more successful than they would have been if he had stayed at NPL (ref. 66 p.407).

There were two tangible results from Turing's time at Cambridge supported by NPL. First, he completed a paper (ref. 141) analysing the way in which cumulative errors can build up in a long sequence of numerical calculations, which was one of the foundations of Wilkinson's future work in this important area. Secondly he wrote a paper entitled *Intelligent Machinery* (ref. 140) as a report to NPL. Partly a speculative essay (including such topics as autonomous robots roaming the countryside) and partly a technical paper on the properties of neural networks, it shows how far ahead of the current state of computing his mind was running. Its subject is the human brain and the way in which its development and many of its capabilities might be paralleled by future computers. He defines a class of machines consisting of networks of logical elements, whose behaviour can be modified using 'reward' and 'punishment' stimuli, and describes how using a paper simulation he found that he was able to 'train' such a machine to behave as a simple computer. The method of training consisted really of discovering how the machine was organised and systematically changing it, and as he said himself 'it is not sufficiently analogous to the kind of process by which a child would really be taught'. Nevertheless his discussion of the training of initially randomly organised artificial neural nets by judicious interference was a remarkable innovation which seems to have gone unrecognised by later workers in this field, as pointed out in a recent paper by Copeland and Proudfoot (ref. 22).

---

[11] On 23 July 1947, when the sabbatical year was being arranged, Darwin had written to Sir Edward Appleton of DSIR: 'On my side I have made with him [Turing] the condition that he is under a gentlemen's agreement to return here for at least two years after the year's absence.' (ref. 100)

At NPL, in early 1948, the development of ACE was still stymied by the organisational separation of the Radio Division and Mathematics Division groups. But the appointment of Colebrook (who, like Thomas and Aughtie, was a long-serving member of NPL staff) as head of the soon-to-be-independent Electronics Section in March 1948 was the turning point. Shortly after his appointment he made the radical suggestion to Wilkinson that the four members of the Mathematics Division group who had been most involved in the Test Assembly work, namely Woodger, Davies, Alway, and Wilkinson himself, should join the Electronics Section team temporarily and all should work together on the construction of a pilot machine. Even more surprisingly, this was agreed by all concerned in Mathematics Division, including Womersley. Thomas was no longer in a position of influence as regards the ACE work, and in fact both he and Aughtie were to leave the section the following year. The new combined team was well balanced, a reasonable size for the job, and soon developed a sense of purpose. After the distressing catalogue of delays, the development of Pilot ACE was about to be properly launched.

Bibliography on early plans for ACE and Turing's work at NPL

1. Technical reports

Turing's 1946 report, ref. 138; see also Carpenter and Doran's analysis of the report, ref. 18.
Womersley's supporting paper, ref. 174.
Notes from a series of lectures on ACE given by Turing and Wilkinson in 1946–47, ref. 5.
Turing's lecture to the London Mathematical Society on 20 February 1947, ref. 139.
Thomas's 1947 plan for ACE development, ref. 135.
Turing's 1948 paper on intelligent machinery, ref. 140.
Turing's 1948 paper on round-off errors in matrix processes, ref. 141
Wilkinson's progress report on ACE in April 1948, ref. 157.
A shorter note on progress by Wilkinson in 1948, ref. 156.

2. First-hand retrospective accounts

Goodwin's short '21 Today' article on the history of Mathematics Division, ref. 58.
Huskey's paper 'From ACE to the G-15', ref. 68.
Wilkinson's 1970 paper 'Some comments from a numerical analyst', ref. 168.
Wilkinson's 1980 paper on Turing's work at the NPL, ref. 171.
Womersley's note on the history of the ACE project, ref. 175.
Woodger's 1958 paper, ref. 178.

3. Historical accounts written by people not personally involved

The introduction to Carpenter and Doran (1986), ref. 19 pp.1–19.
Croarken (1990) ref. 25 pp.93–94.

Hodges (1983) ref. 66 pp.305–307 and 314–389.
Lavington (1980) ref. 83 pp.23–30.
Randell (1972) ref. 127.

4. Papers from NPL files

Many documents from contemporary NPL files are preserved in the Woodger Papers, ref. 180, see particularly folders M11, M12 and M15. The NPL Administration Division file AD 74/01 *Automatic Computing Engine* is preserved in the Public Record Office, see ref. 100.

2.4 Pilot ACE

The logical design for Pilot ACE developed by the combined Electronics Section/Mathematics Division team in 1948 was in fact the 1947 Test Assembly plan with improvements; in Wilkinson's words (ref. 171 p.108) the design 'owed more to the abortive Test Assembly than it was wise to emphasise', considering that work on the Test Assembly had been stopped by the Director the year before. The crucial new element was the availability of the electronic design skills and experience of Newman and Clayden and their colleagues. Pilot ACE was set to be an interesting, quirky, and in the event highly successful machine, still clearly based on Turing's original plans, with a significant speed advantage over its contemporaries and offering great opportunities for programming ingenuity.

It was decided to retain both the 32-bit word length and the timing arrangements proposed by Turing, so that the long delay lines (DLs) each held 32 words and circulated in a *major cycle* of 1024 µs, and the short delay lines (TSs) each held one word and circulated in a *minor cycle* of 32 µs. Eventually there were 11 DLs, five TSs, and also two 'double stores' (DSs), each holding two words and circulating in 64 µs[12]. In February 1954 a magnetic drum was added, with 32 tracks each of 32 words. This drum was replaced later the same year by one with 128 tracks[13]. Each transfer from a complete long delay line to a track, or vice versa, took about 12 ms (though this time was not necessarily wasted because, once initiated, a transfer continued automatically and the computer could be doing other things in parallel with it). The final total memory of Pilot ACE was thus 4457 words, equivalent to

---

[12] As described by Woodger in 1951 (ref. 176), there were at first eight long and eight short delay lines. Soon the number of DLs was increased to ten, the number of TSs was reduced to six, and the two DSs were introduced; this is the stage described by Wilkinson in 1951 (ref. 160), by Davis in 1952 (ref. 37), and by Campbell-Kelly (ref. 15). Later the eleventh DL was introduced in place of TS 11; this is the final stage of development in 1953 as described by Wilkinson (ref. 161) and by Newman et al. (ref. 96) (though both these papers have some internal inconsistencies regarding the stage of development they are describing).

17.8 Kbytes in modern terms—as it happened, well within the size range planned by Turing.

The instruction format consisted of the following fields (the numbers in parentheses give the length of each field in bits):

1. Next instruction source (N) (3)
2. Source (S) (5)
3. Destination (D) (5)
4. Characteristic (C) (2) [replacing the earlier serial digit (s) (1)]
5. Wait (W) (5)
6. Timing (T) (5)
7. Go digit (G) (1)

The basic effect of an instruction was to transfer the contents of delay line S to delay line D starting in minor cycle W and ending in minor cycle T, inclusive; and to take the next instruction from delay line N in minor cycle T[14]. However if C was set to 1 then the transfer was to last for only one minor cycle regardless of the value of T, and if C = 3 it was to last for two minor cycles; the value C = 2 was not used. Since N had only three bits, instructions could only be stored in eight delay lines. Since there were only 18 delay lines in all, there was more capacity in the S and D fields than was needed for straight transfers, and the other numbers were used to specify particular arithmetic, logical or input/output functions. For example, D = 16 meant simply that the contents of S were to be put into TS16, but D = 17 meant that the contents of S were to be added to TS16. Discrimination was indicated by the use of destinations 24 and 25; the effect of D = 25, for example, was that if the content of source S was zero the next instruction was taken from source N at time T as usual, but if the content of S was non-zero the next instruction was taken from source N at time T + 1 (modulo 32). Table 1 gives a list of the 32 sources and 32 destinations (taken with minor corrections from Wilkinson, ref. 161). A completely blank instruction meant something specific: read the next card row, and treat it as the next instruction. This was a neat design trick, because it meant that when the

---

[13] The detailed account of the Pilot ACE drum by Clayden et al. (ref. 21) describes it as having 256 tracks, but I understand from David Clayden and Fred Osborne that this third model in fact never worked reliably enough to be incorporated in the machine. A new (moving-coil) head-shifting mechanism was then developed, which overcame the problem. This arrived too late for Pilot ACE but was used successfully in the first 256-track drum attached to the full-scale ACE; the four such drums eventually used on that machine involved a further modification. After Pilot ACE was closed down its drum was attached to the DEUCE for use as a spare.

[14] Somewhat confusingly, W and T were both expressed relative to the minor cycle of the current instruction, offset by 2, modulo 32; so that for an instruction stored in minor cycle M the transfer lasted from minor cycle W + M + 2 to minor cycle T + M + 2 inclusive, and the next instruction came from delay line N in minor cycle T + M + 2 , all additions being mod 32. This meant that in really optimum coding, with no unwanted delays at all, the values of W would all be zero.

Table 1. Pilot ACE: Sources, destinations and next instruction sources

Sources		Destinations		Next instruction sources	
0.	Input	0.	INSTRUCTION	0.	DL11
1.	DL1	1.	DL1	1.	DL1
2.	DL2	2.	DL2	2.	DL2
3.	DL3	3.	DL3	3.	DL3
4.	DL4	4.	DL4	4.	DL4
5.	DL5	5.	DL5	5.	DL5
6.	DL6	6.	DL6	6.	DL6
7.	DL7	7.	DL7	7.	DL7
8.	DL8	8.	DL8		
9.	DL9	9.	DL9		
10.	DL10	10.	DL10		
11.	DL11	11.	DL11		
12.	DS12	12.	DS12		
13.	DS14 ÷ 2	13.	DS14 add		
14.	DS14	14.	DS14		
15.	TS15	15.	TS15		
16.	TS16	16.	TS16		
17.	~ TS26	17.	TS16 add		
18.	TS26 ÷ 2	18.	TS16 subtract		
19.	TS26 x 2	19.*	MULTIPLY		
20.	TS20	20.	TS20		
21.	TS26 & TS27	21.	Modifies Source 20		
22.	TS26 ≢ TS27	22.	—		
23.	P17	23.	Modifies Source 13, Destination 13		
24.	P32	24.	DISCRIMINATE on sign		
25.	P1	25.	DISCRIMINATE on zero		
26.	TS26	26.	TS26		
27.	TS27	27.	TS27		
28.	Zero	28.	Output		
29.	Ones	29.	BUZZER		
30.	Last row of card	30.*	PUNCH		
31.	—	31.*	READ		

* Independent of source used.

machine was switched on, and was therefore empty, its first (blank) instruction caused it to activate the card reader and take its next instruction from there, the first step in the process of loading a program. Further details of the instruction format and example programs are given in Wilkinson's paper. A slightly earlier stage of the programming system is described in much more detail than is possible here by Campbell-Kelly (ref. 15).

Once the logical structure of a program had been decided, there were two stages to the coding process: first, to express the logic in the form of a program as for any other machine, and secondly to decide where to put each instruction in the memory so as to eliminate as far as possible waiting time between instructions. This process of placing instructions in memory so that they fitted together in time without unnecessary gaps was called *optimum coding*. It was a feature of Turing's original design and was at this time unique to Pilot ACE; in other machines using delay-line storage, retrieving a word from a long delay line involved on average a wait of half a major cycle for the word required to come round. It was this capability for optimum coding which made Pilot

The classical era: 1945–1956

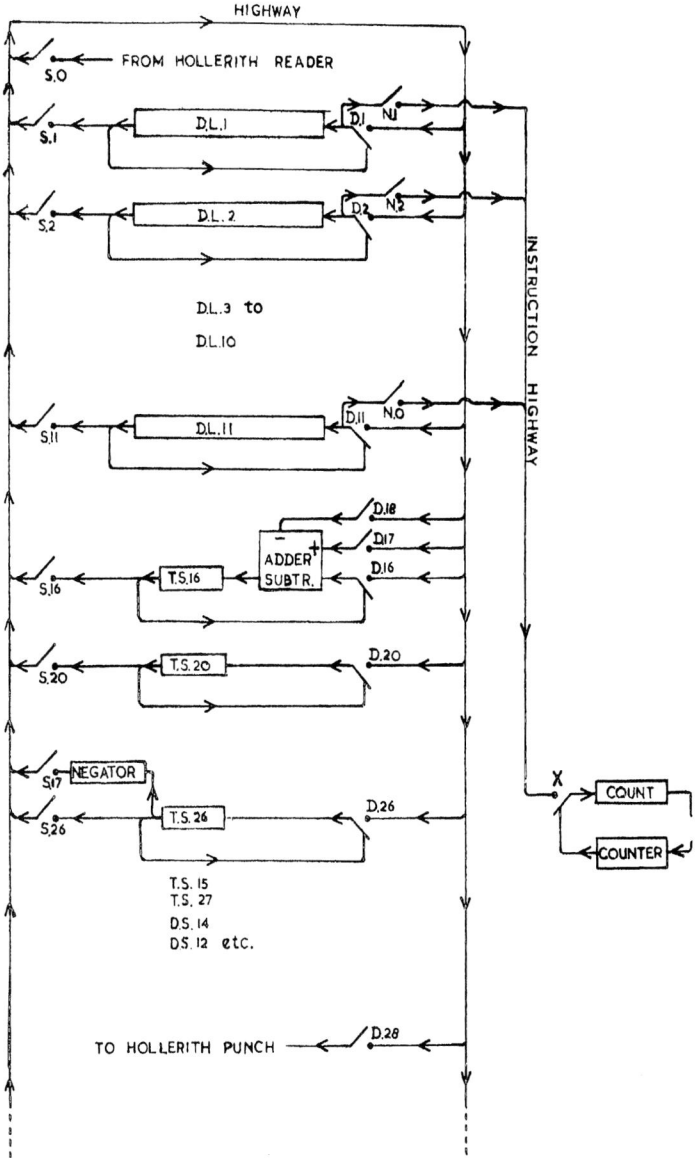

Figure 2. Simplified diagram of Pilot ACE (from Wilkinson ref. 161 p.12).

ACE fast compared with other machines of its generation, at the cost of making programming more intricate and error prone.

A simplified diagram of the machine is shown in fig. 2. It can be seen as a railway marshalling yard in which most of the points (switches S, D, and N) are open, as shown, at any one time; the contents of each delay line then circulate without external interference other than clock pulses to keep them synchronised. When an instruction is to be obeyed, the function of the control circuits (represented by COUNT and COUNTER on the diagram) is simply to extract its component fields and to close temporarily the three switches corresponding to the values of S, D, and N in the instruction; the start times and durations of the closures are determined by W, T and C. The result was that a train of pulses would emerge from the selected source and pass round to the selected destination, and another train would emerge from the selected next instruction source and pass to the control circuits. This was the essence of how Pilot ACE worked. All the details, including arithmetic and logical functions and punched-card input and output, followed from the selection of particular sources and destinations.

The progress of the combined team in formulating these plans and constructing the machine was reasonably rapid. Though he did not contribute to the detailed technical work, Colebrook evidently played an important part in ensuring that everyone worked together harmoniously and had a common understanding of their tasks. The English Electric Co Ltd (whose chairman, Sir George Nelson, was a member of the NPL Executive Committee) provided a small group including G M Davis, R T Clayden (David's brother) and four wiremen to help with the development and construction and to provide a basis for the future commercial exploitation of the design of Pilot ACE; within English Electric this group was responsible to A C D Haley. The legendary ability of W Wilson of Electronics Section to locate scarce electronic components was a great asset to the team. Construction started in early 1949. One by one, some 40 chassis were built, tested, and added to the 'main frame' (a 12×6 ft rack). Newman (ref. 96) describes Pilot ACE as 'a relatively small machine, embodying about 1000 valves, [which] could be comfortably accommodated in a room about 20 ft square'. It ran its first simple program on 10 May 1950; details of the happy event are given in Wilkinson (1980), ref. 171 p.109. He says: 'We switched off for the day knowing that the computer was working. It was a little while before we reached this high peak again and could convince the Director that it was indeed working. He conceded our point but remarked that the program was "scarcely epoch-making". From our point of view he was quite wrong, and history proved us to be correct.'

NPL with Pilot ACE can claim to have been the fourth group in the world to achieve a working general-purpose stored-program electronic digital computer[15]. The clear leaders were Manchester University (UK; F C Williams and T Kilburn), whose prototype ('baby') Mark I machine ran its first program on 21 June 1948 (ref. 90 p.433). They were followed by Cambridge University (UK; M V Wilkes) with EDSAC on 6 May 1949 (ref. 90 p.497) and the National Bureau of Standards (USA; R J Slutz) with SEAC which was demonstrated in April 1950 (ref. 90 p.476). Two other groups also have strong arguments for inclusion. The BINAC, developed by the Eckert-Mauchly Computer Corporation in the USA, was demonstrated on 22 August 1949 but

---

[15] A comprehensive survey of the early history of the stored-program computer is given in Williams (1985) ref. 172, pp.298–381.

The classical era: 1945–1956

Figure 3. Members of the Pilot ACE team at the press demonstration, November 1950. Left to right: E A Newman, F M Colebrook, J H Wilkinson, D W Davies.

appears not to have worked satisfactorily subsequently; Stern (ref. 134) gives a detailed history of the machine from which readers can judge its somewhat debatable status. Secondly and much more substantially, the Whirlwind machine developed by the Massachusetts Institute of Technology evolved over the period 1949–51 (ref. 90 pp.365–384). This machine is also not readily classifiable for different reasons: it was designed and used for large-scale real-time defence applications, and though it was in concept a general-purpose computer no specific claims have been made regarding the date at which its development reached this point as they have for the other machines mentioned above. If both these machines are accepted, NPL and Pilot ACE drop to sixth place. Of course the order of precedence ignores many important aspects of the machines such as size, speed, cost, influence, life span, software capabilities, and range of applications. Ultimately the order is in any case not of great significance; what matters is the far-reaching technical revolution to which all the groups were contributing. But because competition traditionally encourages progress, people have good reason to choose to see such events in competitive terms.

A grand demonstration of Pilot ACE was held between 29 November and 1 December 1950 (fig. 3). Day 1 was for the popular press, day 2 for the technical press, and day 3 for invited guests including Williams, Kilburn and Wilkes. Two main programs were shown, one popular and one serious. As described by Wilkinson (ref. 171 p.110), the popular program 'took in a six-figure decimal number and gave its highest factor. A bottle of beer was offered to any member of the press who could give a six-figure prime,'[16] and 'The serious program traced the paths of rays through a complex set of lenses; it was virtually impossible for

Figure 4. Pilot ACE installed in Mathematics Division, March 1952. The short delay lines are on the central stand and there are two experimental adjustable-length long delay lines on the right. The large box behind the main frame is the temperature-controlled cabinet for the other long delay lines.

anybody not intimately connected with the computer to know for certain whether this was really working.' Luckily the machine, previously distinctly temperamental, behaved impeccably for these three days. It attracted great interest; an album of the resulting press comments, kept in the NPL Museum, contains 78 cuttings.

The success of this demonstration forced a change in the Laboratory's attitude to Pilot ACE. It had been intended literally as a pilot machine, providing experience which would enable a full-scale ACE to be built with confidence, and it would be this big machine which would be used for serious work. However, the demonstration led to an immediate demand for computing services, and it was therefore decided to make a few modifications to the machine including the addition of a multiplier and then to use it to provide a computing service in parallel with the development of the larger machine.

In addition to these changes, new temperature-control equipment was installed during 1951 to improve the reliability of the delay lines. This made the machine dependable enough to be handed over to Mathematics Division, and it was moved from its birthplace in Bushy House to Building 21 in February 1952 (fig. 4). Evening shifts, with occasional Sunday and all-night sessions, were soon introduced, and the performance of the machine was described in the annual report for 1952 as most satisfactory. The work programme of the Division meant that in

---

[16] The representative of the *Richmond and Twickenham Times* was credited with winning the first bottle of beer. Wilkinson describes a second popular program which 'took in a date in decimal from input keys and gave out the corresponding day of the week on a cathode-ray tube'. This is not mentioned in the press reports, and may have been kept in reserve; alternatively, as Tom Vickers believes, it may in fact have been prepared for a later occasion, a visit by Prince Philip on 22 April 1952.

The classical era: 1945–1956

❑ SIDELINE ❑ DETOUR ❑ DIGRESSION ❑ BYWAY ❑ SCENIC ROUTE ❑

The Paris Model

A much reduced version of Pilot ACE was built in 1951 to provide Electronics Section with a basis for experiment and testing once Pilot ACE had been handed over to Mathematics Division, and for use in demonstrations. It had very little memory, a minimal function set, input by keys and output on lights in binary, but was a true stored-program computer. First demonstrated very successfully at the Physical Society Exhibition in London in April 1951, it was known as the Paris Model because it was also shown at the Scientific Instrument Exhibition in Paris in May 1951, although it did not work satisfactorily there because of fluctuations in the power supply.

Keeping track of chassis changes involved climbing to read the top labels. One day Mike Woodger did this without noticing that the power supplies had been removed from the bottom of the Paris Model, making it top heavy. When it fell on him he became probably the first person ever to be injured by a computer. Luckily an oscilloscope took the main impact, so he was not seriously hurt, though he was left with a permanent scar.

spite of Turing's insight seven years earlier concerning non-numerical uses of computers, the tasks given to Pilot ACE were entirely computational. They included the solution of ordinary differential equations by step-by-step methods, the solution of large sets of simultaneous equations, inversion of matrices and the determination of their latent roots, and numerical quadrature (evaluation of integrals). Applications included determination of pressure distribution on aircraft wings, calculations concerned with the phenomenon of flutter, the solution of 129 simultaneous equations for a gravimetric survey, and trajectory calculations. A considerable proportion of the work was defence related. Many of the mathematicians did some programming, but particular mention should be made of Betty Curtis, who was the chief specialist Pilot ACE programmer, starting well before the machine was completed and therefore one of the very first programmers in the UK.

Also in 1952, arrangements were made with the English Electric Co Ltd for the development, for NPL and others, of a production version of the Pilot ACE to be called DEUCE; this machine is considered further below (p.44).

As already mentioned, a magnetic drum store, developed by Electronics Section in 1952–53, was added to Pilot ACE in 1954. This made a big difference to the speed of the machine in many existing applications and considerably extended its scope. Because no other Government establishments had their own computers, the range of applications undertaken became very wide. It included the analysis of stresses set up in the steam catapult retardation structure on HMS *Ark Royal*, an investigation of the optimum setting of traffic signals for the Road Research Laboratory, ray-tracing in optical systems, the analysis of stereograms used in surveying, and statistical work on stress measurement data from the Comet disaster investigation carried out by the Royal Aircraft Establishment. In several cases staff from the establishments concerned worked at NPL, programming their problems and running them on the machine. A program to calculate PAYE tax tables was developed for the 1954 Budget, but the anticipated publicity bonus did not materialise because in the event the tax rates were not changed; however the program was rewritten for DEUCE and used successfully a year later. The Pilot ACE service for users outside NPL, the first external computer service on a significant scale in the world, was organised by Josie Wright (later Mrs Snook).

One of the most influential items of Pilot ACE software was the General Interpretive Program (GIP) written by B W Munday with the associated set of matrix routines written by M Woodger. These allowed a program of matrix manipulations to be specified for the machine by someone not versed in the arcane details of Pilot ACE programming. Space-saving and error-checking facilities were built in. This package also was rewritten for DEUCE and in this form very widely used well into the 1960s.

With the delivery of DEUCE machines to both NPL and the Royal Aircraft Establishment in 1955 the load on Pilot ACE began to ease. One of the more unusual problems tackled this year was the mathematical description of the rapid freezing of a slab of fish packed between two cooling surfaces: it was required to find the time elapsed before the central part of the slab was cooled below a prescribed temperature, the problem being complicated by the latent heat given up as the fish froze. The Annual Report commented 'in view of the assumptions made regarding the homogeneity of the fish, the agreement of the theoretical results with experiment is quite remarkable'. Another new application was the verification of theories regarding the mixing of fresh and salt water in the Thames for the Water Pollution Research Laboratory.

The reduction in demand from other organisations as they acquired their own computers, and the greater reliability of DEUCE, led to the closedown of Pilot ACE in June 1956 after four-and-a-half years of yeoman service to the UK science and engineering community. The machine was dismantled and the main frame, control desk and two delay lines were sent to the Science Museum at South Kensington where they form part of the permanent computer display.

Contributors to the development of Pilot ACE not already mentioned include R F Braybrook, A F Brown, B J Byrne, R G Chalmers, S Gill, W L Gleed, J S Osborn, C F Osborne, L J Page, A J Williams, V Wilmott, and M A Wright.

The classical era: 1945–1956

Bibliography on Pilot ACE

Cautionary note on terminology in these documents: the earlier term 'Test Assembly' was sometimes used to refer to Pilot ACE, particularly during its early development; it was also used as a name for the Paris Model before it went to Paris.

1. General accounts

Woodger's 1951 note in *Nature*, ref. 176.
Newman's paper at the 1951 Manchester conference, ref. 95
Wilkinson's 1953 conference paper, ref. 161.
Goodwin's 1955 paper on applications, ref. 56.
Five historical articles: Woodger (1958) ref. 178, Woodger (1969) ref. 179, Malik (1969) ref. 85, Wilkinson (1975) ref. 170, and Wilkinson (1980) ref. 171.
Brief accounts are also given by Lavington (1980) ref. 83 pp.44–47, Hodges (1983) ref. 66 pp.407–408, Williams (1985) ref. 172 pp.338–346 and Croarken (1990) ref. 25 pp.94–98.

2. Hardware

Second progress report S Gill June 1949, ref. 55.
Wilkinson's 1951 report on the logical design, ref. 159.
Newman et al. on the mercury delay line store, ref. 96.
Clayden et al. on the magnetic drum, ref. 21.
Many patents relating to Pilot ACE are included in the list in Annex B, p.319.

3. Programming

Wilkinson's 1949 paper 'Coding on automatic digital computing machines', ref. 158.
Wilkinson's 1951 report 'Programming and coding for the pilot model of the ACE', ref. 160.
Davis's 1952 programming manual prepared for English Electric, ref. 37.
Wilkinson's 1956 assessment of optimum coding, ref. 163.
Campbell-Kelly's detailed historical paper, ref. 15.

4. Papers from NPL files

Many documents from contemporary NPL files are preserved in the Woodger Papers, ref. 180; see for example the Pilot ACE programs in folders N16–N21. The following four files are still at NPL at the time of writing (1996):
  A.C.E. Test Assembly, ref. MA 26/02 [1948–51]
  A.C.E.—Reports on Pilot Model, ref. CME 27/03 [1949–53]
  Enquiries arising from A.C.E. demonstration etc., ref. MA 26/06 [1950–52]
  Pilot A.C.E.—Disposal of, ref. MA 26/013 [1955–63]

Other members of the ACE family of computers

Besides Pilot ACE and the Paris Model, six different computers were developed directly or indirectly from Turing's plans for ACE: the General Post Office's MOSAIC, the Bendix G-15, the Packard-Bell PB 250, the full-scale ACE, the EMI Electronic

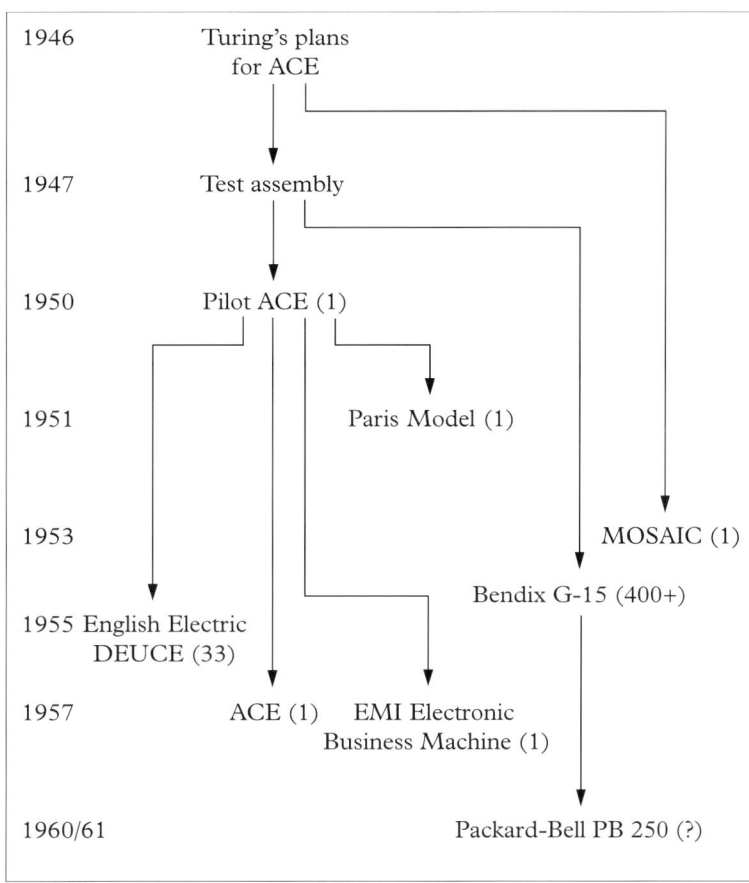

Figure 5. The ACE family of computers. The numbers in parentheses show how many of each machine were built.

Business Machine, and the English Electric DEUCE. The relationships are shown in fig. 5. ACE, which was developed at NPL, is described in section 3.2 below; the other five were all developed elsewhere and are described briefly next.

MOSAIC

The MOSAIC computer was developed by the Post Office Research Station for the Ministry of Supply for the analysis of radar data. Construction started in 1947 and the machine was first operational in 1953. It had 64 long mercury delay lines each storing 16 40-bit words, and four shorter delay lines, three holding one word and one holding two, a total of 1029 words. The instruction format was three-address, similar to the full-scale ACE; optimum coding was recommended as with other members of the family. MOSAIC was slower than Pilot ACE, with a pulse frequency of 570 kHz. Physically it was literally massive: it contained three-quarters of a ton of mercury and 6000 valves, and dissipated 30 kW. When completed it was housed at the Radar Research and Development Establishment (RRDE) at Malvern.

The leaders of the Post Office development team were A W M Coombs and W W Chandler, both of whom had worked with Flowers on Colossus during the war. According to Coombs, in his 1953 paper listed below, 'the mathematical design was by NPL, the engineering design by GPO Research, and the manufacture and assembly by the All-Power Transformer Co.' The Post Office of course had access to Turing's plans because of their abortive work on ACE development in 1946–47, and Donald Davies remembers that they were kept in touch with later developments; for example he went to Dollis Hill with a design for a multiplier, explained it to Coombs and Chandler, and later recognised it in a description of MOSAIC.

The Post Office were evidently more successful in building MOSAIC for the Ministry of Supply than they had been in building ACE for NPL. It is not entirely clear why this was, but three points may be relevant. First, unlike NPL, RRDE were not themselves computer designers, so once the formal link with NPL was broken, the Post Office group were free to make their own decisions on how to implement Turing's design without any risk of the plans being changed or the decisions questioned. Secondly, defence budgets may have provided more funds than were available from NPL. And thirdly it still took them a long time: MOSAIC was three years behind Pilot ACE. Although Donald Davies remembers some working contact between NPL and the Post Office on MOSAIC, it is perhaps surprising there is no record of liaison between NPL and RRDE regarding programming methods, where there must have been many common interests. (There appears to have been a similar gulf between RRDE and their sister establishment at Malvern, the Telecommunications Research Establishment (TRE), where a separate computer development group was at work, led by Dr A M Uttley who was later to join NPL.) The defence establishments' need for security may have discouraged such contacts, or may have simply discouraged references to them in published reports.

Published references to MOSAIC

Campbell-Kelly (1982) ref. 16 pp.129–130 and see his list of references.
A W M Coombs. MOSAIC: the Ministry of Supply Automatic Computer. *Automatic Digital Computation*, HMSO, 1954, pp.38–42.
Lavington ref. 83 p.53.
Malik's 1969 article (ref. 85) about ACE development includes a picture of the MOSAIC memory (p.58).

Bendix G-15

When Hartree helped to arrange Huskey's year at NPL in 1947, his main intention was no doubt to strengthen the NPL group. In this he was successful, but he may not have foreseen the benefits which later accrued to the US computer industry. When Huskey returned to the USA in early 1948 he started work on computers for the National Bureau of Standards. Although his initial design, the 'NBS Interim Computer', was based on his NPL experience, this was later changed by others, and the machine as eventually built (SEAC) was not noticeably influenced by Turing's ideas. Huskey's second project used random-access Williams tube technology and led to the SWAC; it too was unrelated to the ACE tradition. However in 1952–53, while on leave from NBS, he designed a computer which did bear a strong family resemblance to Pilot ACE, which the Bendix Corporation decided to build and christened the G-15.

The memory of the G-15 was a magnetic drum, on which all information was read, erased and rewritten at every rotation, as for mercury delay lines. The drum area was divided into 'lines': 20 long lines of 108 words each and eight shorter lines of various lengths, a total of 2183 words, with serial access to each line. The instruction format included the familiar source, destination and characteristic, and though the timing arrangements were somewhat different the possibilities for optimum coding were very similar to those on Pilot ACE. Logical, arithmetic and input/output functions were selected using the source field, with a particular number (31) in the destination field to show this was not a normal transfer.

The considerable influence of the Bendix G-15 can be judged from the fact that over 400 of the machines were built (the 400th had gold-plated fittings). The one which was installed in Huskey's home for development work has been called the first home computer.

For further details of the G-15, see Huskey (1984), ref. 68.

Packard-Bell PB 250

Bell and Newall (ref. 12 pp.44, 74, 191) say that the design of the Packard-Bell PB 250, which first appeared in 1960–61, was also derived from the ACE plans via the G-15 and Huskey, but give few details. It was a low-cost machine with transistor logic and a memory based on magnetostrictive delay lines, and therefore one of few cyclic access machines in the second generation; its word length was 22 bits.

EMI Electronic Business Machine (CP 407)

Ronald Clayden has already been mentioned as a member of the English Electric group seconded to NPL to help build Pilot ACE and to prepare for the development of its commercial version,

DEUCE. Before DEUCE was complete Clayden left English Electric to return to his former employers EMI. There his task was to produce a computer quickly using known techniques. EMI soon received a firm order for a computer to run the payroll for the British Motor Corporation, and this led to a considerable expansion of the team.

Like Huskey with the G-15, Clayden chose a serial architecture using a drum store in place of mercury delay lines. The main area of the drum held 384 tracks each of 64 36-bit words, a total of 24,576 words. In addition there were 50 tracks called *circulating registers* and one *quick-access track*. The circulating register tracks each had a single writing head followed one word later by a single reading head; as a word was read it was normally immediately re-written so that 64 copies of it would be written round the track. This arrangement meant that a program could read from or write to a register without waiting for the drum to rotate to a selected position, and the version read would in all circumstances be the last one written. A very similar system was used for the 'short lines' on the G-15 drum.

The quick-access track was used to hold the current 64-word segment of program. It had one read/write head and 63 read heads, giving random access without delays to the instructions within the current segment. When another segment of program was needed, the program had to call for the appropriate drum track to be copied into the quick-access track. This random access coupled with the large number of registers largely avoided the need for ACE-type optimum coding, but involved the programmer in a considerable amount of program shunting.

The drum was slower than mercury delay lines, the clock rate being 115 kHz compared with 1 MHz in Pilot ACE. The machine had five magnetic tape units, punched-card input and line-printer output. Only the one machine of this type was built.

R T Clayden. The EMI Electronic Business Machine (undated, typescript).
R J Froggatt. Logical design of a computer for business use. *J. Brit. I.R.E.*, December 1957, pp.681–696.
J Hendry (1989) ref. 64 p.114.

DEUCE

DEUCE was the production version of Pilot ACE, developed by the English Electric Co Ltd between 1952 and 1955. From the programmer's point of view the changes from Pilot ACE were minor: there were 12 long delay lines instead of 11, four TS instead of five, three DS instead of two and two quadruple stores (QS) were introduced. Word length and major and minor cycles were unchanged; timing details in the instruction format were

Figure 6. NPL's DEUCE in about 1956, with Brenda Webber.

improved and simplified. There was a 256-track drum, each track holding 32 words like a long delay line.

Physically the machine looked quite different from Pilot ACE, consisting of a single large cabinet and a control desk. You could walk inside the cabinet, where the chassis were arranged in racks on each side of a short corridor. The logical design was little changed, although the opportunity was taken to make the electronics more robust where possible, and the machine used rather more valves than Pilot ACE (1450 compared with 1000).

Many Pilot ACE programs were rewritten for DEUCE. These included the General Interpretive Program mentioned above which became widely used; it was instrumental in the sale of several DEUCEs, notably to the British aircraft industry.

Altogether 33 DEUCEs were built, of which 11 went to Government establishments, four to universities, six to industrial organisations and the remaining 12 to English Electric itself (these figures were given by George Davis in a lecture in May 1993). NPL's DEUCE was the first to be installed outside English Electric, arriving in May 1955. The last DEUCE was sold in 1962, and the last close-down was in 1967.

Further details of DEUCE are given in Haley's contemporary descriptive paper (ref. 59), and by Campbell-Kelly (ref. 15, pp.157–158).

For most of its long life (1955–66), the NPL DEUCE was the foundation of the Laboratory's computing service. The service was managed by Tom Vickers, with day-to-day matters in the care of Gwen Edwards, Brenda Webber, and (later) Joyce Dickerson.

The use made of the machine by Mathematics Division is outlined in sections 2.5 and 3.9 below.

2.5   Other early work in Mathematics Division

Turing's work, and the subsequent development of Pilot ACE jointly with Electronics Section, can now be seen as the major achievements of the early years of Mathematics Division. But the Division had many other less spectacular activities. What follows is a brief round-up of this other work to set the computer developments in context.

The Division completed its initial period of growth in 1946, and by the end of the year had a staff of 50. The emphasis was on computational services, where there were three main tools: desk machines, punched cards and the differential analyser.

The General Computing Section, relying chiefly on desk machines for calculation, produced specialist mathematical tables, carried out some research on the determination of latent roots and on relaxation methods, and undertook various tasks involving numerical calculations for other Divisions of NPL and for Government departments, including the defence ministries and the Building Research Station.

The technology of punched cards is largely forgotten today because it has been entirely superseded by computers, but in its day it was a powerful and versatile tool which provided the only available means of bulk data processing. NPL had one of the country's strongest facilities, with powerful machines and experienced staff. Besides the basic capabilities to punch, sort, select and tabulate (print from) cards, card-handling equipment could be programmed (using a plugboard) to select numbers from fields on the cards and add, subtract and multiply them, and to keep running counts and totals. Amongst the section's tasks were surveys of electricity consumption for the Electrical Research Association, child development for the Ministry of Health, fire statistics for DSIR, examination results for the Civil Service Commission, and road accidents for the Road Research Laboratory. Using a procedure for Fourier analysis developed in the Division, scientific work carried out included analyses of ionospheric observations and of crystallographic structures. Because of the continued demand for their services, the group survived well into the computer era, only finally closing down in 1984.

The Statistics Section also provided a wide-ranging consultancy service to Government departments and industry, though it only remained in the Division until 1951, when it was transferred to the Ministry of Supply to make room in a fixed staff complement for computer staff. One member, J G Hayes, was left behind and subsequently, in Goodwin's words, 'played a spirited statistical one-man band'.

Other early work in Mathematics Division

Figure 7. Two integrators on the Manchester Differential Analyser (undated, but taken before the move from Manchester).

Digression on differential analysers

The *differential analyser* was a mathematical machine developed by Vannevar Bush at the Massachusetts Institute of Technology in 1930[17]. In spite of its name, the basic function of the machine was integration. Its central unit, the integrator, is shown in fig. 7. This unit usually consisted of a horizontal disc like a record turntable, with, resting on it, a vertical wheel, free to rotate but fixed in position, driving a horizontal shaft. The horizontal disc and its driveshaft were mounted on a carriage so that the disc could be moved, in its own plane, parallel to the shaft of the vertical wheel. The theory of the machine is as follows. Suppose the point of contact between the wheel and the disc is a distance y from the centre of the disc, and the disc is rotated through a small angle δx. Then the wheel will rotate through a small angle $cy.\delta x$ where c is a constant depending on the radius of the wheel. Thus if the disc is rotated and at the same time moved laterally, the total angle through which the wheel rotates will be $c.\int y.dx$. This was the basic principle of the integrator. The variables x and y were represented by the angle of rotation of the disc and its lateral position respectively, and the result of the integration was represented by the angle through which the wheel rotated. The correct functioning of the machine depended very much on the contact between

---

[17] Although Bush is generally credited with this invention, the basic principle was known in 1851 and was considerably developed by Professor J Thomson and his brother William, later Lord Kelvin, in 1876. See:

J Thomson. On an integrating machine having a new kinematic principle. *Proc. Roy. Soc.*, 24, 1876, p.262.

S P Thompson. *The Life of William Thomson, Baron Kelvin of Largs*. Macmillan, 1910, pp.692–694.

The classical era: 1945–1956

Figure 8. NPL's second differential analyser: an operator following an input curve (August 1954).

the wheel and the disc: if this was too light the wheel would not rotate when it should, and if it was too heavy the wheel would not be able to slide freely along the radius of the disc. For complex problems several integrators could be connected together, with the result of one integration forming the input to another. Although the early machines were purely mechanical, some later machines used electrical connections between units.

To input data to the machine, a graph relating x and y would be drawn on paper and fixed to a special table fitted with a carriage carrying a pointer. The operator's task was to follow the line of the curve with the pointer as shown in fig. 8; the resulting motion of the carriage was converted, usually by a mechanical linkage, into the required motion of the integrator's disc described above. A similar machine was used for output, which was in the form of a curve drawn by a pen mounted on a carriage moved under the machine's control.

NPL had two differential analysers. The first, an eight-integrator model, was originally built for Professor D R Hartree at Manchester University in 1935, and taken over by the Ministry of Supply during the war (see ref. 62). As mentioned above, this machine was hired for NPL's use from 1 December 1945, with Hartree's support. It was eventually moved to Teddington in June 1948 and installed in the hut called the Babbage Building. This machine was purely mechanical. It was in use until August 1953, and helped with a wide variety of problems which could be expressed as differential equations, for example the design of the automatic speed control on a ship tank carriage. It is now (1996) in the Science Museum.

A contract with a German firm for the construction of NPL's second differential analyser was signed in March 1949, but its

Other early work in Mathematics Division

Figure 9. NPL's second differential analyser, Building 21, August 1954.

gestation did not go smoothly, and the machine as eventually built had mechanical parts from Germany, electrical parts from Metropolitan Vickers Electrical Co Ltd, and assistance on ancillary units from NPL's Control Mechanisms Section. The machine, a large 20-integrator model, used electrical connections between the units and a plugboard like a manual telephone switchboard to set up the configuration required for a particular job. It was installed in Building 21, and, though it looked impressive (see fig. 9), it was obsolete by the time it was fully working in 1954. Traditionally, its fate was settled when it took a week to solve a problem for the Director which Pilot ACE solved in a few minutes, though J G L Michel, who led NPL's differential analyser work throughout, believes this story to be unfounded. In any case, differential analysers had proved to be an evolutionary dead end, and the machine was dismantled following the decision to terminate its use taken by the Executive Committee in 1957.

History of Mathematics Division resumed

Womersley resigned as Superintendent in September 1950. Following an interregnum with E C Fieller in charge, Dr E T Goodwin was appointed Superintendent on 9 February 1951. This heralded some major changes in the Division. In an exchange of accommodation with Aerodynamics Division, Mathematics Division (except for the Punched Card Section) moved from Cromer House, Teddington Hall and the Babbage Building to Building 21 in October–December 1951. The long saga of ACE development described in 2.3 and 2.4 above was finally bearing fruit; Pilot ACE was moved to Building 21 from Bushy House in February 1952, and quickly came to dominate the work of the Division. The programme was reorganised, with a broad division into mathematics and computation, with the latter subdivided into high-speed computing (Pilot ACE and differential analysers) and low-speed computing (desk machines and punched cards).

Pilot ACE and its successor DEUCE revolutionised the Division's methods and its ability to meet its customers' requests. For example, in 1956 a set of tables of Bessel function zeros which had taken 18 years of desk machine work by various groups was checked by J H Wilkinson using DEUCE over a period of eight months, taking 12½ hours of machine time. As the speed and reliability of computers were appreciated, desk machines were phased out and the staff retrained to use the new technology. Already by the end of 1952 about a third of the staff working on desk machines had transferred to ACE work. The use of punched-card equipment also declined, but as already noted it took much longer to succumb, being for some years more appropriate than computers for applications such as the management and use of mailing lists, where the necessary database software had yet to be developed.

In March 1953 a major international symposium on Automatic Digital Computation was held at NPL, organised jointly by Mathematics Division and Electronics Section. It was the third of a biennial series, the first having been held at Cambridge in June 1949 and the second at Manchester in July 1951, and was attended by over 200 delegates including Hartree, Wilkes, Williams, Turing and Uttley. The proceedings included nine papers by NPL staff (see ref. 104).

The wide range of application of the work undertaken by Mathematics Division at this time can be illustrated by a selection of the problems mentioned in the 1956 Annual Report:

> On the tracing of sound waves through water, for the Admiralty;
> On traffic flow, for the Road Research Laboratory;
> On servo backlash, for Control Mechanisms and Electronics Division, NPL;
> On side-launching of ships, for Ship Division;
> On the density of mercury, for Metrology Division;
> On human colour-matching capabilities, for Light Division;
> On stereogram calculations, for the Ordnance Survey;
> On tax tables, for the Inland Revenue;
> On nuclear scattering, for various universities;
> On crystallography, undertaken by Oxford University staff at NPL;
> On flutter and stress calculations (over 20 separate investigations for aircraft companies);
> On the siting of power stations, for the Central Electricity Authority;
> On the effect of focusing and defocusing of particles in the synchrotron, for CERN;
> On a semiconductor problem, for Standard Telephones and Cables Ltd;
> On the results of a survey of the effects of television on children, for the Nuffield Foundation and the BBC.

Acceptance tests were devised for other organisations' computers. Research topics included 'a successful attack on the numerical integration of the Orr-Sommerfeld equation occurring in problems of fluid flow', 'asymptotic expansion of Weber functions of large order' and similar subjects appropriate to a more specialist history than this one.

The overall picture of Mathematics Division in the mid-1950s is of an organisation making good use of its exceptional computing facilities and skills to provide an important service to Government, universities and industry in the UK, but doing so through many small ad hoc projects rather than through the introduction of radical new methods or the launching of influential initiatives (like the computing service itself). This position was to change, with a flowering over the next decade of the growing talent of the Division in the field of numerical analysis. The developments are outlined in section 3.9.

2.6 Other early work in Control Mechanisms and Electronics

Control Mechanisms Section

A new Section for the study of Control Mechanisms was established in Metrology Division NPL in 1945. Its aim was to 'make fundamental studies of control systems, and to assist industry in the design and synthesis of automatic and manual controllers for industrial processes and plants'.

One of the first tasks of the Section was to give assistance to Mathematics Division on their proposals for a new differential analyser. This work continued on and off until 1953; the plans led eventually to the large machine described above and shown in fig. 9. The role of Control Mechanisms Section was to give advice and assistance, and design some components, the lead throughout being taken by Mathematics Division.

The other initial task was to develop a pilot plant to enable control techniques to be investigated. In the plant, oil was circulated through a lagged tank, and the aim of the system was to maintain its temperature at a constant level despite variations in the flow rate. In 1950 an electronic simulator was developed; it proved a more versatile tool than the pilot plant, which was not heard of subsequently.

A major practical task undertaken by the Section in 1947–48 was the development for Ship Division of automatic speed control equipment for a ship tank carriage. Various ingenious measurement techniques for special situations were also developed by the Section, including the gauging of wires and threads using air-pressure variations and the assessment of the evenness of fine sieves (the results were expressed as a statistical distribution of the actual mesh sizes in relation to the nominal size).

Electronics Section

An Electronics Section was established in Radio Division in early 1947 with two tasks: the construction of a prototype computer for Mathematics Division and the provision of advice to industry on the use of electronics in industrial processes. As described above (section 2.3), the computer development got off to a slow start. The transformation of this position in 1948 when Electronics Section under Colebrook became independent of Radio Division, and four members of Mathematics Division were seconded to join the team, has been described in section 2.4; the development of Pilot ACE took up most of the Section's effort over the next few years, though the advisory work on industrial electronics continued until 1951.

Control Mechanisms and Electronics Division

On 10 June 1954 the Control Mechanisms Section of Metrology Division and the independent Electronics Section were combined to form a new Control Mechanisms and Electronics Division (CME). Colebrook was appointed to head the new Division, but he never took up the post as he was seriously ill; he died on 21 June. R H Tizard was appointed in his place (though he did not formally become Superintendent until that post was created in November 1955). Founder members of the new Division included Ted Newman, David Clayden, Lew Page, John Parks (who was temporarily absent on National Service), Michael Wright and Willie Wilson all from Electronics Section and Dennis Blake from Metrology Division. A strong group of new recruits included Frank Blake, Derek Barber and Wyn Price in 1954 and Roger Scantlebury in 1955, all of whom were to make important contributions to the Division in later years. Pat Woodroffe transferred from Physics in 1955, and CME Division was considerably strengthened by the transfer of Donald Davies from Mathematics Division also in 1955.

The work of the Division for its first three years comes under three headings: computers; control and data handling; and the application of computers to clerical operations.

The Division's major task was its work on computers. It (1) maintained Pilot ACE, and inherited from Electronics Section the tasks of completing and installing the 128-track drum described in section 2.4; (2) collaborated with English Electric on DEUCE and took over the maintenance of NPL's DEUCE from them in 1956; and (3) started on the detailed design of the full-scale ACE, as described in section 3.2.

An additional off-beat computer project was described in the 1954 Annual Report (p.24). 'The Division has made a complete logical design for a small and relatively cheap computer to be made by the Northampton Polytechnic Institute. This machine

Other early work in Control Mechanisms and Electronics

Figure 10. The Electronic Simulator, September 1954.

will use a new system of instructions in which each word has a "tag" appended to it, and is located by reference to this tag rather than to its position in the store.' This design was later described in detail by Newman and Wright (ref. 97); as far as is known it was never implemented.

On control and data handling, the Division's main tool was the Electronic Simulator shown in fig. 10, a large machine whose development had been started by Control Mechanisms Section in 1950. It consisted of many separate units which could be selected and interconnected by means of a plugboard like a telephone switchboard to set the machine up for a particular task, very much on the lines of the interconnections in the large differential analyser. Variables represented in analogue form could be generated, arithmetically processed, and output graphically. Discrimination was achieved by 'an electronic switch which is open or closed depending on the absolute value of a variable'. Altogether the machine included a function generator to approximate to an arbitrary curve, four multipliers, 37 amplifiers, 36 adders, 34 exponential time lags, one time delay, two integrators, four 'dead zone units', and four 'saturation units'. It was used for a wide variety of applications including various mathematical investigations, the study of an existing control system in an oil refinery to examine improved methods of control, an investigation of the effects of load changes in a turbo-alternator, the simulation of economic systems (in conjunction with the London School of Economics), a proposed system for operating the control surface of a high-speed aircraft, flow control in a sugar-refining process, speed control in a wool-carding machine, and others. But the relative versatility and accuracy of digital systems were in the end too much for this technology, and the simulator was last heard of, in use by outside organisations only, in the 1958 Annual Report.

The classical era: 1945–1956

Digital data-handling equipment developed included graph plotters and an interface to an automatic typewriter, and the Division continued to give advice and assistance on electronics to other Divisions in NPL and to outside bodies.

A major IEE convention on digital computer techniques was held in London on 9–14 April 1956. The proceedings included eight papers from NPL staff which are listed below (ref. 69). The introductory lecture by Professor Williams had a memorable conclusion: he held up a card with a seed glued to it, saying: 'This object is so small that I doubt if you can see it, yet it contains all the data and instructions necessary to control the manufacture of an unending and ever-increasing supply of roses.' At that time the structure of DNA had fairly recently been discovered, so that the chemical basis for the encoding of genetic information was no longer a complete mystery, but even so his words must have given some of his audience of computer engineers reason to reflect on what the future of information storage and processing might hold.

Work on clerical procedures

In May 1954, immediately before the formation of CME Division, a group was established in Electronics Section at the request of the DSIR Committee on High-Speed Computers to study the mechanisation of large-scale clerical operations. Michael Wright and Ted Newman of NPL were joined by three part-time contributors, one from the Organisation and Methods Division of the Treasury and two from the Ministry of Pensions and National Insurance (MPNI). The work that developed from this small beginning was to have considerable influence on the early use of computers by most of the civil departments of Her Majesty's Government.

An initial detailed study of the use of DEUCE for payroll work led to the publication by the group in 1956 of a book, *Wage Accounting by Electronic Computer* (ref. 106), which came at the right time and was an immediate success, almost 6000 copies being sold in 1956. Studies were also made of the possible use of computers to access the MPNI's large index of 30 million people, including the problem of variant spellings of names, and of administrative uses of computers in Royal Ordnance Factories and the Central Statistical Office.

In September–November 1957 the group organised a five-week course on office uses of computers, the first four weeks being held at NPL and the final week at the Treasury in London. Representatives from 13 Government departments attended. These 24 people naturally became at once the local experts when they returned to their departments, with the result that several of them later headed major computer projects. One, Douglas Wass, later Sir Douglas, became Joint Head of the Home Civil Service. Nearly forty years later, he remembers the course vividly, in particular 'the enthusiasm and dynamism of an electronics engineer called Ted Newman'. Although his square-root program for DEUCE never did work, he writes: 'I gained a great deal from the course which has stood me in good stead throughout my working life. What it gave me essentially was a sound conceptual framework within which to appraise the scope and limits of computerisation of manual processes generally. As a result of this indoctrination, I have rarely felt ill at ease in looking at systems applications, and have generally known how much detail I ought to get involved in.'[18] This successful and influential course can now be seen as a key event in the introduction of computers to the civil departments of the UK Government.

The use of computers for office work in Government and industry soon developed a momentum of its own, and the NPL group, which had served its purpose of helping to set the ball rolling, was closed down in 1959.

Meanwhile, Tizard had resigned as Superintendent on 31 May 1956, leaving Ted Newman in charge of CME Division until a successor could be appointed. The radical changes which then ensued are described in the next section.

Publications by CME Division on clerical procedures

E A Newman. The use and future in offices of automatically controlled computers. *Management Views,* Remington Rand Ltd, January–February 1954.

E A Newman and M A Wright. The use of a computer for payroll work. IEE Symposium, 1956, see ref. 69.

NPL. *Wage Accounting by Electronic Computer* (ref. 106).

E A Newman. An analysis of non-mathematical data-processing. *Proc. NPL Symposium on the Mechanisation of Thought Processes 1958,* HMSO, 1959, pp.863–876.

---

[18] From a letter to the author dated 15 May 1995.

3 The Uttley era: 1957–1966

3.1 Outline of developments

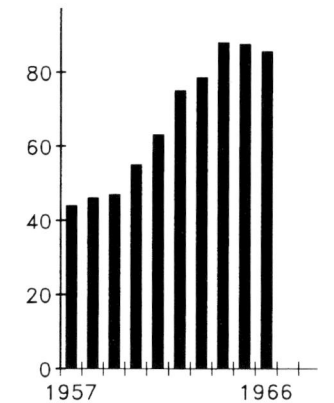

Figure 11. Growth in the Uttley era: CME/Auto staff numbers, 1957–66.

The appointment of Dr A M Uttley as Superintendent of CME Division on 1 January 1957 introduced a period of major transformation in all aspects of the Division: its ethos, programme, accommodation and name all changed within a few years.

Dr Uttley was a mathematician, psychologist and computer designer (see p.312 for a synopsis of his earlier career) who had a passionate interest in the structure and function of the brain. This interest covered physiology, psychology, theoretical aspects of neural nets, and the design of machines embodying and testing these theories. He was a scientist at heart, devoted to investigating the natural world and applying scientific theories in the design of new technology, and was not motivated by policies of Government or opportunities for industrial development, or even by new computer applications except when they were relevant to his chosen field. His vision was of a long-term combined effort by engineers, physicists, mathematicians and life-science professionals to push forward together the technology of computing and the science of the brain; and he aimed to foster a stimulating university-style atmosphere in which these people from different disciplines could work fruitfully together. Many found this idealism inspiring, but it could also provoke irritation in those whose approach to achieving progress was more incremental and who saw him as politically naive.

The Division which he took over had three areas of work: ACE development; control engineering and electronic development, chiefly for other NPL Divisions; and the application of computers to clerical work in commerce and Government. On ACE, design was complete and construction well advanced; this work continued and is described in section 3.2 below. The control work formed the basis of a new group on adaptive control under the leadership of Percy Hammond, described in section 3.3. The work on clerical mechanisation, described in section 2.6 above, continued only until 1959 and was then closed down. An engineering workshop and design office under Fred Osborne, initially working largely on ACE construction but also increasingly undertaking work for other Divisions, also came under Dr Uttley's control but is not covered here except for its contribution to ACE.

The NPL Executive Committee reviewed the Division's work at a crucial meeting on 3 June 1957. Their visiting panel, convinced by Uttley's vision and enthusiasm, made the radical recommendation that the Division should be doubled in size and should have a new building. The conclusion of the Committee's discussion was more guarded, though still positive: 'The Division would have the

Committee's support and encouragement to expand sufficiently to make a proper contribution to the field covered by it.'

With this mandate, Uttley gradually introduced several new projects reflecting his own and his colleagues' judgement of what was potentially important in the field of 'mechanisation of thought processes'; Donald Davies remembers the process of consultation as being 'fairly democratic'. Work on pattern recognition started in 1958 (see section 3.4), on the translation of natural language by computer in 1959 (section 3.6), on cryotrons also in 1959 (section 3.8), and on information retrieval in 1960 (section 3.7). Various smaller projects on aspects of biology and psychology related to recognition and control were undertaken from 1959 onwards and are described in section 3.5. Staff numbers rose accordingly (see fig. 11). Quite separately from Dr Uttley's CME Division, Mathematics Division continued its work on numerical analysis and computing services, and their work in this period is outlined in section 3.9.

Several events in the period deserve special mention. A major conference on the mechanisation of thought processes was held in November 1958, and its proceedings (ref. 109) published the following year. This was a major influence in suggesting areas for the future work of the Division, and many of the new projects listed above can be related to the conference agenda. In April–June 1959 Dr Uttley undertook an extensive series of visits in the USA and Canada which also influenced his future plans considerably: for example, he visited Harvard University which was to provide significant help to the new NPL project on machine translation, and Ramo-Wooldridge where there was work on information retrieval on the same lines as that later started at NPL. His visit report was considered of sufficient general interest to be produced as an NPL report (ref. 147).

In April 1960 the changes in the work of the Division were reflected by renaming it Autonomics Division. This was intended to convey the idea of self-regulation as in the word 'autonomy' and in the established phrase 'the autonomic nervous system', but with hindsight the name was not ideal, because most people did not understand it.

In 1959 it was agreed that the Division, whose groups were scattered round the NPL site, should have a large new building. Design and construction followed, and staff moved in to the new Building 93 in January 1964, with an official opening on 5 April 1965. A booklet (ref. 111) was prepared for this event which gives a useful outline of the Division at that time. The building is shown in fig. 12. In the main block, the ground floor was designed chiefly for the equipment of the Adaptive Control group; there was a room in the north-east corner built as a separate massive concrete box on a spring suspension to minimise outside noise (for psychological experiments). The second floor included a clean-room suite for the cryotron project, and the top (fifth) floor an extensive

Outline of developments

Figure 12. The new Autonomics Building, January 1965.

animal house and facilities for the biological work. The rest of the main block contained laboratories (on the north side) and offices (on the south side). The south wing held the engineering workshops, and the central connecting block the library (on the ground floor), a large open-plan drawing office on the first floor and administrative offices and a lecture room on the second floor. The building, at first known as the Autonomics Building, was later (in 1968) named after the computing machinery pioneer Charles Babbage, as was the earlier Babbage Building, a hut at the north end of the NPL site. In November 1964 a somewhat startling photograph (fig. 13, note the chalk lines!) was taken of the staff parading in front of the building.

❑ SIDELINE ❑ DETOUR ❑ DIGRESSION ❑ BYWAY ❑ SCENIC ROUTE ❑

Floor tiles and the complex plane

*Donald Davies's design for the tiling of the entrance hall floor in the new building is of interest to mathematicians. Complex numbers of the form $a + b\omega$ (where a and b are integers and ω is one of the complex cube roots of unity, $e^{2\pi i/3}$) form a **ring**; that is, if any two are added, subtracted or multiplied you get another member of the set. Some members of this ring are prime in the sense that they cannot be expressed as the product of other members except in trivial ways. The hall floor represents the complex plane, with the origin at the centre of the metal tile and the real axis pointing north. The centres of the hexagonal tiles are the members of the ring; primes correspond to dark tiles and non-primes to light. The pattern can be seen as 12 sectors, each a reflection of its neighbour in their common boundary. It has been used as the basis for the cover design on this book.*

The Uttley era: 1957–1966

Key to figure opposite:

A M Uttley

B de L Burns	P H Hammond	E A Newman			D W Davies
T B Mulholland	D L A Barber	D O Clayden	L J Page	A R Meetham	P R Stuart
A D J Robertson	P A N Briggs	C H Davis	F M Blake	J McDaniel	J S Hill
G O Plumb	D H Stockwell	J R Parks	B A Wichmann	P K T Vaswani	C T H Stoddart
R S Watson		C R Evans	K A Bartlett	W L Price	R A Scantlebury
S A Larcombe	E P H Woodroffe	P W Nye	K R Morris	A J M Szanser	D S Allam
S R Townsend	E R Dymott	G Williams	D S Baker	D M Yates	
P M Scanlan	J S Mortimore	B E Pay	P E Carter		W L Gleed
J I Oates	A T Davies	P J Pobgee		B J Byrne	J S Osborn
	A A Hill	J R Elliott		A M Day	M Longden
	K Wilkinson	R E Rengger		S Whelan	E Oldfield
	L A Pink	K J Barnes		G R Cohen	P W Storey
	B E Aldous		I P Priban	R J Reason	C M Blanchfield
	P K Griffiths	J Kirkby	W F Fincham	C A Walsh	C J Robbie
	P L Mann	D R Manning		C Jenkinson	S A Stirling
	G Hadley	P M Stilliard	S Bastable	D E Orpin	L R Wadsworth
				R Walkinshaw	R E Ward
	E W Anderson	T M Cook	V J Hawtree	I C Scott	I G Norman

This is part of the original picture which also includes, on the right, C F Osborne and about 40 members of the West Workshop and Drawing Office staff; and in the front row W Pascoe, G Allum, W Moss, S Goodbery, J Griffiths and W Clare. The following were members of, or attached to, Autonomics Division at the time but were away that day: J Dawkins, J R Ullmann, D Drage, R J Coombes, K-S Hsu and A F Brown.

Throughout the period NPL held annual Open Days as a means of reporting to all those interested on the Laboratory's stewardship of its resources over the past year. These were major events, with over 3000 guests attending and extensive use of staff time preparing displays and discussing the work with the visitors.

In 1961 a major international conference on machine translation was organised by the Division; it is covered in section 3.6.

Between September 1962 and July 1963 Dr Uttley held a research fellowship at Stanford University; Donald Davies was Acting Superintendent for this period.

On 1 April 1965 the recently elected Labour Government created a Ministry of Technology to promote industry-oriented

Outline of developments

Figure 13. Staff of Autonomics Division, November 1964.

technical development in the UK. It took over most of the functions of the Department of Scientific and Industrial Research, amongst them responsibility for NPL. This followed the publication in October 1963 of the Trend report (ref. 136), which had also recommended the dissolution of the DSIR, though with a rather different new organisation (a Science Research Council and an Industrial Research and Development Authority both coming under a Minister for Science). The change from DSIR to MinTech was far-reaching in three ways: first it emphasised industrial applications at the expense of pure research; secondly it strengthened 'headquarters' at the expense of the individual research establishments; and thirdly it gave the field an explicit place on the political agenda, the Minister of Technology being a member of the cabinet. The Minister was Frank Cousins, and one of his first official duties was to have been the opening of the new Autonomics Building; however a crisis on the day meant that the ceremony was in fact undertaken by his junior minister Lord Snow.

With the change in atmosphere favouring the shorter-term needs of industry, Dr Uttley must have felt that the tide was moving against both his instinct for academic freedoms and his prime interest in the organisation of the brain. He retired on 31 July 1966, shortly before his 60th birthday.

This is a convenient point to describe several areas of work in the Uttley era which for different reasons do not belong under the main project headings.

Advanced Computer Techniques Project

In September 1963 DSIR announced the establishment of the Advanced Computer Techniques Project (ACTP), a new initiative to support the UK computer industry. Donald Davies wrote (*NPL News*, 163, November 1963, p.3):

> The British computer industry, in spite of recent mergers, has no units of research large enough to compete with US companies in all the many directions in which computer research is going. To help the industry maintain its competitive position, DSIR is arranging individual contracts under which 50% of the cost of a research programme is paid for by the Government, 50% by the firm. In this way, firms can put more effort into far-seeing research, and learn something about similarly supported research in other firms and in Government establishments.

NPL acted as the centre for the technical direction of the project, with Davies chairing the Technical Committee. The initial annual budget allowed for Government spending of £250,000 (£100,000 in-house, £150,000 in industry), with the companies putting in another £150,000. The first contract was with Mullard Research Laboratories for work on superconducting computing devices. It was co-ordinated with NPL's work on cryotrons, covered in section 3.8 below, and related work at RRE, both of which were also supported by ACTP.

By 1966 the project had grown into a considerable task for the Division: there were 24 current contracts, of which 14 were supervised directly from NPL. Lew Page was the full-time project leader, and many staff were engaged for part of their time on managing contracts and assessing proposals, in particular Ted Newman and Frank Blake who acted as chairmen of the hardware and software technical committees respectively. Subjects covered by the contracts managed by NPL included integrated circuits, reliability, character and speech recognition, production control in small firms, and optical stores. From the Division's point of view the co-ordination of ACTP was a welcome role which they were well-placed to fill: it kept staff in touch with the needs of industry and broadened their experience, forming a useful complement to their technical work.

ACTP continued into the Davies era, and its later history is covered in section 4.1 below.

Work in Applied Physics Division

When Tizard resigned in May 1956, Ted Newman took charge of CME Division in an acting capacity, and was seen as a strong contender for the post of Superintendent. In the event Dr Uttley was appointed, and this meant, as commonly happens in such cases, that the two had to work together. This was not a great success: Ted worked a good deal by intuition and could not always explain cogently why he advocated a certain view, whereas Uttley was precise and inclined to be impatient and dogmatic. In September 1959 it was agreed that Ted Newman, with five staff including Dennis Blake and Roger Scantlebury, should move to Applied Physics Division. Although Newman was given organisational responsibilities in his new Division (as deputy to the Superintendent), the move was simply an administrative stratagem to solve the problem which had arisen; the work the group undertook had little to do with Applied Physics as the rest of the Division understood it. There were three main areas of work, described below: school timetables, teaching machines, and reliability. The staff transfers lasted until 1963.

School timetables

Scheduling, particularly of factory work, is a logical problem of considerable economic importance, so it was natural for the Division to consider how computers could be used to help. School timetables were chosen as a suitable area for experiment because data were readily available. Programs were written (a pilot version for DEUCE, otherwise for ACE) to read in the requirements for a timetable, check that a solution was not clearly impossible, and then go through a repeated sequence: work out which item to insert next in the timetable, work out where to put it, update the data, and then move to the next item. As this process went on, some items might have only one possible place left in the timetable and had to be put in as soon as this occurred. The current state of the working data was stored at each stage, allowing backtracking if further progress became impossible. Various criteria (heuristics) allowed more promising paths to be tried before less promising ones. This now looks a complex but essentially routine logical task obviously suitable for computers, but in 1960 this was a lesson which had still to be learnt by much of industry and commerce.

Computers were still widely seen as machines for doing predetermined numerical calculations accurately and fast, without their versatility for non-numerical tasks like scheduling being properly grasped.

Publication on school timetables

J S Appleby, D V Blake and E A Newman. Techniques for producing school timetables on a computer and their application to other scheduling problems. *Computer Journal*, 3(4), January 1961, pp.237–245.

Teaching machines

The teaching of a routine task can be structured very like a computer program: take one simple instruction after another, with branching, iteration and subroutines allowed, until the task is complete. However in 1961 it was unthinkable that a machine as expensive to run as a computer should be used to guide a lowly person through a lowly task; if a machine was to be used, it had to be a cheap machine designed for the purpose.

During the war, Ted Newman had written a formal test procedure for radar equipment in book form. The advantages of a formalised approach over informal human instruction were clear to him: a less qualified person could be used to carry out the task since they only had to follow one simple instruction at a time; the teacher was freed to use his skills to better purpose; and mistakes in unfamiliar situations were less likely. But a book is less than ideal; the user may lose his place or get distracted by seeing information which looks relevant or interesting but isn't what he should be reading next.

A prototype teaching machine was developed by Newman and Roger Scantlebury and demonstrated for the first time at the 1961 Open Days. It consisted of a modified film projector with a specially produced film. The user had an answer key which could be turned to 'yes' or 'no'. Each frame of the film contained an instruction, typically some words and a diagram, and two strips containing coded numbers, one for 'yes' and one for 'no'. When the user responded by turning the key, the number in the appropriate strip was read and the film advanced or rewound by the number of frames indicated. The machine was simple, but the subject chosen was not: mending a transistor amplifier, including soldering and use of oscilloscope, for unskilled users. The demonstration worked well and attracted considerable interest from, amongst others, Rolls-Royce. This makes a neat encapsulation of the problems of evaluating the benefits of NPL work in this era. The work was not commissioned by any customer and made no money directly for anyone; but hundreds of visitors from industry had their eyes opened to some new possibilities and may well have put their knowledge to good use later. So did these speculative and unquantified benefits justify the expenditure of taxpayers' money? By the criteria of the day, yes. By today's criteria, certainly not.

Although the machine was called a teaching machine, and could certainly be used as such, it was seen by its developers primarily as an 'intelligence amplifier': a means of using relatively unskilled people to do skilled tasks using the machine to guide their actions, with no expectation that they would eventually learn to do without it. (Seen in this light, the work has a message for those trying to reduce today's levels of unemployment: people working with computer systems to guide them can undertake tasks which would be beyond their powers working alone. Is enough use being made of this principle?)

To assess the machine, the amplifier-mending instructions were also written up as a book and in flow-diagram form, and the effectiveness of the three versions compared. The flow diagram was better than the book, but the teaching-machine program was much better than either. Using it, a completely unskilled person could find faults more quickly than an expert not using the machine. Altogether over 1000 people used the system, including children (one as young as eight) and all mended the amplifier successfully, even when the faults were in subtle combinations—a remarkable record.

Publications on teaching machines

E A Newman, R A Scantlebury and M Longden (inventors). Improvements in or relating to instruction devices. UK Patent No. 968,601, application date 4.5.61.

E A Newman and R A Scantlebury. Teaching machines as 'intelligence amplifiers'. NPL Report Auto 31, May 1967.

Computer reliability

The final item of work carried out by Ted Newman's group during their period of exile in Applied Physics Division was a study of techniques for making computers behave more reliably than usual, for use in applications such as air-traffic control where the extra expense involved would be justified.

For example, a single-bit error in a stored or transmitted computer code would normally mean that the code would be misinterpreted. The effect of such errors can be much reduced, though in principle never entirely eliminated, by the judicious introduction of redundancy. One of the techniques studied by the group was as follows. Consider the binary numbers 0 to 3 written as 00, 01, 10, and 11. If these four pairs of digits are thought of as coordinates in the x,y plane, they represent the corners of a unit square. In the same way the three digits of the binary numbers 0–7 represent the eight corners of a unit cube in x,y,z space, and more generally the set of binary numbers up to n digits long can be viewed as representing the 2^n corners of an n-cube in n-dimensional space. If now the codes used for a particular purpose are selected so that all pairs of codes are at least two edges apart on their n-cube, a single-bit error will always result in an illegal code and will therefore be detected. If the only codes used are say five edges apart by the shortest route, a single-bit error can be corrected (by changing the code to the neighbouring valid code) with some confidence. The implications and ramifications of this and other techniques for enhancing reliability were described in the final report of the study (see below), and the work was continued as part of the cryotron project described in section 3.8 after the group returned to Autonomics Division in 1963.

E A Newman, D V Blake and Maureen Longden. Use of redundancy to increase computer reliability. NPL Report AP6, August 1962 [bound in two parts].

Programming research

In March 1965, partly as a result of a recommendation by an ACTP committee that more resources should be devoted to this subject, a Programming Research group was established in the Division. The founder members were Frank Blake (recently returned from secondment to the Post Office), Mike Woodger and Gerald Alway on transfer from Mathematics Division, Brian Wichmann, and Roger Scowen on recruitment. The initial programme had two threads: an 'expandable compiler' (an aid to the development of new programming languages which allowed language element definitions to be added to a standard core); and an investigation into the new possibilities for program development techniques which were opened up by the advent of interactive display equipment. This latter work needed a dedicated small computer, and in March 1966 an Elliott 4120 was acquired for the group, with (later) a display system with a light-pen and tracker ball. In addition in 1966–67 an experimental modular operating system for KDF9 called DEMOCRAT was developed by the group but proved not to justify full implementation.

The group was not to survive long in this form; its further history is described in section 4.1 below.

B A Wichmann. A modular operating system. In: A J H Morrell (ed.), *Information Processing 68: Proc. IFIP Congress 1968*, held in Edinburgh, August 1968, North-Holland, 1969, pp.548–556.

3.2 ACE

With Pilot ACE successfully launched, and experience in its use accumulating, its designers began in 1953 to consider their plans for its successor, the full-scale ACE. Some of the more important surviving early papers[1] are:

(1) A note on future work by Colebrook dated 20 August 1952, which gives design and development work on ACE as the major task of Electronics Section in the following year.
(2) An overview of the current position by Colebrook dated 4 May 1953, which includes one key passage: [The ACE] '... must be based on well proved components and techniques, even when revolutionary developments seem to be just round the corner. Otherwise the [Mathematics] Division will get nothing but a succession of pilot models.'
(3) A brief record of a meeting on 6 June 1953 attended by the Director and Secretary with Goodwin, Fox, Wilkinson and Davies of Mathematics Division and Colebrook and Newman of Electronics Section, which accepted Colebrook's document as a good case for the development of ACE.
(4) A three-page Mathematics Division note 'Proposals for full-scale ACE', dated 10 August 1953, giving technical details of their requirements.

The design and construction of the machine was the task of CME Division, and their first formal meeting on the subject, held on 15 October 1954, had before it a provisional specification prepared by David Clayden on the basis of 'the original Maths Division proposals' (which probably refers to item (4) above and not to any earlier document such as Turing's original proposal). Development continued in the following years (see fig. 14); the machine was doing some useful work in late 1958, and was described in the 1960 NPL Annual Report (p.60) as 'a fully working computer'. Its existence was eventually terminated on 14 February 1967. Thus although ACE started under Colebrook and Tizard, its useful life extended right through the Uttley era and it is accordingly described here.

As with Pilot ACE, the architecture of ACE was dominated by the fact that the main memory medium was mercury delay lines. The word length was 48 bits; each instruction occupied one word. Each of the 24 long delay lines held 32 words, and circulated in 1024 microseconds (one *major cycle*), so a new word became available from a delay line every 32 microseconds (one *minor cycle*). This was the time taken to execute a single instruction; so the maximum possible instruction rate was one every 32 microseconds, about 31,000 per second, twice the rate of Pilot ACE. In addition to the long delay lines there were seven single-length (one-word) delay lines, four double-length and five quadruple-length. The contents of these shorter delay lines of course came round for use correspondingly more frequently than words in the long delay lines, and they were used for temporary storage.

---
[1] At the time of writing (1996) these papers are in NPL file CME 27/03.

The Uttley era: 1957–1966

Figure 14. ACE under construction, May 1957, with (l. to r.) Frank Blake, Lew Page and Bill Gleed.

In addition to the delay-line store there was a backing store consisting of four drums. Each drum had 256 tracks, and a track held 32 words, the equivalent of a single long delay line. So the total drum capacity was 32,768 words. It may help to compare ACE with modern computers if these figures are expressed in 8-bit bytes (although these were not an ACE concept). In these terms the immediate access store of ACE could hold 4818 bytes, roughly one thousandth of the corresponding memory on a typical home computer at the time of writing; and the drums held 196,608 bytes, perhaps one five-hundredth of the capacity of a home computer's hard disc. On processing speeds a fair comparison is more difficult, but on any showing ACE would come out far slower than today's machine. The most startling change though is perhaps in physical size: ACE occupied a room the size of a lecture theatre.

An ACE instruction consisted of ten fields:

> Wait; Source A; Source B; Function; Destination; Stop;
> Next; J; Time; Ch

These are best explained by an example. If the values of the ten fields were:

> 11   18   4   2.1   25   0   2   0   11   0

this would mean:

> Wait till the next time minor cycle 11 comes round;
> then take the contents of the words from delay lines 18 and 4;
> add them (2.1 meant add);
> put the result into delay line 25 (one of the single-length ones);
> and take the next instruction from delay line 2,
> also in minor cycle 11.

(The uses of the fields Stop, J, and Ch can be ignored for the moment; they were often zero, as here.)

The instruction thus included four addresses (two sources, a destination, and a next instruction source).

If this instruction could be stored in minor cycle 10, that would be ideal because no time at all would be wasted in waiting for minor cycle 11. On the other hand, if for some reason this instruction was stored in, say, minor cycle 12, it would still work but a delay of nearly a major cycle would be caused by the wait. A thousandth of a second may not seem long to wait, but of course if this was in a loop of instructions obeyed many times when the program was run, the effect on the total time taken could be considerable. If a programmer carefully minimised these delays, that was called 'optimum coding', and involved a significant (and nowadays totally useless) skill. 'Tight' coding of this kind had its disadvantages, since if the programmer found an extra instruction was needed between two which were already the minimum time apart, either a big delay had to be introduced or the whole section of code rewritten.

The final field in the instruction, Ch (Characteristic), opened up some powerful possibilities. If set to zero, as normally, the operation of the instruction lasted for one minor cycle (W) only; 1 gave two minor cycles (W and W+1); 2 gave up to 32 minor cycles (from W to T inclusive); and 3 gave four minor cycles (W to W+3 inclusive). Using this facility some quite lengthy operations could be called for in a single instruction.

The logical circuits were based on valve technology, a unit the size and shape of a light bulb corresponding to a minute dot inside a present-day microchip. This of course accounts for the great physical size of ACE, and also for the fact that the units generated so much waste heat that a system of plumbed-in car radiators (Riley) was needed to cool them.

The drum store, multiplier and divider were independent units in the sense that once an action involving one of them had been initiated by an instruction it would continue until complete, and in that time other instructions could be obeyed, provided they did not need the result of the independent operation. In this way an element of parallelism was introduced.

Input and output were initially by punched cards (though paper tape was soon added). A six-deck magnetic tape system, with a 32-word core-store buffer, was introduced in 1962; without it the work on machine translation and information retrieval, described later, would not have been possible.

The machine was contained in ten long cabinets arranged fanwise so that anyone working on them could maintain visual contact with the operator at the control console in the centre (see fig. 15). These cabinets had vast doors which slid vertically upwards when opened, worked by hydraulic hoists.

The Uttley era: 1957–1966

Figure 15. ACE, July 1959.

Several useful features for program testing were provided at the console. The instruction currently being obeyed was shown in binary on a row of 48 lights. Normally these would flicker too fast to be read but the operator could run a program slowly, or even one instruction at a time ('one shot'), for debugging purposes. Corresponding with the lights were 48 switches on which a new current instruction could be set up and activated by a special key ('external tree') if the operator decided to divert the program. These switches had another vital use: the operator could set up an instruction (or part of an instruction) on them and then request that the program stop when it reached an instruction of this form. Another useful key was one which stopped the program at any instruction with a 1 in the Stop field. The contents of the short delay lines (and others, on request) were permanently displayed on small CRT screens (in binary of course). There were loudspeakers which gave an indication of what the machine was currently doing; if you were used to the program this could be quite informative, particularly as regards drum operations.

There was no operating system or other permanently resident software, but an interpreted Autocode was developed by Mike Woodger assisted by H R Whiteley (1961 Annual Report p.136 and ref. 180 section O), Woodger and Clifford Nott wrote an Algol translator for ACE (1962 Annual Report pp.136–137 and ref. 180 folders L1, L14, L15), and there was a considerable library of mathematical subroutines (ref. 180 folder N10).

Once a programmer had decided on the sequence of instructions in the program, and allocated them to fixed places in the store using pre-printed coding sheets, the program had to be prepared on punched cards for input to the machine. This was done one instruction per row, the instructions for one long delay

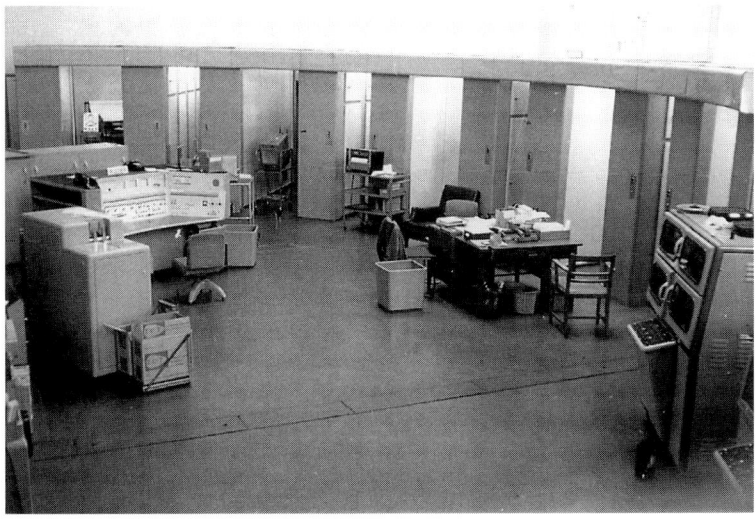

Figure 16. An informal picture of ACE in about 1963. Note the graph plotter (on trolley, centre), the hand card punch (on desk), and the magnetic tape decks (right).

line fitting on three cards. A key depression on the hand card punch corresponded to a single bit; thus to punch the instruction:

11   18   4   2.1   25   0   2   0   11   0

the programmer had to 'type' on the appropriate key for the card row:

01011   010010   000100   010   001   011001   [tab]   00010   [tab] 01011   [return],

quite a lengthy and error-prone business for a long program. The card punch made small rectangular holes, and for each hole, of course, it also produced a small rectangle of waste card, a 'chad'. If a hole was made by mistake when punching, a chad could with care be inserted in the hole and by rubbing with the thumb nail, persuaded to stay in at least long enough for the card to be copied on a reproducer—another now quite useless skill!

Once ACE was complete it was passed to Mathematics Division, like Pilot ACE before it, to be run as a computing service, under Tom Vickers and more directly under the eagle eye of Brenda Webber; this service is described briefly in section 3.9. Maintenance responsibility remained with Autonomics Division, and in 1962 a new team was established for this purpose, led by Keith Bartlett on transfer from RRE, with Les Pink, Derek Baker and Peter Carter.

By the time ACE came into use, core stores and transistors were showing their superiority over delay lines and valves respectively, and the machine was beginning to look what it eventually proved to be, something of a dinosaur both in size and as an evolutionary dead end. Yet it was a reasonably powerful machine for its day, with many unique features and considerable charisma. This was particularly in evidence during a night-time session, with the operator in a solitary and silent battle with the intricacies of his program, and the huge dark aisles of the machine around him like a mediaeval cathedral.

Following the arrival of KDF9 in 1964 the use of ACE gradually became restricted to one or two groups with a large investment of programming, and as already mentioned the machine was finally closed down on 14 February 1967, with appropriate ceremonies.

Besides Donald Davies and David Clayden, those most involved in the design of ACE were Frank Blake, Lew Page and John Stringer. Fred Osborne designed and developed the drum mechanisms. Wyn Price and C H (Bob) Davis designed the magnetic tape system, using Decca tape decks. Mention should also be made of Pat Woodroffe and Peter Pobgee, and of Bill Gleed, who was an invaluable expert in the process of giving drums their magnetic coating. A large workshop team under Fred Osborne was responsible for the construction of the units of ACE, and many of those already named contributed to their assembly into a working machine.

Publications and internal documents on ACE

F M Blake, D O Clayden, D W Davies, L J Page and J B Stringer. Some features of the ACE computer. In: *Data Processing & Automatic Computing Machines,* Proceedings of a Conference held at Weapons Research Establishment, Salisbury, South Australia, 3–8 June 1957, Australian Defence Scientific Service Dept of Supply, Session II, pp.224-1 to 224-29.

NPL. Building of DEUCE and ACE. NPL file MA 26/1/01 [still at NPL in 1996].

NPL. ACE—Reports on Pilot Model. NPL file CME 27/03 [in spite of its title, this file includes several papers relating to full-scale ACE. It too was still at NPL in 1996.]

NPL. ACE News. Issue no. 1 (4 May 1959) to issue no. 18 (November 1963).

NPL. ACE Programming Manual. Mathematics Division, NPL, ref. Ma/48, 1 November 1959 with later additions [a ring binder].

J H Wilkinson and D W Davies. The Automatic Computing Engine at the National Physical Laboratory. *Nature,* 183, 1959, pp.22–23.

M Woodger. The history and present use of digital computers at the National Physical Laboratory. *Process Control and Automation,* November 1958, pp.438–443. Reprinted in Carpenter and Doran (1986) ref. 19, pp.125–140.

The Woodger Papers (ref. 180). These include many original documents relating to ACE; see especially folders K14, N11, N12 and N23.

3.3 Adaptive control

As understood in the early years of CME Division, the essential first step in industrial process control was to develop a mathematical model of the process to be controlled. Using this model, often embodied in a machine, settings for the controls could be chosen with confidence as to what the resulting behaviour of the system would be. There were two weaknesses in this approach: it implied a complete theoretical understanding of the process which could not always be achieved, and it failed to allow in any systematic way for fluctuations in the process arising from causes outside the operator's control. Methods by which these problems could be addressed were given the name *adaptive control*; the phrase appears first in the Annual Report for 1959, though the main line of the work evolved without a break from the control mechanisms development which was one of the main concerns of CME Division from its inception.

One of Dr Uttley's first projects was however a complete change from the CME control tradition. This was the further development, in co-operation with Dr A M Andrew, of the so-called *conditional probability computer* on which he had been working at RRE before his move to NPL. It was not a computer in the sense that the word is now used; it was a learning device. What it did was to read in data, in the form of two-level signals, on several channels in parallel, and to count the number of events on each channel and each group of two or more channels, a total of $2^n - 1$ counts for n channels. From these counts it could calculate the probability of events on one channel given the simultaneous state of one or more of the other channels. In other words, if any one or more channels was unavailable, it could 'infer' their most likely state, provided of course it still had at least one active channel. In a sense, it had 'learnt' something about the statistical behaviour of its inputs from the 'training' phase. It could therefore be used as a control device without needing any model of the process under control, calculating the required control settings from its observations during the preliminary training phase. Dr Uttley had considerable faith in this simple concept because of the parallels he saw between its action and that of elements in the brain. The 1957 and 1958 reports refer to planned applications in an oil refinery and a distillation-column model respectively, but nothing more was heard of it after 1960; although it could learn, its learning powers were only useful in practice in very simple situations. But Uttley's underlying belief in the relevance of neural principles in this field has proved to be justified: neural networks are now (1996) being used in real time process control in industry as he was proposing they should be 35 years earlier.

The mainstream work of the group included both industrial process control, described below, and the biological control systems work discussed in section 3.5. It started with the arrival from RRE in March 1959 of Percy Hammond, who was to be the leader of the group throughout its subsequent life. He had been attracted to NPL by Uttley's enthusiastic vision and bold plans for the Division, but he was also well aware that the group had to show its relevance to current industrial needs if it was to prosper. He

The Uttley era: 1957–1966

Figure 17. Adaptive control: the distillation column, August 1964.

writes: 'I well remember the heady days of 1958/9 . . . and the task of trying to reconcile the very sensible and logical approach to control systems of the indigenous CME staff with the imaginative but, from an engineering viewpoint, then essentially impractical ideas of Albert Uttley!'

Hammond and his group adopted a pragmatic approach to the design of industrial control systems: (1) that a *cost function* should be defined for the process under control, including for example the financial benefits of faster output, the costs of extra power, the cost of any departure from specification in the quality of the product, and so on; and (2) that the object of the control process was to minimise this cost function. The minimising process could take the form of trial and error: make a small change in something, see if it helps, if it does keep it and if it doesn't revert to the state before the change. This would clearly be a possible strategy by itself, but might take a long time to find the optimum position. A better approach might be a judicious compromise between this method and the use of a mathematical model of the process to predict the effect of any change.

To put these ideas to the test, two items of equipment were developed: an adaptive controller and an analogue model of a simple distillation column, with satisfactory results described in the 1961 Annual Report. In parallel with these experiments and further theoretical studies, the group developed an actual distillation column (see fig. 17) to bring their work nearer to the needs of industry. This was in operation by November 1962. Its use required the development by the group of some novel instrumentation: for example an infra-red composition detector to measure the ratio of alcohol to water in a mixture (by D L A Barber and D Stockwell), and a tilting bucket mass flowmeter to measure the

Adaptive control

Figure 18. Adaptive control: the Ferranti Hermes computer, May 1968.

mass flow of the mixture (by G O Plumb). More significantly for the history of information technology at NPL, the group found that an integrated data-handling system was a useful concept: common standards between their data loggers, paper-tape punches, digital channel multiplexers and so on allowed greatly increased flexibility in putting together a combination of equipment to meet a new need. In charge of this data-handling work was Derek Barber, and the later history of standard interfaces and networks can be traced directly back to this early work for the adaptive control group.

A refinement of the theory was described in the 1962 Annual Report. The idea was to make simultaneous small *periodic* variations in the control variables, with a different frequency for each, and look for corresponding variations in the cost function; the theory showed that there would be no such correlation when the cost function was minimised.

By 1963 it had finally been decided that 'the trial and error approach on its own is unlikely to have general application in industry' because of the time taken to optimise. On the other hand the computation involved in accurately modelling complex processes was also too slow to be feasible, and the main challenge was seen to be the selection of an approximate description of a process which was both good enough for control and computationally tractable. In 1964 the group acquired a Ferranti Hermes computer (see fig. 18) to carry out these real-time calculations; it could control either the distillation column or an analogue computer simulating other processes. In the same year the group and their distillation column and other equipment moved to the new

Building 93 from a nearby hut, gaining in facilities but losing something of the pioneering spirit which their more primitive accommodation had fostered.

Theoretical studies showed that both the periodic variations in control signals mentioned above and random variations could yield useful information to guide the control process. A combination was devised, the so-called *pseudo-random binary signal* or PRBS, in which (1) there is a regular sequence of instants at which a change from one level to the other can occur; and (2) after a certain time the random pattern so generated is repeated. In 1965 the PRBS technique was used successfully on the heat control of the distillation column, and extensions of the technique to multivariable systems were being investigated. The group advertised its usefulness widely, and at the time of writing (1996) it is still applied routinely in many areas of engineering and medicine, and research in the field continues.

In 1964 the standard method of interconnecting data-handling devices developed by the group in collaboration with Dennis Blake, then of Ship Division, was adopted for use throughout NPL, and became known as the *NPL Standard Interface*. It consisted of a twelve-way parallel connection: eight data wires for an eight-bit character, one wire to indicate 'character ready', one to indicate 'character received', one to prepare (e.g. switch on) remote equipment, and an earth. This connection was for one-way transmission of data (socket for data source, plug for data receiver). The interface also included circuits at each end to eliminate the effects of interference in the link. Standard interfaces proved very successful and were fitted to a wide variety of equipment including paper-tape readers and punches, digital voltmeters, analogue-to-digital converters, keyboards, typewriters, a CRT display, computers including Hermes, and, experimentally, an infra-red link over a line of sight of about 400 metres between Hermes and KDF9.

Since the requirement for flexibility in interconnecting data-handling equipment was a common one, this work attracted considerable interest. A new British Standards committee was established in 1965, chaired by Derek Barber, to consider the NPL proposal and relevant work elsewhere. A draft specification of a *British Standard Interface* was issued by the committee the same year. They extended the NPL design to an eighteen-way parallel connection for one-way transmission of data, the extra lines allowing for more sophisticated error checking and correction than the earlier design. While logically very sound, the committee's deliberations took time and it was not until 1969 that the new British Standard 4421 was finally published. Two months later it was put forward as a candidate for international standardisation, but was rejected by the narrowest of margins.

BS 4421 was not adopted wholeheartedly by the market. There were three reasons for this: first it added extra cost to products, secondly its effect was to allow interchangeability and hence freer competition which implied risks for manufacturers, and thirdly its existence tended to inhibit further interface development. Set against this of course were the arguments that wide adoption of such a standard would open up the market for everyone, and that the freer competition was beneficial. In spite of the manufacturers' lukewarm support, BS 4421 proved very useful to its devotees: it was widely adopted in UK universities and was an invaluable element in the first NPL Network. As with several later national and international standards in IT, while not realising its proponents' ambitions, it met part of the market need and served to raise awareness of the issues and techniques so that later and commercially more successful equivalents had the ground prepared for them.

By 1966 it was clear that the design of standard interfaces had developed a momentum and significance of its own, independent of the control group. The ideas were also very relevant to the exciting possibilities for computer networks which were then opening up. Derek Barber and the other staff working on data handling were accordingly moved to form the nucleus of the new Data Communications group, whose work other than BS 4421 is described in section 4.2 below.

Returning to the mainstream work of the group, considerable further extensions of control theory were described in the Annual Report for 1966 (pp.163–168). At the same time new applications of the techniques were explored, including a blast furnace (with the British Iron and Steel Research Association), a production distillation column at an oil refinery (with BP Ltd), a town gas reformer (with the East Midlands Gas Board), and a nuclear reactor used for training by the Royal Naval College. The Uttley-inspired title Adaptive Control was dropped at this time and the group was renamed, first as Systems Research and then as Automatic Control Systems.

Throughout its life the group included a changing population of Research Fellows, Guest Workers, and students, who maintained its strong links with universities and contributed a good deal to its liveliness. A list compiled in 1967 (of the whole group including the biological control work) shows that there were then as many as 17 of these short-term workers: eight Guest Workers, three Research Fellows, three sandwich-course students and three other paid temporary workers, in addition to 13 permanent members of staff, making a total of 30.

With the detachment of the Data Handling Section the remaining work of the group had become more closely related to the industrial research programme of the Warren Spring Laboratory at Stevenage than to that of NPL. Accordingly the work programme and the core of the group, eight members of staff including Percy Hammond, were transferred to Warren Spring on 1 April 1968. Together with the indigenous chemical engineers, they formed there a new Control Engineering Division under Hammond's leadership.

Besides those named above, the following made major contributions to this work: P A N Briggs, N W Rees, E P H Woodroffe, K R Godfrey and E R Dymott.

Selected publications on adaptive control

1. Conditional probability learning machine

A M Andrew. The conditional probability computer. *Proc. NPL Symposium on the Mechanisation of Thought Processes 1958*, HMSO, 1959, pp.945–946.

A M Uttley. Conditional probability computing in a nervous system. *Proc. NPL Symposium on the Mechanisation of Thought Processes 1958*, HMSO, 1959, pp.119–152. [This paper includes (p.147) references to Uttley's work in this field before he joined NPL].

A M Uttley. The design of conditional probability computers. *Information and Control*, 2(1), 1959, pp.1–24.

A M Andrew. Learning in control systems. *Control*, 3(28), 1960, p.100.

A M Andrew. A method for long-term storage of analogue information. *Control*, 3(29), 1960, p.118.

2. General adaptive control

R E King. A transportation lag circuit for analogue computation. *J. British Institution of Radio Engineers*, 24(2), 1962, pp.111–115.

J Dawkins. Control measurement in the presence of noise. *J. of Electronics and Control*, 15(3), 1963, part I p.245, part II, p.255.

P H Hammond and M J Duckenfield. Automatic optimisation by continuous perturbation of parameters. *Automatica*, 1(2), 1963, p.147.

N W Rees and R E King. Optimization studies on an electronic analogue of a simple still. *Trans. Soc. Instrument Technology*, 15(1), 1963, p.59.

P H Hammond and N W Rees. Self-optimising and adaptive control systems. NPL Report Auto 6, July 1964.

P A N Briggs, P H Hammond, M T G Hughes and G O Plumb. Correlation analysis of process dynamics using pseudo-random binary test perturbations. *Proc. IME*, 179, 3H, 1965.

P A N Briggs and K R Godfrey. Pseudo random signals for the dynamic analysis of multi-variable systems. *Proc. IEE*, 113, 1966, p.1259.

K R Godfrey and P A N Briggs. An examination of some pseudo random signals for multivariable system dynamic analysis. NPL Report Auto 14, April 1966.

D W Clarke. Digital learning models using sensitivity methods. NPL Report Auto 16, May 1966.

D W Clarke. Self-optimizing systems involving the estimation of cost-function slope using pseudo-random binary perturbations. NPL Report Auto 20, June 1966.

D W Clarke. Generalized-least-squares estimation of the parameters of a dynamic model. NPL Report Auto 26, November 1966.

B J Williams. Multivariable system identification using P.R.B.S. NPL Report Auto 23, November 1966.

P A N Briggs, D W Clarke and P H Hammond. An introduction to statistical identification methods in control systems. NPL Report Auto 24, December 1966.

B J Williams. The design of digital compensators for chemical processes. NPL Report Auto 29, April 1967.

P A N Briggs, K R Godfrey and P H Hammond. Estimation of process dynamic characteristics by correlation methods using pseudo-random signals. *Proc. IFAC Symposium on the Problems of Identification in Automatic Control Systems*, Prague, June 1967.

K R Godfrey and P H Hammond. Identification in automatic control systems—a review. *Control*, 11(112), October 1967, p.480.

P H Hammond. On-off control. In: A R Meetham and R A Hudson (eds), *Encyclopaedia of Linguistics, Information and Control*, Pergamon Press, 1969, pp.136–140.

G W Lange. Man-machine in control systems. In: Meetham and Hudson as above, pp.307–311.

A Hazlerigg. Optimization of industrial processes. In: Meetham and Hudson as above, pp.345–348.

P A N Briggs. Use of pseudo-random binary signals in correlation analysis of dynamic systems. In: Meetham and Hudson as above, pp.433–437.

3. Distillation column and associated instrumentation

D L A Barber. Infra-red composition measuring equipment. *Control*, 6(55), 1963, p.96.

G O Plumb. A mass flowmeter. *Control*, 6(56), 1963, p.103.

N W Rees. Dynamic optimization of a continuous distillation system. NPL Report Auto 5, March 1964.

D L A Barber and P H Hammond. The use of an on-line digital computer to evaluate the dynamic response of a pilot-scale distillation column. *Trans. Soc. Instrument Technology*, 17(3), 1965, p.59.

B J Williams. Optimal control of a distillation column. NPL Report Auto 21, July 1966.

P H Hammond and B J Williams. On determining the dynamic model of a binary distillation column using a computer program. *Proc. IEE Convention on Advances in Computer Control*, Conference Publication 29, IEE, 1967.

B J Williams. The estimation by computer of composition from temperature and pressure measurements in a binary distillation system. NPL Report Auto 27, January 1967.

B J Williams. The computer control of a distillation column. NPL Report Com Sci 37, July 1968.

4. Data handling

D V Blake and D L A Barber. Punched paper tape for experimental data. *Computer Bulletin*, 7(3), 1963, p.82.

D L A Barber. A versatile data processing system. NPL Report Auto 2, January 1964.

D L A Barber, G O Plumb and E P H Woodroffe. The interconnection of computers and peripheral equipment. *Computer Bulletin*, 8(1), 1964, pp.23–27.

A T Davies. A technique for the transmission of digital information over short distances using infra-red radiation. *Radio and Electronic Engineering*, 29(6), 1965, p.369.

E P H Woodroffe. Digital recording on quarter-inch magnetic tape. NPL Report Auto 11, July 1965.

D L A Barber and E P H Woodroffe. The NPL Standard Interface. NPL Report Auto 13, July 1966.

D L A Barber and E P H Woodroffe. Some aspects of a highway interface. NPL Report Auto 28, April 1967.

5. **BS 4421**

D L A Barber and D V Blake. The implementation of the British Standard Interface at NPL. NPL Report Com Sci 38, May 1968.

BSI. British Standard Specification No. 4421: a digital input/output interface for data collection systems. BSI, April 1969; reproduced in Davies and Barber's 1973 book (ref. 33), pp.531–551.

D L A Barber and D V Blake. The derivation, description and application at NPL of British Standard Specification 4421. NPL Report Com Sci 43, February 1970.

3.4 Pattern recognition

Communication in both speech and writing depends on one of the most fundamental human information-processing capabilities: that of recognising *patterns,* such as printed characters in a visual scene, or phonemes in a stream of sound. It was therefore natural for those interested in the mechanisation of thought processes in the 1950s to consider whether machines could be made to recognise patterns; if so, the foundation would be laid for means of computer input which matched human behaviour and abilities much better than the currently available media of punched cards and paper tape. This type of parallel between man and machine was typical of Dr Uttley's approach, and soon after his arrival work started at NPL in the area of automatic pattern recognition.

The NPL Report for 1958 records (p.56): 'The Division has purchased an industrial television camera for feeding pictorial information into DEUCE. The special equipment needed to link the camera to the DEUCE has been designed and constructed, but it has not yet been connected to the computer. With the aid of this equipment it is intended to investigate methods of automatically reading and recognising printed characters and, in particular, written numbers.' But assuming such an image has been captured in a computer's memory, how exactly is the software to distinguish an image which we would classify as the numeral '2', say, from other images, given the great variability that can occur in style, clarity and size?

The first approach was as follows:

- draw the ten numeric characters 0–9 in a supposedly standard form;
- select 12 common character components, either straight-line segments or circular arcs, fixed in position, size and orientation;

Pattern recognition

- measure the degree of overlap or correlation between each standard character and each component, thus defining 12 numbers for each of the ten standard characters;
- for an unknown character, measure the same 12 correlations with the components;
- identify the character as the one whose 12 numbers are the closest match with its own.

According to the 1959 Annual Report, this whole procedure was carried out on DEUCE; the program probably used data collected off-line as John Parks does not remember a camera being connected to DEUCE in spite of the plans mentioned above. The procedure sounds a reasonable first approach, but was found to be too vulnerable to differences in size and position between the unknown character and the reference set.

The next idea, developed by Max Clowes, was more cunning. Instead of correlating the unknown character directly with stored reference data, it was first correlated with various shifted copies of itself, a process known as *autocorrelation*. The idea is shown in the figure on the left: if for example a character has a line element at a certain angle, it will correlate more strongly with a copy of itself shifted at that angle than it would if it had no such element. This remains true whatever the size and position of the character. The set of correlation factors resulting from shifts in several directions can then be matched with reference sets as before to identify the character. A hand-operated optical system for measuring auto-correlations was developed in 1960 using high-contrast 35 mm negatives of individual characters. This system was used to develop and refine the autocorrelation technique.

By 1961 an electronic character-recognition machine using these principles was being designed. It used a *flying-spot scanner* (a device to sweep a spot of light across the character being read several times, like a television raster scan, with a photocell to

❑ SIDELINE ❑ DETOUR ❑ DIGRESSION ❑ BYWAY ❑ SCENIC ROUTE ❑

Magnetic ink character recognition

In 1960 the London Clearing Banks were handling 3.3 million cheques on an average day. Each cheque had to be returned to its home branch, and the banks planned to use a magnetic ink character system to enable the cheques to be sorted automatically.

There were three contenders: a French system from Machines Bull, an established American system known as E-13B, and the FRED system from EMI Ltd; samples are shown in the diagram (in this order in each quadrant).

Autonomics Division was given a six-month contract by the banks to assess these three systems as regards the logic of the reading process, the printing methods, and the effect of printing faults on recognition. Donald Davies and David Clayden carried out the investigation; although the details were confidential, the outcome can still be seen in any cheque book over 35 years later.

The Uttley era: 1957–1966

Figure 19. Pattern recognition: John Parks with the 'Bird's Nest' Cyclops prototype, May 1964. The flying-spot scanner is on the right.

Figure 20. Pattern recognition: Cyclops 1 with Roger Manning, June 1968.

observe the variations in the brightness of the light reflected). To carry out an autocorrelation, the output from the scanner was compared with copies of itself subjected to appropriate delays. The final stage matched the output from the autocorrelator against the outputs for a standard set of characters, and on this basis selected the most probable identity of the input character. Although parts of this process were validated by computer simulation, the whole design was implemented in purpose-built electronics.

The system was designed for reading printed numerals presented rapidly one at a time. A prototype known as the Bird's Nest, shown in fig. 19, was completed in 1964. It was followed in 1965 by the full version, called Cyclops 1, shown in fig. 20. It was claimed that Cyclops could read 3000 characters per second of poorly printed numerals with an error rate of about 1 in 10^5 (NPL Annual Report for 1967, p.170), though in retrospect this appears optimistic. Products based on Cyclops 1 were developed by Plessey Automation Ltd and marketed successfully as the Plessey 4200 series (OCHRE).

Reading continuous text is a good deal harder than reading single numerals, for two reasons: the larger set of characters gives more scope for confusion, and the segmentation of words into individual characters often proves to be a problem. In 1963, in parallel with the development of Cyclops 1, investigation started into the design of a new machine to read continuous printed text. The idea was to process a whole line of text at a time, without any preliminary attempt to divide it into its component characters. Features such as horizontal line segments were found by auto-correlation as before, and their positions recorded. Then many searches were made, each for a particular combination of features occurring within a small distance of each other. When such a combination was found, say the crossover typical of an X, the likelihood of an X in that position was stepped up. Finally, the results of this process for the whole line were scanned, and a most probable sequence of characters identified. This ingenious attempt to overcome the segmentation problem in parallel with the process of character recognition was known as Cyclops 2.

So in 1966, at the end of the Uttley era, Cyclops 1 was complete and had been transferred to the industry for exploitation, and the Cyclops 2 technique was being investigated. The prime movers in the work were Max Clowes (until his departure in 1963), David Clayden and John Parks, with Julian Ullmann specialising in the theory. Other contributors included Peter Pobgee, Ralph Rengger, Rosemary Elliott (later Mrs Lewis), Bob Davis and Roger Manning. Pattern recognition research continued in the Davies era, and this work is described in section 4.5 below.

Publications on pattern recognition 1958–66

M B Clowes and J R Parks. A new technique in automatic character recognition. *Computer Journal,* 4(2), 1961, pp.121–126.

E A Newman. Some comments on character recognition. *Computer Journal,* 4(2), 1961, pp.114–118.

M B Clowes. The use of multiple auto-correlation in character recognition. *Proc. ONR-NBS Symposium on Optical Character Recognition,* Spartan Books, Washington, 1962, pp.305–318.

J R Ullmann. Consistency techniques for pattern association. *IRE Trans. on Information Theory,* IT-8, 5, 1962, pp.74–81.

M B Clowes. Towards versatile reading machines. *New Scientist,* 19(348), 1963, p.122.

M B Clowes and J R Parks. Character recognition. *Proc. Electronic Data Processing Symposium, October 1961,* Pitman, 1963, p.558.

J R Ullmann. A basic approach to pattern recognition. *Computer Journal*, 7(4), 1965, pp.282–289.

D O Clayden, M B Clowes and J R Parks. Letter recognition and the segmentation of running text. *Information and Control*, 9, 1966, p.246.

J R Parks. An analogue technique for the recognition of low quality printed characters. PhD thesis, City University and NPL Report Auto 17, August 1966.

Reading aids for the blind

Braille and 'talking books' (audio tapes) can only cover a small fraction of all printed material. As long ago as 1920 a device called an *optophone* was marketed for producing sounds from ordinary printed text, not by recognising the characters but by making a sound analogue of the shape of each letter. For example an 'n' would sound like a chord followed by a single note of medium-to-high pitch followed by a repeat of the original chord. One particularly skilled operator could read 30 words per minute using this machine, but it was never widely used because the sounds were hard to learn and also if you read very slowly you tend to forget what the beginning of a sentence is before you get to the end. From 1960 to 1964 St Dunstan's supported a research programme in Autonomics Division to investigate ways of improving on the optophone technique.

Four preliminary ideas were put forward: to change the mapping of shapes on to sounds so as to improve discrimination; to try stereophonic presentation of more than one letter at a time; to develop a tactile 'display' using moving pins; and to tackle the problem of how to follow lines of print across the page.

In the event work concentrated on the first area. Equipment was constructed to read characters from a film one at a time (to avoid location, delimitation and cross-talk problems) and store the images on paper tape. The tape was used as input both to shape analysis programs on ACE and to several alternative sound-generation systems. The output sounds were compared in a series of careful experiments to measure how easy they were to learn. The conclusion was that people could distinguish better between artificial speech-like sounds (even though they were not related to the 'natural' sound of the character) than between the various musical chirps produced by the optophone.

The work was carried out by Keith Ellis and Pat Nye (Guest Workers) and Ralph Rengger.

Publications on reading aids for the blind

P W Nye. Aural recognition time for multi-dimensional signals. *Nature*, 196, 1962, p.1282.

K Ellis. Some experiments on reading aids for the blind. *Journal of the British Institution of Radio Engineers*, 25(2), 1963, p.188.

P W Nye. Reading aids for blind people. *Medical, Electronic and Biological Engineering*, 2(3), 1964, p.247.

P W Nye. An investigation of audio outputs for a reading machine. NPL Report Auto 8, February 1965.

3.5 Biology and psychology related to recognition and control

Dr Uttley's interest in the working of the brain, and his belief in its relevance to the design of artificial recognition and control systems, led to the arrival at NPL of specialists in several fields alien to its traditional culture of 'hard' science and technology. Most were either Guest Workers (unpaid) or Research Fellows (on fixed-term contracts). The principle proved ultimately to be too idealistic and long-term for its time and place, but the new people, notably perhaps Seymour Papert, raised the level of intellectual stimulation, much as a university educates in part through its mix of people with different viewpoints. Dr Uttley relished this effect, always seeing his role as that of the professor in charge of a university research department. Although the direct influence of the 'soft' science on the contemporary hard technology was not as great as he had hoped, the work had a lasting effect on the Division through the recruitment of Chris Evans.

There were four main areas of work: human visual perception, biological control systems, brain physiology and learning systems.

Human visual and auditory perception

The starting point for this work was the observation that the same pattern can appear different to a human observer at different times depending on the context. This looked likely to be a useful trait in artificial recognition systems, and so in 1959 investigations were begun into this aspect of human perception. The particular phenomena chosen were 'figural after-effects': for example, if you stare for a while at a point on a curved line and then look at a straight line, it may appear curved in the opposite direction. There was a theory that this was a by-product of the process by which pattern recognition is learnt, but experiments in 1961 did not find any improvement in discrimination associated with a figural after-effect. If you stare at a tilted line for a while your judgement of verticality is temporarily impaired. This effect was measured in experiments reported in 1962, but again no relevance to recognition was established.

In normal use, the eyes are constantly moving, both voluntarily and involuntarily. What role, if any, do these movements have in pattern perception? One way to find out is to eliminate the effects of the movements and see what happens to perception. To do this,

The Uttley era: 1957–1966

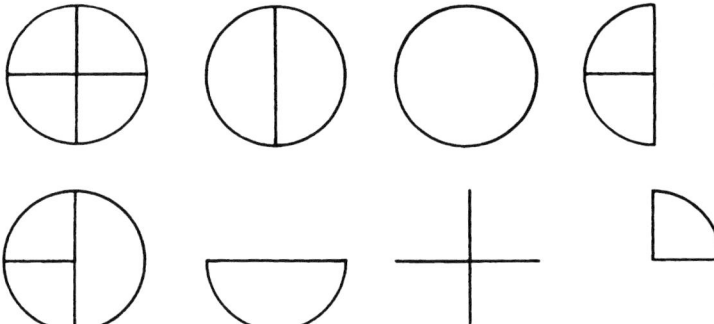

Figure 21. Visual perception: an initial after-image (top left) and later fragmented versions of it.

Figure 22. Visual perception: equipment for studying after-images, with P Stilliard as the subject, November 1964.

an image needs to be stabilised on the retina. Contact lenses can be fitted with a small attachment to produce a focused image, but this is uncomfortable for the subject. In 1963 Chris Evans was recruited to work on a better idea: to produce a stabilised image by firing a flash gun behind a transparency of the required pattern. This of course produces an after-image, which is fixed in position on the retina and disappears after some minutes. The interesting thing is that it does not necessarily fade uniformly: neat chunks disappear and reappear, leaving equally neat, symmetrical pieces behind (see fig. 21). The experimental set-up is shown in fig. 22; when this was first published Chris was at pains to point out that the eye patch was to ensure that the subject saw the flash with one eye only, and should not be taken to indicate a recent eye injury!

Results from this work reported in 1964–65 were:

- when a stereoscopic pair of images is flashed on the two eyes, the images fuse but depth perception is largely inhibited, thus suggesting that depth perception depends in part on the normal regime of eye movements;

> ❑ SIDELINE ❑ DETOUR ❑ DIGRESSION ❑ BYWAY ❑ SCENIC ROUTE ❑
>
> **Computers and dreams**
>
> Sessions of rapid eye movements (REM) associated with dreaming are a feature of human sleep. In 1960 it was found that deprivation of REM sleep caused psychological disturbances, and that when allowed REM sleep again, subjects spend more time than usual dreaming. In other words people seem to need to dream, or perhaps to need some process of which dreaming is a result. In 1964 Ted Newman and Chris Evans created considerable interest by suggesting that this process was analogous to program modification, file restructuring and suchlike housekeeping tasks on computers; see refs 41, 42, 44.

- a correlation was found between periods of disappearance of the stabilised image and the occurrence of alpha rhythm in the brain;
- a straight-line after-image may fragment into segments in a way which suggests the presence in the human perceptual system of units sensitive to straight-line segments subtending about 1° at the retina.

In 1967 (at last, one might think) the technique of retinal stabilisation was applied to numerals and letters of varying typefaces and designs to investigate the ways in which they fragmented and to consider whether these fragments were relevant to the design of automatic pattern recognition systems. An 'artificial retina', an array of light-sensitive elements on which an image could be projected together with associated logical circuitry, was also developed (and patented, see Annex B).

In a parallel investigation of auditory perception, experiments were carried out in which subjects listened to many repeats on the same word, using a loop of tape. Previous experiments by others had shown that words appear to change as they are repeated in this way, with subjects sometimes finding it hard to believe that the change is only in their perception and has no external reality. The idea behind the NPL work was that the ways in which consonants appeared to change might throw some light on the sound classification system used in auditory perception, and that this in turn might help in the design of speech recognition systems. As with the work on stabilised retinal images, the results are reported in the papers listed below but their relevance to the design of artificial recognition systems does not seem to have been established.

Publications on visual perception

M B Clowes. Some factors in brightness discrimination with constraint of retinal image movement. *Optica Acta*, 8(1), 1961, p.81.

J A Wilson. Is the figural after-effect accompanied by changes in discrimination? *Quart. J. of Experimental Psychology*, 13(4), 1961, p.219.

M B Clowes. A note on colour discrimination under conditions of retinal image constraint. *Optica Acta,* 9(1), 1962, pp.65–68.

J A Wilson. Apparatus for recording figural after-effects. *Quart. J. of Experimental Psychology,* 14(2), 1962, pp.119–121.

C R Evans. A comparison of the behaviour of geometrical shapes when viewed under conditions of steady fixation, and with apparatus for producing a stabilized retinal image. *British Journal of Physiological Optics,* 20, 1963, p.261.

C R Evans. Subjective fading under steady fixation. *Science,* 144, 1964, p.1359.

C R Evans et al. Perception of pattern and colour in the stabilised retinal image. *Nature,* 203, 1964, p.1200.

C R Evans and G K Smith. Alpha-frequency of electroencephalogram and a stabilized retinal image. *Nature,* 204, 1964, p.303.

C R Evans. A universally fitting contact lens for the general study of stabilized retinal image phenomena. *British Journal of Physiological Optics,* 22(1), 1965, p.39.

C R Evans. Some studies of pattern perception using a stabilized retinal image. *British Journal of Psychology,* 56(2,3), 1965, p.121.

C R Evans and T B Mulholland. An unexpected artefact in the human EEG relating to alpha occurrences and the position of the eyes in the head. *Nature,* 207, 1965, p.36.

C R Evans and J R Ullmann. A proposed behavioural test for distinguishing between the perceptual judgement mechanisms of humans and those of a machine. *Trans. IEEE (HFE),* 6(1), 1965, p.86.

J A Wilson. Adaptation and repulsion in the figural after-effect. *Quart. J. of Experimental Psychology,* 17(1), 1965, p.1.

C R Evans. New approach to pattern perception. *Discovery,* 28(8), 1966, p.17.

C R Evans and R P Marsden. A study of the effect of perfect retinal stabilization on some well-known visual illusions using the after-image as a method of compensating for eye movements. *British Journal of Physiological Optics,* 23(4), 1966, p.242.

C R Evans. Prolonged after-images employed as a technique for retinal stabilization: some further studies of pattern perception and some theoretical considerations. NPL Report Auto 25, November 1966.

J M Clegg and C R Evans. Binocular depth perception of 'Julesz patterns' viewed as perfectly stabilized retinal images. *Nature,* 215, 1967, p.893.

J J Kulikowski and J R Parks. Contrast-transfer characteristics of n-tuple models of retinal receptive fields. *Proc. IEE,* 114(1), 1967, pp.156–159.

C R Evans and A M Wells. The perception of stereoscopic targets when viewed as binocular stabilised images. NPL Report Auto 33, June 1967.

C R Evans and J M Clegg. The perception of depth in binocular stabilised images. NPL Report Auto 34, July 1967.

C R Evans and J Wicks. A study of the effect of perfect retinal stabilization on the ability to shift 'attention' in a visual display. NPL Report Com Sci 39, May 1968.

C R Evans. Fragmentation of patterns occurring with tachistoscopic presentation. NPL Report Com Sci 40, November 1968. Reprinted in *Proc. IEE/NPL Conf. on Pattern Recognition,* held at NPL July 1968, IEE, 1968, pp.250–263.

C R Evans. Perceptual breakdown with stabilized images. In: A R Meetham and R A Hudson (eds), *Encyclopaedia of Linguistics, Information and Control,* Pergamon Press, 1969, pp.388–391.

Publications on auditory perception

C R Evans, M Longden, E A Newman and B E Pay. Auditory 'stabilized images'; fragmentation and distortion of words with repeated presentation. NPL Report Auto 30, January 1967.

C R Evans and A Kitson. An experimental investigation of the relation between the 'familiarity' of a word and the number of changes in its perception which occur with repeated presentation as a 'stabilised auditory image'. NPL Report Auto 36, September 1967.

C R Evans and J Wilson. Subjective changes in the perception of consonants when presented as 'stabilised auditory images'. NPL Report Com Sci 41, November 1968.

Biological control systems

In industrial processes, control parameters are varied on the basis of regular measurements of key variables, with the aim of optimising the behaviour of the system in some defined and measurable sense. There are clear parallels between this situation and the operation of many biological mechanisms: the maintenance of oxygenated blood supply by varying heart and respiration rates, the maintenance of body fluid levels by regulating the sensation of thirst, and countless others. Although physically very different, artificial and biological systems must have some common ground in control systems theory.

On this basis, a group funded by the Medical Research Council to investigate human breathing control was housed in Autonomics Division from 1963 to 1969. The leaders of the group were Ian Priban and Bill Fincham, with up to three supporting staff at any one time. All were Guest Workers.

The mechanism regulating human respiration adjusts both the depth and the frequency of breathing in order to keep nearly constant the partial pressures of oxygen and carbon dioxide in the blood, even when moderate exercise changes the rate at which the oxygen is used up. In addition the depth and frequency of breathing are balanced to minimise effort. Other factors are involved in breathing control, including temperature, level of consciousness, speech and swallowing. Breathing had been found to exhibit two regular cycles, one with a period of 3.5 *breaths* and one with a period of 40–50 *seconds* (independent of the breathing rate), and this provided clues as to the nature of the control process.

The group set out to construct a formal model of the breathing process. Data logging equipment was used to record the depth and frequency of breathing both in healthy subjects and in patients suffering from respiratory disorders. The information was processed on the Adaptive Control group's Hermes computer.

The complex model, involving four feedback control loops, was duly formulated and although seen as successful 'exposed clearly definable gaps in our knowledge that have to be filled before the model can be said to represent the respiratory system as a whole'. The work undoubtedly benefited from the expertise and equipment available in the Adaptive Control group, but there is no record that it led to any new ideas for industrial process control.

In addition to this major project, various studies were made of subjects engaged in reactive tasks involving hand movements, such as tracking a target using a joystick. Psychological work of this type was mentioned briefly in most Annual Reports from 1959 to 1963. In 1964–65 studies were made of physiological tremor, the small regular variations in muscular force which occur when you try to exert a steady pressure, in this case a side thrust with the wrist. Data recorded included eye movements as the subject watched his or her own actions, and both ACE and Hermes were used to analyse the observations. In collaboration with St Thomas' Hospital, the group made studies of the use by disabled people of head and eye movement for control purposes.

Selected publications on biological control systems

P H Hammond. An experimental study of servo action in human muscular control. *Proc. 3rd Int. Conf. on Medical Electronics, 1960*, IEE, 1961, p.190.

I P Priban and W F Fincham. Self-adaptive control and the respiratory system. *Nature*, 208, 1965, pp.339–343.

P H Hammond. The control of artificial limbs. *Discovery*, 27(3), March 1966, pp.21–25.

P H Hammond. Control by eye and head movement. *Control*, 11(103), January 1967, p.31.

P H Hammond. Control in living systems. *IEE Electronics and Power*, 13, 1967, p.338.

K Oatley. The role of thirst in regulating the state of body fluids. NPL Report Auto 32, May 1967.

I P Priban. Self-adaptive control of respiration. In: A R Meetham and R A Hudson (eds), *Encyclopaedia of Linguistics, Information and Control*, Pergamon Press, 1969, pp.132–136.

Brain physiology

In 1961, plans were made for direct investigations of the working of the nervous system. The first attempt was to study learning in earthworms, but they proved ineducable, so attention turned to higher animals. It was assumed that the physical basis of learning was alteration in the connection between neurons in the brain. In a series of experiments in 1962–65 electrical activity around individual neurons in the cat's cerebral cortex was observed, and statistical models describing the activity were constructed. It was found that repeated use of a synaptic pathway between neurons did not facilitate the transmission of further impulses, and that the conductivity of a pathway between two cells depended on several aspects of their recent activity. Those involved in this work were Professor B de L Burns (on a senior temporary appointment), Dr G K Smith and A D J Robertson. The work ended with

Dr Uttley's departure in 1966, and the specially designed accommodation on the top floor of Building 93 was eventually converted to office use.

Selected publications on brain physiology

A M Andrew. An electrophysiological investigation of learning in the earthworm. *Proc. of the Symposium of the German Society for Electronics*, held at Karlsruhe, S Hirzel, Stuttgart, 1961, pp.158–166.

G K Smith and D R Smith. Spike activity in the cerebral cortex. *Nature*, 202, 1964, p.253.

C R Evans and A D J Robertson. Single-unit activity in the cat's visual cortex: modification after an intense light flash. *Science*, 147(3655), 1965, pp.303–304.

C R Evans and A D J Robertson. Prolonged excitation in the visual cortex of the cat. *Science*, 150(3698), 1965, p.913.

G O Plumb. Pulse height analysis for electrophysiology. *J. of Physiology*, 179(1965), p.16.

A D J Robertson. Anaesthesia and receptive fields. *Nature*, 205, 1965, p.80.

A D J Robertson. Correlation between unit activity and slow potential changes in cat's unanaesthetised cerebral cortex. *Nature*, 208, 1965, p.757.

Learning systems

In parallel with the biological work, studies of artificial learning systems were undertaken. This was done on the basis that such systems deserved investigation in their own right, regardless of whether they turned out to be useful models of brain function, though of course it was hoped that the two lines of inquiry might suggest fruitful experiments for each other, with a possible long-term convergence. Models of neural activity based on the computation of probabilities in individual neurons had been Dr Uttley's main research interest in the three years before he joined NPL in 1957, and his work led to the development of the so-called conditional probability computer, already described on p.73 because of its relevance to control systems. To demonstrate its capability for simple learning, this machine was connected to the small trolley or 'tortoise' shown in fig. 23. The tortoise carried two optical sensors using which it could tell whether it was straddling a boundary in the floor pattern or was in a black or white area. At first it wandered randomly, but after a time successfully learnt to follow the curving boundary. Another device photographed by NPL on the same day is shown in fig. 24, apparently more versatile judging by the lamp and recorder. In NPL's photographic records this is given the cryptic title 'Hungarian machine (Tortoise)'. It has been suggested that it may have been the work of a Hungarian Guest Worker, but no record has been found of such a person and nothing is known at present of the capabilities of this device or of its connection with Hungary.

The Uttley era: 1957–1966

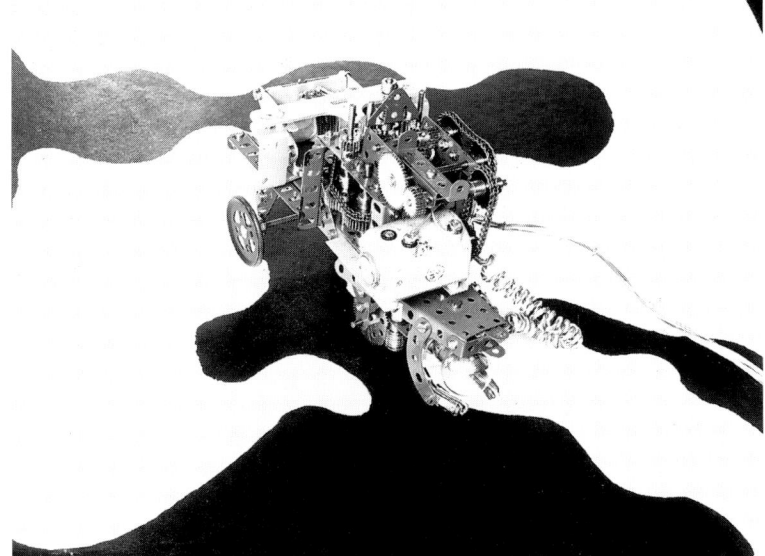

Figure 23. Learning systems: the NPL tortoise, November 1958.

Figure 24. Learning systems: the 'Hungarian machine (Tortoise)', November 1958.

The NPL Annual Report for 1960 mentions (p.59) a mathematical model covering several different artificial learning systems, including the conditional probability computer (CPC), and the 1961 Report, after an account of the limitations of the CPC (p.68), outlines theoretical studies of *plastic* neural nets, in which the properties of the cells change as a result of their activity. Details of this work, carried out by Alec Andrew, Seymour Papert and others, are given in the reports listed below. Uttley's pioneering work on neural nets, which started well before he joined NPL, has been unfairly neglected compared with that of Rosenblatt and others, and a recent paper by Copeland and Proudfoot (ref. 22), though it concentrates on the similar neglect of Turing's contribution to the same field, also mentions Uttley's work and is a welcome move towards setting the record straight.

Publications on learning systems

A M Uttley. Computing in the nervous system. *Impulse*, 6(6), 1958, pp.6–9.

A M Andrew. Learning machines. *Proc. NPL Symposium on the Mechanisation of Thought Processes 1958*, HMSO, 1959, pp.473–509.

S Papert. Capacity and redundancy in logical nets. *Proc. Bionics Symposium 1960*, Wright Air Development Division, Technical Report 60-600, p.181.

A M Uttley. Self-organizing systems. *Proc. Interdisciplinary Conf. 1959*, 2, Pergamon Press, 1960, pp.319–322.

A M Andrew. Self-optimizing control mechanisms and some principles for more advanced learning machines. *Automation and Remote Control*, Butterworths, 1961.

S Papert. Some mathematical models of learning. *Proc. 4th London Symposium on Information Theory*, 1960, Butterworths, 1961, p.353.

S Papert. Centrally produced geometrical illusions. *Nature*, 191, 1961, p.733.

A M Uttley. Discrete learning in automata. *Proc. Symposium of the German Society for Electronics*, held at Karlsruhe, S Hirzel, Stuttgart, 1961.

A M Andrew. An experimental comparison of some algorithms for self-organizing systems. *IRE Trans. on Information Theory*, IT-8, 5, 1962, pp.163–168.

A M Uttley. Properties of plastic networks. *Proc. Int. Biophysics Conf.*, Stockholm, 1961, *Biophys. J.*, 2(2), Pt. 2, Supp., 1962, pp.169–188.

J R Ullmann. Cybernetic models which learn sensory-motor connections. *J. of Medical Electronics and Biological Engineering*, 1, 1963, pp.91–100.

D R Smith. On the capabilities and limitations of learning networks. NPL Report Auto 3, February 1964.

See also the list of publications on the conditional probability computer on p.78. A list of Uttley's publications in this field before he joined NPL is given in Feigenbaum and Feldman (1963), ref. 51 pp.517–518. After leaving NPL he published a book on information transmission in the nervous system (ref. 148).

3.6 Machine translation

The possibility of using a computer to translate from one natural language to another was mooted at least as early as 1948[2]. It raises in a neat form many of the challenges of artificial intelligence, since the original text can readily be input to the computer and the output printed, but the transformation from one character string to another depends, at least as far as human translators are concerned, on an understanding of the meaning of the text. The subject caused considerable controversy in the 1950s, with some saying that the task was clearly beyond the powers of any

---

[2] The use of an electronic dictionary to aid human translators was suggested by A D Booth of Birkbeck College London in 1946; one of the first references to the possibility of translation by computer was in Turing's 1948 paper on intelligent machinery (ref. 140 p.9 of original); and the first proposal for practical work was by Warren Weaver of the Rockefeller Foundation in 1949, following discussion with Booth and others. The early history of machine translation is described in Mounin (1964), ref. 92 pp.15–27.

conceivable computer-based system, while others said the problem could at least be attempted. The opposition cited examples of 'untranslatable' sentences to support their point, which were usually one of three types: allusions to the culture of the source country which did not make sense in the target language without extra explanation; ambiguities both intentional and unintentional; and metaphors, puns, poetry and similar artistic uses of language. This controversy was apparent at the NPL Thought Processes conference in 1958 (ref. 109 pp.303–307), and Donald Davies saw that machine translation (MT) was a challenging area where a practical approach might produce a rough but useful solution while the philosophers were still arguing that ideal translation by computer was impossible. He started to give some thought to how ACE could be used in an NPL machine translation project.

Russian-to-English technical translation was selected early on as the task to be attempted, primarily because there was substantial technical literature in Russian not readily available to Western science and industry. Restricting the task to technical papers removed many of the objections to MT mentioned above, because the culture of science is international and language is being used in a relatively straightforward way with few if any literary quirks. Also Russian as an Indo-European language has many basic similarities with English (in the sense of common concepts of word classes and sentence structure, not in the sense that individual words are similar), whereas in, say, Japanese more of the concepts are different and even the character set forms a considerable obstacle because it is not a small fixed alphabet.

Contact was established in 1958–59 with Harvard University, where a group led by Professor Oettinger had been working on Russian–English MT since 1956. He gave the nascent NPL work a great boost by offering Donald Davies a free copy of the Russian–English dictionary on magnetic tape which had been developed as part of their project. This offer was gratefully accepted. The Univac-format tapes were inevitably incompatible with the magnetic tape system planned for ACE and were therefore converted to punched cards for transfer.

Russian is a highly inflected language, often using differences in word endings to carry meanings expressed in English with extra words. The designer of a computer-readable dictionary therefore has to decide whether to include all the possible forms derived from a single stem as separate entries, or to have a single entry for the stem with a note of which affixes it can take. The latter method, chosen by both Harvard and NPL, saves greatly on space while adding complexity to the process of looking up a word in the dictionary. Donald Davies showed something of his polymath virtuosity by devising a detailed scheme for the organisation of the dictionary entries, involving a comprehensive study of Russian grammatical forms, which was published in 1960 (ref. 28, and the first item in the list of publications below). He estimated that an adequate dictionary might need 100,000 entries, each on average 1500 bits long, say 20 Mb in modern parlance. This far exceeded the capacity of the ACE drums, so a serial storage medium had to be used, and clearly magnetic tape was the best choice for speed and durability.

A team was gradually assembled to build on these ideas. The leader of the MT group for most of its life, John McDaniel, was recruited in 1958 and worked initially on the mechanisation of clerical processes before moving to MT in July 1959. Two experts on Russian, Steve Whelan and Adam Szanser, arrived in 1959 and 1961 respectively, while those who knew more about computers than Russian were Wyn Price, who moved from ACE magnetic tape work to MT in 1961, Tony Day and David Yates.

One of John McDaniel's early tasks was to organise the first international conference on MT, which was held at NPL in September 1961. This conference was well timed: it came at a point when there were many groups in the USA and several in Europe newly active in MT and keen to share ideas. The basic facts that there were 169 delegates, 123 of whom were from outside the UK, and that the proceedings (ref. 112) run to 747 pages give some idea of the size of the event and the interest and enthusiasm that MT aroused at the time.

When designing the dictionary entry layout, the group devised a neat scheme for coding the affixes that a particular stem could take in a single 48-bit ACE word: each possible affix corresponded to a bit position, which was set to 1 if the stem could take that affix and 0 otherwise. The affix actually present in a text word was coded similarly; then only a single logical AND operation between the two words was needed to check whether the affix matched. The Harvard dictionary needed considerable modification to make use of this scheme and the associated rules for delimiting affixes; also it was found necessary to add many new words to the dictionary to make its coverage in its field (electronic engineering and related topics) reasonably comprehensive.

When translating, to start at the beginning of a text and find one word at a time in a dictionary held on a serial medium like magnetic tape would involve a prohibitive amount of time in running up and down the tape. A better plan is to sort the text words into the same alphabetical order as the dictionary, make one pass through the dictionary appending copies of all relevant dictionary entries to each text word, and then re-sort the text back to its original order using serial numbers inserted at the outset. This was the method adopted by the NPL group; the resulting text-with-dictionary-entries-appended was called *augmented text*.

Alphabetical order of complete words can not be completely maintained in a stem dictionary. (For example in English the stems *hit-* and *hitch-* would appear in that order, but the derived words *hits* and *hitches* if sorted alphabetically would appear in the opposite order.) Several interrelated considerations of this kind arising from the intricacies of Russian affixes made both the dictionary organisation and the look-up process more complex than they appear at first sight.

In Russian as in English new technical terms are often created using prefixes like *thermo-, radio-, electro-,* and so on. Such prefixes were identified by the text input program and both the full and truncated (without prefix) forms sent forward for look-up, the position being resolved once the words had been sorted back into text order. This provision meant that many long words which otherwise would not have been found in the dictionary were translated correctly. In a somewhat similar way Russian uses freely many suffixes like the English *-ness* and *-ological,* and if such a suffix occurred in a word not found in the dictionary it was translated. Sometimes both these circumstances occurred together, creating unforeseen pseudo-English forms like *non-contactness* which might well help the reader to understand an otherwise obscure passage.

For a group of Russian words forming an recognised idiom (in other words the preferred translation of the group is different from the sequence of translations of individual words), the details were included in one of the dictionary entries, much as is done in a conventional dictionary. Once the augmented text had been created such idioms were searched for, and when found the sequence of items was replaced with a single item with grammatical information and English equivalent taken from the idiom definition. Over 500 such idioms were added to the dictionary.

The group's basic overall plan for translation was a pragmatic one: to create an augmented text in the way outlined above and then to produce as output the English equivalents taken from the dictionary entries, in order. This was what would now be called the default option; naturally extra words would sometimes need to be inserted, or the word order changed, to reflect English grammatical conventions.

The first acceptable translation was produced in late April 1963, the sentence:

МЫ ГОВОРИМ ДРУГ О ДРУГЕ.

being rendered as:

WE SAY ABOUT ONE ANOTHER.

This is believed to be the first computer translation produced in the UK using a real dictionary (i.e. a full-size one, not one compiled to suit a particular text). The other two sentences in the same short text produced gobbledegook ('BETWEEN PHOSE I DAM YOU THIS . . .') for a variety of reasons, but the breakthrough had been made.

In subsequent development, a partial syntactic analysis was carried out on the augmented text to delimit word groups and resolve some ambiguities, using for example the requirement in Russian that adjectives and the nouns they qualify must agree in case, gender and number. The results of this analysis were expressed in the form of a tree-like list structure for each sentence, showing how the word groups nested within one another. In the final stage of the process, the synthesis of the English output, each type of word group had its own subroutine to carry out such tasks as re-ordering, word insertion, and inflection. These routines called each other freely and recursively as determined by the tree structure. There was found to be an interesting parallel between human short-term memory, which limits the depth of nesting found in naturally occurring sentences, and this program's requirements for push-down storage.

As a result of these processes of Russian analysis and English synthesis, various improvements were made to what would otherwise have been a crude word-for-word translation. Examples are:

- Russian verb forms were translated into the appropriate English constructions using auxiliary verbs, like *will not be taken*.
- English correspondents for Russian prepositions were chosen according to the case governed, and *of* was inserted where appropriate to represent the Russian genitive case.
- English inflections were created (using information coded into the dictionary to ensure, for example, that *write* was modified into *writing, wrote,* or *written* and not *writeing* or *writed*).
- Certain participial phrases were moved after the nouns they qualified (because in Russian you may say, for example, *the written last week paper*).

Where the dictionary gave alternative English equivalents (up to three were allowed), these were output in a vertical column, to be read as alternatives. Words not found in the dictionary were simply transliterated into English letters, and marked with an asterisk. An example of the unedited printed output is shown in fig. 25.

The software was written in ACE machine code, and the processes of creating and updating the dictionary, and debugging and developing the translation software, involved considerable difficulties, bearing in mind that valves and early magnetic tape systems were much less reliable than their equivalents today. Development aids were unknown: there was no facility, for example, for printing out an ACE program, much less viewing it on a screen; outside the computer it existed only as a pack of punched cards and the original manuscript coding.

A serious attempt was made to evaluate the quality of the translations resulting from the process outlined above.

```
Sources of mutual interferences of radio(s) and of radar



Engineer - podpolcovnic P. A. Arutyunov
                         *                *



Unlike conducting network of electrical connection    radio communication and
                                           communication

radar utilize one general medium, in which occurs  transmission of signals.
                 common                            results  transfer

And  although way(s), which pass electromagnetic waves, transferring message(s)
also                                                    transmitting

to definite   correspondents, and also length of waves not always coincide,
   defined
   determined

nevertheless some stations can mix       to work       onto reception to other
              only                interfere  performance for

stations.


These mutual interferences have own causes and  depend on power   , quantity and
                                           also            output

distance(s) of transmitters from receiving equipment, location    of their
                                                      arrangement

aerials, difference(s) of frequencies of transmitters or their harmonics from


frequencies of receivers and  , finally, from intensity of radiation
                         also

transmitting and  amplification of receiving directed aerials in non-desired
passing       also

directions .
trends
```

Figure 25. Machine translation: example of unedited results, 1967. For some words, the program gives alternative translations under the first choice, and any words not found in the dictionary it marks with an asterisk.

Participants were invited to send in Russian papers, which were put through the translation process; the results were returned to the senders with an invitation to assess their usefulness on a stated scale. The majority verdict was summed up in the final report, perhaps a little rosily, as 'mostly good enough, with a few obscurities'. This report, included in the list below, can be recommended to anyone interested in more detail.

Although there were many plans for further developments, including better syntactic analysis and the selection of English equivalents on the basis of co-occurrence statistics, these would realistically have involved rewriting the software for a more modern machine. As it happened, the level of funding for MT in the USA was at the same time being sharply reduced as a result of a critical report by the National Academy of Sciences (ref. 2); in fact, as subsequent developments have shown, machine translation was at a low point in the cycles of popularity and understanding which afflict many long-term enterprises. Practical work on MT at NPL came to an end with ACE on 14 February 1967. Besides those already mentioned, those who worked on the project included Albert Hill, Margaret Turney and Celia Jenkinson (later Mrs Searle).

Publications on machine translation

D W Davies. The organization of a Russian-English stem dictionary on magnetic tape. *Journal of Language and Speech,* 3(4), 1960, pp.193–222.

D W Davies and A M Day. A technique for consistent splitting of Russian words. *Proc. 1961 Int. Conf. on Machine Translation of Languages and Applied Language Analysis,* NPL, HMSO, 1962, pp.343–362.

J McDaniel and S Whelan. The grammatical interpretation of Russian inflected forms using a stem dictionary. *Proc. 1961 Int. Conf.* as above, pp.363–377.

J McDaniel. Translation by computer. *Electronics Weekly,* 304(7), 1966.

W L Price. Machine translation at NPL. *Научно-техническая Информация,* 9, 1966, pp.27–30. [in Russian]

A J M Szanser. Machine translation research at the National Physical Laboratory, Teddington. *The Incorporated Linguist,* 5(4), 1966, p.102.

D M Yates. A linguistic model for Russian–English machine translation, and its use in the synthesis of the English output. PhD thesis, University of London, 1966.

J McDaniel. Machine translation of natural languages. *Bulletin of the Institute of Information Scientists,* 5(3), 1967, p.5.

J McDaniel, A M Day, W L Price, A J M Szanser, S Whelan and D M Yates. Translation of Russian scientific texts into English by computer—a final report. NPL Report Auto 35, July 1967.

J McDaniel, W L Price, A J Szanser and D M Yates. An evaluation of the usefulness of machine translations produced at the NPL with a summary of the translation methods. *Deuxième Conférence sur la Traitement Automatique des Langues,* University of Grenoble, August 1967.

D M Yates. A computer model for Russian grammatical description, and a method of English synthesis in machine translation. *Deuxième conférence sur la traitement automatique des langues* as above.

J McDaniel, A M Day, W L Price, A J Szanser, S Whelan and D M Yates. Machine translation at the National Physical Laboratory, Teddington, Middlesex, England. In: A D Booth (ed.), *Machine Translation,* North-Holland, 1967, pp.229–266.

W L Price. Computer translation—is it worthwhile? *Electronics & Power,* September 1967, pp.343–345.

A J M Szanser. Machine translation—the evaluation of an experiment. *The Incorporated Linguist,* 6(4), 1967, pp.90–95.

D M Yates. Work on Russian–English machine translation at NPL. *Машинный перевод и прикладная лингвистика*, 10, 1967, pp.126–135. [in Russian]

A J Szanser. Machine translation at the NPL. *Physics Bulletin*, 20, March 1969, pp.92–94.

D M Yates. Computational linguistics: machine translation. In: A R Meetham and R A Hudson (eds), *Encyclopaedia of Linguistics, Information and Control*, Pergamon Press, 1969, pp.51–54.

3.7   Information retrieval

Any library needs some means by which an enquirer can locate those particular documents in the collection which are relevant to an enquiry. Indexes of titles and authors' names are obvious first steps, but if the enquirer does not have this information a subject index is needed. A librarian makes a subject index by choosing for each document one or more keywords or *descriptors*, and then creating an index showing for each descriptor which documents are relevant. (The Universal Decimal Classification system (UDC), for example, is a structured set of descriptors in wide use.) An enquiry relating to a single descriptor can then be answered readily, but in practice this is not adequate, and some means is needed of dealing with requests for documents which match all or most of a specified group of descriptors. In the 1950s conventional technology could offer the so-called 'peekaboo' system, in which each descriptor corresponded to a position along the top edge of the index cards; those cards for which the descriptor did not apply had a hole in this position, while those for which it did apply had a slot extending to the edge of the card. To answer a multidescriptor enquiry, rods like knitting needles were inserted into the pack of cards in the appropriate positions and lifted; like magic just the required cards would be left behind. Computers were clearly potentially a more powerful and versatile tool for tackling this problem, and in 1960 Dr Uttley initiated an investigation of the possibilities for automatic indexing and retrieval, undertaken by Peter Vaswani, then newly arrived, with help from Seymour Papert. Vaswani and Roger Meetham were the main contributors to the subsequent project. The underlying motivation for the work was the understanding that successful industrial research and development depended on ready access to relevant technical information; if computers could help, that would contribute to UK competitiveness.

Amongst the possibilities considered at the outset were (1) for the computer to have available a thesaurus of technical terms, so that it had some basis for assessing the degree to which two descriptors were related in meaning; and (2) for both the indexer and the enquirer to have the possibility of assigning weights to descriptors indicating their relative importance for the document or enquiry concerned. The computer system's output in response to an enquiry could then be a set of references to documents, rank-ordered according to the probability of their being relevant to the enquiry.

However, no suitable thesaurus of technical terms had been published, and in 1961 initial attention was being concentrated on the possibility of using a computer to create its own thesaurus by relating pairs of keywords together if there was a tendency for the two words to occur in the same document. A collection of 1600 abstracts in the field of radio technology had been prepared on punched cards for input to ACE, and programs written and run to find and list all the keywords (those not in a 'reject dictionary' of common words, truncated to eight letters or less). There were 1400 such words (later reduced to 1000). Preparations were in hand for the counts of word-pairs.

By 1962 these ideas had developed into a plan to use a set of over 10,000 abstracts, each of about 30 words, 11 of which on average were keywords in the above sense. The intention was to study the statistical association of pairs of keywords (whether their degree of co-occurrence was significantly higher or lower than would be expected by chance). Words would then be grouped under a conceptual 'thesaurus heading' either if they tended to co-occur, or more subtly if there was a sufficiently large number of other words with which each separately tended to co-occur. These artificial thesaurus headings would be used as descriptors in indexing and retrieval experiments, the idea being that this method would find documents which were relevant to the enquiry without necessarily using the same words. This was an exciting prospect, because the meaning of words is a notoriously slippery concept and this looked like a way in which computer-based systems could gain a foothold in the field of semantics.

In 1964 a new model of the thesaurus concept was introduced. The idea was to consider each keyword as corresponding to a point in space, with a line joining two points if the keywords were statistically associated; then a subset of the points with many interconnections (a *cluster*) corresponded to a thesaurus grouping. The attraction of this model was that there was an existing body of pure mathematics—graph theory—whose theorems could provide a reliable framework for working with the co-occurrence data in this form. For computing purposes, the data were expressed in the form of a matrix, with element *(i,j)* being the statistical association of keywords i and j. To reduce this 1000×1000 matrix to a size manageable on ACE, a threshold was applied to the numerical values to produce a binary matrix.

Various techniques were tried both for the statistical measure of association between an ordered pair of two words and for creating a 'useful' set of clusters, that is one which covers the ground without individual clusters being too big or many clusters being too small. Techniques were tried in pilot experiments using sections in a school geometry textbook as the document collection

(156 documents with a restricted technical vocabulary of only 146 words). A full-scale evaluation experiment was planned using the set of 12,288 abstracts (which had been keypunched in a marathon exercise by Val Hawtree).

Trials in 1965 showed that improvements were needed to restrict the effect on cluster formation of those keywords which associated most widely with others, and to allow enquirers to insist on certain keywords being present in the documents retrieved. It was decided this was the point at which to rewrite the software for the recently arrived KDF9 computer, the attractions compared with ACE being its speed, reliability, longer life expectancy, and less idiosyncratic store arrangements. To transfer data, including the document texts and the large binary matrices representing word-association data, a direct link was established between ACE and KDF9, using the NPL Standard Interface on each machine and purpose-written software: an early instance of the design and use of a host-to-host protocol.

The work on graph theory briefly developed a life of its own outside the document retrieval field; it was used for example to find structural similarities between complex organic molecules.

In 1967 and 1968 the final stage of the project consisted of a major series of experiments using various indexing and retrieval strategies and 93 enquiries from 21 subjects. These experiments are described in detail in the project's final report, which makes recommendations about the best choice of strategy in different circumstances. The overall conclusion (in the 1968–69 Annual Report) was that the best single strategy was to use keyword matching alone, but that strategies based on word associations could find considerable extra relevant material, and should be used to supplement, rather than replace, the use of keywords.

Besides those already mentioned, contributors to the work on information retrieval included John Cameron, Derek Baker, Hsu Kung-Shih, Carol Walsh (later Mrs Corby), and Roger Reason.

Publications on information retrieval

A R Meetham. Preliminary studies for machine-generated index vocabularies. *Journal of Language and Speech,* 6(1), 1963, p.22.

A R Meetham. Probabilistic pairs and groups of words in a text. *Journal of Language and Speech,* 7(2), 1964, p.98.

P K T Vaswani. Mechanized storage and retrieval of information. *Revue Internationale de la Documentation,* 32(1), 1965, pp.19–22.

A R Meetham. Algorithm to assist in finding the complete subgraphs of a given graph. *Nature,* 211, 1966, p.105.

A R Meetham. Graph separability and word grouping. *Proc. 21st National Conf. of the ACM,* Thompson, 1966, pp.513–514.

P K T Vaswani. Information storage and retrieval. *Научно-техническая Информация,* 3, 1967, pp.9–16 [in Russian].

A R Meetham. Partial isomorphisms in graphs and structural similarities in tree-like organic molecules. In: A J H Morrell (ed.), *Information Processing*

68: *Proc. IFIP Congress 1968,* held in Edinburgh August 1968, North-Holland, 1969, pp.210–213.

P K T Vaswani. A technique for cluster emphasis and its application to automatic indexing. *Proc. IFIP 1968* as above, pp.1300–1303.

A R Meetham. Communication theory and the evaluation of information retrieval systems. *Information Storage and Retrieval*, 5, 1969, pp.129–134.

A R Meetham. *Information Retrieval.* Aldus Books, 1969.

P K T Vaswani. Information storage and retrieval. In: A R Meetham and R A Hudson (eds), *Encyclopaedia of Linguistics, Information and Control,* Pergamon Press, 1969, pp.223–232.

P K T Vaswani and J B Cameron. The National Physical Laboratory experiments in statistical word associations and their use in document indexing and retrieval. NPL Report Com Sci 42, April 1970.

3.8 Cryotrons

By 1957, with the design of ACE complete and its construction well under way, thoughts began to turn to what future role the Division should have in computer design. There was no doubt that ACE was to be the last computer built at NPL: the growing computer industry had successfully taken over the development and manufacturing tasks from the pioneers. One way to help the industry would be to investigate novel technologies for computer components, and any implications they might have for systems design—a proposal which fitted in well with NPL's capabilities in physics and materials.

The fundamental computer component is the *switch,* a device to use a current in one conductor to allow or prevent current in another conductor. Early computers used thermionic valves as switches; by 1957 transistors had provided an alternative which was proving vastly superior in all the four important parameters: speed of operation, cost, reliability and size. Nevertheless further improvements would be demanded by the market, and any technique which looked like being able to offer improvements deserved investigation. In 1955 Professor Buck of MIT had suggested that superconductivity, the property whereby certain conductors lose all electrical resistance when cooled sufficiently, could be used to make a fast switch, because electrical resistance reappears in a superconductor if it is subjected to a sufficiently strong magnetic field. A superconductive switching element based on this idea is called a *cryotron.* It had also been suggested that a computer memory element, with non-destructive read-out, could be made from a superconducting loop containing two cryotrons with a current permanently circulating round it. In 1957 cryotrons looked very promising for use as computer components as regards speed and size; cost and reliability were little known. Donald Davies studied the available information and recommended that this was an area which deserved priority attention and where NPL's particular resources, including the availability on site of a

The Uttley era: 1957–1966

helium liquefier, offered a good foundation. A High Speed Computing group was accordingly established in CME Division in 1958, led by Dr Peter Stuart, to investigate these ideas.

The group designed a suitable basic configuration of crossed thin strips of tin and lead deposited on a substrate, separated from each other electrically by a thin insulating film, and began to develop equipment to make circuits of a few such devices by vacuum deposition, cool them to their working temperature within a few degrees of absolute zero, and allow their performance to be studied.

Initial results with individual cryotrons were not as good as had been expected from the properties of bulk superconducting materials, and in 1959 studies were undertaken of the many factors during manufacture which could affect the performance of the devices, in particular the way in which the fine structure of the deposited films was influenced by the residual gases in the evaporation plant. By 1961 an external contract was placed to study the feasibility of making cryotrons by the alternative techniques of chemical or electrodeposition, but this produced films with less satisfactory properties, apparently because of chemical impurities. In parallel with the development work, design studies were undertaken in 1962 of logic circuits using cryotrons to access a superconductive store.

In 1963 the work was brought under the DSIR Advanced Computer Techniques Project (see 3.1 above), which encouraged collaborative work. By this time it had been decided that it would be difficult to make crossed-strip cryotrons with time-constants less than 50–100 ns, and that parallel-strip devices should be investigated. Also the use of polymer insulating films was tried, in place of the silicon monoxide previously used, to improve the stability of the film under thermal stress and reduce the occurrence of disastrous pinholes in the insulation. (The insulation had to be thin to keep the switching time short.) The group was realising that it might not be possible to produce cryotron planes in which all the cryotrons functioned correctly, and therefore studied the extent to which circuit redundancy and component redundancy techniques could be used to give a satisfactory yield of usable planes. The goal of a completely superconductive computer was now seen as a long-term objective, and attention was focused on the use of cryogenic techniques in large random-access stores and their addressing circuits. A superconductive continuous film store was investigated jointly with RRE.

The 1964 Annual Report shows continued technical optimism but increasing concern about the economics of cryotrons: 'There is still no reason to doubt that cryotron storage elements and circuits can be made to function in a predictable manner, and the future of the cryotron now seems to be determined mainly by economic considerations, of which a particularly relevant factor is the yield in the fabrication process.' Concentration of effort on

Figure 26. Cryotrons: a vacuum evaporation unit with the bell-jar raised, April 1964. The operator is Christine Blanchfield.

polymer insulating films curtailed the ultra-high vacuum and alloy film work previously undertaken. Detailed studies were made of cryotron 'selection trees' for addressing a random-access cryogenic store, and evaporation masks were made for a small-scale tree and store consisting of 82 cryotrons for a store of eight words (see fig. 27). Even for this relatively simple circuit the stencil masks required were complex and found to be difficult to implement without introducing errors, and a program was written to help with mask production.

In 1965 the nettle was grasped: 'It is now considered unlikely that economic fabrication of cryotron stores will be achieved by the evaporation of circuit patterns through stencil masks.' The group turned to photoresist and etching techniques, and used these to construct the same small-scale tree and store circuit successfully achieved, but with a poor yield of circuits, by

The Uttley era: 1957–1966

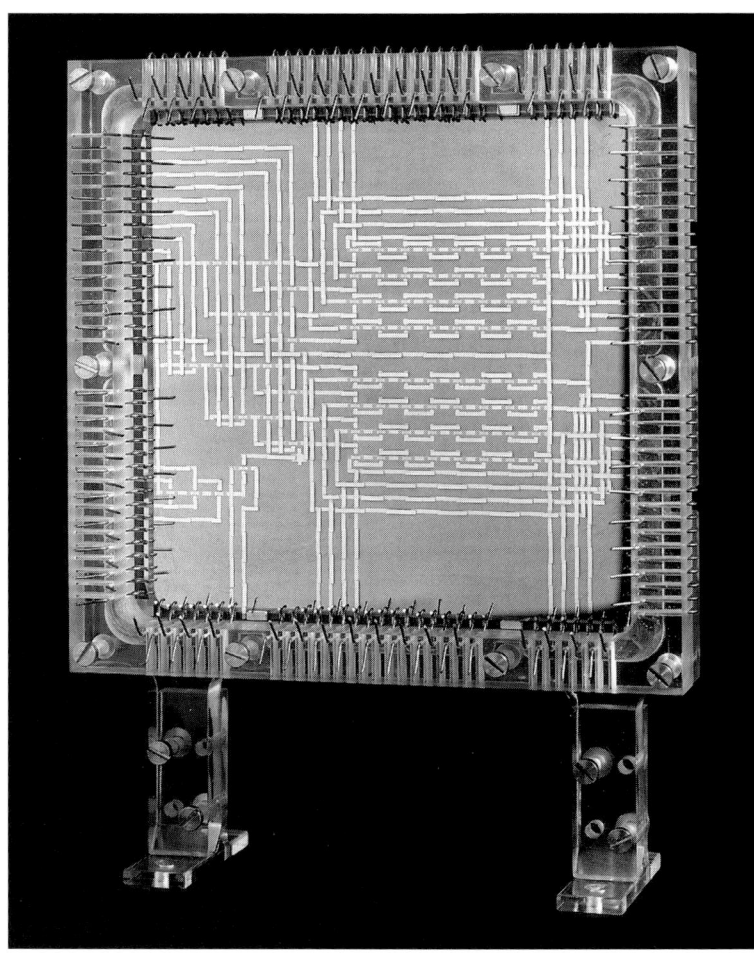

Figure 27. A cryotron selection tree (left) and dummy store, September 1964. The circuit consists of eight superimposed layers vacuum-deposited through stencil masks on a substrate 100 mm square.

evaporation techniques the previous year. The theoretical work on circuit redundancy was developed considerably by Maureen Longden (later Mrs Vaswani), Lew Page and Roger Scantlebury in investigations into 'triplicated redundancy' in which a logic chain is divided into sections each of which is triplicated, with 'voting' circuits interposed between the sections; the voting circuits may themselves be triplicated.

There remained serious concerns about yield, liquefier reliability, the effects of thermal cycling on the thin films, and the problems of replacing any units which might develop faults. Also semiconductor integrated circuits were developing fast and looked likely to remain reliable and cheap compared with cryogenic equivalents. On these grounds Mullard, the industrial partner in the ACTP collaboration, decided not to develop a prototype store, and NPL's work on cryotrons was ended in 1966. Staff whose expertise lay mainly in the properties of thin films moved to the NPL Inorganic Materials Unit, where new work in that area was undertaken; those with a computing background remained in Autonomics Division.

Contributors to this work included John Hill, Colin Stoddart, Roger Scantlebury, Lew Page, Keith Bartlett, Derek Allam, Bill Gleed, Joe Osborn and Maureen Longden (later Mrs Vaswani); the group was led throughout by Peter Stuart.

Selected publications on cryotrons

P R Stuart. The planar cryotron. *Automation and Control*, 13(3), 1960, p.43.

J S Hill. The cryotron—a superconducting computer component. *Automation Progress*, 6(11), 1961, p.377.

D W Davies. Parallel binary adders using the crossed-film cryotron. *Proc. IEE*, 110(6), 1963, pp.999–1007.

M Longden, L J Page and R Scantlebury. Circuit redundancy as an aid to making functioning cryotron circuits. NPL Report Auto 1, January 1964.

M Longden, L J Page and R A Scantlebury. The effect of circuit and component redundancy on the reliability of cryotron circuits. NPL Report Auto 4, February 1964.

D W Davies. Heat transfer from a cryotron. NPL Report Auto 7, July 1964.

M Longden, L J Page and R A Scantlebury. An assessment of the value of triplicated redundancy in digital systems. NPL Report Auto 9, January 1965.

D S Allam, C T H Stoddart and P R Stuart. Polymer insulating films for cryotron fabrication. NPL Report Auto 10, July 1965.

M Longden. Majority logic. NPL Report Auto 12, December 1965.

H F Lovesey and P R Stuart. An optical comparator for checking and locating stencil masks used in the vacuum deposition of microcircuits. NPL Report Auto 18, April 1966.

W L Gleed, J S Hill, K H Hursey and P R Stuart. A bakeable vacuum evaporator for the deposition of large area cryotron circuits. NPL Report Auto 19, August 1966.

R A Scantlebury and K A Bartlett. The fabrication of lead/tin cryotron circuits by photolithographic methods. NPL Report Auto 22, September 1966.

A F Brown and M Vaswani. The calculation of current waveforms in a binary cryotron tree. NPL Report Auto 15, May 1967.

3.9 Computing aspects of the work of Mathematics Division

In 1957 Mathematics Division was on a reasonably even keel. DEUCE was in full swing as the mainstay of the computing service; Pilot ACE had gone, the differential analyser was on the way out, and ACE was a promise for the future. Dr Goodwin had been Superintendent for six years. The staff were organised into two main groups: scientific staff, doing individual mathematical work with minimal management responsibilities, and experimental/assistant grade staff providing computing services and support to the scientific staff as required. Within the scientific staff, there was a broad division into numerical methods (for general use) and applied mathematics (focused on specific areas). Lectures given to outside bodies (typically 30–40 per year) formed an important means of passing on knowledge and skills, and publications increased from 14 in the year 1957 to 50 in 1966 (though the number of publications, as always, is of limited significance; what matters is that a few of them, covered below, were exceptionally influential). As explained in the Introduction, detailed consideration of the mathematical work is outside our scope; the aim here is to describe those aspects of the programme which are significant for the general development of computing, and to select outline examples only of the very wide range of mathematical tasks which formed the bulk of the Division's work.

Numerical methods: use of Chebyshev polynomials

In the pre-computer era, the publication of printed tables of values of functions was one of the major objects of numerical mathematics. The Royal Society had a Tables Committee which covered the fundamental functions; in addition to assisting this committee, NPL found a particular role for itself in producing tables of other functions which the Division had found useful in its work. In all, eight volumes of the NPL Mathematical Tables series were published over the period 1956–66.

But the advent of computers was changing the nature of the demand: a particular function value might well be needed by a program running on a computer, not by an engineer at his desk. Should the program have the set of tables available, or should it calculate the value required?

C W Clenshaw, building on earlier work by Lanczos and others, developed practical methods for expressing many mathematical functions as sums of series of Chebyshev polynomials[3], each with a numerical coefficient. The significance of this is that if the Chebyshev polynomials are truncated at degree n, the resulting approximation to the function being calculated can be shown to be a good one compared with other polynomial approximations of the same degree. This development meant that printed tables of many functions were redundant for computing purposes, since a program could calculate a required value using the Chebyshev expansion sufficiently accurately in a reasonable time and using much less memory than a table of the values. With others, notably A R (Joe) Curtis, Geoff Miller, and Susan Picken (later Mrs Hodson), Clenshaw extended the application of Chebyshev polynomials to the solution of ordinary differential equations, numerical integration (quadrature), and the fitting of curves and surfaces to numerical data.

C W Clenshaw. The numerical solution of linear differential equations in Chebyshev series. *Proc. Cambridge Philosophical Soc.*, 53, 1957, pp.134–149.

---

[3] The *Chebyshev polynomial* of degree r in x is defined as $\cos(r \cos^{-1} x)$.

C W Clenshaw. Curve fitting with a digital computer. *Computer Journal*, 2, 1960, pp.170–173.

C W Clenshaw and A R Curtis. A method for numerical integration on an automatic computer. *Numerische Mathematik*, 2, 1960, pp.197–205.

C W Clenshaw. Chebyshev series for mathematical functions. NPL Mathematical Tables Series Vol. 5, HMSO, 1962.

Numerical methods: linear algebra and error analysis

In any method of representing numbers in a computer, only certain numbers can be held exactly. For example, in the usual (*floating point*) method, 9.125 can be held exactly (because it is 1001.001 in binary; the binary fraction terminates) but 9.1 cannot be held exactly (because the binary fraction does not terminate). Thus although 91 and 10 can be held exactly, the result of dividing 91 by 10 cannot be held exactly, and must be rounded; a small error has therefore been introduced by the process of division. Very small errors of this kind are logically unavoidable in most computer arithmetic. Because complex numerical processes involve many successive arithmetic operations, the errors, though individually small, could accumulate as a calculation progresses and in some cases could invalidate the process completely. In the early days of computers, this matter caused considerable gloom: theoretical investigation showed that errors could quickly get out of hand and long calculations on computers were therefore not reliable.

Against this dragon Mathematics Division produced St George in the shape of Jim Wilkinson. In a brilliant series of investigations starting in the mid-1950s, building on the work of Givens and von Neumann, he showed how a more accurate picture of the build-up of errors over a calculation could be obtained, and that the pessimism of the early 1950s was, as a general view, unjustified. It would be too much to claim that the dragon was slain, but it was

---

❏ SIDELINE ❏ DETOUR ❏ DIGRESSION ❏ BYWAY ❏ SCENIC ROUTE ❏

Numerical instability

Conventional mathematics courses do not always warn their students of the dangers that may lurk in apparently innocent situations. Consider one of Wilkinson's examples (ref. 166, pp.42–43), the polynomial:

$$(z-1)(z-2)\ldots(z-20)$$

Clearly its zeros are 1, 2, ..., 20; and the coefficient of z^{19} is readily calculable as −210. One might think that a small change in this coefficient would lead to a small change in the zeros, but in fact a change as small as a multiplication by $1 - 2^{-23}$ produces a polynomial whose zeros include five conjugate complex pairs, including for example the pair $19.502 \pm 1.940\,i$. The essence of caging the dragon of cumulative errors is recognising and avoiding processes where such instabilities are hiding.

truly caged, and thanks to Jim the world now has the means of keeping it firmly under control.

His methods are described in particular in the two influential books listed below. It would be well beyond our scope to consider them in detail, but the broad outline is that instead of investigating the way errors develop as a calculation proceeds, he considered the computed result as the accurate outcome of a calculation slightly different from the required one, and examined the consequences of the differences between the two processes; in other words a 'backward error analysis' compared with the conventional forward view. In his hands this idea became a powerful tool which threw light on a whole range of numerical processes including the solution of linear equations, matrix inversion, computing eigenvalues of matrices and calculating zeros of polynomials. In particular he was able to show why certain existing methods had produced unreliable results and how the pitfalls could be avoided. He showed that the problem was really one of assessing the numerical stability of an algorithm (see above box), and of suggesting preferable alternatives if potential instabilities were found.

This work and its subsequent developments led to many honours and awards; an outline of Jim Wilkinson's distinguished career is given on p.314.

J H Wilkinson. Error analysis of direct methods of matrix inversion. *JACM*, 8, 1961, pp.281–330.

J H Wilkinson. *Rounding Errors in Algebraic Processes. Notes on Applied Science No. 32*, HMSO, 1963.

J H Wilkinson. *The Algebraic Eigenvalue Problem*. Oxford University Press, 1965.

Modern Computing Methods

The accumulated wisdom of Mathematics Division on numerical methods was distilled into an influential book, *Modern Computing Methods*, first published in 1957. This first edition, written by L Fox, E T Goodwin, J G L Michel, F W J Olver and J H Wilkinson, was based on a series of lectures given as part of an Imperial College vacation course, 'Computers for Electrical Engineering Problems'. The topics covered included linear equations and matrices, zeros of polynomials, finite-difference methods, differential equations and evaluation of integrals. The NPL Annual Report for 1957 noted that it was selling well. In 1959 a major revision was reported, including new chapters on error analysis and Chebyshev polynomials. This second edition, written by Clenshaw, Goodwin, Martin, Miller, Olver and Wilkinson was published in 1961 and was an even greater success than its predecessor. One reviewer wrote: 'the book . . . is admirably written in a straightforward manner and is entirely free both from vexatious vagueness and from puzzling profundity'[4]. The book was launched at a symposium held at NPL in June 1961 attended by over 200 college and university lecturers. In all, over 20,000 copies of the two editions of *Modern Computing Methods* were sold, representing a notable educational achievement by an outstanding group of numerical analysts.

NPL. *Modern Computing Methods. Notes on Applied Science No. 16*, HMSO, 1957; second edition completely revised 1961.

Algol

From the earliest days of computers it had been understood that there would be many advantages in writing programs in a universal language: rewriting programs for different machines could be avoided, so long as each machine was provided with a translator from the universal language to its own instruction set; the language could be designed to suit the user instead of being constrained by the requirements of the machine; and it would provide a useful means of expressing algorithms unambiguously for human communication. Fortran had gone some way towards these aims but was seen as IBM-oriented and unnecessarily cumbersome. Algol was for many years one of the most successful attempts to overcome these problems. Helped by a decision to exclude as far as possible provision for mundane matters like data input, printing and file structure, it achieved considerable clarity and great elegance. In particular the technique used in the language definition for specifying formally what was valid Algol, now known as Backus–Naur Form (BNF), set new standards of excellence. Although it had both earlier and later history, the most influential form of Algol was ALGOL 60, developed by an international committee of which Mike Woodger was a member. He said himself that most of the work was done by Peter Naur of Copenhagen, but his own contribution was also significant, and his name stands as one of the co-authors of the Report on the Algorithmic Language ALGOL 60 (ref. 94), one of the milestones of computer history.

M Woodger. An introduction to ALGOL 60. *Computer Journal*, 3, 1960, pp.67–75. Reprinted in P Wegner (ed.), *Introduction to System Programming*, Academic Press, 1964, pp.56–72.

M Woodger. The description of computing processes: some observations on automatic programming and ALGOL 60. In: R Goodman (ed.), *Annual Review in Automatic Programming 3*, Pergamon Press, 1963, pp.1–15.

M Woodger. ALGOL. *IEEE Trans. on Electronic Computers*, EC-13, 4, 1964, pp.377–381.

P Naur. The European side of the last phase of the development of ALGOL 60. In: R L Wexelblat (ed.), *History of Programming Languages*, Academic Press, 1981, pp.92–139.

The Woodger Papers (ref. 180) include much historical material on Algol; see folders J3, K16, K18, K20, K22, K26, L1–L30, and W2–W8.

---

[4] M T L Bizley, *J. Institute of Actuaries*, 87, 1961, pp.397–399; quote is on p.398.

Applied mathematics

This group, led by Jack Michel, worked in areas of mathematics related to the programmes of other NPL Divisions or the needs of outside organisations. There were two sections, one using classical methods and one on Theoretical Physics, both staffed largely by recruitment; notable among the recruits and comparatively recent arrivals were Ernie Albasiny (1954), David Martin (1956), Paul Dean (1957) and John Cooper (1959).

An example of the work in classical applied mathematics was work on two problems concerned with the shapes of ships' hulls, undertaken by Geoff Hayes originally in the numerical analysis group, for Ship Division NPL. The first problem, known as *ship fairing*, was to provide a mathematical representation of the shape of a hull, working from data taken from standard design drawings. This could be used, for example, in the control of frame-bending and plate-cutting equipment in shipyards. Deviations from the data were permitted within stated limits to help make the surface satisfactorily smooth and to avoid unnecessary points of inflection. Programs to carry out this work were written for ACE, and the system was approved by the British Ship Research Association.

The second maritime problem was how to minimise the resistance to the motion of a ship caused by its passage through the water. Work started with a statistical analysis of resistance data for trawlers, compiled by Ship Division from experiments with models. An empirical equation was obtained relating the resistance to various hull-shape parameters, and as a direct result methods were found for reducing resistance by up to 25 per cent. These methods became part of Ship Division's standard recommendations, and many trawlers were built in accordance with them with corresponding savings in fuel consumption. At the request of the Food and Agriculture Organisation of the United Nations, Hayes, working with D J Doust of Ship Division, later developed the work considerably for international use.

A crystalline substance consists of an ordered lattice of atoms or molecules. In glasses, in contrast, the atoms form a disordered structure. The ways in which the atoms in these structures can vibrate is of considerable interest in understanding the properties of the materials, and theoretical models showing how the degree of disorder influences the atomic motion would be of great benefit in understanding the spectra and related properties of real substances. Work in this area was undertaken by Paul Dean and Jim Bell, and makes a good example of the work of the Theoretical Physics Section. They saw the relevance of the Division's recent advances in linear algebra and used first DEUCE and later ACE and KDF9 to explore the problem and make predictions about the behaviour of substances with particular types of disordered lattice structure. More details are given in their *New Scientist* article listed below.

J G Hayes and L O Engvall. Computer-aided studies of fishing boat hull resistance. FAO Fisheries Technical Paper No. 87, Food and Agriculture Organization of the United Nations, Rome, 1969.

P Dean and R J Bell. A model approach to glasses. *New Scientist*, 45(684), 15 January 1970, pp.104–106.

Computing services

The General Computing group under Tom Vickers had four main areas of work: programming (for DEUCE and later ACE and KDF9), computer operation, desktop calculating machines and punched cards.

DEUCE was a sturdy workhorse from its delivery in 1955 to its final closedown on 31 July 1966. Its configuration, described in section 2.4, remained unchanged apart from the installation of twin magnetic tape decks in 1958–59. (An abortive attempt to install magnetic tape units had been made in 1957, described by Mathematics Division as 'unsuccessful' and by CME Division as 'experimental'!) The first mention of ACE in the Annual Reports for Mathematics Division was in 1959 when up to 20 hours per week were available and the 'reliability of the computer itself was impressive', presumably implying that the drums were still unreliable. Like Pilot ACE before it, ACE was then handed over to Maths by CME for use as the basis of a computing service. A full description of the machine is given in section 3.2 above.

Night-time working on ACE was soon needed, and as the demand for computing services continued to increase, an order was placed in 1962 with the English Electric Co Ltd[5] for a KDF9 computer for delivery early in 1964. The Algol compiler for ACE completed in 1963 was designed to take input paper tape in exactly the format required for KDF9, thus reaping one of the great benefits of using a high-level language: the avoidance of unnecessary reprogramming costs when hardware is changed.

On both DEUCE and ACE, while system management including most operation was the responsibility of the General Computing group, experienced users were encouraged to do their own operating. This was particularly helpful to the user in program testing, where anything can happen and the programmer knows best what action to take. On the other hand permanent operating staff are better at keeping an expensive machine busy. For KDF9 this balance was judged to have changed over, and it was decided that the new machine should from the beginning be operated as a 'closed shop'.

---

[5] Following a merger with Leo Computers Ltd, the company became English Electric – Leo Computers Ltd on 1 April 1963, and subsequently English Electric – Leo – Marconi, which eventually formed part of ICL.

The Uttley era: 1957–1966

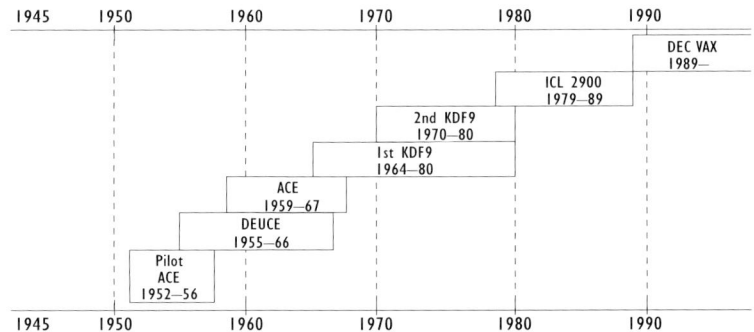

Figure 28. NPL central computers.

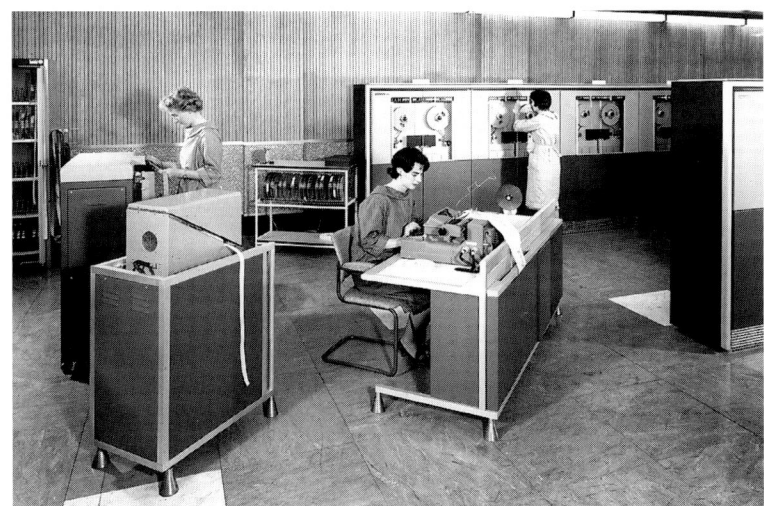

Figure 29. The KDF9 computer, August 1964, with (left to right) Joyce Dickerson, Brenda Webber, and Monica Trumble.

The KDF9 was eventually delivered on 29 June 1964. It had 32 K words of core store (the equivalent of 192 K bytes), four magnetic tape decks, paper-tape reader and punch, and line printer, with no time-sharing capability. It was installed in a large room at the southern end of the Glazebrook Hall building. Acceptance tests were completed on 1 August. Two flavours of Algol were provided: one (WALGOL) for development use, with fast compilation but slow object code, and the other (KALGOL) to produce a version for operational running, slower to compile but producing much faster code. Program development was done using the POST batch system: everybody's source code was kept (serially of course) on magnetic tape, and instructions for corrections, Usercode assembly and Algol compilation were submitted by users on paper tape. Once a day, these tapes were arranged by the operators in the right order, and the run carried out—more complicated than the simple one-program-at-a-time regime used on ACE and DEUCE, but a much more efficient use of expensive resources.

KDF9 was soon heavily used, without there being any significant diminution in the demand for ACE and DEUCE. The first issue of *KDF9 Weekly*, the forerunner of *NPL Computing*, appeared in November 1964. By 1965 the machine was handling 200 jobs per day. NPL Standard Interfaces (see p.76) were fitted, allowing direct connection to ACE, Hermes, or an extra tape reader. In a major enhancement in June 1966, the KDF9 was fitted with a disc (3.9 M words or about 24 Mb), card reader and two extra tape decks. This meant that the serial POST system for batch program development could be replaced by the random-access PROMPT system—a great simplification for the operators. It also allowed use of the EGDON operating system, but as this was punched-card oriented and so did not suit many NPL users' reasonable preference for paper tape, it was only run for one session per week. The KDF9 system was now handling 330 jobs in a 13-hour day. The remaining users of DEUCE were almost entirely from outside NPL, and DEUCE was finally closed down on 31 July 1966.

Staff particularly involved in the management of ACE and DEUCE and in the establishment and running of the KDF9 service were Brenda Webber, Gwen Peters, Joyce Dickerson (later Mrs Brick), and Margaret Price.

This outline of the history of mathematics and computing services at NPL continues in section 4.7.

4 The Davies era: 1966–1978

4.1 Outline of developments

The news that Donald Davies was to be transferred to Ministry of Technology Headquarters on 31 December 1965 came as something of a shock to Autonomics Division, as he had been generally seen as the natural successor to Dr Uttley, who was due to retire during the next year. However it soon became clear that his transfer was not what it seemed; the appointment was simply intended to give him some temporary experience of Headquarters work. In the event, although he is said to have had his name on a door in London, that was about the extent of his involvement, and he duly succeeded Uttley as Superintendent of Autonomics Division on 1 August 1966.

His appointment, like that of Uttley almost ten years before, soon led to a major transformation in the Division's programme of work; this time, in addition to his own ideas of what the Division should be doing, the incoming Superintendent had a new climate to operate in because of the establishment of the Ministry of Technology by the Labour Government of the day.

Uttley had been an idealist, fired by his scientific interest in the brain and in means of mechanising its capabilities and processes, and also by his wish to foster a lively academic group in this and related fields. Davies had a more practical and complex range of motivations and talents: he had a thorough grasp of the political and industrial realities which formed the context and justification of the Division's work, enjoyed intellectual challenges and puzzles and logical design, and had wide scientific and engineering interests with a polymath's urge to understand how things work and a particular expertise in data communications.

A symbol of the new regime was the abolition of the idiosyncratic name Autonomics Division and its replacement by the more reasonable Division of Computer Science on 1 April 1968; at the same time the Division's building was renamed after the nineteenth-century computing pioneer Charles Babbage.

The main areas of work which were stopped or moved away in the years following Donald Davies's appointment were biology, cryotrons, machine translation, information retrieval and adaptive control; all are described in section 3 above. In addition, the end of responsibility for the maintenance of ACE in 1967 made several further staff available. New work was started in data communications (see section 4.2), in information systems (section 4.3), in Palantype transcription (section 4.4), and, somewhat later, in man–machine interaction (section 4.6). In fact the only projects surviving the Davies wind of change were pattern recognition (sections 3.4 and 4.5), ACTP (sections 3.1 p.62 and 4.1 p.125),

Figure 30. Staff numbers in Auto/Com. Sci., 1966–77.

and, for a time, pattern perception (section 3.5) and programming research (sections 3.1 p.66 and 4.1 p.124). Staff numbers were gradually reduced (see fig. 30).

One of Donald Davies's first actions as Superintendent was to confirm Ted Newman and Percy Hammond as his deputies, in posts which would later be known as Branch Heads. When Hammond moved to Warren Spring in 1968 he was succeeded in this role by Derek Barber, and when Barber was appointed Director of the European Informatics Network in 1973 he was followed by David Yates (at first in an acting capacity as it was not known whether Barber would return). Newman retired in December 1977, and his Branch Head post was taken the following year by David Schofield.

The Division's task was not only to carry out its technical programme but also to ensure as far as possible that its results, both intellectual property and professional skills, were used effectively in the national interest, a process which had become known as *technology transfer*. In this era ACTP was probably the largest single item under this heading (through the use of Divisional staff both to manage the scheme and to monitor individual contracts), but consultancy work and direct exploitation contracts were also important, and the traditional communication routes of publication, lectures, conferences and Open Days continued.

As regards publications, besides an increasing mass of technical papers several books were published by members of the staff: Roger Meetham's encyclopaedia (ref. 89) to which several of his colleagues also contributed; Donald Davies and Derek Barber's highly influential book on communication networks (ref. 33); a book by Julian Ullmann on pattern recognition (ref. 146); and Brian Wichmann's study of Algol compilation and assessment (ref. 153).

Several major conferences were organised by the Division, sometimes jointly with other bodies. Those on the following subjects were all held at NPL: attention in neurophysiology (1967 ref. 46, the last sign of the biology work); pattern recognition (1968 ref. 70); computer applications in Government (1969); man–computer interaction (1970 ref. 71); and machine perception of patterns and pictures (1972 ref. 73).

In most years in the period 1966–72 the Division ran a Schools Programming Course for local sixth-formers. At that time computers were too expensive for most schools to own one, so this imaginative scheme was a worthwhile contribution to local computer literacy, and the courses were understandably popular. In 1969, for instance, 110 young people spent five days at NPL being initiated into the mysteries of computer programming; three days of theory were followed by two of practice.

One particular consultancy contract deserves mention: in 1972 the British Steel Corporation commissioned the Division to survey the likely development of computer technology up to 1980 and the effect this would have on the Corporation's use of computer systems. This was a major project involving most of the Division's senior staff, co-ordinated by Frank Blake. The various written contributions were produced, and combined into a two-volume final report, using the Scrapbook system (see pp.152–158) developed in the Division—one of its largest single tasks and a convincing early demonstration of how useful a shared computer-based text-management system could be.

In 1967 the Laboratory decided to change the pattern of Open Days. From 1946 to 1966 these had been held annually for the whole Laboratory, and they had become very large events which took up a disproportionate amount of staff effort. The new plan was to have a four-year cycle, with a third of the Laboratory on show each year for three years, followed by one fallow year. Thus in 1967 only the Measurement group of Divisions was on display, with the others on standby to deal with any questions from the visitors in their areas. In 1968 it was the turn of the Engineering Sciences group, including the Division of Computer Science, followed by the Materials group in 1969. The computing work was again on display in 1972 and 1976. In an Open Day year, much effort went into designing display boards and handouts; the surviving sets of handouts form a useful historical record (ref. 114). The benefits of Open Days were notoriously difficult to quantify, but they clearly helped to draw the attention of industry, universities and the press to the work in progress, and management and staff were agreed that once every four years was about right, certainly more appropriate than every year.

Guest Workers continued to play an important part in the life of the Division. Though the biologists departed with Dr Uttley, and the Medical Research Council team left in 1969, a group of architects from the Ministry of Works joined the Division in 1969 to work with the Man–Machine Interaction group. In January 1974 a successful and long-running association was established between the Division and the Hoger Informatica Onderwijs at Enschede in the Netherlands whereby each year one or two of their students worked in the Division as Guest Workers for a period of five months as part of their industrial training. This arrangement has been very useful to the Division because of the consistently high standard of the students' work; it continues at the time of writing (1996).

A less welcome event had occurred in 1971 with the publication in *Nature* of an editorial article (ref. 8), unsigned but in fact written by the Editor, Dr A Jones. It was a brief analysis of what the UK should do to maintain a place in world computer developments, and in passing it criticised the Laboratory for not fulfilling national expectations in that respect. The section concerned refers to 'the attempt in the past few years to use the National Physical Laboratory as a focus for creative research and development', and was thus arguably a reference to ACTP rather than the Division as a whole. Whatever his exact intended target, such is the influence of the Editor of *Nature* that the remarks caused an understandable shudder in the NPL Directorate and must have done some damage to the Division's reputation, at least amongst readers not in a position to assess its work for themselves.

Historical awareness

One of Donald Davies's many interests was (and is) in the history of computing, and although as a subject this was not on the Division's agenda he recognised the benefits of his staff and others having some idea how computer technology came to be the way it was. The fruits of this interest appeared in several ways: first in his reprint of Turing's 1946 report (see ref. 138), which effectively rescued this crucial paper, hitherto widely ignored because it had remained unpublished; secondly in an occasional series of lectures by computing pioneers (see list below; no. 2, which was never published, was by Konrad Zuse); thirdly by his (private) membership of the A M Turing Trust which encouraged Andrew Hodges in the compilation of his biography of Turing (ref. 66, see pp.536–537); and finally in his personal interest in old cryptographic machines like Enigma, part of a wider interest in data security which eventually led to a major new programme of work for the Division.

I J Good. Early work on computers at Bletchley. The Pioneers of Computing No 1, NPL Report Com Sci 82, September 1976. Reprinted with an Addendum under the title 'Pioneering work on computers at Bletchley' in Metropolis et al., ref. 90 pp.31–46.

M V Wilkes. The EDSAC. The Pioneers of Computing No 3, NPL Report Com Sci 90, June 1977.

T H Flowers. Electronic computers and telephone exchanges. Number 4 in Lectures on 'The Pioneers of Computing', NPL Report DNACS 24/80, January 1980 [the lecture was given on 1 July 1977].

The Fulton report

NPL, as part of the UK Scientific Civil Service, has always had a grading structure to provide a basis for the balanced staffing of projects and the management of individual careers. In the late 1960s this system was suffering from an over-rigid division into three classes (scientific, experimental and assistant) corresponding to the administrative, executive and clerical classes in the administrative Civil Service. There were some overtones of the traditional military separation into officers, NCOs and men: all senior posts were in the scientific class, but elsewhere there were considerable overlaps between the classes in pay and responsibility, particularly between the two lower grades of the scientific class (then SO and SSO) and most of the experimental class. The problems with the system were the hurdles of class-to-class promotion which it involved for the many individuals whose skills did not fall neatly and permanently into one of the categories, and its unhelpful and unnecessary divisiveness. The separation into three classes was abolished following the publication of the Fulton report (ref. 53) in 1968, with staff being assimilated to a new unified grading structure on 1 January 1971; this was generally seen as a welcome reform of benefit to government research establishments including NPL.

The Rothschild report and its effects

In November 1971 a Government Green Paper was published containing an influential report by Lord Rothschild entitled *The Organisation and Management of Government R. & D.* (ref. 131). This put forward the view that where public money was to be spent on research with a practical objective, there were benefits to be gained from separating the functions of those who required the work to be done from those who did it. In other words, the Minister responsible for the expenditure should act as a proxy customer on behalf of the taxpayer, commissioning work which would be of public benefit if successful, with the research establishments and others acting as his contractors; this became known as the *customer–contractor principle*. The implication was that the existing mechanisms for the management of civil R & D were too cosy, with (for example) the control of NPL's programme in the hands of an Executive Committee which might very easily identify itself more closely with the Laboratory than with the interests of the taxpayer. The (Conservative) Government of the day endorsed Rothschild's recommendations, and in July 1972 published a White Paper putting his principles into practice.

In NPL's parent department (by then the Department of Trade and Industry) the problem with implementing this policy was that neither the Minister nor his Civil Service advisers had the technical background needed to play the role of proxy customer over the very wide range of their research stations' activities. A set of permanent advisory boards was therefore established to recommend to the Department in detail how its role of proxy customer should be discharged. To be effective, these bodies had to comprise members of the industrial and academic communities noted for their far-sightedness, commercial acumen, high professional expertise, and willingness to give their time for the public good. The boards were called Requirements Boards, since their task was to specify pro-actively what work was required in each area in the public interest. The Board responsible for programmes in the computing area was the Computers, Systems and Electronics Requirements Board (CSERB). The first submission from NPL to the Board was considered at its second meeting on 22 February 1973.

The Requirements Board system was to last with modifications until 1988, though it turned out not to work in practice quite as its propounders had hoped. On the plus side it did introduce a genuinely independent voice into the process of determining the Division's programme of work, and many outstanding people were persuaded at different times to serve on the Board and its working groups. The problems were threefold. First, the Board never acted (as it was intended to) on its own initiative to state some new 'Requirement'. Instead it made decisions as a response to proposals submitted by the Division and others. These were often accepted, sometimes after one or more cycles of modification, and occasionally rejected; but the effect of the Board's deliberations was in essence negative: they were a hurdle that a proposal had to surmount, rather than a source of new ideas. Secondly they introduced a considerable bureaucracy: in addition to the apparatus of the Boards and working groups themselves, a great deal more of the time of the Division's senior staff was taken up with preparing proposals and reports for the Board than had been needed for the old Executive Committee, with little visible relative benefit. Thirdly and most importantly, the research groups, once their programme was agreed, had their horizons and freedom of action inevitably much reduced: targets were clearer, but individual responsibility was formally limited to meeting them. In effect, vision was encouraged only when compiling a new two- or three-year programme for the Board, and even then it had to be expressed and justified in detail, not always a helpful discipline for a seedling idea. (Although in principle 10 per cent of the Laboratory's budget could be used to develop new research ideas, this was hedged round with administrative barriers and was chronically under-used.) The introduction of Requirements Boards thus had an immediate deadening effect on the Division's readiness to take a long-term view, on the likelihood of it producing good ideas and on its ability to capitalise quickly on them when they did arise. The Division, fortunate to have someone of Davies's calibre in charge, was in no doubt that the taxpayer would have had better value for money if the Superintendent had been given a policy remit and allowed to get on with the job of directing the Division's work on that basis, with regular checks on his stewardship. As it was, he was diverted from his basic tasks—maintaining awareness of national needs, programme selection, technical challenges and management—by the requirement that the Board's agreement had to be obtained for any significant move. Overall, the establishment of the Board, intended to focus effort better on to national needs, was of no help to the Division in that respect and a significant hindrance in others, though the position might have been different with a less able Superintendent or a less authoritarian interpretation of the Rothschild principle.

The existence of the Boards greatly weakened the role of the NPL Directorate: if a Superintendent and his staff could get a proposal agreed by the Board it would happen and not otherwise, with the Directorate no longer in practice part of the dialogue. The change thus gave substantive form to the shift of power from NPL to 'headquarters' started by the formation of the Ministry of Technology in 1965. A symbolic consequence was the disruption and eventual discontinuation of the Laboratory's series of public reports (ref. 99). From 1900 to 1964 these had been, formally, the Annual Reports of the NPL Executive Committee. This Committee was abolished when the direct link with the Royal Society was broken in 1965, and the series of reports, though it continued briefly, was replaced in 1969 by triennial reports, those in the computing area covering 1969–71 and 1972–74. By 1974 the establishment of the Requirements Boards had introduced a whole new fragmented technical reporting structure, and the triennial series was itself then discontinued. Presumably public reports were seen as superfluous when more detailed reports were going to proxy customers representing the public interest; in any case from 1975 no regular reports for the whole Laboratory were produced until, in a different political climate, commercial-style annual reports were introduced in 1984.

The end of the Davies era

The establishment of the Requirements Boards also greatly changed the nature of the Superintendent's job. Donald Davies found that besides the new restrictions on his freedom of action he was able to spend less and less of his official time on the technical work in which his real interests and special talents lay. Instead, his days were increasingly taken up with Requirements Board business in addition to the traditional responsibilities for technology transfer, staff reporting and careers, financial affairs, participation in the Laboratory management, safety matters, and the multifarious administrative details of accommodation, purchasing of equipment, foreign travel approvals, and so on. This was part of a general trend, throughout the whole period covered in this book, for senior and later middle-ranking staff to have to spend more time on justificatory, commercial and miscellaneous matters, and less on actually managing research—and even less, if any time at all, as active personal contributors in their own fields. For example, one of the many tasks of Pilot ACE was to carry out calculations connected with the then Director's personal research interests. In the 1970s the days when the Director could afford time for such interests had long gone, and the Superintendents were finding they were being pushed the same way. (The process has continued, and at the time of writing (1996) even the Section heads often spend more time seeking their next customer than in innovative technical work, but that is to anticipate.) As a result of this shifting emphasis, Davies became less happy with his job, and by the mid-1970s a change to more specialist duties would have been welcome.

This ambition was eventually realised as a result of a quite unrelated decision by the Laboratory management to reduce the effort devoted to mathematics. What they decided to do was to combine the Division of Computer Science with the remaining mathematical work in a new Division of Numerical Analysis and Computer Science (DNACS) under Ernie Albasiny. This freed Davies, who was put in charge of a short-lived independent Computing Technology Unit (CTU) until his regrading as an Individual Merit (rather than an organisational) DCSO could be arranged. These changes, together with the related formation of the Computing Services Unit, came into effect on 1 June 1978 and are shown in fig. 1. They brought the Davies era, though not of course his career at the Laboratory, to an end, and the next phase in the Division's history is described in section 5.

Programming research

For the first eighteen months of the Davies era this group continued on the lines started under Dr Uttley, with two broad areas of work: one on programming language structure, and one on graphical display software and its use in interactive design. There was a gradual increase in numbers: Blake, Woodger, Alway and Scowen were joined by John Sexton and by two more Research Fellows, Fraser Duncan and Peter Wilkinson.

Under the heading of programming language structure there were several work items only loosely related to each other by a common perception that the currently available languages were not in practice as useful as they should be because of inadequacies in their formal specifications. This applied both to definitions of the form of language statements (syntax) and to definitions of their meaning (semantics). Fraser Duncan made a comparative study of programming language specifications. He showed that the number of definitions in these specifications could often be significantly reduced without changing the language. Each language was illustrated by a ball-and-stick model like a chemist's model of a molecule. These at least brought home to the uninitiated that language definitions did have a structure, with each element being defined in terms of certain others, and that languages varied considerably in complexity, but it is not clear that they added anything to the experts' understanding. Mike Woodger continued his contribution to international collaboration on programming languages, particularly on Algol. Roger Scowen developed the Babel language, which was like Algol but with a modular structure which allowed the introduction of new language elements; it also had a novel form of semantics whereby the meaning of a program was defined as its effect when run on a specified hypothetical computer.

The work on graphical display software and its applications was led by John Sexton. Today it is taken for granted that a computer screen can show pictures as well as words, and that a pointing device, now usually a mouse, will be useful as well as a keyboard; but these were novel ideas in the late 1960s. Visual display units, with upper-case letters and numbers only, were slowly becoming more familiar, but these were seen as 'paperless printers' and as such needed no special software development. In contrast, the display of diagrams on a screen, and the need for the user to be able to create and modify them in ways which suited the particular application, called for radically new methods of representing shapes in two or three dimensions in a computer. The group's Elliott 4120 computer was equipped with a graphical display with a light pen (for 'drawing' on the screen) and a tracker ball (a 'mouse on its back', like the pointer on some present-day portable computers but using a much larger ball). Sexton's software is described in section 4.6 below; the NPL Report for 1968/9 records its use for electronic circuit drawing and program development.

When the Central Computer Unit was established in 1967 (see section 4.7) it was decided that it should include its own software research group. The existing group in Autonomics Division was therefore split; Blake, Alway, and Scowen, together with Brian Wichmann from the Pattern Recognition group, joined the new unit while Woodger, Sexton, Duncan and Wilkinson remained in the Division. Shortly afterwards, Wilkinson was also moved (to Data Communications) and Duncan left at the end of his Fellowship, and in 1969 the Programming Research Group as such was disbanded. However, Woodger and Sexton both continued their work as part of a new group on Man–Machine Interaction, whose programme is described in section 4.6.

ACTP

The Advanced Computer Techniques Project was aimed at providing Government support to the UK computer industry. It was introduced in 1963 as described on p.62, and continued to be a major task for the Division throughout the Davies era. Besides providing overall technical management, the Division had to assess new proposals and supervise individual projects. By 1969 there were 38 current contracts of which 20 were managed directly from the Division, and the total annual cost of the project was £1.2 million, of which the Government paid half. The whole range of information technology was covered, including

The Davies era: 1966–1978

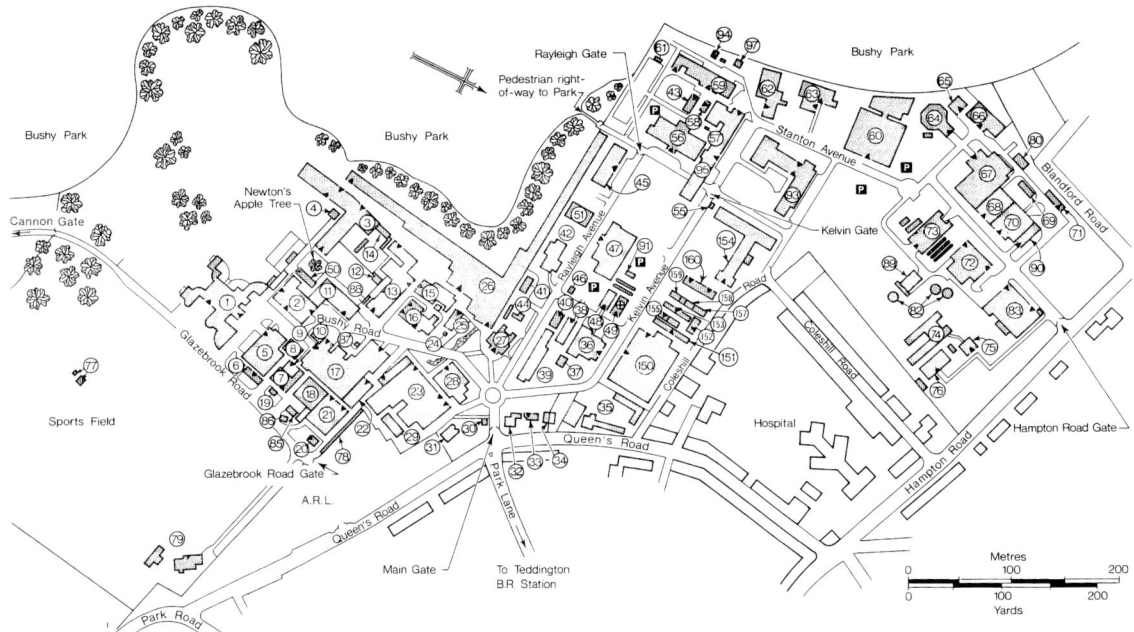

Figure 31. The NPL site in 1970. Buildings mentioned in the text are:
- *1 Bushy House, built 1710.*
- *21 Mathematics Division. Built 1916, demolished 1990.*
- *23 Glazebrook Hall. Built (as wind tunnel and workshop) 1918; converted to restaurant etc. 1961.*
- *74 Babbage Building huts. Built 1945, now demolished.*
- *75 Cromer House. Ground lease bought 1921, taken over by NPL 1945, no longer in NPL and derelict 1996.*
- *76 Teddington Hall. Bought 1946, no longer in NPL and in disrepair 1996.*
- *93 Charles Babbage Building. Built 1964, vacated by CMOT ISE Branch 1996 and likely to be demolished.*

processors, memory, peripherals, software, manufacture and testing. Full-time staff included Frank Blake, chairman of the software technical committee, who moved to Brussels in 1969 and was replaced by Michael Wright; Lew Page, project leader, who sadly died in 1970; and his successor David Clayden who also became chairman of the hardware technical committee.

4.2 Data communications

Ever since wet clay tablets were impressed with symbols and then baked, people have been developing new technology to help them handle information. The invention of computers in the 1940s can now be seen as one of the key steps in this long evolution, comparable with the rediscovery of printing with movable type in Europe in the fifteenth century, and the inventions of telegraphy in the 1830s and radio in 1895. It was followed within twenty years by another momentous step, not as spectacular but in the long term also of the greatest significance: the marriage of computers with communications technology. This marriage has already led to the worldwide Internet with its key ability to promote the establishment of international communities of interest, and the explosive growth of applications of the technology continues. In this great enterprise, as with the earlier invention of computers, NPL was in the forefront of developments during the formative years.

In the first computers, information to be input had to be physically taken to the machine in a medium such as punched cards, and output information taken away often in printed form. For special purposes data could be transmitted to or from a computer over a telephone link using modems, or one computer could be connected to another. Such data transfers required appropriate programs to be written for the computer(s) involved, and prior agreement between the parties on the technical details and the timing of the transfer, so that both systems were ready at the appointed time.

By the early 1960s it was realised that for some applications it would be useful to have remote connections of this kind on a routine basis, not just as one-off arrangements. For example in software development, much of the cost and delay involved in the usual movement of people and paper could be avoided if each user of a machine had access to a *terminal* (typically at that time a teletypewriter comprising keyboard, printer, and paper tape reader and punch) connected to the computer by a communication channel. For such a system to be economic it was essential for several terminals to be usable simultaneously. This meant that complex software had to be developed to share the resources of the computer amongst the apparently simultaneous users; this was possible because each individual user was slow compared with the central computer, so that it could share its time between them, in principle without them even needing to be aware that they did not have its undivided attention.

In addition to this specific need for *time-sharing* services, it was slowly understood that the use of terminals had the potential to transform businesses such as banking and airline seat reservations, where the ability to access and change stored data remotely would be of great commercial advantage so long as it could be done reliably. In addition, if appropriate standards could be developed and adopted, the terminals could be used to access different computer services at different times; and in some circumstances (such as a large company with several computers in different locations) routine interconnection of one computer with another over telecommunication links would be useful. (At that time of course terminals were not themselves small computers, as they are today, but simply remote peripheral devices of the central machine.) In 1965, Donald Davies saw that existing telecommunication systems, which had evolved to meet quite different demands, would need to be supplemented by new services if they were to meet these new computer-related communications requirements in a cost-effective and technically sensible way; and he had some specific and novel ideas on the services required and how they should be provided.

To develop these ideas, and so open up the possibilities for future work in the promised land of computer network applications, a Data Communications group was established in

The Davies era: 1966–1978

Autonomics Division in 1966, led by Derek Barber. Other key founder members were Roger Scantlebury and Keith Bartlett; David Clayden was briefly attached to the group before moving to ACTP full-time. Pat Woodroffe, Keith Wilkinson and others moved with Barber from the Automatic Control Systems group; Les Pink came with Bartlett from ACE support; and Peter Wilkinson joined the group from Programming Research in 1968 to provide much-needed software expertise. Donald Davies maintained his direct personal involvement, and with this strong team the group quickly became the Division's flagship.

Initially, work concentrated on three topics: the development of Davies' novel ideas for the technology of computer networks, the design and construction of a local network on the NPL site to put these ideas to practical test, and the metamorphosis of the NPL Standard Interface into the British Standard Interface. Over the next few years three further lines of work developed: the use of computer simulation in network design; research into the problem of how networks of different types should be interconnected; and the European Informatics Network (provision of the main UK input to this project, including connection to the NPL Network). With the exception of the British Standard Interface, which has already been described in section 3.3 as it was directly derived from work in the Adaptive Control group, these developments are now described in turn.

Packet-switching

From their origins in 1837, the world's telecommunication services evolved to provide two basic services: first *telegraphy*, in which messages are one-way and timescales are not of the essence provided sequence is maintained, and later (from 1875) the familiar *voice telephony*, in which communication is two-way and preservation of the internal timescales of messages is essential. Voice telephony was based on *circuit-switching*, in which for the duration of a call an electrical circuit is in effect established between the two subscribers; since the circuit is reserved for their use, there is no difficulty in meeting the strict timing requirements. Telegraphy could also use switched circuits, but where there was heavy traffic it was more economic for it to use *message-switching*, in which messages can be stored briefly at the nodes in a network, traditionally on paper tape, and if necessary queued up to be sent on to the next appropriate node as soon as a link to it is available.

Donald Davies's big idea was that to support time-sharing and other data transfers involving computers, what was wanted was not circuit-switching but a fast message-switching service, with one critical special feature: that long messages would be automatically split into chunks sent separately, so that they could when necessary be interleaved with chunks of other messages; this would avoid the excessive delay to other users which would otherwise be caused by a long message. The chunks were called *packets,* and the technique became known as *packet-switching.* There was a clear and close analogy with computer time-sharing services, where the time of the processor is also divided into short chunks, one for each active user in turn, thereby preventing a user with a long job holding up the rest. Clearly each packet had to be labelled with its destination address, an identifier of the message it was part of, and a sequence number to allow the receiving device to reassemble the original message. To provide the rate of throughput required, the message-switching devices would themselves have to be computers. The four big questions were feasibility, reliability, demand and cost—it was clearly a good idea logically, but it could still fail on any of these four grounds.

Though Davies was not aware of it, the principle of packet-switching had been put forward independently in 1964 in an outline design for a military communication network by Paul Baran of the RAND Corporation (ref. 10). As Baran made clear, the technique is well-suited to distributed networks (those with no single centre through which all messages pass). Distributed networks are more suitable for military use than the star-connected variety because a single switching centre makes a network very vulnerable to attack. Baran's ideas were not put into practice.

In the UK there were some political dangers in entering this field, because the provision of telecommunication services was a monopoly of the Post Office, and they might reasonably ask why NPL, part of another Government department, was involving itself with matters that were not its concern. Davies's combination of professional expertise and political awareness successfully avoided this pitfall: it was understood that NPL would simply carry out research in the area, build an experimental local network on its own site, and would restrict public pronouncements to these technical matters. While it might make suggestions on UK telecommunications policy, responsibility for decisions in that area, which depended on commercial as well as technical judgements, of course lay solely with the Post Office. On this basis good working relations were maintained: the Post Office awarded a study contract to the Division in 1973 and staff were also seconded in both directions.

Being careful simply to make technical suggestions and not to appear to be putting pressure on the Post Office, Davies put forward a proposal for a national communications network using the packet-switching technique in a paper (ref. 30) circulated privately in December 1965. The paper was followed in March 1966 by a seminar attended by over 100 people including representatives of the Post Office and telecommunications suppliers. The level of interest shown encouraged Davies to produce a more detailed proposal (ref. 31), which he circulated widely in

The Davies era: 1966–1978

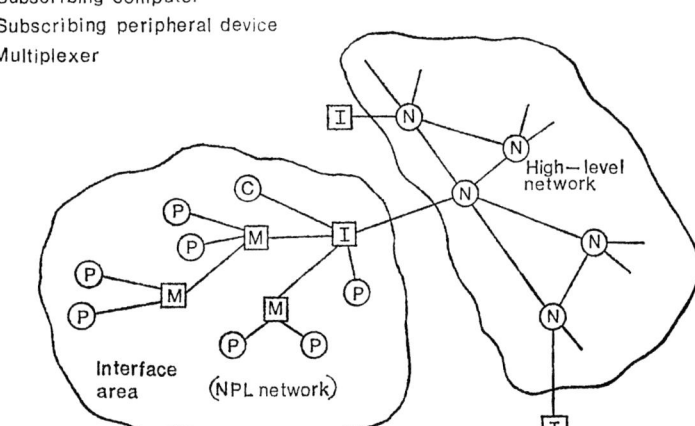

Figure 32. The planned NPL Network, showing its connection to the proposed high-level national network (from the NPL Annual Report for 1967, p.177).

June 1966. This paper, which was the first to use the term *packet* in the technical sense, included performance and cost estimates for the proposed national packet-switched network. It made it clear that 'dumb' devices like printers or visual display units could not be connected directly to such a network because they would not be able to create outgoing packets or disassemble incoming packets to form complete messages. Local 'interface' computers were therefore needed to carry out these functions, managing communications with groups of individual devices on one side and exchanging packets with a node of the national network on the other. The resulting two-level system is shown in fig. 32.

One of the key events in the origins of packet-switching was a symposium held by the US Association for Computing Machinery at Gatlinburg, Tennessee in 1967. Larry G Roberts of the Advanced Research Projects Agency (ARPA) of the US Department of Defense described a requirement for a network in broad outline, saying that message-switching was likely to be important. NPL's paper (ref. 32), presented by Roger Scantlebury, put forward a detailed design for a packet-switched network which fitted ARPA's needs well. ARPA accordingly adopted NPL's ideas enthusiastically and the two groups established regular contact. The first practical networks using packet-switching were the ARPANET and the NPL local network. The ARPANET evolved into the Internet, and the packet-switching technique forms the undisputed basis of the worldwide complex of computer communication systems in use today.

As more people became enthusiastic about the future of interactive computing and the computer networks needed to support it, a group known as the Real Time Club, led by Professor Stanley Gill of Imperial College, was formed and began active lobbying to encourage the Post Office to provide a pilot packet-switched service. They organised a major event of lectures and demonstrations, 'Conversational Computing on the South Bank', held in London in July 1968, to promote awareness of the possibilities. Davies contributed technical advice and planning although he had to leave it to Gill and others to present the public case for action to implement his ideas. Another sign of the growing appreciation of the importance of packet-switching came in August 1968 when a whole session of the 1968 Congress of the International Federation for Information Processing (IFIP) was devoted to papers on the subject all from NPL (see below and p.135). The Post Office showed continuing technical interest but evidently saw no justification for prompt commercial activity; their Experimental Packet Switched Service was announced in 1973 and formally introduced in 1977. In the meantime, NPL could still develop their own network, and this major project is the subject of the next section.

Papers on packet-switching and general network design

D W Davies. Proposal for a digital communication network. NPL, June 1966.

D W Davies, K A Bartlett, R A Scantlebury and P T Wilkinson. A digital communication network for computers giving rapid response at remote terminals. *Proc. ACM Symposium on Operating System Principles,* Gatlinburg, USA, 1967.

D W Davies. Some design aspects of a communication network for rapid-response computers. *Computer Technology,* IEE Conference Publication 32, 1967, pp.200–205.

D W Davies. Communication networks to serve rapid-response computers. In: A J H Morrell (ed.), *Information Processing 68: Proc. IFIP Congress 68,* held in Edinburgh August 1968, North-Holland, 1969, pp.650–658.

D W Davies. The principles of a data communication network for computers and remote peripherals. *Proc. IFIP Congress 68* as above, pp.709–715.

D W Davies. A communication network for real-time computer systems. *The Radio and Electronic Engineer,* 37(1), January 1969, pp.47–52.

D L A Barber. Computer networks. *Science Journal,* 6(10), 1970, pp.60–64.

D W Davies. Packet switching in a public data network. In: C V Freiman (ed.), *Information Processing 71: Proc. IFIP Congress 71,* held at Ljubljana, August 1971, North-Holland, 1972, pp.622–627.

Davies and Barber's 1973 book, ref. 33.

D W Davies. Packet switching, message switching and future communication networks. In: J L Rosenfeld (ed.), *Information Processing 74: Proc. IFIP Congress 74,* held in Stockholm, August 1974, North-Holland, 1974, pp.147–150.

D W Davies. A review of computer communications technology. In: R L Grimsdale and F Kuo (eds), *Computer Communications Networks,* Leyden, Nordhoff, 1975, pp.1–17.

The NPL Data Communications Network

In designing and building the first NPL network, the Data Communications group had three aims: to show that packet-switching worked in practice, to gain experience of network

The Davies era: 1966–1978

development and use as a basis for future work, and to provide a versatile data-transmission service for the NPL site. The first Annual Report to mention the proposed network is that for 1966: besides providing for 'a variety of peripherals attached to the main computer service' it would 'allow a number of small computers in different Divisions of the Laboratory to make use of a central file system on disks'. With notable foresight, coaxial cables linking various NPL buildings were being laid as early as February 1966, initially to enable ad hoc data links to be set up easily, but also with the needs of the future network in mind. Dialogue with potential users, including an open meeting for NPL staff held on 25 October 1967, led to a considerable widening of the proposed applications in the 1967 Report (p.178): 'Using the network, it will be easy to connect telemetering, data logging and automatic control equipment to remote computers anywhere in the establishment. Through the medium of graphical displays and enquiry stations, a number of improvements in information dissemination and human computer usage will result. The administration services of the Laboratory are also likely to benefit in the long term.' The 1968–69 Report (p.194) adds a further idea: 'we hope to make arrangements for the network to be connected to various externally available computing facilities'. A vision of a brave new world was slowly clarifying.

As described above, Donald Davies's proposal was for a two-level system (fig. 32): a high-level national packet-switched network together with lower-level local networks, each of which could exchange packets with a node of the high-level network and could also pass data to and from local terminal devices using more traditional techniques. The first NPL network was a prototype of such a local network, though with no high-level network to connect to. Its function was to interconnect on request any pair of the terminal devices connected to it, enabling them to exchange information in character form reliably, and taking care of any inherent difference in speed between them. Logically, the network was star connected (more than one node was not necessary). It used the packet-switching technique, but only internally in the central message-switching computer.

To enable changes of equipment to be made easily, devices were connected to the new network using the British Standard Interface described in section 3.3. Multiplexers, to a design patented by Scantlebury and Bartlett, were used to enable several slow devices to share a single cable where possible. Communication between a terminal and the message-switch followed a set of rules called a *protocol*; Scantlebury and Bartlett were apparently the first to use this word in this sense (see separate section on protocols below, p.145). By the end of 1969 the design was complete and delivery of the message-switching computer (a Honeywell DDP-516) was imminent. The message-switch software by Wilkinson and others worked well (though it was not easy to make changes to this first

Figure 33. The NPL Network, February 1972.

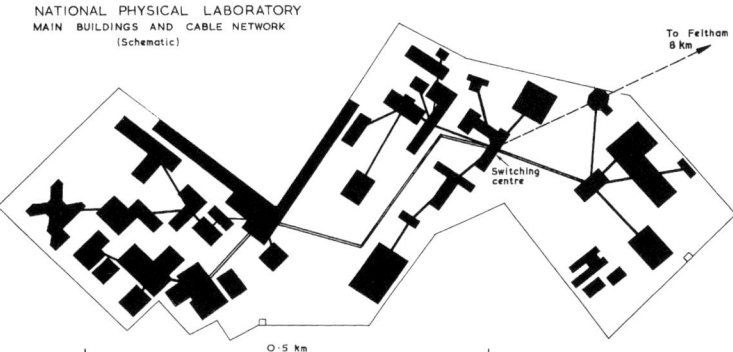

version as it was written in a low-level assembly language). Early in 1970 a network of 'some half dozen simple terminals' could be demonstrated (ref. 116 p.38); with hindsight, this can be claimed as the first local-area network in the world. A limited service was soon being offered to sympathetic users, and on 21–23 July 1971 the network was formally unveiled in a series of demonstrations to the press and other interested parties.

By late 1971 the KDF9s of the central computing service had been connected, as had a second Honeywell DDP-516 intended for the future file-store service and a Modular 1 computer running the first version of Scrapbook (see section 4.3). Using a Post Office line and modems, the network had been extended to Ship Division at Feltham (see fig. 33). A major public demonstration of the network and its services, together with a series of lectures, was held at the Institution of Electrical Engineers building in central London on 19 January 1972, using a Post Office line to NPL hired for the occasion. This Mark I version of the NPL network had one major limitation: it allowed only one-to-one connections, like the telephone system, whereas computers providing a time-sharing service on a network needed many-to-one connections. The interim solution was for such computers to have several network ports, so that would-be users had to 'ring round' manually to find a free one, but a new design to improve this position was clearly needed.

A radical redesign of the network architecture was accordingly started in January 1972, and continued until June 1973 when a fully tested Mark II service was successfully introduced. The new design is shown in fig. 34. It made a clear distinction between computers providing multi-access services on the one hand, and simple terminals, which could establish only one connection at a time, on the other. The service computers, called User Machines (UMs), handled their input and output using packets, and each such machine therefore had to include packet assembly and disassembly software. The packets sent by the UMs were received and redistributed by a central packet-switch software module. Communication with simple terminals, which could not deal with

The Davies era: 1966–1978

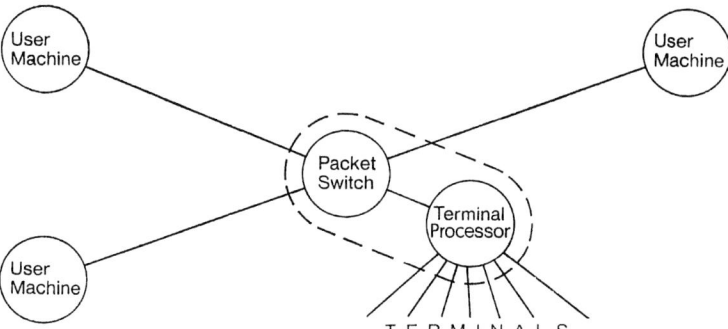

Figure 34. The Mark II NPL Network.

packets because they had no processing capability, was handled by a software module called the Terminal Processor (TP); this module was treated like an ordinary UM by the packet-switch, although the two lived in the same computer. Two protocols were required, one governing the exchange of packets between a UM and the packet-switch, and one for communication between two UMs (one of which could of course be the TP); these protocols are discussed further below (p.145). The two software modules were written in the PL-516 language developed by Brian Wichmann and Donald Bell (see p.196); this provided many high-level features without sacrificing run-time efficiency and proved a much better tool for the purpose than the machine language used for the Mark I network software. The software structure was considerably more advanced than that used in the Mark I network, being based on the principles of communicating processes for real-time software developed by Dijkstra and others; more details are given in Davies and Barber's 1973 book, ref. 33, in a chapter contributed largely by Peter Wilkinson, pp.458–523. The Mark II software involved 10–12 programmer-years of effort, compared with just over four programmer-years for Mark I.

The hardware of the network consisted of the central computer, a tree-like data transmission system of coaxial cables and multiplexers, and, for each terminal, a Peripheral Control Unit (PCU-A) and a British Standard Interface. The User Machines on the Mark II network needed a different network termination unit, a PCU-B. Standard modules were used throughout to allow for ease of replacement and extension. The PCU-A units included a group of four illuminated buttons with which users established and closed down connections (analogous to picking up and replacing the receiver in a telephone system, with refinements). There was a Central File Store, a User Machine providing (in 1974) 60 Mbytes of file storage for other User Machines on the network. The file store software was written under contract by Computer Analysts and Programmers Ltd.

By June 1974 the Mark II system was 'deemed proven'. The network now served about 80 character terminals and ten User Machines, and was expanding steadily. There were terminals in eleven different buildings round the NPL site, and they generated traffic at a rate of about a million packets a day. Maintenance of the network was passed to a contractor, Computer Field Maintenance Ltd, and the management and development of the network as a service to the Laboratory was handed over to the Computing Branch of the Division of Numerical Analysis and Computing in October 1974. This new stage in the life of the network is described in section 4.7.

The successful development of the NPL Network was led by Roger Scantlebury, who had become head of the Data Communications group following Derek Barber's promotion in 1969. Peter Wilkinson was in charge of the software work, assisted by John Laws (on loan from DNAC), Carol Walsh (later Mrs Corby), Keith Wilkinson, Rex Haymes and three contract staff from CAP Ltd, including Mike Gentry. Keith Bartlett led the hardware design and development team which included Pat Woodroffe, Les Pink, Peter Carter, Alan Davies, Iain Leitch and Brian Aldous. Alan J Gardner, on loan from the Post Office, made a valuable contribution, as did the CAP Ltd team producing the file store software, which included Bryan Wood and Pat Bailey.

Publications on the NPL Network

D W Davies, K A Bartlett, R A Scantlebury and P T Wilkinson. A digital communication network for computers giving rapid response at remote terminals. *Proc. ACM Symposium on Operating System Principles,* Gatlinburg, USA, 1967.

R A Scantlebury and K A Bartlett. A protocol for use in the NPL Data Communication System. NPL Tech. Memo. Auto TM 4, August 1967.

K A Bartlett. Transmission control in a local data network. In: A J H Morrell (ed.), *Information Processing 68: Proc. IFIP Congress 68,* held in Edinburgh, August 1968, North-Holland, 1969, pp.704–708.

R A Scantlebury, P T Wilkinson and K A Bartlett. The design of a message switching centre for a digital communication network. *Proc. IFIP Congress 68* as above, pp.723–727.

P T Wilkinson and R A Scantlebury. The control functions in a local data network. *Proc. IFIP Congress 68* as above, pp.734–738.

R A Scantlebury and P T Wilkinson. The design of a switching system to allow remote access to computer services by other computers and terminal devices. *Proc. ACM/IEEE Second Symposium on Problems in the Optimization of Data Communication Systems,* held in Palo Alto, October 1971, ACM/IEEE, 1971, pp.160–167.

R A Scantlebury and P T Wilkinson. The National Physical Laboratory Data Communication Network. In: J Borge Hansson et al. (eds), *Proc. Int. Conf. on Computer Communications 1974,* held in Stockholm, August 1974, ICCC Secretariat, 1974, pp.223–228.

P A Bailey and B M Wood. A central file store for the data communication network at the National Physical Laboratory. In: J Borge Hansson et al. (eds), *Proc. Int. Conf. on Computer Communications 1974,* held in Stockholm, August 1974, ICCC Secretariat, 1974, pp.229–238.

K A Bartlett and P T Wilkinson. The effect of a data communications network on a large laboratory site. In: D L A Barber (ed.), *Communications Networks* [papers presented at the European Computing Conference on

Communications Networks held in London, September 1975], Online, 1975, pp.95–111.

R A Scantlebury and P T Wilkinson. The National Physical Laboratory Data Communication Network. NPL Report Com 85, December 1976.

M Campbell-Kelly (1988), ref. 17 pp.233–239.

Network simulation

Designing the shape of a new data network is like designing a road network from scratch: given a set of cities, and for each pair of cities an estimate of the volume of traffic expected between them, what links and interchanges should be built? Because breakdowns and hold-ups can occur, alternative routes should be available where possible, but on the other hand the cost of the network should be kept to a reasonable minimum. Clearly the tool needed to investigate these questions is a computer simulation which will allow various designs to be tried, and their cost and performance compared.

Whatever design is chosen, a packet-switched data network, like a road network, will become congested if it is given too much traffic. The queues of packets waiting at each node will become full and the performance of the network will at best deteriorate and at worst collapse. Two elements in the network design can help to avoid these problems: *flow control*, which is analogous to regulating the admission of new traffic to a road system showing signs of jamming, and *routing algorithms*, which are rules for directing traffic through the network, and in particular diverting it round a congested or faulty area. In both cases various possible strategies could be devised, and it is not clear which would be the most effective. Here again, computer simulation of the alternative approaches will provide information to allow an informed choice to be made.

To investigate these ideas, simulation studies were started in 1968 by Roger Healey with guidance from Peter Wilkinson. Healey wrote programs in Algol 60, run on KDF9, to simulate the performance of a hypothetical 18-node UK national network. These pioneering studies showed just how the performance of the network would degrade as more traffic was offered to it. Simulation of a half-second's events took over two hours of computer time. The work was revived in 1970 when Wyn Price joined the Data Communication group and a research contract was placed with Plessey Telecommunications Research. Their studies showed that the choice of routing algorithm made little difference to network performance, but that flow control was critical and that the best performance was obtained if the number of packets in transit was kept low, in fact to less than one eighth of its maximum possible value.

In a distributed network with no central supervision, it is not obvious how the number of packets in transit can best be controlled. Donald Davies suggested that the network should contain a fixed number of packets, initially empty; then a node could only introduce a new data packet to the network if it could find an available 'empty'. When the data packet arrived at its destination and was delivered, the packet of course became empty again and at the disposal of the node concerned. This constant-number or *isarithmic* method of flow control was investigated in a series of simulation experiments starting in 1971; particular attention was paid to finding the best strategy for distributing the empties so as to avoid unnecessary shortages.

In parallel with this work, Peter Wilkinson and others were developing the idea of a *link protocol* between adjacent nodes in a network whereby (1) a packet sent from one node to another should be acknowledged, and (2) if it is not, for example because the receiving node is too full to accept it, the sending node should retransmit it after a fixed delay. When a network using this protocol was simulated, it was found that to avoid congestion the nodes had to reserve some capacity for inter-node traffic as opposed to locally arising traffic; they also had to reject local traffic if the appropriate output queue was full. This design worked well: throughput increased with increasing applied load up to a maximum level, after which further offered traffic was made to wait, with the network showing no signs of congestive failure. With this system, additional control using the isarithmic method was unnecessary.

Studies were also made of the effect of random transmission errors on throughput, and of the way in which reducing the packet size could reduce the effect of such errors (because less material has to be retransmitted). More significantly, the effect of complete failure of a link was studied. The idea was that a special test packet should be sent regularly along each link if there was no normal traffic along it. If the receiving node did not receive a test packet when one was expected, it treated the link concerned as faulty. This meant that the routing tables which normally determined where an incoming packet was sent next were automatically amended to exclude the faulty link, and information identifying the link was broadcast to all neighbouring nodes for them to take similar action. In this way news of the problem spread rapidly across the network. These techniques ensured that any data packets lost because of a link failure would be recreated with no harm done other than a short delay; if receipt acknowledgments were lost, duplicate data packets could be generated but the duplicates could be identified as such and deleted by the eventual receiving system.

In collaboration with Logica, further studies were made of simulated hierarchical networks, for example a two-decker system in which there are several separate multinode local networks, each with a link to a multinode national network. These studies showed that it was less easy to avoid congestion in such systems than with a single level. Other collaborative work was undertaken with GMD in Germany and with Reuters.

The simulation projects were very fully documented, as the following bibliography shows. The best summary is probably Wyn Price's 1977 paper in *Computer Networks* (ref. 125). He led the work from 1970, and other main NPL contributors were Costas Solomonides and Godfrey Cowin.

Selected publications on network simulation

D W Davies. The control of congestion in packet-switching networks. *Proc. ACM/IEEE Second Symposium on Problems in the Optimization of Data Communications Systems,* held in Palo Alto, October 1971, ACM/IEEE, 1971, pp.46–49; reprinted in *IEEE Trans. on Communications,* COM-20, 1972, pp.546–550.

W L Price. Simulation of data transit networks. NPL Report Com Sci 56, April 1972.

W L Price and C O Baillie. Further simulation studies of an isarithmic data transit network. NPL Report Com Sci 58, July 1972.

W L Price. Survey of NPL simulation studies of data networks, 1968–72. NPL Report Com 60, November 1972.

W L Price (ed.) Logical description of a program for the simulation of computer networks. NPL Report Com 62, December 1972.

R Healey. Computer network simulation study. NPL Report Com 64, January 1973.

W L Price. Simulation of a packet-switched data network operating with a revised link and node protocol. NPL Report Com 68, April 1973.

W L Price. Simulation of a packet-switched data network operating under isarithmic control with a revised link and node protocol. NPL Report Com 71, September 1973.

W L Price. A study of bifurcated routing in a data network and the effect of isarithmic flow control in this context. NPL Report Com 72, March 1974.

W L Price. Design of data communication networks using simulation techniques. *Computer Aided Design,* 6(3), July 1974, pp.171–175.

W L Price. Simulation studies of an isarithmically controlled store and forward data communication network. In: J L Rosenfeld (ed.), *Information Processing 74: Proc. IFIP Congress 74,* held in Stockholm, August 1974, North-Holland, 1974, pp.151–154.

W L Price and G W Cowin. The effect of link errors and of selective upgrading of link and node speed on network performance. NPL Report Com 76, September 1974.

W L Price and G W Cowin. Simulation studies of the effect of link breakdown on data communication network performance. NPL Report Com 77, February 1975.

W L Price. Further simulation experiments on adaptive routing using locally available parameters. NPL Report Com 81, December 1975.

I H Kerr, G R A Gomberg, W L Price and C M Solomonides. A simulation study of routing and flow control in a hierarchically connected packet switching network. In: P K Verma (ed.), *Advancement through resource sharing: Proc. Third Int. Conf. on Computer Communications,* held in Toronto, August 1976, ICCC, Washington, 1976, pp.495–501.

W L Price. Data network simulation: experiments at the National Physical Laboratory 1968–76. *Computer Networks,* 1(4), May 1977, pp.199–210. Reprinted in W W Chu (ed.), *Advances in Computer Communications and Networking,* Artech House, Dedham, Mass., 1979, pp.291–308.

W L Price. Simulation of the 10-node data communication network operating with link speeds of 9.6 kb/s. NPL Report Com 87, January 1977.

W L Price. Simulation methods in communication network design. NPL Report Com 92, September 1977.

W L Price. Adaptive routing in store-and-forward networks and the importance of load-splitting. In: B Gilchrist (ed.), *Information Processing 77: Proc. IFIP Congress 77,* held in Toronto August 1977, North-Holland, 1977, pp.309–314.

J D Haenle and W L Price. Some comments on simulated datagram store-and-forward networks. *Computer Networks,* 2(1), February 1978, pp.70–73.

W L Price. Simulation studies of data communication networks operating in datagram mode. *Computer Journal,* 21(3), August 1978, pp.219–223.

G Murphy, I McCurragh, W L Price and C M Solomonides. A design study for Reuters' packet switched network using simulation techniques. *Proc. Fourth Int. Conf. on Computer Communications,* held in Kyoto, September 1978, pp.443–448.

W L Price. Simulation of routing doctrines, flow control and congestion avoidance. In: S Schoemaker (ed.), *Computer Networks and Simulation,* North-Holland, October 1978, pp.141–153.

W L Price. A review of the flow control aspects of the network simulation studies at the National Physical Laboratory. In: J-L Grange and M Gien (eds), *Flow Control and Computer Networks,* North-Holland, February 1979, pp.17–32.

G R A Gomberg, I H Kerr, W L Price, J Richards and C M Solomonides. A design study of a hierarchically connected packet-switching network using simulation techniques. *Computer Networks,* 3(2), April 1979, pp.114–135.

Network interconnection

After the completion of the Mark II NPL network, and particularly following its handover to DNAC in 1974, the focus of the Data Communications group's attention moved to the interconnection of the NPL network with others. Donald Davies's tidy two-level model of national computer communication, put forward in 1966, had still not been realised; but other networks were being developed throughout the Western world, and the potential benefits of interconnecting them, in terms of access to services and ease of communication, were very clear. Internationally, the main forum for discussion was the International Federation for Information Processing (IFIP) Technical Committee 6 (Data Transmission) Working Group 1. This group (chaired by Vint Cerf of ARPA 1972–75 and by Derek Barber 1976–79) studied the interconnection of packet-switched networks, and in particular 'host-to-host' protocols to enable computers on different networks to communicate. On technical grounds, the obvious vehicle for an experiment in this area would have been an interconnection between the NPL Network and the ARPANET, both of which were well established. However, a European collaborative research venture, COST, had identified a European Informatics Network (EIN) as a priority subject for investigation, based on preliminary work by Derek Barber, with NPL as the UK centre. At the same time the Post Office's plans for their Experimental Packet Switched Service (EPSS) were taking shape, and as a prime mover in the area NPL expected to contribute to its development and to take advantage of its existence as soon as possible. Given that the group did not have the resources for all three projects, it was clear that for policy rather than technical reasons links to EIN and to EPSS should take precedence over a link to ARPANET.

When two computer-based systems use a packet-switched network to exchange a sequence of messages constituting a single transaction, the messages are said to form a *virtual call* (because of the obvious analogy with a telephone call). In contrast, the nodes of the network operate in *datagram* mode, that is to say they handle individual packets without needing any concept of the virtual calls (if any) to which the packets belong. EPSS was designed to offer a service to users with simple terminals as well as those with computers. Because of this it was decided, arguably mistakenly, that all users would have to work in virtual call mode; in other words the EPSS nodes, called Packet Switching Exchanges (PSEs), required their external users to conform to a prescribed protocol for opening, handling, and closing calls, even those who were capable of handling packets directly.

In connecting the NPL network to EPSS, the aim was to ensure that a virtual call could be established between a machine at NPL and an EPSS subscriber without either party needing to know about the conventions of the other party's network. To meet this requirement, a *gateway* computer was needed, connected to both networks, which would carry out a translation between the NPL computer-to-computer protocol and the EPSS customer protocol. The machine used for the gateway was a Computer Technology MiniMod sited at NPL with a 48 kilobit/sec link to the London PSE on EPSS. As a testbed for this configuration, a similar link was established in 1974 between NPL and the Computer Aided Design Centre at Cambridge, using the proposed EPSS protocol, and the lessons learnt were fed back to the EPSS team in the Post Office. The establishment of EPSS incidentally made communication between the NPL network and ARPANET possible after all, because University College London had a satellite link to ARPANET and was also on EPSS.

The units linking the high-speed line to the MiniMod were designed by Peter Carter with guidance from Keith Bartlett. Bartlett and Les Pink carried out a detailed study of the incidence of transmission errors on the Cambridge link. The main contributors to the design and development of the EPSS gateway software, which was called METHOD, were Ian Dewis, Nick Dawes, Vince Hathway, Mike Gentry (CAP Ltd) and Carol Walsh.

Publications on the connection to EPSS

D W Davies. Introduction to the Post Office Experimental Packet Switched Service. NPL Report Com 70, September 1973.

K A Bartlett and L A Pink. Error analysis of a Datel 48k link between NPL Teddington and CADC Cambridge. NPL Tech. Memo. Com Sci 87, November 1974.

N W Dawes, I G Dewis and M Gentry. An EPSS interface service for the NPL data communication network. In: D L A Barber (ed.), *Communications Networks* [papers presented at the European Computing Conference on Communications Networks held in London, September 1975], Online, 1975, pp.65–80.

P E Carter. A line protocol unit for the Post Office Experimental Packet Switched Service. NPL Tech. Memo. Com Sci 90, July 1975.

European Informatics Network (EIN)

In 1968 the Scientific and Technical Research Policy Committee of the European Economic Communities proposed a number of research projects suitable for international collaboration. These were taken up in 1969 by COST (Coopération Européenne dans le Domaine de la Recherche Scientifique et Technique), a group with a wider membership of nations than the EEC, which established study groups to examine the proposals in more detail. The group for COST Project 11, 'A European Informatics Network', was established in December 1970 with Derek Barber of NPL as chairman. It produced a report in mid-1971, and later in the same year an agreement to establish a network was signed. This agreement eventually had 11 signatories: France, West Germany, Italy, the Netherlands, Norway, Portugal, Sweden, Switzerland, the United Kingdom, Yugoslavia, and Euratom. It came into force in 1973 after it had received the necessary minimum number of ratifications. Barber was appointed Director, and was seconded by NPL to Euratom on 1 May 1973, though he remained at NPL which provided accommodation for his Executive Body. His deputy was Geoff Tootill, who 25 years earlier had worked on the development of the early Manchester computers. The costs of the Executive Body and of the network itself were met by the signatories jointly. There were five Primary Centres, each managing a node of the network and meeting its own costs; these were the Centro Rete Europea di Informatica (CREI) of the Politecnico di Milano, for Italy; the Eidgenössische Technische Hochschule (ETH) in Zürich, for Switzerland; the Institut de Recherche d'Informatique et d'Automatique (IRIA) at Rocquencourt, Paris, for France; the European Communities Joint Research Centre (JRC) at Ispra, Italy, for Euratom; and NPL for the UK. There were also seven secondary centres permanently connected to the EIN via their country's primary centre; the only secondary centre in the UK was the Atomic Energy Research Establishment (AERE) at Harwell. Other establishments could readily be connected temporarily using the telephone network, for

The Davies era: 1966–1978

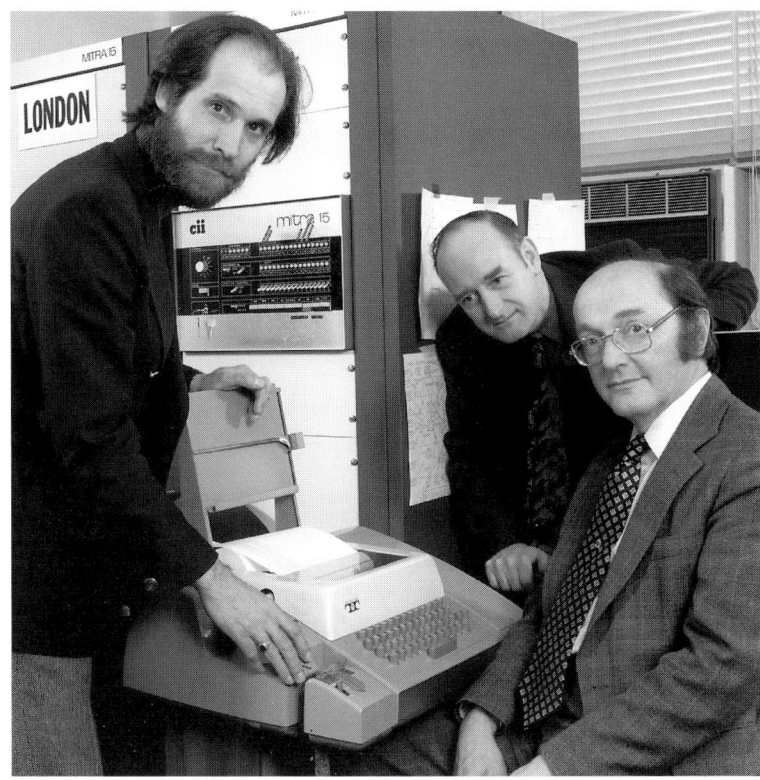

Figure 35. The NPL node computer of the European Informatics Network, 1977, with Roger Scantlebury, Derek Barber and Donald Davies.

example by calling a modem attached as a terminal on the NPL network, or through EPSS.

The aims of the EIN project were to link participating centres by a computer network, and thereby 'to facilitate research into data processing problems, to permit the sharing of resources, to allow the exchange of ideas and the co-ordination of research programmes, to facilitate the comparison of ideas for national networks, to promote the agreement of standards, and finally to be a model for future networks, whether for commercial or other purposes'. As a research project, it was not intended to provide a permanent service.

The node software was developed under contract by Sesa (France) and Logica (UK). The nodes were French CII Mitra 15 computers (see fig. 35), linked by leased 9.6 kilobit/sec lines with a capability to upgrade these to faster links if necessary. The Centres could not agree whether the network should provide a pure packet-switching service using datagrams, or a virtual circuit service. In the end both were included in the specification, though the virtual circuit capability was little used in practice. The network was handed over to the centres on schedule on 26 May 1976.

Besides providing the Director and accommodation as mentioned above, and playing a major part in the collective decisions of the Primary Centres, NPL made two specific technical contributions to EIN. These were the gateway system connecting the NPL EIN node to the NPL network, and the design and development of the Network Control Centre which monitored traffic, diagnosed faults, took corrective action where possible, and collected performance statistics.

The gateway was simpler than that needed for the EPSS link because both EIN and the packet-switch on the NPL network worked in datagram mode; this meant that the gateway had only to pass packets in both directions. A small CTL MiniMod computer was used for the purpose, as in the case of EPSS. However, an exchange of messages between two computers involves a virtual call, as discussed above, and software is needed in each machine to provide this virtual call service, using the basic datagram service provided by the network. This software was called a *transport station*; the rules governing the interaction between the two transport stations conducting a virtual call were an instance of an *end-to-end* protocol. If a standard protocol could be agreed for this purpose, there would be no problem, but unfortunately each network had its own rules. Clearly each computer on the NPL network could not be expected to implement an EIN transport station, and pending an agreement on standards a protocol translation was carried out on a separate machine on the NPL network. Because of the lack of internationally agreed standard protocols, connecting to EIN had turned out to be nearly as complicated as connecting to EPSS, in spite of its superior architecture.

As a test-bed for the plans for EIN, a successful link was established between the NPL network and the French Cyclades network in 1975. Although further progress was sometimes slow because of the need to get agreement between the primary centres, EIN worked well. Figure 36 shows a message broadcast

Figure 36. Teletext in Europe via the NPL Network and the European Informatics Network, July 1976.

by the BBC on Ceefax, made available on the NPL network as part of the Teletext service (see p.158), and accessed via EIN in the course of a demonstration at Ispra on 9 July 1976. A few weeks later a similar demonstration was given at the ICCC Conference in Toronto, the link being via PTT lines to Cyclades and thence via EIN and the NPL network to the Teletext receiver at NPL and so to the BBC. A development of more lasting significance, shown on the same occasions, was the use of NPL's Scrapbook system as an on-line information clearing-house, so that for example documents kept on the system at NPL could be consulted and edited at meetings at other EIN centres, a capability now taken for granted but at that time a startling innovation.

EIN was not itself used by researchers outside the network field to any great extent; it was not set up to provide services which would attract them, and the bandwagon which would later lead to the Internet had only just started to roll. But it showed the way ahead as it was meant to do; and later European networks were able to change the emphasis from innovative communications technology to the provision of practical information services. EIN was closed down, and the final report on the project published, in 1980.

Roger Scantlebury was in charge of NPL's contribution to EIN, assisted by John Laws, who with Carol Walsh developed the gateway and the protocol converter. Keith Wilkinson developed the Network Control Centre. At the time of writing (1996) the detailed records kept by the EIN Executive Body are held by Derek Barber.

Publications on the European Informatics Network

D L A Barber. The European Computer Network Project. *Proc. First Int. Conf. on Computer Communications,* held in Washington October 1972, ICCC Secretariat, New York, 1972, pp.192–200.

D L A Barber. Progress with the European Informatics Network. In: J Borge Hansson et al. (eds), *Proc. Second Int. Conf. on Computer Communications,* held in Stockholm August 1974, ICCC Secretariat, 1974, pp.214–219.

M Gien, J Laws and R A Scantlebury. Interconnection of packet switching networks: theory and practice. In: D L A Barber (ed.), *Communications Networks* [papers presented at the European Computing Conference on Communications Networks held in London, September 1975], Online, 1975, pp.241–260.

D L A Barber. A European Informatics Network: achievements and prospects. In: P K Verma (ed.), *Advancement through Resource Sharing: Proc. Third Int. Conf. on Computer Communications,* held at Toronto, ICCC, Washington, 1976, pp.44–49.

J Laws. An experience of connecting to the European Informatics Network. In: D L A Barber (ed.), *Proc. Online Conf. on Data Communications Networks,* held at West Drayton in May 1977, Online, 1978, pp.257–266.

EIN. Cost Project 11: A European Informatics Network: Report on the Project. Ref. EIN/80/001, 1980. [This final report on the EIN project includes a full bibliography (pp.25–49).]

Protocols

The first use of the term *protocol* in the technical sense of a set of rules governing communication appears to be in the title of Scantlebury and Bartlett's paper in April 1967 (see list below). The term is now in worldwide use. Because the concept underlies all the later work of the group, it is worthwhile bringing together here some of the key early developments.

When units of information such as single characters are transmitted over an untrustworthy channel, more accurate communication will be achieved if the receiving equipment is required to acknowledge correct receipt of each unit, and the sender is required to retransmit if an acknowledgement is not received. To ensure that units sent and acknowledgements match exactly, it would be possible to give each unit a serial number and require the acknowledgement to quote it. The longer these serial numbers are, the more of the channel capacity is used in transmitting them, so the question arises how short such a serial number can safely be made. In a classic paper published in 1969 (ref. 11), Bartlett, Scantlebury and Wilkinson showed that reliable transmission could be achieved if the units sent were simply labelled alternately 0 and 1, and the acknowledgements likewise. This became known as the *alternating bit protocol*; it was used in the first NPL network which was then being designed, and has since become well known as a result of its wide use as an example in teaching.

In the Mark II NPL Network computers communicated using packets. This required a new *link protocol*, described in Wilkinson's 1975 paper listed below, to govern the exchanges between the User Machines and the packet switch. The protocol laid down the format of packets and the rules for detecting and correcting errors in transmission. This was the protocol whose use between the nodes in a distributed network was simulated by Wyn Price as discussed above (p.137). Together with IBM's SDLC, it was an important precursor of the eventual standard link protocol HDLC (High-level Data Link Control), which was used in EIN, and which formed Level 2 of CCITT Recommendation X.25 (ref. 20). A link protocol is conducted by a software module in each machine, which communicates with its peer in the other machine using the physical medium to do so. Because faulty or missing packets can in general be detected and retransmitted, the service provided by the link level module to other local software is a reliable packet transmission service, much more useful than the raw transmission capability provided by the medium itself, and in this sense it can be seen as providing a value-added service.

Virtual calls between systems in subscriber computers on a network need an end-to-end protocol to enable the parties to indicate and recognise the beginning and end of a call, and the beginning and end of the individual messages within it. This protocol will first require the calling party to identify who is being called. For each message it may require the sending party to indicate which call the message belongs to (because the receiving party may be conducting several virtual calls at once). These matters are logically quite separate from the requirements of the particular communications media in use, such as the need in packet-switched networks to conduct a link protocol over each link used. In each of the communicating computers there will be a module of software to conduct this end-to-end protocol with its peer in the other system. Of course it cannot talk directly to its peer, but must do so using the service provided by the local link level module. Its purpose is to provide a virtual call service to other local software. An example is the EIN Transport Station software mentioned above; a simple end-to-end protocol was also used between User Machines in the NPL Mark II network, allowing them to conduct multiple interleaved packet communication with as many correspondents as necessary. As with link protocols, the early transport protocols led eventually to standards, many of their functions corresponding to those of Level 3 of CCITT Recommendation X.25.

This concept of a layered architecture, whereby a layer of software conducting a particular protocol uses a service provided by the layer below and provides a value-added service to the layer above, is fundamental to present-day computer communications systems. At the bottom is a physical communication capability; at the top is applications software, for example that providing electronic mail facilities to human users. The layered model is just an instance, though a classic one, of the usual method of tackling a complex problem: break it down into sub-problems with well-defined interfaces. It was clearly stated by Keith Bartlett as early as 1968 (in his IFIP paper, see list on p.135): 'If interfaces between adjacent levels can be defined, improvements in technology at any one level do not involve redesign or change at any other level.' The model soon led to the concept of Open Systems and the next phase in the work of the group, which is described in section 5.2.

Publications on protocols

R A Scantlebury and K A Bartlett. A protocol for use in the NPL Data Communication System. NPL Tech. Memo. Auto TM 4, August 1967.

K A Bartlett, R A Scantlebury and P T Wilkinson. A note on reliable full-duplex transmission over half-duplex links. *Comm. ACM*, 12(5), May 1969, pp.260–261.

P T Wilkinson. Link protocols for use in packet-switching networks. NPL Report Com 78, February 1975.

R A Scantlebury (ed.). Second European users' workshop on network protocols, Computer Science Division, NPL, 7 & 8 October 1976. NPL Report Com 84, November 1976.

N V Stenning. A data transfer protocol. *Computer Networks*, 1(2), 1976, pp.99–110.

Network job control

A network considered as a whole is a complex resource, with users, capabilities (software) and information (data) all being geographically distributed. A critical item in the set of tools needed to use this resource was thought at the time to be a capability for remote job control: that is a means by which a local computer system can ask a remote computer to run a particular program with defined input, and tell it what to do with the output if any. To explore this further, the first consideration is what facilities the human user might need; a *network job control language* can then be defined to enable these requirements to be expressed precisely, and the design of the high-level protocol between the two computer systems can then follow. These possibilities were studied by Dave Rayner in 1975–77, as described in the papers listed below.

D Rayner. Recent developments in machine-independent job control languages. *Software Practice and Experience*, 5, 1975, pp.375–393.

D Rayner. An introduction to Network Job Control Language. NPL Report Com 88, March 1977.

D Rayner. Past and present solutions to the problems of network job control. NPL Report Com 96, December 1977.

4.3 Information systems

In the late 1960s, the use of magnetic discs as a computer memory medium had developed to the point where substantial amounts of text and/or numeric information could be stored: for example, the 24 Mbyte drive added to NPL's KDF9 in 1966 could have held the works of Shakespeare at least three times over. Compared with magnetic tape, discs had the key advantage of allowing random access to any point in the stored data in about a tenth of a second. But the development of techniques for representing, updating and consulting information on the discs was still in its infancy. Although storing plain running text on-line could be useful in studies of language and literature, most potential applications involved large bodies of more structured information, typically sets of completed forms or the like. It was clear that if such a *database* was kept on a computer it would be possible to get answers to factual questions about the data stored which would be prohibitively time consuming if undertaken manually. This capability became known at the time as *fact retrieval,* in contrast with the existing document-retrieval systems which were designed for finding out which documents in a library were relevant to a given query; database management systems and query languages are the more modern terms for fact retrieval.

In the longer term, *information utilities,* large bodies of information stored on-line and available over communication links, were seen as a realistic possibility for the future, supplying information on demand as existing utilities supplied water or electricity. The potential importance of this idea meant that the whole subject was judged to be in the evolutionary mainstream. Subsequent developments have confirmed that view, even though the availability and power of home computers, and the general swing away from centralised public services in favour of free enterprise, have led to a form and ethos for the Internet rather different from the more sober and orderly utilities foreseen by the researchers of the late 1960s.

With this background, it was natural that fact retrieval was made the prime target of the Information Systems Group established in Autonomics Division in 1967 following the completion of the work on machine translation. The new group was led initially by John McDaniel, and then by David Yates following McDaniel's resignation in August 1968. To ensure that the work matched real needs and to avoid any undue tendency to the academic, it was decided to involve users in the first project, and various possible applications were considered. The interesting one eventually selected emerged from discussions between Donald Davies and Mr A G McDonald of the Police Research and Planning Branch of the Home Office.

Helping the police with their inquiries: the SHREWD system

To help with criminal investigations, the police need to keep records of past crimes in their area, people who have come to their attention in connection with crime, suspect vehicles, and so on. This information, usually held on card indexes in the 1960s, formed a promising basis for a fact-retrieval project: typical collections were a reasonable size, they had a well-defined overall structure, and the efficient use of the data stored was very much in the public interest. A collaborative project was accordingly established in 1967 to develop an experimental fact-retrieval system suitable for the police application, with NPL responsible for the software systems design and programming, and the Police Research and Planning Branch of the Home Office, later the Police Scientific Development Branch (PSDB), responsible for the hardware procurement and police aspects. (This Branch was staffed by police officers on secondment and scientists working together, an unusual and productive arrangement.)

The first stage of the work was to study the police application. This was completed in late 1967; it gave the NPL staff involved a memorable and privileged insight into the everyday work of the police on criminal investigations. At the same time thought was being given to the overall shape of the experiment. The computer to be used had to be secure and under police or Home Office control. Since the expense of buying a dedicated machine could not be justified for such a speculative project, it was decided to use an existing ICL 1900 series machine already installed for unrelated batch-processing work by the Home Office and Metropolitan Police Joint Automatic Data Processing Unit (JADPU) in central London. Extra disc drives and core memory would be added, and Post Office lines would be installed to connect the machine to the two police units selected for the pilot scheme. In parallel with these plans by the Home Office, an outline systems design was being prepared at NPL.

SHREWD (System for Holding and REtrieving Wanted Data) was to be a software package for on-line data storage and retrieval, written in the PLAN assembly language of the 1900 series computers. It enabled users to build up a database in the remote computer, and to alter and interrogate the stored data, using visual display units—a pattern now so familiar that it is hard to appreciate the futuristic flavour of these proposals at the time. Although designed with the police application in mind, the system could be used in other fields, because the specifications of data structure and query vocabulary were parameters of the program and not built in.

In the police application there were to be five files: people, places, crimes, vehicles and events. To insert new records, the user called for and completed a form-like display, and an existing record could be modified by editing the completed form. Each record was stored as a hierarchical data structure with the twigs of the tree being *attribute–value pairs* like 'place of birth: Plymouth'. The records were cross-linked by allowing the values of certain attributes to be the names of records elsewhere in the database. Free-text comments could be included. Names of attributes and common values were stored as numerical codes to save space, and the system would keep indexes of selected attribute–value pairs to save time on queries. Records were held on the disc in encrypted form to reduce the risk of information getting into the wrong hands.

Simple queries to retrieve a named record were expressed by a code followed by the name of the record; more complex queries were expressed in a subset of English, and this was where the greatest research interest of the system lay. A query had to consist of a *preamble* defining the information required and a string of *features* defining the set of records from which this information was to be extracted. For example, the query:

> GIVE DATE OF BIRTH FOR ALL BALD BANK ROBBERS LIVING IN TEDDINGTON

consists of a preamble (up to and including the word ALL), followed by three features. Simple features such as these each indicated an attribute and a value; the word BALD, for example, meant to the system 'records in which the attribute *hair* has the value *bald*'; and BANK ROBBERS meant 'records in which the attribute *convictions* has the value *robbery (bank)*'. A feature could define more than one value for an attribute, either explicitly using the word OR, or implicitly by using a blanket term. More complex features could be used which referred to another of the five files, for example:

LIST ALL PICKPOCKETS WITH RED SPORTS CARS

The system clearly had to have available to it a *dictionary* containing all words or word-groups which could be used in queries to refer to particular attributes, so that it could understand which attribute was involved. Words or word-groups referring solely to values, however, did not have to be in the dictionary if the context made their role clear. The result of looking up the words forming a query in this dictionary was a set of 'jigsaw pieces' with which the program attempted to build a tree-like data structure representing the meaning of the query. This tree formed the basis of the subsequent search in the indexes and files to find the records satisfying the user's specification; the particular information called for was extracted from each one for display on the VDU screen. To avoid delays caused by users inadvertently asking questions with very long answers (like 'LIST ALL MEN'), the program found the records matching the query one at a time, only finding the next one on request.

Altogether there were four main uses of tree-like data structures by the software: the database definition, the items in the dictionary, the stored records themselves, and the queries. Handling these structures efficiently was clearly a key requirement of the system, and a set of list-processing PLAN macros called Treemaster was developed for the purpose by Derek Baker.

In addition to the group's main task of designing and developing the retrieval system, a study was made by Malcolm Robinson of a possibility for the future: that the system in its idle moments should look for unexpected 'patterns' in its database. An example of such a pattern would be the existence of several tenuous links between a particular person and a particular crime where none of the links in isolation would have been surprising enough to attract attention. Informally, a 'pattern' was thought of as any combination of facts which would make the user say 'Aha!' and take some action when it was pointed out, but it was clearly less easy to provide an effective formal definition. One possibility worth exploring was closed chains of records in which each record concerned was linked to its neighbours either by explicit reference or by having an attribute–value pair in common. Although the effective identification of such patterns was a highly ambitious goal, the potential pay-off both for the police and for the study of artificial intelligence made it a promising research area.

Information systems

Figure 37. Sgt Colliar, Thames Valley Police, with a newly-installed SHREWD terminal, December 1970.

The plans for the main project appeared satisfactory, but their realisation was to prove more difficult. The main problem was the painful slowness of developing software with no ready access to an appropriate computer: every interaction took at least a day and in practice often much longer. Secondly, the time-sharing aspects of the software, the use of VDUs, the use of discs and the use of communications lines, though all supported by the computer manufacturer, were still in various degrees of infancy and made performance sadly unreliable when combined in one system. Thirdly, although the users recognised the potential value of the experiment, they had many other duties and their patience with a system which offered possible jam tomorrow, but only certain hassle today, could not be inexhaustible. Finally, the English-like queries proved to be too adventurous; with hindsight it would have been more practical, though less interesting, to have started with a more formalised method of specifying retrieval requirements and only extended this to freer-form queries after successful trials.

The slowness of the early software development, though frustrating, did not affect the timetable directly because the hardware delivery was only completed in February 1971, and by then software was available for the users to start to input their records (see fig. 37). A two-year experiment was planned, to end in February 1973 when the extra computer equipment was scheduled for other purposes. But in practice, because of the problems already mentioned, further progress both with data input and with the completion of the query-answering software was too slow. Though the experiment was extended by a few months, and the query system did eventually work, the users could not be expected to devote much effort to learning and using an unreliable system with incomplete data and only a short future life. The experiment ended in August 1973.

Although the experiment had not achieved its intended goals, many useful lessons had been learnt. First, dedicated computer systems with a reasonably long planned life were needed for the police application; it had proved unsatisfactory to bolt it on to a batch-processing operation. Secondly, reliability was of the essence, more important to them than sophisticated features. Thirdly, as regards facilities, SHREWD matched the primary needs well (it was used as a basis in the specification of the future systems); queries however should be more formalised than in SHREWD to ensure that the users could distinguish between valid and invalid queries more readily. NPL had also learnt important lessons, in particular the need to have system development tools, both hardware and software, readily available; and the group's ideas on what were the primary features of the information systems of the future had for some time moved away from fact retrieval, as will be seen in the next section.

The SHREWD software was developed by Roger Reason, Malcolm Robinson, Celia Searle, Derek Baker, Willy Russell (Home Office), and David Yates who was also the overall software systems designer. Keith Wilkinson, Sylvia Larcombe and Eddie Dymott also contributed at various times. The Home Office staff most closely involved were Willy Russell, Ross Tristem (in the early stages), Alan Holt, Barry Blain and Sheilagh Keddie. Though the project started on a collaborative basis, NPL in common with other Government research establishments came under pressure in 1971 to get funding from primary beneficiaries of projects where these could be readily identified, and accordingly the Home Office met the full costs of the project in its later stages.

Documents on the SHREWD system

D M Yates and W Russell. On-line data retrieval for a local police intelligence unit. *Police Research Bulletin*, 16, October 1970, pp.4–12. [Also presented at the XVII International Conference of the Institute of Management Science, 3 July 1970.]

M G Robinson. Notes on pattern-searching. NPL Tech. Memo. Com Sci TM 53, April 1971.

D M Yates. SHREWD: an on-line data storage and retrieval system with natural language queries. NPL Tech. Memo. Com Sci TM 62, April 1972.

NPL. SHREWD system documentation. 11 sections, dated between April 1972 and January 1974. Unpublished, prepared for internal Home Office and NPL use.

E R Dymott. Computer retrieval of incorrectly spelled surnames. NPL Report Com 83, October 1976.

Scrapbook

From the establishment of the Information Systems group in 1967, it had been understood that the group should in time

Information systems

Figure 38. One of the Division's CTL Modular One installations, with Vince Hathway and Angela Stephens, October 1971.

develop its own information system as a basis for future work exploring the uses of such systems and extending their capabilities. The key requirements were:

(1) that the system should provide a versatile tool allowing its users to create, modify and access stored information so as to help them in the course of their everyday tasks;
(2) that it should be as straightforward as possible to use;
(3) that it should be flexible, allowing new facilities to be added without the existing ones being upset; and
(4) that it should make use of the newly developed NPL Network.

The proposed system soon acquired the name Scrapbook, as users were to be able to stick in anything they liked; the earliest notes on system requirements to survive use this name and were written between July 1970 and February 1971.

Learning from their experience with SHREWD, the group were clear that a dedicated small computer installed in their own laboratory was essential; the Modular One (Mod 1) system from the UK manufacturer Computer Technology Ltd (see fig. 38) was eventually chosen. As with SHREWD, the users' terminals were to be visual display units (VDUs); although these had a screen and a keyboard making them superficially similar to today's personal computers, they of course had no processing capability—all the computing was done by the central Modular One. Initially four VDUs were connected directly to a single Mod 1; use of the network, and more Mod 1s, came later.

A Scrapbook user could create *records* on the computer's hard disc by typing on a VDU keyboard. Each record—document would be the modern term—had a unique name chosen by the

153

user; then as now these names were usually divided up by several '/' characters so that the name defined the place of the record in a hierarchical classification system. Once created, a record could be retrieved by quoting its name and then read, altered or printed. The alteration or editing process differed in some respects from a modern word processor because the computer could not 'see' every key depression, only a sequence of such depressions ending in a 'return' character. This meant, for example, that to insert new text in a paragraph one had first to make some space at the point of insertion by giving an appropriate command, then type in the new text, and finally give a 'pack' command to tidy up the paragraph. The process would seem slow and clumsy today, but it did allow text to appear on the screen, be modified and apparently disarranged, and then magically be reformatted into a new tidy paragraph. Up to that time text had always been seen as something inherently fixed in position on the printed page; the idea that it could be made to flow and move around and rearrange itself on demand was an amazing revelation to many who saw it on Scrapbook for the first time, particularly as they were being told that this was to become an everyday tool.

Because Scrapbook was designed to serve a community rather than a single user, it was realised from the outset that it could be used for message-passing. In a crude form, this could have been achieved without any special provisions: two users could agree on a name for a record to be used as a mailbox and then each write into that record any message for the other; the receiver would of course have to look at the record to see any incoming message. From an early stage, however, Scrapbook provided more sophisticated facilities than this, giving each user an identifier (the modern term would be 'e-mail address') and a mailbox record, and showing each user the latest contents of his or her mailbox at the start of each Scrapbook session. Messages could be 'broadcast'—i.e. sent to a named list of users simultaneously—or sent to a single user.

An important aim of Scrapbook was to give its users the ability to create, and to use, databases of information on particular topics. A database user wants to move from one record to another without typing the name of the new record. For example, if a piece of text gives some information and ends with a question: 'Do you want more information on this topic?', the user will expect to be able to type 'yes' or 'no', not some long and clumsy record name. Similarly in the common case where a menu of choices is offered, typing a single letter or number to indicate the choice should be enough. To achieve this, Scrapbook allowed the creator of a record to include in it *user response definitions*. These simply associated the name of the next record required with each expected user response, and the actual definitions were not shown on the screen except when the record was being altered. User response definitions proved very versatile; they allowed questionnaires and teaching texts to be devised, and, for illustrative purposes only, 'non-linear fiction' in which the reader makes choices to determine the next twist of the plot; such a story can of course have a complex structure with several different endings depending on which turns in the maze the reader has taken. The modern term for the user response facility is *hypertext*.

To enable users to keep track of what records existed, Scrapbook maintained a hierarchy of *directories* using the record names, exactly like the directories kept by the later operating systems for personal computers, such as DOS and Windows. Scrapbook also maintained a log for each user called a *trace record,* showing the sequence of records accessed and (using the user response technique) allowing the user to return readily to an earlier point in his travel through this primitive version of cyberspace.

Careful thought was given to security. A record could be read by any user unless it had been marked as 'private', but it could only be altered by a user authorised to do so. Each user had a password. A Scrapbook system had a *database administrator,* who kept a *permit record* for each user of the system. This recorded (1) which groups of records the user could read even if they were private; and (2) which groups of records the user could create and alter (and mark private). In this context, a group of records was usually those appearing in a particular directory (including lower level directories).

Scrapbook records could be sent to a printer over the network (only one font and size of print were available); and they could be input or output using other terminals such as paper-tape devices. On-line help, appropriate to the particular process in use, was available if a user had problems. Scrapbook even had a feature called Windows, though it did not mean what it means today; it simply allowed editing to be restricted to a defined rectangular area or *window* on the screen, useful for example to deal with text in columns.

The final step in the evolution of Scrapbook came in 1976 when several Scrapbook systems, each with their own database administrator and population of users, could be linked across a network; there were three at NPL. This meant that records could be accessed and edited as if they were on one's 'home' system without the user having to be aware that they actually lived on a remote system. Crucially, this applied to the hypertext system outlined above as well as to basic retrieval and editing—a prototype of some aspects of the present-day World Wide Web and as far as is known a unique capability at the time. There were many ideas for further development, but these were discouraged by the Requirements Board which felt that further evolution should be left to the industry. Given the policy framework and state of knowledge of the day, this may have been a defensible decision, but with hindsight it was unfortunate (warning—the author is not an impartial witness on this issue!).

The Davies era: 1966–1978

> ❑ SIDELINE ❑ DETOUR ❑ DIGRESSION ❑ BYWAY ❑ SCENIC ROUTE ❑
>
> ### An early e-mail
>
> *When Scrapbook was shown to the Director, the latest message in the demonstrator's mailbox appeared as usual on the screen. This was a known risky moment, though what appeared could have been worse: it was a message from a colleague announcing that he had lost his umbrella and would welcome information leading to its recovery. This caused different reactions: the Director was concerned at the impression that the system dealt with trivia, whereas the team thought it showed how well fitted Scrapbook was to everyday needs. 'John Stockton's umbrella' accordingly found its small niche in computing history: trivial at one level, but quite significant at another. And yes, he did get it back as a result of the message.*

In software design, Scrapbook was able to take advantage of recent progress in the understanding of real-time systems due to Dijkstra, Hoare and others. This gave a firm theoretical basis for the development of systems in which several 'simultaneous' activations of a module of software might be needed, for example because several users are using the same module (on different data) at the same time. Such modules, called *processes,* required only one copy of the program code, though of course each activation would need its own data. A central operating system was needed to establish and delete activations of processes and to enable messages to be passed between them; the operating system in Scrapbook was called (arbitrarily) Lemons. The Scrapbook software was written in BCPL, a language developed by Martin Richards at Cambridge and incidentally an ancestor of the modern C language, for which a compiler was available for the Modular One.

In the first version of Scrapbook (early 1971), four terminals were connected directly to the Mod 1. The earliest account of the Lemons executive is dated 28 April 1971 (and is printed in upper case only, because the VDUs then in use could only display upper-case characters). In August 1971 the vital step of using the Mark I NPL Network to connect the terminals to the computer was taken, and as already mentioned Scrapbook was used from central London in a network demonstration on 19 January 1972. The first version of the Users' Guide to survive is dated 6 December 1972; this includes editing, user responses, trace and security. By 23 May 1973 directories and mail were apparently also in use, as they were described in a lecture on the system given on that day, subsequently published as ref. 130. By June 1973 the Mark II NPL Network was available, involving the Scrapbook team in the development of 'User Machine' software, as described above (section 4.2). The users of the early versions of Scrapbook were mainly within the Division of Computer Science, but a more organised Laboratory-wide service was introduced in September

1973 following the inauguration of the Mark II Network. By 1974 this service had 90 users, of which five to ten were usually connected at any one time (ten was the limit on a single system, so as to prevent the system becoming unacceptably slow). Further facilities were added gradually; a teleconferencing subsystem called Conclave, by Mark Dowson and Andrew Newman, was added in 1975 but little used. By 1977 there were three systems with 220 registered users, including several scattered through Europe connected to NPL through the European Informatics Network. The final state of the facilities is described in the last version of the Users' Guide, dated 4 July 1983; and the NPL Scrapbook systems were closed down on 20 July 1984.

The NPL Scrapbooks were used mainly for word processing, particularly of documents with several authors, for the organisation and maintenance of program texts and documentation, for databases such as address lists, and for e-mail. Within the Information Systems group the system was also used for the development and compilation of new processes; the BCPL compiler was itself a process.

A contract between NPL and Triad Computing Systems Ltd for the commercial exploitation of Scrapbook was signed on 1 August 1975, on Triad's side thanks chiefly to the interest and vision of one of the directors of the company, Michael Bevan. By present-day standards hardware costs were high, which meant that no mass market was available, which meant in turn that software prices were high as the costs had to be recovered over fewer sales. Nevertheless, the customers that Triad was able to attract made up in influence for their lack of numbers. They included Shell (UK) Ltd, the National Water Council, the Ministry of Defence (two systems), British Telecom, Murray Clayton Ltd, E C Baumann (a German newspaper publisher), and the Commission of the European Communities. On 1 May 1983 Triad sold their rights under the contract to British Telecom, whose subsidiary Milepost Business Systems extended the system for BT's use. Michael Bevan had by then founded Xionics Ltd which developed and marketed a new generation of systems whose facilities showed Scrapbook's influence on their designers[1]. In 1984 Milepost commissioned a study by NPL of how a single-user Scrapbook system might be implemented on a BBC Microcomputer; the resulting report showed how this could be done, but the idea was not followed up by the company.

---

[1] Mike Bevan writes: 'The Scrapbook-derived system developed by Xionics, based on much less expensive hardware than had been available at the time of the Triad agreement, took [the Scrapbook] ideas on to considerable commercial success. The system had its largest installation at the Greater London Council (1280 daily users at peak), its most prestigious at the Cabinet Office, and its most widely dispersed at the London, Los Angeles, New York and Tokyo offices of Security Pacific National Bank, in a WAN/LAN "Intranet" system serving its derivatives trading team.'

The Davies era: 1966–1978

In modern terms, Scrapbook provided user-friendly screen-based word processing and a common database for a working community, including electronic mail and hypertext facilities. These capabilities individually were not in all cases as novel as they seemed at the time, but considered as an integrated package Scrapbook gives NPL a claim to have been again amongst the world leaders in a key area of computer development. Because of the number of visitors whose eyes it opened, and because of its heavyweight customers, Scrapbook was very influential. Many of the ideas it incorporated were later to sweep the world when computers became cheap; but exactly what part it played in contributing to this complex evolution will only become clear when other threads in the pattern have been clarified.

The facilities to be offered by Scrapbook were decided by group discussions. The principal software designer, and author of the central Lemons operating system and many of the key processes, was Malcolm Robinson. The other major contributors to the software development were Vince Hathway, Peter Cashin and Michael Stevens, with contributions from Dave Eason, Mark Dowson, Andrew Newman, Sue Olding (later Mrs Chorley), Steve Hambly, and others. Celia Searle (later Mrs Kirkby) was the Data Base Administrator, and the group was led by David Yates.

Documents on Scrapbook

M G Robinson and D M Yates. The Scrapbook information system. *The Information Scientist,* December 1973, pp.135–143.

P M Cashin, M G Robinson and D M Yates. Experience with Scrapbook, a non-formatted data base system. In: J L Rosenfeld (ed.), *Information Processing 74: Proc. IFIP Congress 74,* held in Stockholm, August 1974, North-Holland, 1974, pp.1012–1016.

NPL. Scrapbook Users' Guide. Produced in several editions dated between December 1972 and July 1983. Unpublished; for internal NPL use.

S E Olding. Augmentation of a text retrieval system with an intelligent graphics terminal. NPL Report Com 86, January 1977.

M Dowson. The CONCLAVE computer teleconferencing system. NPL Report Com 107, May 1978.

Teletext and Viewdata

In UK television transmission, not all the 625 lines are used for the picture: 22 are used for control purposes and 28 are spare. It is these spare lines which are used to transmit the pages of text and simple graphics now familiar in many homes as Teletext. This service was pioneered by the BBC in the early 1970s; transmissions started in September 1974. It was soon realised that Teletext would form a useful addition to the information services on the NPL Network, and with the co-operation of the technical departments of the BBC and Mullard Applications Laboratory a Teletext receiver was linked to a port on the NPL Network to provide a single-user Teletext service. The user had to specify the channel and page numbers using a simple dialogue, and the required page then appeared on his VDU. This service was established in 1976 and is still in use at the time of writing (1996).

Networks, being essentially transparent, need services before they can be demonstrated effectively, and Teletext made a useful addition to the repertoire. As mentioned above (section 4.2) NPL's Teletext service was used via the European Informatics Network in July 1976, and the following month this link was further extended temporarily from Paris to Toronto as part of a demonstration at an international conference. Although arranged specially for the occasion, this extension of NPL and BBC services via France to Canada was not simply a communications showpiece; there was an important message that if effective standards could be developed many different information-carrying technologies could be routinely linked, to the benefit of the world's information users.

Viewdata, later called Prestel, was an information service established by the UK Post Office in the late 1970s. Terminals, each consisting of a television set and a keyboard, were connected via a black box and a telephone line to a central computer on which the information was stored. This too was experimentally interfaced to the NPL network but never evolved into a local service, probably simply because the cost of doing so was felt not to be justified (Teletext was of course free to holders of a television licence).

Teletext and Viewdata were interfaced to the NPL network by Alan Davies; technical details are given in the two reports listed below.

A T Davies. Teletext interfacing to a Data Communication Network. NPL Report Com 91, October 1977.
A T Davies. British Post Office VIEWDATA interfacing to a Data Communication Network. NPL Report DNACS 1/78, August 1978.

Distributed databases

It was realised in the mid-1970s that even with good data communication facilities it was difficult to exchange information between database systems if they were organised differently. A study was therefore carried out by Mike Woodger and others of the possibility of using a common standard form of data-structure description as a means by which one system could request and obtain data from a remote system with a different internal organisation—a lingua franca approach. The Relational Model developed by E F Codd in 1970 was adopted as the most appropriate basis for such an interface. Further details are given in the reports listed below.

The Davies era: 1966–1978

> M Woodger. Problems of representation of information in data bases with special reference to the relational model of Codd. NPL Report Com 103, May 1978.
>
> M Woodger. A menu-controlled interface to data bases and an interface generator. NPL Report Com 104, May 1978.
>
> M Dowson. Database interworking. NPL Report Com 106, May 1978.

4.4 Palantype transcription

In mechanical shorthand systems, an operator uses a machine like a small typewriter on which several keys can be depressed simultaneously like a musical chord. Each such chord or *stroke* represents (normally) a single spoken syllable: the left-hand keys represent the initial consonant(s), the middle keys the vowel, and the right-hand keys the final consonant(s). A stroke causes a row of letters corresponding to the selected keys to be printed across a vertical paper band, and the band to be advanced one line. Repeating this process, a skilled operator can keep up with normal speech, and thus produce a paper band recording, for example, the proceedings in a court of law. The band can then be

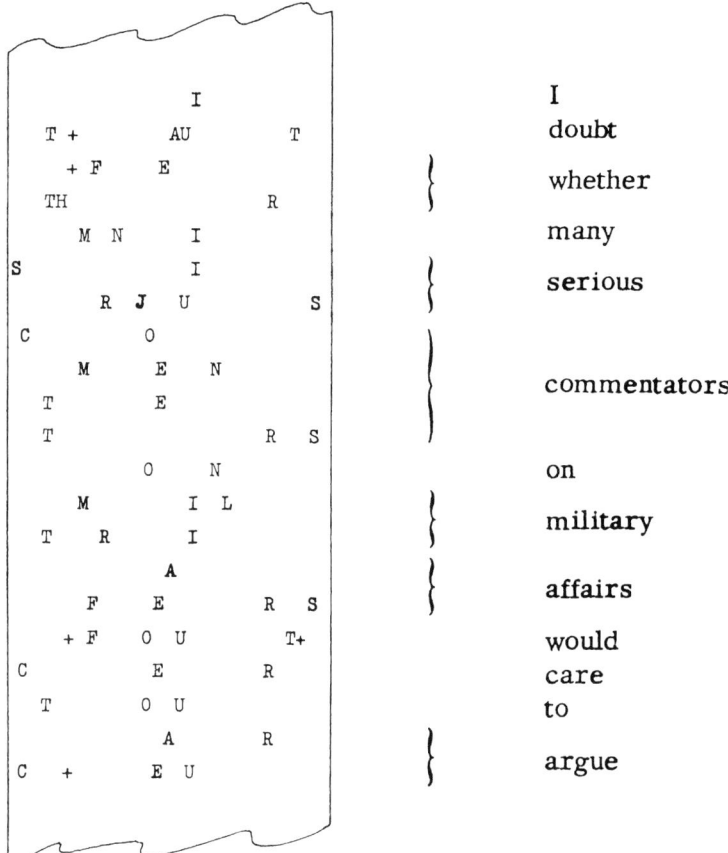

Figure 39. Section of a Palantype paper band with its English transcription. Note that T+ stands for D, +F for W, and C+ for G.

Palantype transcription

transcribed to produce a printed report, a process which takes four or five times as long as the original recording. An example of a band with its English transcription is shown in fig. 39.

The idea that a computer could be used to do the transcribing, thus producing immediate printed output, first arose in the United States, and work at Harvard and IBM based on the US Stenotype system was reported from 1959. In the UK a different system called Palantype was in use; and in 1966 it was decided that, following the completion of the machine translation work, a small group led by Dr Wyn Price should be established at NPL to develop an experimental computer-based Palantype transcription system and investigate the possibilities for its application. Among those interested were the Lord Chancellor's Office, the House of Commons Hansard Department, and organisations for helping the deaf.

Existing Palantype machines were purely mechanical, and an early task for the group was to modify a machine so that in addition to the printed paper band it produced digitally coded electrical output at an NPL Standard Interface. This could then be connected to a computer or to a paper-tape punch, directly or

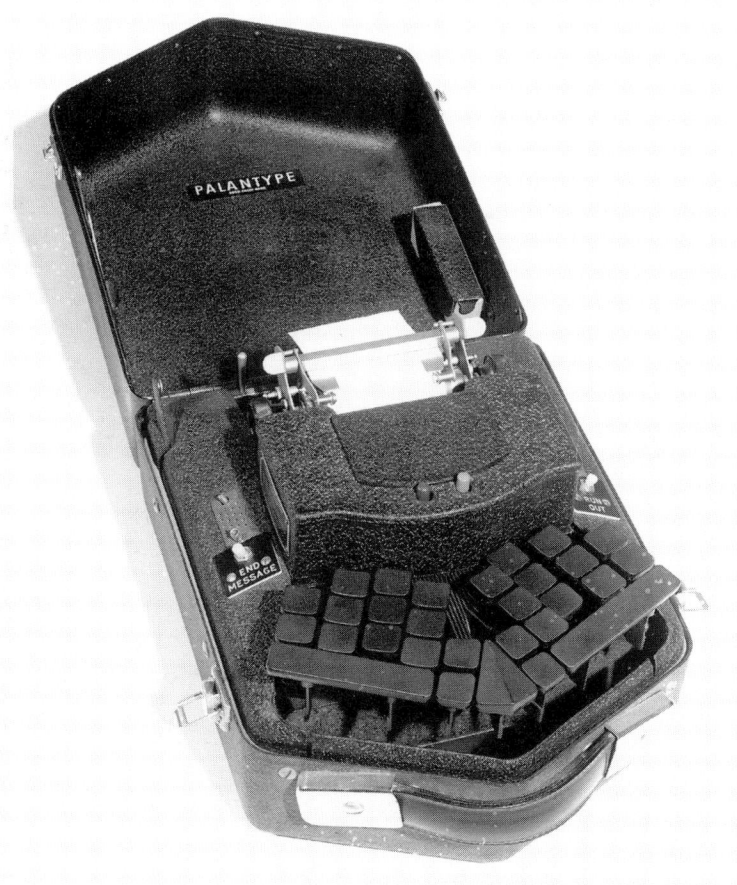

Figure 40. The Palantype machine modified for computer input.

via a telephone line, for eventual transcription. A single stroke, typically corresponding to one spoken syllable, was represented by a group of eight bytes at the interface; once in the computer, these eight bytes were converted to a 29-bit pattern corresponding to the 29 keys on the machine's keyboard. The machine's paper-advance mechanism was used to determine when a stroke ended. The modified machine is shown in fig. 40.

The computer transcription system clearly had to have available a comprehensive Palantype-to-English dictionary, and the fact that the NPL KDF9 had a large disc store which would allow random access to this dictionary made it the obvious choice of computer for the experimental system. The next tasks for the project were to decide the format of this dictionary, and to create it.

The choice of dictionary structure was governed by the fact that word boundaries are not represented in Palantype. A study showed that the best strategy for the system was to accept at each point the longest sequence of strokes for which a match could be found in the dictionary, to record that identification, and then to start again looking for the longest possible match from the first unmatched stroke. Some errors would occur (for example, the word *canteen* would be wrongly identified in the sequence of three strokes representing the successive words *can teenage*), but on the whole the strategy worked well, and provided they were not too frequent such errors could be dealt with at the final editing stage. This critical decision on the best look-up strategy determined that the dictionary entries should have a branching structure, with each possible initial stroke leading to a set of possible second strokes and a default English identification if none of the second strokes appeared; each possible second stroke led (in general) to a set of possible third strokes and a default identification, and so on to a maximum 'depth' of about eight. If an initial stroke occurred which led to no match in the dictionary it was simply transliterated into the output (and distinguished by being printed in upper case).

Having decided how such a structure could best be represented in the computer, the next considerable task was the actual construction of the dictionary. The first thing needed was a list of English words, which could be given to a Palantypist to record the possible ways of Palantyping each word. Ordinary dictionaries were unsuitable as a basis for the word list because they did not include, for example, inflected forms of verbs. It was found that Pitman's Shorthand Dictionary did include these forms, so with the permission of the publishers this work was used as the basis for the word list. Some rare words were excluded and some names of people and places added, and the resulting list of 71,000 words punched on paper tape by an agency. After correction, a printed copy of this tape was given to a Palantypist using the specially modified machine to produce another paper tape, and the two

Figure 41. Sample of output from the experimental Palantype transcription system.

```
                Which I consider to be one of the most damnable, mean,
con TEV PTI PL, Indefensible clauses that has EFR been placed
in a bill in the House of Commons. When I say this I say it
deliberately, I say it is a 3A STRD child of panic buy'by cower
DIES, AND the Cod Yao ? godmother is I GNO RNS. I'm sorry to
say these harsh words, but I think that the house is not fully
seized of the importance of clause'claws three, both ass it
affects the school children AND ass it affects the industry
which is going to be "E ? severely hit ass a result of this
panic measure. I hope that after reflection, I do not ask at
this stage of course for the government to drop the bill, but
I do suggest that when clause'claws three goes to another place
the government will have second thoughts AND it will come=back
minus clause'claws three. If that is so, I believe there would
be a sigh of relief from members on this side of the house,
and also from more enlightened members on the other side. .
```

tapes together were fed to the dictionary-construction software which had been written for KDF9.

The basic task of the transcription program was to read in a group of strokes, look up the dictionary to find the longest match as outlined above, print out the English equivalent (or transliterate the initial stroke if no match was found), and start the next dictionary look-up, reading in more data as required. For some strokes, or sequences of strokes, there would be more than one English equivalent in the dictionary: for example *by* and *buy* are Palantyped in the same way. In such cases the possible equivalents were printed in a row and the choice left to the editor. Other cases for editorial action were words not in the dictionary (a frequent problem with proper names, where the dictionary was not, and could never be, comprehensive); words not Palantyped in the same way as the dictionary entry, which would also of course be treated as if they were not in the dictionary at all; and errors by the operator. These last two categories were found to be more frequent than expected: human transcribers may hardly notice such inconsistencies provided the sense is not obscured, but with the computer transcription system they were all too clear. The system was fully working by 1970. An example of the unedited output is shown in fig. 41.

With this feasibility demonstrated, the technical part of the NPL project was complete. Studies were made of several possible organisations where the system might be used. These showed that it would only be commercially viable in most cases if less editing was needed, which would mean the development of the computer system to include syntactic analysis and automatic error correction, and if possible changes in the Palantype conventions to reduce ambiguity. It was also clear that the economics would be much improved by the development of smaller and cheaper computers, which indeed appeared over the following years. Further work was done at Southampton University and at Leicester Polytechnic, who were both provided with copies of NPL's dictionary. One application of the Southampton system was in the House of Commons, where the Rt Hon. Jack Ashley MP, later Lord Ashley, was provided with a continuous transcript of the current proceedings which enabled him to take part in debates in spite of his profound deafness. Another application of the Southampton and Leicester systems was to the Teletext subtitling of television programmes for use by the deaf.

In addition to Wyn Price, those who worked on this project included Adam Szanser, Peter Carter, Tony Day, Steve Whelan and Celia Searle. The Palantype Organisation, represented by Isla Beard, also made a vital contribution.

Publications on Palantype transcription

D W Croisdale. Unitran. *O. and M. Bulletin,* 22, 1967, pp.94–96.

W L Price. Unitran II. *O. and M. Bulletin,* 23, 1968, pp.139–143.

W L Price. The transcription of machine shorthand by computer. Automated Publishing Systems Seminar, Univ. of Newcastle, 1969.

W L Price. Minimising the editor's task in computer transcription of machine shorthand. Automated Publishing Systems Seminar, Univ. of Newcastle, 1969.

W L Price. The viability of computer transcription of machine shorthand. *Man-Computer Interaction,* IEE Conference Publication No. 68, 1970, pp.1–6.

W L Price. Palantype transcription by computer—a final report. NPL Report Com Sci 45, February 1971.

W L Price. Palantype transcription at NPL and afterwards. *NPL News,* 348, Winter 1980, pp.9–12.

Automatic error correction

Spelling mistakes do not generally mean that a text is misunderstood, unless they are very frequent. This robustness arises because all practical representations of natural language, including printing and Palantype, involve redundancy. This is important in Palantype, because the speed at which the operators are working means that some mistakes are bound to occur, and the redundancy almost always allows these errors to be corrected at the transcription stage. The question arises whether this human capability for error correction can be simulated by a computer process, which could then, for example, be included in the Palantype transcription software.

Adam Szanser investigated this question in a series of studies over the period 1968–73. He developed a technique called *elastic matching,* based on dividing both the suspect word and the dictionary words into segments each of which was in alphabetical order before comparing them, and he showed that this enabled various common types of misspelling to be identified and corrected. Even with the assumption that there was not more than one error in a word, this could lead to more than one acceptable candidate, and to resolve such cases he devised techniques based both on syntactic criteria (*I havr not* must be a mistake for *I have not* and not for *I hair not* because the latter is syntactically unacceptable), and on word frequencies.

This work demonstrated that the automatic detection and correction of spelling errors by computer was practical, and so foreshadowed in important respects the spell checkers included in modern word processors.

Publications on automatic error correction

A J Szanser. Error-correcting methods in natural language processing. In: A J H Morrell (ed.), *Information Processing 68: Proc. IFIP Congress 68,* held in Edinburgh, August 1968, North-Holland, 1969, pp.1412–1416.

A J Szanser. Automatic error-correction in natural languages. *Information Storage and Retrieval,* 5, 1970, pp.169–174.

A J Szanser. Automatic error correction in natural texts—Part 1. NPL Report Com Sci 46, May 1971.

A J Szanser. Automatic error correction in natural texts—Part 2. NPL Report Com Sci 53, December 1971.

A J Szanser. Elastic matching in automatic pattern recognition. *Proc. Conf. on Machine Perception of Patterns and Pictures,* held at NPL, April 1972, Institute of Physics, 1972, pp.328–333.

A J Szanser. Bracketing technique in elastic matching. *Computer Journal,* 16(2), May 1972, pp.132–134.

A J Szanser. Automatic error correction in natural texts—Supplement. NPL Report Com 63, January 1973.

A J Szanser. Paragraph structure: a preliminary study. NPL Report Com 67, March 1973.

4.5   Pattern recognition

In 1966 the main line of development in the Pattern Recognition group was the Cyclops 2 system described in section 3.4. This system was simulated by computer, but was not in the end implemented in hardware, because the simulation showed that spurious letter identifications, due mainly to 'cross-talk' between characters, could not be eliminated sufficiently, however carefully the detailed parameters of the process were selected. The goal of reading single-font printed text a line at a time had proved to be too ambitious.

Attention therefore moved back to the classical problem of recognising single characters which had already been delimited. A new system was devised, to be known as Cyclops 3, aimed at the recognition of poor quality characters, primarily hand-printed numerals. A flying-spot scanner was still used as an input device,

The Davies era: 1966–1978

Figure 42. Pattern recognition: John Parks using CHIT connected to the Honeywell DDP-516 computer, October 1971.

and the two first stages remained logically similar to those in Cyclops 2, namely the identification of line segments followed by the identification of features such as line endings and junctions. These stages were implemented in special-purpose hardware and produced a list of features which was input to a DDP-516 computer for the final stage of identification. Various techniques were tried for this identification process. First an attempt was made to compile a dictionary of the feature lists of known characters in which the unknown character's list could be looked up, with a controlled degree of mismatch permitted. Unfortunately the size of the dictionary soon threatened to get out of hand. The next approach was to try the common-sense method of flowchart-type logic. For example, if a left-pointing line ending is present the character may well be 7, 3 or 2. The hypothesis that it is a 7 is tested first by looking for an acute angle in the area to the right of the line ending, and if this is found further tests are applied to the lower part of the character to confirm the identification. If these fail the hypotheses that it is a 3 or a 2 are tested successively, and so on. This was more effective than the dictionary method, though its reliance on intuitive judgement as to what features ought to be present in a particular character type was felt to be less than ideal. The method eventually selected was a modified version of this which first ranked the possible characters in order of likelihood (on the basis of feature counts irrespective of position), and so was able to save time by using the ranking to determine the order of testing. The system was demonstrated at the Open Days in May 1972.

The special-purpose hardware of the initial stages of Cyclops 3 was developed by Gerry Plumb, and the recognition software of the final stage was written by Donald Bell and others in the PL-516 language developed by Bell and Brian Wichmann and described in section 4.7. Julian Ullmann continued his work on the theoretical principles of pattern recognition, and the group was led by John Parks.

Publications on general pattern recognition and Cyclops 3

J R Parks. Automatic recognition of low-quality printed characters using analogue techniques. *The Radio and Electronic Engineer*, 34(2), August 1967, pp.67–80. [This paper won the IERE Bulgin Prize.]

E A Newman. Character recognition—the way ahead. *Electronics and Power*, 13, 1967, p.84.

L Tatham. Pattern recognition at the NPL. *Data Processing*, September–October 1967.

R E Rengger and J R Parks. A survey of handprinting. NPL Tech. Memo. Auto TM (68)9, March 1968.

D A Bell. Computer aided design of image processing techniques. *Proc. IEE/NPL Conf. on Pattern Recognition*, held at NPL July 1968, IEE, 1968, pp.282–289.

J R Parks, J R Elliott and G Cowin. Simulation of an alphanumeric character recognition system for unsegmented low quality print [Cyclops 2]. *Proc. IEE/NPL Conf. 1968* as above, pp.295–105.

B A Wichmann. A method of choosing operators in pattern recognition. *Proc. IEE/NPL Conf. 1968* as above, pp.191–196.

J R Parks. A multi-level system of analysis for multifont and hand-block printed character recognition. NPL Tech. Memo. Com Sci TM 13, August 1968.

D A Bell and J R Parks. The 2-ness of a '2'. *New Scientist*, 38(602), 1968, p.624.

E A Newman. Similarity. In: A R Meetham and R A Hudson (eds), *Encyclopaedia of Linguistics, Information and Control*, Pergamon Press, 1969, pp.535–539.

D A Bell. Shape analysis and character recognition. NPL Report Com Sci 47, March 1971.

D A Bell. A versatile program text editor for a small computer. NPL Report Com Sci 51, July 1971.

E A Newman. The theoretical structure of pattern. *Machine Perception of Patterns and Pictures*, proc. of a conf. held at NPL April 1972, Conference Series No. 13, The Institute of Physics, 1972, pp.285–293.

J R Ullmann. Correspondence in character recognition. *Machine Perception of Patterns and Pictures* as above, pp.34–44.

D A Bell, G W Cowin, S E Olding, G O Plumb and R S Watson. The Cyclops III reader for handwritten numerals. NPL Tech. Memo. Com Sci 72, November 1972.

J R Ullmann. *Pattern Recognition Techniques*. Butterworths, London, 1973.

D A Bell. Decision trees, tables and lattices. In: B G Batchelor (ed.), *Pattern Recognition: Ideas and Practice*, Plenum Press, 1978, pp.119–141.

CHIT

In about 1970 the group carried out a study, with support from the Inter-Bank Research Organisation and the National Research Development Corporation, on means of verifying people's identities automatically. The aim was to find a method which was effective, socially acceptable, reasonably cheap, and did not suffer from the key weakness of existing systems using plastic cards or personal identification numbers—the ease with which these items can fall into the wrong hands. The study identified the recognition of dynamic signatures[2] as the most promising approach. This fitted in well with work already started at NPL on the design of a device which could capture basic data describing a dynamic signature.

The device was a tablet consisting of a flexible membrane stretched close to, but not touching, a solid surface. Both the membrane and the solid surface had a uniform surface resistivity, so that a voltage applied between opposite edges produced a linear potential gradient. When the user wrote on paper placed on the membrane, the pressure of the pen caused local electrical contact to be made between the membrane and the surface.

The tablet worked as follows. First a voltage was applied between the left and right edges of the solid surface. If writing was in progress, this caused the membrane to adopt a potential proportional to the distance between the pen and the left-hand edge. The device converted this potential to digital form and output it. Then the voltage was applied instead to the top and bottom edges of the membrane, so that the solid surface adopted a potential proportional to the distance of the pen from the bottom edge. Again this potential was converted to digital form and output. This cycle was repeated, normally 50 times per second, so that a stream of co-ordinate pairs was produced. The tablet was fitted with a British Standard Interface so that the data could be captured on paper tape or input directly to a computer.

This device, invented by Peter Pobgee, was called CHIT (CHeap Input Tablet). It was first described in the 1969 patent application listed below, and was shown at the Physics Exhibition in London in March 1970 and elsewhere; the NPL Report for 1969–71 (ref. 116, pp.8–10) gives a full description. It soon attracted commercial interest and derived products were produced and marketed under licence by Quest Automation Ltd under the names of Datapad and Micropad.

P J Pobgee (inventor). Graphical input apparatus for electrical apparatus. UK Patent No. 1 310 683, date of application 6 August 1969. Improvements were described in three further patents: 1 559 173 (21 October 1975), 1 597 374 and 1 597 375 (both 9 March 1977).

P J Pobgee and J R Parks. Applications of a low-cost graphical input tablet. In: C V Freiman (ed.), *Information Processing 71: Proc. IFIP Congress 71,* held at Ljubljana August 1971, North-Holland, 1972, pp.737–741.

A M Day, J R Parks and P J Pobgee. On-line written input to computers. *Machine Perception of Patterns and Pictures,* proc. of a conf. held at NPL April 1972, Conference Series No. 13, The Institute of Physics, 1972, pp.233–240.

---

[2] A *dynamic signature* is a record of the signing process which includes timing information, as opposed to the familiar *static signature* which carries only spatial information.

Pattern recognition

Computer verification of signatures (Verisign)

With the tablet developed, the next problem was the design and development of software to verify signatures. The software's task was to compare a candidate signature with stored reference information and accept or reject it. The aim of any such system is to keep to a minimum both the *false acceptances* (forgeries accepted as genuine) and the *false rejections* (genuine signatures rejected as forgeries). There is a trade-off between the two, and the optimum balance will vary with the application. At a point of sale, for instance, the emphasis is on minimising the number of false rejections because customers find them embarrassing, and if the system still detects most forgeries it will remain a good deterrent. On the other hand, if the device is used to guard a secure area in a building, the main aim is to detect would-be intruders, so that it is false acceptances which matter most: if the chance of a forgery being detected can be kept high, the extra inconvenience caused by rejecting a few valid signatures will probably be a price worth paying.

The first stage of the work was to study a wide range of signatures to find measurements of any kind which remained fairly constant within a group of genuine signatures by one individual, but took different values for forgeries or quite different signatures. 10,000 dynamic signatures were collected and studied, and ten measures chosen. Software was then written to compute these measures from data derived from CHIT, and to compare the resulting ten numbers with the reference values for the person whose identity was being claimed. These reference values might for example be read from a plastic card presented before the signature was written, or found in a computer file on the basis of

Figure 43. Verisign and Datapad with Celia Searle, July 1974.

a typed-in identity number. The signature validation system was thus being proposed for *checking a purported identity,* not for identifying an individual from amongst a large population which is a much harder task. Depending on how well the measured numbers matched the reference set, the computer would signal appropriate action by indicating acceptance or rejection on a screen to a cashier, asking the person to sign again, unlocking the door, ringing the alarm bell, or whatever.

This software system was given the name Verisign (see fig. 43). The cost of the development was met jointly by NPL and the National Research Development Corporation (NRDC), with the Inter-bank Research Organisation contributing a lesser amount but also allowing their premises and staff to be used for signature collection. As with CHIT, the NPL work was under John Parks' direction until his departure in 1974; after that Bob Watson and Peter Pobgee were responsible for NPL's continuing interest in the system. Bernard Chorley and Sue Olding also made important contributions. Peter Hawkes of NRDC managed the commercial exploitation of the system; three companies, including Quest, took licences and produced commercial products.

Anon. Verisign: an NPL project on automatic signature verification sponsored by IBRO and NRDC. National Research Development Corporation, March 1975.

R S Watson and P J Pobgee. Is that you? A computer to check signatures. *IEE Spectrum*, 12(138), 1976.

Automatic inspection

In 1973, partly as a result of encouragement from the Requirements Board to widen their interests, the group made a study of how the image-handling techniques developed for character recognition could be applied in other areas. Amongst the possibilities considered were X-ray image analysis, aerial photograph analysis, fingerprint recognition, parcel handling, and the inspection of timber, fruit, dials and integrated circuits. On the basis of its economic importance, automatic inspection during manufacturing processes was chosen. Initial consideration was restricted to parts which were either flat or cylindrically symmetric, because in these cases the object's silhouette would provide enough information for a useful assessment to be made, and this restriction would help to keep costs down. The plan was to develop a system which could first be 'trained' by showing it a sequence of correct components, and then left to monitor new components, which would be presented to it on a moving belt at rates up to 10 pieces per second. Conventional computer interaction using a keyboard would be eliminated in normal running. Discussions with interested companies showed that such a system could well be a good economic proposition.

A second possibility, investigated by John Yardley with support from industry, was to monitor the operation of a machine tool carrying out an automatic process. The idea was that if, say, waste material got caught up in a punch, the machine would react with a pattern of vibrations which might well be recognisably different from normal. The system would be like a car driver, sensitive to any unfamiliar and potentially expensive rattle or squeak.

On visual inspection, a pilot system was developed which monitored Meccano parts using a television camera looking vertically down on to them. The measurements taken were independent of the orientation of the part (for example, its perimeter length and total area; the number, area and perimeter length of any holes; and the distances of any holes from the centroid of the object). This successfully demonstrated the feasibility of the system. The next step was to replace the video camera with a row of 512 light-sensitive elements (photodiodes). The parts in this case were moved on a transparent turntable, lit from below to enhance contrast, with the photodiode array placed radially above it. Because of the circular motion, the image of a rectangular object built up in the computer from successive scans of the photodiodes was banana shaped, but the software could of course allow for this distortion. A production version of NPL's prototype was developed by Gays (Hampton) Ltd and Triad Computing Systems Ltd with NPL collaboration, and exhibited under the name SCANAFORM at the Machine Tool Exhibition in Birmingham in September 1976. In this version each part was removed from the turntable by one of two air blasts under the computer's control, one for 'good' and one for 'bad'. It incorporated an Intel 8080 microcomputer, the software for which was developed on the Honeywell DDP-516 using the group's own EASI 80 tools.

This work was started by John Parks and Donald Bell in 1973, and was continued by Bell, with Bernard Chorley, Sue Olding and Bob Wanek, after Parks left NPL in 1974.

J R Parks and D A Bell. Sensory devices and industrial robots. *Conference on Electronic Control of Mechanical Handling*, held at Nottingham, July 1971, Conference Proc. No. 21, IERE, 1971, pp.361–373.

D A Bell. The extraction of continuous boundaries and contours from a raster scan. NPL Report Com 66, April 1973.

B J Chorley and S E Olding. EASI 80: an editor, assembler and simulator for the Intel 8080 microprocessor. NPL Report Com 80, September 1975.

D A Bell. On unbending a banana. *NPL News*, 320, December 1976, pp.6–9.

J R Parks. Intelligent machines—commercial potential. *The Radio and Electronic Engineer*, 47(8/9), 1977, pp.355–367 [published after Parks left, but covers NPL work].

The Davies era: 1966–1978

Ermintrude

As a spin-off from the experience with the 8080 microprocessor mentioned above, a flexible microcomputer system called Ermintrude was developed by the group for general use in NPL laboratories. It consisted of a rack into which a selection of cards could be slotted to suit a particular application. As shown at the Open Days in 1976, there were six different types of card: processor, random-access memory, read-only memory, parallel interface, serial interface, and clock. It worked well but never attracted a wide clientele, probably because it was a research group's product: the NPL customers felt that commercial devices, even though they were less flexible, would be better supported in the long term.

R Wanek. A flexible microcomputer system. NPL Report Com 95, November 1977.

Ending of work on optical pattern recognition

Although applications work was allowed to continue, NPL's core work on optical pattern recognition was ended in 1974 by the withdrawal of Requirements Board support. This decision caused particular concern because it was apparently based on an opinion on the underlying aims of the Division rather than the quality of this particular project. And if long-term work on what Uttley had called the mechanisation of thought processes was no longer seen as appropriate, what was the Division for? Discussions continued, but in the short term the decision led directly to John Parks's departure and so caused lasting damage to the Division's capabilities. By an ironic twist of career development, Parks's next appointment involved acting as Secretary of the same Requirements Board.

Speech recognition

Speech is our fastest and most natural means of communicating information, and in some circumstances it would be handy to be able to use it to communicate with a machine if the means of doing so could be made cheap and reliable. Unfortunately the automatic recognition of speech sounds is arguably an even more difficult task than the recognition of written or printed characters. Work on the problem started at NPL at least as early as 1958[3]; it gets an occasional mention in subsequent Annual Reports, but was only established as a major project in the mid-1960s.

---

[3] The first work was apparently done by Ted Newman during his time in Applied Physics Division (see p.63), probably in an attempt to help with the routine calibration of thermometers. There is an NPL photograph (CS 12190) showing a machine, but it was apparently unsuccessful as it was not heard of again.

Pattern recognition

Figure 44. Speech recognition: Brian Pay using a PDP-8 computer, October 1971.

The first phase of the work was a study of vowel sounds. These are formed by moving air being forced to vibrate in the mouth, and the characteristic frequencies, called *formants,* which determine which vowel sound is heard, are generated by regulating the shape of the mouth cavity. If the speech waveform is analysed electronically to produce a *sonogram,* a diagram showing how the distribution of sound intensity over the frequency spectrum varies with time, the resonant frequencies of the complete mouth cavity and of the space behind the tongue can be readily identified. The matter is complicated by the fact that for some vowel sounds it is the absolute value of the formant frequency which determines the vowel heard, while for the majority it is the ratios of the intensities at the formant frequencies that count rather than their absolute values. Formant frequencies also vary from speaker to speaker. In spite of these complications, the facts clearly provide a basis for the automatic recognition of vowel sounds.

A vowel-recognition system based on these ideas was developed at NPL in 1969–70. It consisted of two stages. The first, realised in purpose-built electronics, identified the formant frequencies and represented them digitally. This was done 100 times per second, and the resulting data stream was divided into 8-bit bytes and presented at a British Standard Interface for input to a DEC PDP-8 computer (see fig. 44). The second stage consisted of software in the PDP-8. It examined three features: the frequencies of the two major formants, the *voicing* (whether or not the mouth airflow has been energised by the larynx, determined by the ratio of low-frequency power to high-frequency power), and the duration of the sound. These values were compared with standard values derived from earlier experiments to determine which vowel was being heard.

The next system was aimed at the recognition of a limited vocabulary, relying mainly on the vowels. It consisted of two parts, with no computer involved. The first part, called SID (Speech Input Device), was a development of the earlier system. It could detect nine elements: six vowels, *f*, *s*, and silence, and its output was a sequence of these elements. The second part was also purpose-built hardware, and consisted of logic to compare SID's output with predetermined sequences corresponding to items in the vocabulary; it recognised an item whenever it received its sequence correctly. The sequences were set by plugging. At the Open Days in 1972 this device was used to demonstrate a voice-controlled slide projector with six commands ('turn on', 'next slide please', and so on). This performed well for its master (Brian Pay) but could be somewhat temperamental for others, particularly if they were new to the system; the overall performance figures reported were 8 per cent rejects and 0.1 per cent errors.

In an interactive application the restriction to a small vocabulary is not as limiting as it sounds, because the vocabulary used to analyse the responses to one question can be replaced by another for the next question. Another important possibility is the use of verification, whereby the system can if necessary check that it has heard correctly. By 1974 these points were being made, showing that attention was being given to future practical applications as well as the basic recognition techniques. SID Mark II had been developed, with improved vowel recognition, a wider range of other phonetic features including 'stop consonants' such as *p* and *b*, and improved timing flexibility. Research was under way on identifying elements embedded in continuous speech, and on more features of consonants.

At the 1976 Open Days a speech-recognition system for use in avionics was described. The idea was that in a situation where the pilot's eyes, hands and feet were all busy, the use of speech could be a helpful extra capability. This led to successful trials allowing helicopter pilots to set instruments by speech. Another exhibit involved the use of SID over a telephone line. In 1978 a speech-based variant of Chris Evans's medical interviewing system, described in the following section, was tried out but proved less easy for the patients than the usual push-button version.

In face-to-face conversation, listeners get help in their speech-recognition task by being able to see the speaker's mouth. This means that when cartoon characters are speaking, the animator has to synchronise appropriate changes of mouth shape with the recorded speech if the results are to be realistic. This provided a novel application for the NPL speech-recognition system reported in February 1978. The script was first read aloud and recorded, and the recording was fed to the system to produce a phoneme sequence (on punched paper tape). This was then used to control the sequence of mouth shapes on the cartoon frames. Results were described as 'little short of excellent'.

Work on speech recognition throughout this period was led by Brian Pay with Ralph Rengger, Roger Manning and John Yardley, and guidance from Ted Newman. The work continued in the Albasiny era, and the story is taken up again in section 5.7.

Publications on speech recognition up to 1978

R E Rengger and D R Manning. A device to enable a computer to accept human speech, 'SID Mk I'. NPL Tech. Memo. Com Sci TM 79, October 1973.

R E Rengger. Speech controlled equipment. NPL Tech. Memo. Com Sci TM 80, November 1973.

B E Pay. Phase locked lips [film animation]. *NPL News,* 334, February 1978, pp.2–3.

E H Budgett. An investigation of man-computer interaction using an automatic speech recognition system [medical interviewing]. NPL Report Com 105, May 1978.

B E Pay. Analysis of pilots' voice records for automated speech recognition. NPL Report DNACS 2/78, August 1978.

B E Pay and C R Evans. An approach to the automatic recognition of speech. NPL Report DNACS 7/78, October 1978. Reprinted in *Int. J. Man-Machine Studies,* 14(1), 1981, pp.13–27.

4.6 Man–machine interaction

When a machine for human use is being designed, both physical and psychological aspects of the way it is to be used need to be taken into account if the final product is to be fit for its purpose. Under the name of ergonomics, the systematic study of these aspects of engineering design was a fairly novel subject in the 1960s. It was clear that the same systematic approach ought to be useful in the design of computer-based systems, but no one was very sure where to start in applying it. As it happened, one of the questions facing Donald Davies at the start of his period as Superintendent was how to make best use of the talents of the psychologist Chris Evans, who had been studying retinal afterimages for quite long enough. Two and two were put together, and in 1969 a Man–Machine Interaction Section, soon put under Chris's leadership, appeared on the Divisional staff charts for the first time. This marked the start of a major thread in the Division's subsequent programmes of work traceable through to the present day.

The Davies era: 1966–1978

The main item in the new programme was 'studies of computer interaction by naive users and the development of programs and technical equipment to facilitate this interaction', which was to be Chris Evans's own area. The other items were taken over from the former Programming Research group: John Sexton's work on facilities for the graphical display programmer, and Mike Woodger's work on levels of language in programming. The overall objective, 'to develop models of man in interactive situations enabling the performance of such systems to be predicted', was understood to be a long-term aim, and indeed is still far from being achieved in any integrated sense.

As a signal of NPL's involvement in the area and an opportunity to show some of the first results, a conference on man–computer interaction (ref. 71) was held at NPL on 2–4 September 1970, the first event of its type in the UK, managed by the IEE with Chris Evans as chairman of the organising committee. This energetic and publicity-conscious approach was typical of Chris, and the early success of the group owed a great deal to his personality and infectious enthusiasm.

Computer interaction by untrained users

In 1970 computer systems were designed to be used by trained people, either computer specialists or those in jobs which called for computer use. Most people would have found it hard to imagine how a computer could possibly be usable by an untrained person, or what the object of such use could be. Chris Evans realised that there were in fact many situations where it could be useful for a naive user to interact with a computer, and that this was quite feasible if careful thought was given to the design of the interface. He found a simple way of showing what could be done, using three tools. The first and most important tool was the widely available and well-named BASIC language. This enabled inexperienced programmers in his group to develop programs which would conduct interactive interviews; the questions in the interviews were framed so that the responses were restricted to 'Yes', 'No', and '?' ('?' covered both 'Don't know' and 'Don't understand'). The second tool was a commercial on-line BASIC service, which could be used anywhere where there was a telephone: the usual terminal was a teletypewriter linked to the telephone line through either a modem or an acoustic coupler (a box into which the handset of the telephone fitted). The third tool was a simple hardware gadget developed at NPL: a mask which fitted over the Teletype keyboard with three big buttons labelled 'Yes', 'No', and '?', with a mechanical linkage inside connecting these buttons to three of the keys on the hidden keyboard. The choice offered to the interviewee at each step was thus kept as simple as possible, a vital consideration. The set-up is shown in fig. 45.

Man–machine interaction

Figure 45. 'Tell me, does the pain ever wake you in the early hours of the morning?' Peggy Anderson, July 1971.

The key element in the success of this approach was the design of the dialogue, which had to achieve the aim of the interview accurately and at the same time seem as natural as possible to the interviewee. Here Chris's talents as a communicator really came into their own: he was able to develop scripts which asked straightforward questions expressed so as to put the subjects at their ease.

The classic application was a medical interview designed to interrogate patients with suspected gastric ulcers, first reported at the 1970 conference. Doctors' interrogations were observed and distilled by Chris into a structured dialogue which was then programmed in BASIC. Fig. 46 shows part of the record of a session with this system. It was used experimentally by patients at the Southern General Hospital in Glasgow, and the results were compared with those obtained by human consultants. The conclusion was that this evidence could be elicited by the computer with about the same precision as the human doctors. The program was not doing diagnosis, simply saving the consultants' time by relieving them of the routine history-taking part of their work; an added advantage was that patients could be screened by the computer without having to wait for an appointment with the consultant. By early 1971, 200 patients had been interviewed and the method had been shown to be acceptable and effective; indeed

Figure 46. Medical history-taking: an extract from the record of a session, September 1970.

```
TELL ME DOES THE PAIN EVER WAKE YOU IN THE EARLY HOURS OF
THE MORNING? PLEASE PUSH 'YES' OR 'NO'? 0


I SEE.  WHEN IT WAKES YOU UP, DO YOU FIND THAT HAVING
A LITTLE SNACK - MILK, BISCUITS OR PERHAPS SOME WARM WATER -
GIVES YOU RELIEF? 0


NOW I'D LIKE YOU TO THINK RATHER CAREFULLY BEFORE YOU ANSWER
THE NEXT QUESTION.  JUST IMAGINE THAT I ASK YOU TO POINT OUT
THE AREA WHERE YOU FEEL THE PAIN IN YOUR STOMACH - NOW CAN
THIS AREA BEST BE INDICATED WITH ONE OR TWO FINGERS, OR
WITH THE FLAT OF THE HAND.
IF WITH ONE OR TWO FINGERS, PRESS 'YES'
IF WITH THE FLAT OF THE HAND, PRESS 'NO'
IF YOU DON'T UNDERSTAND OR IF YOU FEEL THAT YOU COULD NOT
EASILY INDICATE THE AREA WHERE THE PAIN IS THEN PRESS '?'? 1
```

some patients said they felt more open and relaxed talking to the polite machine than they did when facing a doctor, who could be daunting or impatient or make them feel embarrassed when sensitive topics were being discussed. There was also a suggestion that the responses might be more honest: for instance, the answers to a question from the computer about alcohol consumption were twice as high as those given to a doctor asking the same question.

Structured interactive questionnaires of this kind could also be used for training, the basic technique being to explain the subject a step at a time, and to ensure that each step was understood before going on to the next. To test the idea, a GCE history lesson was programmed and tried out in two local schools. The questionnaire technique also lent itself to personality, intelligence and aptitude tests, and various examples were developed with the co-operation of the Civil Service Commission and others. A 'programmed audio tape recorder' having some similarities to Newman and Scantlebury's early teaching machine was tried in the Glasgow hospital as an alternative to the computer-based system. These developments are all reported in the 1969–71 triennial report (ref. 116 pp.19–22), and it is typical of Chris Evans's approach that so many interesting projects were being started that they could never all be pursued in much depth.

By 1974 interactive programs had been developed for the investigation of respiratory complaints (tested at the Western Hospital, Fulham), psychiatric patient interviews (at Guy's Hospital, London), and antenatal care (at the West Middlesex Hospital). A system using video recordings of interviewing doctors speaking in minority languages was successfully tested in Bradford, and cartoons by Bill Tidy, shown using an automated slide projector, were used experimentally to help reduce patients' tension in the psychiatric interviews. In the training area, new applications included the instruction of insurance claims assessors in a large insurance company and the teaching of computing in schools.

Man–machine interaction

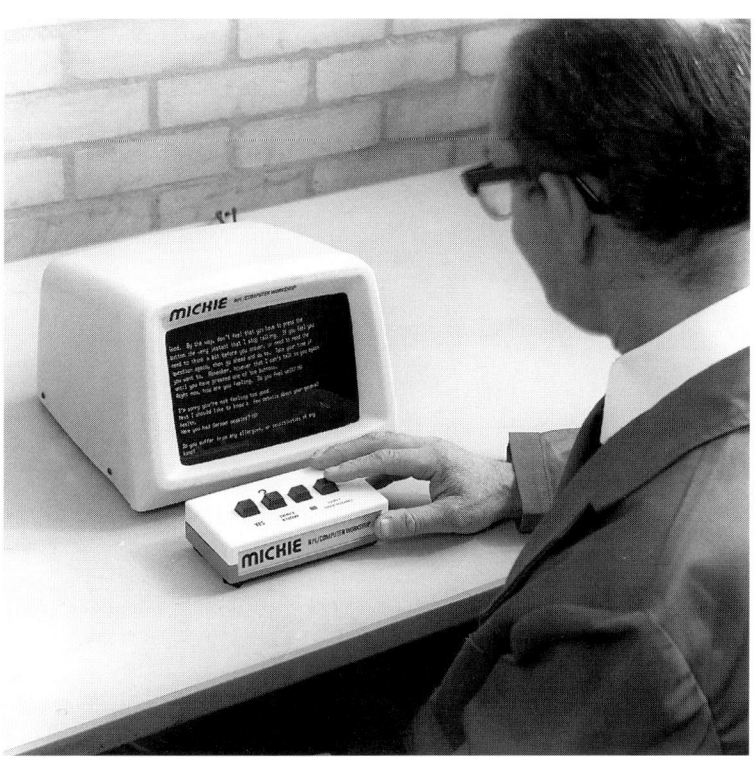

Figure 47. MICKIE the Medical Interviewing Computer, September 1978.

The advent of small desktop computers in the mid-1970s provided a much more convenient and reliable basis for the interviewing systems than the use of on-line terminals and telephone links. No immediate changes were needed to the software because BASIC interpreters were available for the new small machines. Work on these lines was first mentioned in the 1972–74 triennial report, and by 1977 a compact system had been developed and christened MICKIE (see fig. 47). A simple script language was provided for doctors who wanted to prepare their own interviews. MICKIE had a small screen, a keyboard with four buttons ('Don't know' and 'Don't understand' had been separated), and a strip printer which produced a summary to be given to the doctor at the end of the interview. By 1980 MICKIE was being marketed under licence to NPL by Abies Informatics.

To contribute to these projects Chris Evans attracted a considerable entourage of Guest Workers and students at NPL and also collaborators in other institutions, several of whom appear as co-authors in the list of publications below. NPL staff contributing included Jackie Wilson throughout, Peter Whittle on the early BASIC systems, Gerry Plumb on video-based interviewing, Peter Pobgee and Nigel Bevan on MICKIE, and Angela Stephens on measuring user performance. The history of the group is continued in section 5.7.

Publications on computer interaction by untrained users

W I Card, G P Crean, C R Evans, B Wilson James, Mary Nicholson, G Watkinson and Jackie Wilson. On-line interrogation of hospital patients by a time-sharing terminal with computer/consultant comparison analysis. *Proc. IEE Conf. on Man-Computer Interaction*, Conference Publication No. 68, IEE, 1970, pp.141–147. Reprinted in a slightly updated form as NPL Report Com Sci 52, November 1971.

C R Evans and P B Whittle (inventors). Improvements in or relating to the operation of keyboard machines [the 'Yes/No/?' mask for a conventional keyboard]. UK Patent No. 1 359 657, date of application 1 September 1970.

C R Evans and J Wilson. A program to allow computer based history-taking in cases of suspected gastric ulcer. NPL Report Com Sci 49, May 1971.

C R Evans, P A Purcell and J Wood. An investigation of design activities using analytic time-lapse photography. NPL Report Com Sci 50, July 1971.

C R Evans. Psychological assessment of history-taking by computer. *Proc. British Computer Society Conf. Spectrum 71*, held at Bristol, Butterworth, 1971, pp.9–22.

C R Evans. An automated medical history-taking project—a study in man-computer interaction. NPL Report Com Sci 55, March 1972.

D J McLeod, R M Burrell, E J Nicholas, J P Harris and C R Evans. An experimental study of specialised instruction by computer involving a non-mathematical topic. NPL Report Com Sci 59, August 1972.

M C Bott, J Box, C R Evans and J Wilson. An investigation of computer administration of a psychological test to psychiatric patients. NPL Report Com 61, November 1972.

C R Evans, H C Price and J Wilson. Computer interrogation of patients with respiratory complaints in a London hospital. NPL Report Com 69, June 1973.

C R Evans and P B Whittle. An inexpensive programmed video tape system for automated medical history-taking. *Proc. IERE Conf. on Video and Data Recording*, held at Birmingham July 1973, paper no. 26, IERE, 1973, pp.249–251.

C R Evans, C G J Kinchin, H C Price and P B Whittle. Some preliminary experiments in the use of a programmable videotape recorder as an automatic history-taking device in a chest clinic. NPL Report Com 73, March 1974.

W I Card, C R Evans and Jackie Wilson. A comparison of doctor and computer interrogation of patients. *Int. J. of Biomedical Computing*, 6, 1974, pp.175–187.

K D Dietz and C R Evans. An automatic terminal simulating user function on a large multi-access computer. NPL Report Com 75, July 1974.

D W Davies, C R Evans and D M Yates. Human factors in interactive teleprocessing systems. In: J Borge Hansson et al. (eds), *Proc. Int. Conf. on Computer Communications 1974*, held in Stockholm, ICCC Secretariat, 1974, pp.491–496.

C R Evans. Dreams of computers. *J. of the Royal Society of Arts*, November 1974, pp.830–836. [The text of a lecture given to the Society on 5 June 1974.]

C R Evans, N Masters, H B Milne and M Hashim. An automated medical history-taking project with videotape interviewing of immigrant psychiatric patients. NPL Report Com 79, April 1975.

C R Evans. Chatting with computers. *Electronics and Power*, 17 April 1975, pp.430–432.

G O Plumb. Automated interviewing by videotape. NPL Report Com 93, October 1977.

C R Evans, P J Pobgee and S S Somerville. MICKIE—an automated interviewing system. NPL Report Com 97, December 1977.

C R Evans, G O Plumb, S Somerville and S P Whitfield. Some experiments in automated interrogation of immigrant patients in their own language. NPL Report Com 101, March 1978.

D W Davies and D M Yates. Human factors in display terminal procedures. *Proc. Int. Conf. on Computer Communications*, 1978, pp.777–783.

N Bevan. Meet Mickie, the well-mannered micro. *Personal Computer World*, 1(8), December 1978, pp.34–36; reprinted in M Whitbread (ed.), *Microprocessor Applications in Business and Industry*, Castle House, 1979.

C R Evans. Improving the communication between people and computers. *Theoria to Theory*, 13, 1980, pp.271–294.

NPL. MICKIE—Medical Interviewing Computer. NPL leaflet DNACS/1a, 1980.

N Bevan, P Pobgee and S Somerville. MICKIE—a microcomputer for medical interviewing. *Int. J. Man-Machine Studies*, 14(1), 1981, pp.39–47.

Graphical software

John Sexton's work on software for interactive graphics, previously carried out in the Programming Research group disbanded in 1969, was in all respects a contrast with the work of Chris Evans's section. The early interviewing software described above was openly cheap and cheerful, with no claims to distinction as software engineering and maximum publicity. A new application meant a new program. Sexton's work on the other hand was necessarily far more complex, expertly designed for flexibility, and with publicity low in his order of priorities. A new application was built on an existing body of software.

The hardware of a graphical display provides basic facilities for programmers to control the brightness of individual minute areas of the screen (*pixels*). This capability is at too low a level for the convenience of the applications programmer developing, say, a package for computer-aided design. This programmer wants facilities enabling him to define elements in a picture (like lines or boxes or symbols or diagrams), to vary them by translation, rotation, magnification and so on, and to copy and combine them with other elements to form new ones treated as single units. It may be useful for the screen to display a set of rectangular windows, each showing a selected area of a much bigger 'virtual drawing board'. It should be possible to represent three-dimensional objects, and to display them on the screen from various angles and in cross-section. These facilities are needed in many graphical applications packages, and it was the function of Sexton's software to provide them. The key concepts in the software design were (1) multiple levels, carefully kept separate, and (2) modularity. The basic level software was called DISPAC, later DISGOL, and the second-level modules GIPSY; their major application was to architectural design software, as described below. The work was very much a solo effort by John Sexton, and ended when he resigned in February 1975.

Publications on graphical software

J H Sexton. DISPAC—a macro system with a data-structure aid for display programming. *Proc. IEE Conf. on Computer Science and Technology*, Conference Publication No. 55, IEE, 1969, p.306.

J H Sexton. Multi-level software for interactive graphics and computer-aided design. *Proc. IEE Conf. on Man-Computer Interaction*, Conference Publication No. 68, IEE, 1970, pp.181–187.

J H Sexton. An introduction to data structures with some emphasis on graphics. *Computer Bulletin*, 16(9), September 1972, pp.444–447.

Architectural design

In 1969 the UK Ministry of Public Building and Works (soon to be renamed the Department of the Environment) had one of the largest architectural design offices in the world, spending £200 million per year. They realised that the use of computers could lead to increased efficiency in building design, and to explore the possibilities a group of their staff was seconded to the Division of Computer Science as Guest Workers in 1969–71. The long-term aim of their project, called CEDAR, was to develop an architectural design package incorporating NPL's DISGOL graphical software described above. Those seconded to NPL included architects John Parsons and John Chalmers, and quantity surveyor John Brown. The work is described in the following paper:

J W Parsons and J R Chalmers. The development of a computer-aided design system for a large-scale user. *Proc. IEE Conf. on Man-Computer Interaction*, Conference Publication No. 68, IEE, 1970, p.160–165.

Levels of language

One of the most basic concepts in software engineering is that of the *module,* a chunk of software designed to carry out a sub-task, with a specification and a well-defined interface so that it can be used without the user having to worry about how it works inside. Adopting a modular structure makes programs simpler to construct, understand and if necessary modify; it also often saves duplication of effort. As mentioned in section 2.3, these ideas were very familiar to Alan Turing. In a particularly complex task it may help to organise the modules into a hierarchy of levels, with modules at one level calling on others at the next lower level and providing a service to those at the next higher level. These concepts of modularity and level were well exemplified in John Sexton's graphical software described above.

In work first reported in 1971, Mike Woodger developed these ideas from principles of good practice in software design to principles of programming language design, believing that the programmer's basic tool, the programming language, should reflect the same structural concepts as the software to be written using it. At the highest level, a program should consist of a formal description of its task using terms appropriate to the application; these terms correspond to modules in the level below. Successive lower levels introduce more detail, with the modules at the lowest level using language directly executable by the hardware. Each level has its own terminology and is not cluttered with either text or concepts appropriate to other levels. Further details are given in the NPL triennial report for 1969–71 (ref. 116 pp.18–19) and in this paper:

M Woodger. On semantic levels in programming. In: C V Freiman (ed.), *Information Processing 71: Proc. IFIP Congress 71*, held at Ljubljana, August 1971, North-Holland, 1972, pp.402–407.

4.7 Mathematics and computing services

Organisation: CCU, DNAM and DNAC

In November 1967 the increasing importance of computing services to the Laboratory was recognised by the establishment of a Central Computer Unit (CCU), hived off from the rest of Mathematics Division, which was renamed the Division of Numerical and Applied Mathematics (DNAM) in April 1968. (This name followed a trend in NPL at the time, which many regretted, to replace short Divisional names with arguably more accurate but clumsier ones.) The establishment of CCU however did not go smoothly, because the Director, Dr Dunworth, could not convince Headquarters that a post at SPSO level should be created for the head of the new Unit. To avoid delay, he persuaded Paul Dean (then an Individual Merit SPSO) to become acting head temporarily while he continued to argue for the new post. After six months, the post was still not approved and Dean wished to return to his research, so Goodwin was given the position of officer-in-charge of CCU while remaining Superintendent of DNAM. The two groups were now separate in little more than name.

By 1971 NPL was being told to reduce staff numbers, and as a result the work in DNAM on theoretical physics was closed down and the staff involved dispersed. Without some further reorganisation this would have left the Division unacceptably small. At the same time there was still no agreement on the creation of a post of head of CCU. The attempt to separate mathematics and computing services was therefore abandoned, and in April 1971 CCU and DNAM were re-merged to form the Division of Numerical Analysis and Computing (DNAC). The new Division, led by Dr Goodwin, consisted of a Computing Branch under Jack

Michel and a Numerical and Mathematical Analysis Branch under Ernie Albasiny. The organisational dance is shown in fig. 1.

In the computing services area the short-lived CCU had one lasting positive effect: a new acknowledgement of the importance of innovative non-numerical software, signalled by the inclusion of Brian Wichmann and Roger Scowen in the Unit on its formation. In the mathematical work, the loss of the highly regarded theoretical physics group was a major blow. The organisational changes did not have much effect on the rest of the technical programme, and in the following outline the work of CCU, DNAM and DNAC is described under the natural headings of Mathematics and Computing Services.

Goodwin was promoted and appointed one of the Deputy Directors of the Laboratory on 13 December 1971; he remained in charge of DNAC until his successor as Superintendent, Ernie Albasiny, was appointed on 27 November 1972. David Martin took over Albasiny's former Branch Head post in April 1973.

Mathematics

In the core area of numerical analysis, this period was one of steady building on the substantial foundations established in the previous ten years and described in section 3.9. Jim Wilkinson in particular extended his already very high reputation with a continuing flow of influential papers, and he was appointed a Fellow of the Royal Society in 1969. Applied mathematics fared much less well. Work on theoretical physics, on the elasticity of structures and on ship hull design was all discontinued or moved to other Divisions between 1969 and 1974.

When the Requirements Boards system was established in 1973 (see p.121), the mathematical work had no natural home because the Boards were organised according to industrial sectors. At first the work was considered by a special Chief Scientist's Board; later it was given to the Computers, Systems and Electronics Board as being the best available. They recognised the high standing of the work but were less convinced that industry needed it. They eventually approved the programme, but called for an increase in the proportion of work paid for from non-Government sources, to demonstrate relevance to industrial needs. The staff were concerned that the longer-term work (on the past success of which their current expertise was based) was being dangerously undervalued: they felt the Board was concentrating on the golden eggs and neglecting the goose.

The four main threads in the numerical analysis programme were partial differential equations, linear algebra, data fitting and optimisation. As in other periods it is outside our scope to consider this work in detail, but some flavour can be given.

The essence of progress in physical science is the construction of mathematical statements to represent theories based on observations. The power of such statements lies in the fact that they enable predictions to be made, on the basis of which the theories they symbolise can be tested and so reinforced, modified or discarded. A theory which consistently passes such tests can be used with confidence in engineering design, still represented in its mathematical form. In a wide variety of situations, these key mathematical statements take the form of *partial differential equations*. The best-known example is probably Laplace's Equation, which describes many phenomena including magnetic fields, the flow of heat through solid bodies, and even water percolation through earth dams. In any particular problem, the equation will apply to a variable within some specified area or volume, and there will be *boundary conditions* specifying constraints on the variable on the boundaries of this region. The Division's role was to bring its armoury of numerical methods and software to bear on the very wide range of such problems on which its advice was sought, finding the solution of the equation concerned which satisfied the given boundary conditions. Staff involved included Geoff Miller, John Lockett, Bill Murray, Alan Burton, and George Symm who was co-author of an influential book on the subject published in 1977 (ref. 81).

Another group of physical phenomena can be modelled as sets of linear equations. In school algebra, simultaneous equations seem straightforward: n equations can be solved for n unknowns, at least if n is 2 or 3. If n is 100, one might expect a computer to be able to cope. Indeed it can (provided the equations are not inconsistent or otherwise ill-behaved), but many subtle considerations arise. For example, the matrix of coefficients may be sparse (that is have many zero elements), or it may be symmetrical, or the elements may be complex numbers instead of real, and in all these cases the preferred method of solution will be different. Perhaps most significantly, the individual coefficients may be subject to small errors, in which case the effect of these errors on the solution will certainly be important. All these matters, and many further ramifications, come under the heading of *linear algebra*. This was one of Jim Wilkinson's particular areas of expertise, and many of the pioneering procedures he devised were published in 1971 in the Linear Algebra volume of the *Handbook for Automatic Computation* (ref. 169). He was assisted by Roger Martin, Gwen Edwards (later Mrs Peters), and Hilary Bowdler (later Mrs Symm).

Another area familiar in a rudimentary form at school is *data fitting*, the process of finding a smooth curve or surface to fit as well as possible some numerical data derived from experimental work. The reason for wanting to do this may be to enable further computation to be carried out, to calibrate an instrument or to control a machine tool. The curve or surface identified will often consist of many segments, each of which has a simple algebraic form (such as a polynomial curve) and fits smoothly with its neighbours; such segments are called *splines*. A measure of goodness of fit with the data will be needed; that usually adopted is the *least-squares* criterion (that the sum of the squares of the distances of the points from the curve or surface should be minimised). In this area too the Division established itself as a centre of excellence, thanks to the work of Charles Clenshaw, Geoff Hayes and Maurice Cox.

The final major thread in the mathematical work in this period was that of *optimisation*. Here the problem is to find the minimum or maximum value of some function of several variables given (in general) a set of constraints on the values these variables can take. Such problems arise very widely; examples are minimising the weight of an engineering structure with stated mechanical properties, maximising the accuracy of an optical filter, or minimising the cost of some process. Major conferences in this area were held at NPL in 1971 (ref. 93) and 1974 (ref. 54). The work was particularly associated with the names of Philip Gill, Walter Murray and Susan Picken (later Mrs Hodson). A separate class of problems, known as *integer programming*, arises if the variables are restricted to integer values. Work in this area was carried out by Ed Brocklehurst, Keith Dennis and Margaret Wagland.

Perhaps the most important development in numerical mathematics in this period was one which applies to all the above areas: the development of formal libraries of numerical software, complete with specifications and guidance on which algorithm to use in given circumstances. The most important such development in the UK started with a meeting in 1968 between Jim Wilkinson of NPL and Brian Ford of the University of Nottingham. This meeting led to the establishment in 1970 of the Nottingham Algorithms Group Project, a collaboration between six UK academic centres to produce a library of routines, particularly in linear algebra, for use on ICL 1900 series computers. NPL was not formally a participant at this stage but Wilkinson's strong support was influential in getting the work going. The project developed into the Numerical Algorithms Group (NAG) Library, initially funded by Government but later, as NAG Ltd, financially self-supporting. The NAG Library was made available on the NPL KDF9s in 1974. As NAG evolved from an academic co-operative to a commercial service, NPL began to use it as an important way of making its numerical software available to industry, and in recognition of the Laboratory's major contribution David Martin of NPL was appointed to the NAG Council and Executive.

In parallel with the NAG development, NPL's own collection of routines, which had been growing and evolving since the Turing era, was organised and documented systematically as the NPL Algorithms Library, with John Cooper as the prime mover. Algol 60 was the language in general use for writing mathematical software at NPL, but by 1976 most routines in the NPL Library were available also in Fortran because this was the language most used in industry—a significant change from the 1971 *Handbook for Automatic Computation,* which used Algol only. An important subset of the NPL Library was made commercially available as the Numerical Optimization Software Library (NOSL).

The next stage in the history of mathematical software at NPL is covered in section 5.6.

Computing services

At about the same time as the Central Computer Unit was formed in November 1967, approval was given for the purchase of a second KDF9 to meet the Laboratory's steadily increasing demand for computing services. After various delays, a second-hand machine was bought from the National Computing Centre in Manchester, and installed in the Charles Babbage Building, starting in September 1969; acceptance tests were finally completed in February 1970. The original machine was then moved from Building 23 to join it, and was working in its new home by mid-June.

In October 1969 a new multiaccess operating system, Eldon, developed at the University of Leeds, had been installed on the original KDF9. This allowed a major transformation in computing services to begin: the introduction of on-line terminals scattered round the NPL site connected directly to KDF9. By February 1970, 15 terminals were connected, rising to 27 by the end of the year and to 32 in 1971; all were Teletypes and all were connected to the first machine, with the second one acting as a 'slave' to run batch jobs and jobs off-loaded from the first machine. Eldon, which was considerably extended at NPL by Tony Hillman and others, allowed terminal users to create and modify program texts, and to call for specified programs, including compilers, to be run. Data could come either from the terminal or from an existing file in the machine, and likewise results could be sent either to the terminal or to a file. The main languages used were Algol and KDF9 Usercode. Basic and Babel (see below) were introduced in 1971, and the (initially very limited) Fortran capability was gradually improved. Traditional batch-mode operation became less important. By 1973 there were on average 800–900 on-line jobs per day, and Eldon had proved to be a very effective way of using the KDF9s. To increase the power of the system further, there were demands for a new machine to control the time-sharing, a 'front-end processor', but this never materialised. A PDP-8 machine was however used as a front-end to handle code conversion and similar routine operations.

Besides the terminals connected directly to KDF9, there were in 1971 nine Teletypes in NPL connected to modems for use with external commercial on-line computing services, in particular the de la Rue-Bull service (later called GEIS and Honeywell). These services were first used at NPL in 1967 before KDF9 offered an on-line service; the main languages available on them were Basic, Algol and elementary Fortran. Like Eldon on KDF9, they enabled new software to be developed, and established software, including libraries of standard programs, to be run.

The first KDF9 was connected to the NPL Network by late 1971. As the network developed, this gave access to the machine from a much larger population of terminals, though the maximum of 32 connected at any one time still applied. Some of the network terminals were VDUs, though these were not ideal for use with Eldon because they had no local printing or paper tape facilities; also Eldon necessarily drove them in a scrolling mode like a Teletype, which did not make good use of their capabilities.

An NPL Computer Users' Panel of Divisional representatives was established in 1967 (with David Martin as the first chairman) to promote communication between the then Computing Branch of Mathematics Division and the computer users in other Divisions. This proved a useful mechanism and lasted until 1994. In parallel with it an equally long-running Data Handling Panel made recommendations on the selection of data-handling equipment such as VDUs, kept a pool of standard equipment, and its members vetted all relevant NPL purchases to avoid unnecessary diversity and so allow interchange and keep maintenance costs down.

Courses and advice services on computing matters were provided for NPL staff. In January 1968 the existing newsletter for KDF9 users in NPL, *KDF9 Weekly*, was replaced by a new publication *NPL Computing* (ref. 113), covering all computing services. This was still produced every few weeks in 1995.

When the NPL Network developed by the Division of Computer Science in 1967–73 had settled down as a useful and growing service, its management was taken over by DNAC Computing Branch. The formal handover was in October 1974, but the groups had been collaborating closely for some time. New services, most notably the Editing Computer, were developed for the network by DNAC; these are described further below. The population of computer users widened quickly, so that the network came to underpin a major part of the computing service operation. By 1976 there were about 30 computers, over 100 VDUs, and about 20 high-quality and line printers attached to the network, with many other devices including Teletypes, paper-tape readers and punches, magnetic tape cartridges and cassettes, and data loggers. Later network services included DART (Data Acquisition in Real Time), installed in 1977 to help experimentalists by carrying out calculations on data as it arose, an idea soon rendered obsolete by the arrival of cheap desktop computers. A maintenance contract for the network and associated equipment had been placed with Computer Field Maintenance Ltd well before the handover to DNAC, and the maintenance of the KDF9s was added to this contract in April 1974.

Frank Blake succeeded Jack Michel as head of the Computing Branch of DNAC in August 1976. Throughout the CCU and DNAC era Tom Vickers, assisted by Dickie Bird, Betty Curtis and others, managed the KDF9s and the service based on them. Dennis Blake managed the expanding NPL Network before and after its handover to DNAC in 1974. Software for new services was designed and developed by Brian Wichmann, David Schofield, Roger Scowen, Tony Hillman and others.

DNAC. Computing documentation. NPL DNAC DOC A2, April 1972.
A L Hillman and B A Wichmann. Experience with the Eldon operating system for KDF9. In: C A R Hoare and R H Perrott (eds), *Operating System Techniques,* Academic Press, 1972, pp.337–340.
DNAC. Introduction to the Data Communication Network. NPL DNAC DOC N1, first published May 1973.

Graphical output

By 1968 computers could produce graphical output using *graph plotters,* devices based on the pen-and-paper tradition of draughtsmanship. The computer controlled the position of the pen and whether it was raised or lowered, and in some devices could also scroll the paper backwards and forwards. A Benson-Lehner plotter was available on KDF9, and a software package, the NPL Graphical Output System, was developed by Brian Heap and Clifford Nott to help programmers take advantage of it. This package, written in KDF9 Usercode, provided routines for drawing curves, boxes, histograms and a range of symbols, and was demonstrated at the 1968 Open Days. By 1972 an Algol interface was available, providing much more advanced facilities; they included perspective drawings of three-dimensional surfaces, with or without the removal of 'hidden lines' (those on the far side of solid objects); contouring algorithms; and stereoscopic drawings to be viewed through spectacles with red and green lenses. More types of plotter were available, and output could also be on microfilm or on a Tektronics 611 storage tube display. This storage tube, driven through British Standard Interfaces either directly from paper tape or via the NPL Network, was a strikingly fast device thanks to special-purpose line-drawing electronics developed by Pat Woodroffe. By 1976 an impressive new output device had been acquired, an HRD-1 display/plotter developed under an ACTP contract by Laser-Scan Ltd. This used laser technology to produce output on microfiche, and was driven by a PDP-11 computer. It could draw more than 100 times as fast as the incremental plotters, and was far more accurate (it could position its 16 micrometre diameter spot to 1 micrometre), but plotters remained in use because of the convenience of direct output on paper.

The Davies era: 1966–1978

By 1978 the NPL Graphical Output System was available with a Fortran interface, and the advanced facilities, by now converted into Fortran, were passed to the Numerical Algorithms Group to form the basis of the graphics routines in the NAG Library. The system was also one of the sources for the GINOSURF package developed by the Computer-Aided Design Centre at Cambridge. Through these channels it made a substantial contribution to many early applications of practical computer graphics in the UK as well as being a widely used tool within NPL.

Reports on graphical output services

B R Heap and C W Nott. Users' Guide to the NPL Graphical Output System. NPL Report Ma. 63, March 1968.

B R Heap and Margaret Laws. Construction of the characters available in the NPL graphical output system. NPL Report CCU 1, May 1968.

C W Nott. A brief guide to the NPL graphical output system. NPL Report CCU 2, June 1968.

B R Heap and Monica G Pink. Some character designs for the Russian alphabet for use with a graphical output device. NPL Report CCU 4, February 1969.

Joyce Dickerson and B R Heap. A simple program for drawing flow charts. NPL Report CCU 5, February 1969.

Joyce Dickerson, C W Nott and B R Heap. A software scheme for text output on visual display devices. NPL Report CCU 8, December 1969.

C Hall. An algorithm for the production of an isometric projection of a three-dimensional surface with hidden line removal. NPL Report NAC 41, November 1973.

DNAC. Useful graphical programs. NPL DNAC DOC L5, May 1976.

C Hall. An algorithm for the production of an isometric projection of a three-dimensional surface. NPL Report NAC 75, March 1977.

Text editing: Pages and Edit

One of the major uses of the Eldon system on KDF9 was the management of program texts, including the storage of prepared text on disc for subsequent modification, printing, and compilation. These editing facilities could with difficulty be used for ordinary documents as well as programs, but were not designed for this purpose. They provided a disc filing system, with file names and file ownership, and allowed the editing and merging of files, but line boundaries were fixed, and there was no division of the text into pages. In 1971 David Schofield and Brian Wichmann developed some new software to help in document production. This allowed the automatic insertion of line and page boundaries in sensible places before the document was printed. The user could include control characters in his text to indicate where headings, new paragraphs and so on occurred, and also style codes to determine page size and layout, and page numbering. The system would even prepare contents lists (using the marked headings) and indexes (including only words marked in the text for indexing). A rough copy could be output on the KDF9 line printer, or a better copy on an electric typewriter controlled by paper tape. This scheme was advanced for its time (though complete originality was not claimed for it)[4], and there were many practical problems, not least that nearly all the Eldon terminals dealt in upper-case characters only. Early documents refer to this software simply as the KDF9 Text Output Scheme, but it later became known as Pages.

As the first step to overcoming some of the practical problems with the KDF9 scheme, a DEC PDP-11 computer to provide a Text Editing Service was ordered in 1971 and delivered in 1972. The Editing Computer, soon known as Edit, was first advertised as a service on the NPL Network in October 1973. It offered all the features of the KDF9 Text Output Scheme in a much more convenient form. Instead of the KDF9 disc, the network Central File Store was used for long-term storage. New time-sharing software was written, which could cope with up to 16 simultaneous users, later extended to 30. Pages was incorporated and its facilities slowly extended. Although many of the terminals on the network were VDUs, compatibility with Teletypes was retained for some time, and this meant a line-at-a-time editing philosophy which could not take full advantage of the display screen. Printing from Edit was carried out via the network, usually in this era on an electric typewriter for good quality or a line printer for drafts, as for KDF9.

Apart from a small kernel, the Edit software was written in Palgol, a cut-down version of Algol 60 developed by David Schofield which was in effect a machine-independent system implementation language. This gave the advantage of ease of training for staff who already knew Algol, while retaining the run-time efficiency of a low-level language.

Documents could also be prepared using the Scrapbook system described in section 4.3, and there was therefore some rivalry between the two in the area of overlap. Pages included several special document production features such as automatic index preparation, with which Scrapbook did not compete. Likewise Scrapbook had its hypertext and electronic mail facilities which at the time were unique. The most important initial difference between the two as regards basic document preparation was that the editing facilities on Scrapbook were designed from the outset solely for use on VDUs. This meant that paragraph reformatting, for example, could be carried out directly on the screen as it is on a modern word processor. People found this so useful that a version of it was eventually incorporated in Edit, and from then on

---

[4] Computer-based document production systems had been described in the literature for some years, and the KDF9 scheme was in part inspired by the 'runoff' command in MIT's CTSS system (see Crisman (1965) ref. 24, section AH.9.01 pp.9–13).

Edit was clearly more appropriate than Scrapbook for all major document preparation.

Besides this main role of document production, Edit was developed as a front-end to other services, helping their users by providing them with a single consistent interface. For example, there was a standard 'help' facility whereby the user could always type '?' and be shown a list of the currently available options. Files could be moved between the Central File Store and KDF9, an Algol syntax checker written by Brian Wichmann was available, and SOAP and WATER (see below) could be applied to any files which appeared to need them. Small BASIC and Fortran programs could be run on Honeywell computers on the network using the simple SNIPE executive developed for network services on these machines.

The development of Edit was led by David Schofield. Tony Hillman was a major contributor, and others involved included George Tondryk, Steve Wilson, Roger Millard, Rita Stevens and Mike Parsons. SNIPE was developed by Nick Dawes.

Publications on Edit and related topics

D Schofield and B A Wichmann. A text output system for production of reports and manuals. NPL Report NAC 5, revised version February 1972.

DNAC. Editing Computer User Manual. NPL DNAC DOC S1, first published January 1974.

N W Dawes. A Simple Network Interacting Program's Executive (SNIPE). NPL Report NAC 66, May 1976. Reprinted with modifications in *Software Practice and Experience*, 7, 1977, pp.341–345.

DNAC. Word processing manual. NPL DNAC DOC W1, September 1976.

A L Hillman and D Schofield. EDIT—an interactive network service: design and implementation. NPL Report NAC 70, October 1976. Reprinted with modifications in *Software Practice and Experience*, 7, 1977, pp.595–611.

A R Lawrence and D Schofield. SFS—a file system supporting Pascal files: design and specification. NPL Report NAC 88, February 1978.

Documentation aids: SOAP, WATER and the Fog Index

A program can be made easier to understand, and therefore easier to modify safely, if its text is laid out in a neat and consistent style, with nested structures systematically indented. Roger Scowen realised that software could be written to improve programs in this way automatically, without any change to their effect when run. His implementation of this idea, SOAP (Simplify Obscure Algol Programs), was first described in 1969 and publicised more widely in 1971; because SOAP was itself written in Algol it was machine-independent (except for input and output) and was widely used outside NPL. An optional extra, SOAP-index, provided further aids to the programmer, including an automatically generated index of the occurrences of each identifier and constant in the program. A version for Babel (BLEACH) was introduced in 1972, one for Fortran (FROTH) in 1973, and one for Basic (SCRUB) in 1977.

WATER (Where Are Typographical ERrors) was a precursor of the spell checkers now routinely available in word processors. It created a list of all the words used in a text in alphabetical order, with the line number of the first appearance of each word and the frequency of occurrence. It was useful for finding spelling mistakes and inconsistencies, and for checking that the first use of an acronym or unfamiliar term was adequately explained.

A bonus when using WATER was that it automatically calculated the 'Fog Index' of the text, a measure of its obscurity depending on the length of the sentences and the proportion of long words[5]. A value over 20 could be symptomatic of a predilection for excessively circumlocutary phraseology; under 10, and you might be trying too hard to keep it snappy.

Publications on documentation aids

R S Scowen, A L Hillman and M Shimell. SOAP—Simplify Obscure ALGOL Programs. NPL Report CCU 6, 1969.

R S Scowen, D Allin, A L Hillman and M Shimell. SOAP—a program which documents and edits ALGOL 60 programs. *Computer Journal*, 14(2), 1971, pp.133–135.

R S Scowen. Pangloss: a system for reading and checking files. NPL Report NAC 59, January 1975.

R S Scowen. SOAP—Simplify Obscure Algol Programs. NPL Report NAC 60, April 1975.

R S Scowen. Some aids for program documentation. NPL Report NAC 76, March 1977. Reprinted with modifications in *Software Practice and Experience*, 7, 1977, pp.779–792.

A R Lawrence. SCRUB—Systematically Clean and Renumber Users' BASIC. *Software Practice and Experience*, 8, 1978, pp.227–232.

Clothesline store

The amount of random-access memory any computer can accommodate is limited by the length of the address field in the instruction format. But in some applications the memory is often being accessed sequentially rather than randomly: communication systems for example spend a lot of time reading or writing bytes sequentially in buffer areas. The so-called clothesline store, designed by John Rodgers and David Schofield in 1976, was a neat device taking advantage of this fact to free some random-access memory, and so allow programs to run more efficiently. It was a hardware element appearing to the programmer as a

---

[5] The Fog Index was defined as:

$$0.4 \times \left\{ \frac{\text{number of words}}{\text{number of sentences}} + 100 \times \frac{\text{number of words} > 8 \text{ letters}}{\text{number of words}} \right\}$$

The idea came from F Whitehouse, *Documentation*, Business Books, 1971.

variable length string of bytes; only the ends of the string were directly addressable. Thus it could be used as a stack (last in, first out) by reading from the end last written, or as a buffer (first in, first out) by reading from the other end. Yet it only required two addresses, one for each end, however long it was. Internally, it consisted of conventional random-access memory components, together with addressing circuits to make the device behave as a clothesline store. To demonstrate its effectiveness, 64 clothesline stores each of 256 bytes were successfully added to the Editing computer, but the idea was not taken up by computer manufacturers.

J L Rodgers and D Schofield (inventors). Improvements in or relating to Computer Stores. UK Patent No. 1 525 045, date of application 11 February 1976.

J L Rodgers and D Schofield. The clothesline store. NPL Report NAC 83, October 1977.

Programming language studies

When CCU was established in 1967, its role was not restricted to running computing services; research and development were also on the agenda provided they were relevant to the Unit's main purpose. Several items of work on programming languages were carried out on this basis. The main ones were Roger Scowen's development of Babel, Brian Wichmann's work on performance measurement, and the development by Wichmann and Bell of the language PL-516, all of which are described below. There were also several smaller projects, and these can best be recorded by simply listing the reports concerned:

B A Wichmann. A note on the use of variables in ALGOL 60. NPL Report NAC 14, February 1972.

R S Scowen. Debugging computer programs: a survey with special emphasis on ALGOL. NPL Report NAC 21, 2nd edition January 1973.

B A Wichmann. Some validation tests for an ALGOL 60 compiler. NPL Report NAC 33, March 1973.

R S Scowen and B A Wichmann. The definition of comments in programming languages. NPL Report NAC 34, May 1973. Reprinted with modifications in *Software Practice and Experience,* 4, 1974, pp.181–188.

I D Hill, R S Scowen and B A Wichmann. Writing algorithms in ALGOL 60. NPL Report NAC 48, April 1974. Reprinted with modifications in *Software Practice and Experience,* 5, 1975, pp.229–244.

R S Scowen. The diagnostic facilities in ALGOL compilers. NPL Report NAC 52, July 1974.

B A Wichmann. A syntax checker for ALGOL 60. NPL Report NAC 53, August 1974.

R S Scowen. The diagnostic facilities in Algol and Fortran compilers. NPL Report NAC 81, July 1977.

Babel

When Roger Scowen joined CCU as a founder member in 1967 he continued the development of the Babel language on which he had been working in Autonomics Division. As already mentioned (p.125), this was an Algol-like language designed to allow extensions to the language to be made readily, and to make it as easy as possible to produce correct and efficient programs. It attracted a loyal band of followers in NPL, but did not catch on more widely.

R S Scowen. Babel, a new general programming language. NPL Report CCU 7, October 1969.
R S Scowen. The Babel compiler. NPL Report CCU 10, March 1970.
R S Scowen. The use of decision tables in Babel. NPL Report NAC 8, December 1971.
R S Scowen. Babel and SOAP, an application of extensible compilers. NPL Report NAC 13, February 1972. Reprinted with modifications in *Software Practice and Experience,* 3, 1973, pp.15–27.
R S Scowen. Testing the diagnostic features of the Babel compiler. NPL Report NAC 57, September 1974.

Computer performance measurement

One major factor in choosing a new computer is how fast the rival machines are. To compare their performance fairly, what is needed is a *benchmark,* a standard task designed to be representative of the intended workload, which can be run on each machine, and the runs timed. If the benchmark is written in the language used for the real workload, the performance of the compiler as well as that of the hardware will be automatically taken into account. In the 1970s, designing a benchmark for scientific computing was more straightforward than for commercial data processing, because input and output were relatively unimportant.

In work first reported in 1969, Brian Wichmann studied the run-time frequency of the major features of Algol 60, and then composed a benchmark which included the features in the same proportions. Care was needed to ensure that a clever compiler could not take advantage of the program's unusual structure to take short cuts which would not be possible in a normal program. The performance of various computers, together with their Algol compilers, was measured using this benchmark, and the results, together with measurements using other benchmarks, were reported in the papers listed below. A thorough discussion of the whole area is given in Brian Wichmann's book, ref. 153. The later work was undertaken in collaboration with the UK Government's Central Computing Agency (later CCTA), which took a close interest because of its responsibilities for computer procurement.

B A Wichmann. A comparison of ALGOL 60 execution speeds. NPL Report CCU 3, January 1969.

B A Wichmann. Some statistics from ALGOL programs. NPL Report CCU 11, August 1970.

B A Wichmann. The performance of some ALGOL systems. In: C V Freiman (ed.), *Information Processing 71: Proc. IFIP Congress 71,* held at Ljubljana August 1971, North-Holland, 1972, pp.327–334.

B A Wichmann. Basic statement times for ALGOL 60. NPL Report NAC 15, May 1972. Second edition NPL Report NAC 42, November 1973.

B A Wichmann. Five ALGOL compilers. *Computer Journal*, 15, 1972, pp.8–12.

B A Wichmann. Estimating the execution speed of an ALGOL program. NPL Report NAC 38, June 1973.

B A Wichmann. *ALGOL Compilation and Assessment.* Academic Press, 1973.

B A Wichmann and B Jones. Testing ALGOL 60 compilers. *Software Practice and Experience*, 6, 1976, pp.261–270.

H J Curnow and B A Wichmann. A synthetic benchmark. *Computer Journal*, 19, 1976, pp.43–49.

P Verstege and B A Wichmann. An experimental data base for computer performance information. NPL Report NAC 62, second edition July 1976.

B A Wichmann. How to call procedures, or second thoughts on Ackermann's function. *Software Practice and Experience*, 7, 1977, pp.317–329.

B A Wichmann and J du Croz. A program to calculate the GAMM measure. NPL Report NAC 86, December 1977; reprinted in *Computer Journal*, 22, 1979, pp.317–322.

System implementation languages: PL-516

Systems software—operating systems, compilers, communications software and the like—has to be efficient because it is run so often, which is a strong argument for writing it in a low-level language. On the other hand, it is also complex and liable to change, and clarity, reliability and speed of production are important, all good reasons for using a high-level language. In 1968, following initial work by others, Professor Niklaus Wirth of Zürich developed a language called PL-360 for systems software development on the IBM 360 computer which was a cunning compromise: a low-level (and therefore machine-dependent) language which nevertheless managed to incorporate many of the features of high-level languages. At NPL it was realised that this approach would be useful in several areas, in particular in the software for the Mark II NPL Network. What was needed was a language on the same lines as PL-360 for the Honeywell DDP-516 computer which was to form the network switching centre. This new language, PL-516, was developed by Brian Wichmann and Donald Bell in 1969–71. It was used successfully in three NPL projects: the Mark II NPL Network software by Peter Wilkinson and others, the Central File Store development by CAP Ltd (both described in section 4.2 above), and Pattern Recognition, Bell's home group (see section 4.5). Further details are given in the reports listed below.

B A Wichmann. PL 516, an Algol-like assembly language for the DDP-516. NPL Report CCU 9, April 1970.

D A Bell and B A Wichmann. An ALGOL-like assembly language for a small computer. *Software Practice and Experience*, 1, 1971, pp.61–72.

D A Bell. Collected papers on the development of the PL-516 programming language. NPL Report Com Sci 44, January 1971.

D A Bell. Modifications to the PL-516 compiler during 1971. NPL Report Com Sci 54, January 1972.

D A Bell. PL-516 in PL-516, the text, syntax and informal description of a high-level assembler. NPL Report Com 65, January 1973.

5 The Albasiny era: 1978–1987

5.1 Outline of developments

The computing work at NPL was reorganised on 1 June 1978. A new Division of Numerical Analysis and Computer Science (DNACS), with Ernie Albasiny as Superintendent, was formed by combining most of the Division of Computer Science with the mathematical branches of DNAC. At the same time the Computing Branch of DNAC became an independent Computing Services Unit (CSU), remaining under the charge of Frank Blake. In addition a small and short-lived Computing Technology Unit (CTU) was established under Donald Davies to undertake work on data security and to manage ACTP. These three were each responsible to one of the Deputy Directors of the Laboratory, Dr J K Foreman.

Ernie Albasiny thus found himself with unexpectedly wide responsibilities. He was a talented numerical analyst who, unlike many mathematicians, was able and willing to take on management tasks; and on this basis, during six years as Superintendent of DNAC, he had successfully kept the mathematical work on the general course set by his predecessor Dr Goodwin. However he had little experience of non-numerical computing, and though here too he maintained the work programme, he had no background on which to base any innovations. The Requirements Board saw a relatively inexperienced hand on the tiller.

The Board's views were also coloured by a gradual and deep-seated shift in political attitudes. When computing work started at NPL in the closing days of the Second World War, Britain's long-established tradition of public service had been strengthened by the wartime necessity of working together for the common good. This applied both to the Government's approach to their new challenges and to many individuals' perception of their place in the world: most of the founding members of Mathematics Division, for example, had moved smoothly from Government service in support of military aims to Government service at NPL for civil aims. They saw serving the country directly as a more satisfying, perhaps even worthier, basis for a career than serving any particular company. There was an ethos of professionalism and also a comforting sense of permanence and security. But in the 33 years since 1945, public perception had changed, and was to change much further.

From being the instrument of the corporate will of the people as expressed in Parliament, and as such to be if not applauded at least respected, the Civil Service had come to be seen by many as a necessary evil in a society which drew its strength from its capitalist economy and the ethic of commercial competition. The

Figure 48. DNACS/DITC staff numbers 1978–87.

fact that by definition the Civil Service had no competitors was now seen as an inherent serious weakness which meant that its scope should be kept to a minimum. From the late 1960s, cuts had been made in public services including NPL.

In this critical spirit, the Requirements Board looked increasingly hard at the reasons why a proposed programme of work should be carried out in the public sector. Faced with a new proposal, there were several questions they had always addressed: was it a good idea which deserved to be developed in the national interest? Were the right skills and resources available? Had the exploitation route been properly considered? What was happening elsewhere in the world? With all these questions the Division was on familiar ground. But now there was a new emphasis: was it really necessary to undertake the work in the public sector? Why shouldn't market forces be left to determine whether it was done or not? In earlier years the computing Divisions had been confident of their roles; like children in a stable family, they knew they were wanted. The familiar Civil Service framework guarded a space within which useful work could be done, given the right people. But now the children were growing up fast and the world began to look less friendly. Technological and commercial arguments were no longer enough: a programme of work had to be politically correct as well, and it was much less clear exactly what that meant. The Division had to seek its own role, appropriate to a national institution, as far as possible distinct from anything private industry or the universities could offer and yet with practical goals and clear potential benefits. Government policy for research establishments, as construed by the Requirements Boards, gradually took on an underlying negative slant—that if others could offer it, it should be left to them—which contrasted sharply with the positive atmosphere of opportunity in the earlier postwar years.

As a result of these pressures and cuts the balance of the Division's work changed and many of its more public fringe activities contracted. The shift away from electronics to software and technical politics, already apparent in the Davies era, continued, until by 1987 there was little hardware capability left. Recruitment to NPL became sporadic, and staff numbers were reduced (see fig. 48), particularly in the mathematical area. As the scientific status of the Laboratory declined under the political pressures, it became more difficult to attract and retain really high-calibre recruits. Formal public reports had already been abandoned in 1974, and there were marked decreases in the numbers of general lectures by members of staff and the frequency of Open Days. Research Fellows became extinct, and Guest Workers and sandwich-course students were endangered species. Taken together, these changes amounted to a major contraction of the Laboratory's visible role as a public institution. In the computing area there were other problems: the technology had become so pervasive that no single institution other than the major manufacturers could have much influence in the short term, but the Requirements Board saw long-term scientific work as inappropriate. And by 1987 the word privatisation had entered the vocabulary, and public sector institutions were themselves beginning to look like a species under threat.

Against this generally unfavourable climatic trend, there was a notable temporary thaw in 1981–82. In a strategy paper written in 1980 (ref. 9 pp.475–478), Kenneth Baker MP argued that, in the face of competition from the United States and Japan, co-ordinated Government action was needed to promote all aspects of information technology in the UK, including application, training and research as well as the hardware and software industries themselves. The Prime Minister accepted this case and appointed him to the Government as Minister of State for Industry and Information Technology in January 1981. The subject took on a new, though sadly temporary, political priority. The Minister visited the Division on more than one occasion, and members of the Division even attended regular briefing meetings for him, a privilege entirely unheard-of before or since. The year 1982 was designated Information Technology Year, and on 11 November the Division held its first Open Day since 1976. Perhaps the most important lasting effect of this brief fit of leadership and interventionist confidence was a transformation in the level of computer literacy in British schools. This came about as a result of a Department of Industry (DoI) scheme to give them financial help with the purchase of microcomputers, in many cases BBC machines manufactured by Acorn Computers Ltd[1]. The Division made an important though unforeseen contribution to this celebrated scheme because one of those most involved in DoI was Donald Bell, whose up-to-date technical expertise was derived directly from his recent NPL career.

This broad respite in the political weather was short-lived, but there were also some positive elements in the longer-term changes in the Division's technical programme. The bounds of the programme were squeezed, on one hand by the traditional ban on work competing with industry and on the other by the swing against work with an academic flavour, but in the middle ground there were two favoured areas: standards-related work and centres of excellence.

On standards, it was widely accepted that many of the potential advantages of information technology would only be realised if

---

[1] The reaction of the Department of Education and Science to this initiative shows how far Government departments can forget what they are there for when distracted by departmental rivalries. According to Mr Baker's memoirs (ref. 9 p.61), instead of welcoming the benefits for British children, they actually resented what they saw as interference in their patch and 'every obstacle was put in the way' of the scheme. In their defence it should be said that they had other plans using different hardware, but even so their priorities were surely at fault.

effective standards could be agreed; network protocols are the obvious example but there are many others. The organisation responsible for defining such standards in the UK is the British Standards Institution, and the Division had always contributed to its committee work. Now however this was identified as an area where the Division could make a special contribution by carrying out related technical work, for example by devising tests to help establish whether or not systems conformed to standards, and by encouragement and assistance in the establishment of testing and certification services. Details of NPL's view of its role in this area are given in ref. 182. Memberships of BSI committees increased from nine in 1973 to 24 in 1985.

Another role which was seen as still politically acceptable was that of constituting a centre of excellence in some technical area useful to UK industry. Mathematics Division and its successors had of course long fulfilled this consultancy role in their own field, as had Donald Davies and his colleagues in the area of data communications, but this was now extended to the use of micro-computers in novel fields and to data security.

The problem with these good causes was, and is, that they require high-calibre staff who can only be attracted in the first place by an element of real technical innovation in their work. Not many of the brightest graduates would be attracted by standards and advisory work alone, and indeed they would not be competent in these areas without technical experience. Many more would accept advisory and standards elements in a research-oriented job. The programme had therefore to include a considerable proportion of technical work aimed between the industrial and the academic and trying, with mixed success, to be relevant to both while encroaching on neither.

The Requirements Board system was given a shake-up twice in this period. First in 1981 the number of Boards was reduced and their membership changed. The new Board responsible for the computing area was the Electronics and Avionics Requirements Board (EARB). However the EARB decided that its area of responsibility was too wide for a single body, and set up committees to be responsible for individual areas; the one dealing with the NPL computing programme was the Computing and Communications Committee (CCC). As with its predecessor the CSERB, this Committee succeeded in attracting some distinguished members, including Professors Brian Randell, Cliff Jones and Roger Needham. In 1986 the Requirements Board system was again reorganised with a single high-level Board, the Technology Requirements Board, and the committee which dealt with the NPL computing programme was renamed the Computing, Software and Communications Committee (CSCC).

In December 1981, reflecting the continuing reduction in the mathematical work, DNACS was renamed the Division of Information Technology and Computing (DITC), a name it was to keep for a record 14 years; and on 1 April 1983 the Numerical Analysis Branch of DITC was abolished as such, though its work continued at a reduced level in a Mathematical Analysis and Software group.

5.2   Protocol standards

By 1978 it was becoming more widely understood that the marriage of computers and communications which had been achieved over the previous decade could have a major impact on society: it made possible dramatic improvements in the availability and mobility of information and so held out exciting prospects for many human activities including education, science, culture, entertainment and personal communication, with corresponding new commercial opportunities. The first step in the realisation of these possibilities had to be the development and adoption of effective standards for the communication process. Protocol standards became a hot topic. There were two approaches. One, favoured by the United States, was that market forces could and should be left to come up with an appropriate and timely solution. The other camp, European-led, saw this as likely to perpetuate the dominance of IBM and the rest of the US computer industry in world markets, and it therefore favoured the development of standards by agreement in international bodies. Very narrowly the relevant committee of the International Organization for Standardization (ISO) voted in favour of undertaking the work; a new committee on Open Systems Interconnection (OSI), TC97/SC16, was established and started work in February 1978.

This provided a new and valuable context for NPL's work on protocols. Following the considerable early achievements of the Communications group, described in section 4.2, and the departure of Derek Barber and Roger Scantlebury who had led many of them, the group took a little time to sort out a new sense of direction. When it came this had three threads: the establishment of a unit to coordinate UK work on higher-level protocols, the development of methods of testing protocol implementations for conformance with standards, and a distinctive contribution to the standards-making process based on this conformance-testing viewpoint. These three topics are described in turn below.

Data Communication Protocols Unit (DCPU)

On 1 October 1978 a unit with this title was set up at NPL under Keith Bartlett to coordinate the development of higher-level protocols in the UK and to promote their improvement and application. 'Higher-level protocols' meant those of concern to the user or applications programmer, levels four and above in the OSI model. An immediate aim was to ensure as far as possible that the limited national effort available was devoted to compatible projects, to avoid unnecessary waste of effort and to ensure that systems built in accordance with the plans could communicate with each other. There was also an underlying aim: international standards for protocols were already under discussion, and it would clearly be beneficial for the UK IT industry and its customers for the interim protocols in use in the UK and the eventual international standards to be as similar as possible.

Four specifications were eventually adopted by the Unit: the 'Yellow Book' Network-Independent Transport Service published by the Post Office PSS User Forum in 1980; the 'Blue Book' File Transfer Protocol originally developed by a collaborative UK academic group in 1977; the 'Red Book' Job Transfer and Manipulation Protocol developed by a DCPU working party in 1980; and the 'Green Book' Character Terminal Protocol developed by the British Telecom PSS User Forum in 1981. UK universities made a major contribution to these developments, and the suite of Coloured Book protocols was a vital element in the successful JANET network established by their Joint Network Team in the early 1980s. The DCPU promoted the development and use of these protocols, and ensured that the lessons learnt from them were input to the international standards-making process.

Bartlett's vigorous approach and firm grasp of the politics as well as the technical aspects meant that the DCPU fulfilled these aims as far as could be expected given that in the international arena there were other, often more powerful, interests to be accommodated. Even within the UK, there was ample scope for argument on what the Government's technical policy should be in this area, and in 1981 there was discussion of the possibility that the Unit, with Bartlett, should move from NPL to the department responsible for such policy matters, IT Division in DTI headquarters. In the event Bartlett was moved on promotion to DTI's Electronics Applications Division, with quite different responsibilities, and what was left of DCPU, chiefly Peter Linington of Cambridge University on contract to NPL, remained NPL's responsibility for a further year. In 1982 the situation was rationalised by the establishment of an IT Standards Unit in IT Division, with Bartlett as its head. The new Unit's task was to promote a strong UK role in the international development of OSI standards and to encourage the use in the UK of stable drafts of the eventual standards (this was known as the 'intercept' strategy). The Coloured Books were no longer supported, though they remained in wide use as the mainstay of JANET. Under Bartlett's successor, George Sidey, ITSU continued its responsibility for DTI support for IT standards-related work in the UK in the late 1980s and early 90s, and was NPL's customer for much of the work on Open Systems described in section 6.2 below.

Protocol implementation assessment

On 14 November 1979 NPL submitted to the Requirements Board a proposal for a two-year programme of work to establish a capability for testing implementations of standard protocols, specifically the current interim standard Transport and File Transfer protocols. This proposal was accepted, and work on the project began officially in January 1980. It proved to be the first of a long-running and influential series of NPL projects in this area which continues at the time of writing (1996).

One of the group's first moves was to stake its claim to an international role in this area by making the major technical input to a Workshop on Certification of High-Level Protocols held at NPL under the auspices of DCPU in January 1980. Amongst the 50 people attending was Dr Tim Wells of the National Computing Centre (NCC) in Manchester; this contact was to lead to a long and fruitful collaboration between NCC and NPL. The idea was that NCC should run services using testing tools developed at NPL (and perhaps elsewhere). The potential customers for the testing services would be both suppliers of products incorporating protocol implementations, who could cite test results when advertising their products, and their customers, who could use testing services as part of their acceptance procedures.

The scheme proposed by NPL for testing protocol implementations consisted of embedding the *implementation under test* (IUT) in a software environment which would subject it to a systematic and rigorous series of checks to confirm as far as possible that its behaviour conformed to the rules of the protocol. The software conducting the tests, the *test driver*, would be connected to the IUT over a communications system and so would in general be geographically remote from it; a second (relatively small) module of test software, the *test responder*, would be needed at the IUT's site to play the part of the user of the service provided by the IUT. For further detail, the interested reader is referred to the papers listed below. This 'philosophy and architecture' of protocol testing formed the main foundation of the subsequent work of the group. It was first proposed by Dave Rayner in the 1981 report listed below, and was presented at an international workshop on protocol testing held at NPL in May the same year (the first of an influential series of IFIP workshops on Protocol Specification, Testing and Verification).

The first application of the philosophy and architecture was in the design and development of a prototype system to test implementations of the 'Yellow Book' Transport Service mentioned above (although called a transport service, this corresponded more closely to the network service in the eventual OSI model). This work formed NPL's contribution to a collaborative project on protocol testing research supported by the European Commission in 1982–84; the other participants were the Agence de l'Informatique in France and the Gesellschaft für Mathematik und Datenverarbeitung in Germany. This contract was to prove important as a foundation for later European collaboration and Commission involvement. A prototype Yellow Book test system was running in-house at NPL by December 1982. It made a major contribution to a commercial test system for the OSI Transport Protocol later developed by NCC, many elements, notably the test description language and the test management protocol, being preserved intact.

In February 1986 a UK consortium on OSI testing was launched, comprising NCC, NPL, British Telecom, and three major computer manufacturers—IBM, ICL and DEC, with other organisations free to join later. The idea was that financial support from the manufacturers and BT would enable NCC to offer commercial products and services (based to a considerable extent on NPL's work); in return for their support the members would get the opportunity to influence the direction of the work, advance information and early testing opportunities; they could, and did, also send secondees to NPL and NCC. NPL's initial role was to develop a system to test implementations of the OSI File Transfer, Access and Management (FTAM) protocol; the subsequent progress of this work is described in section 6.2.

NCC, together with other European computing centres, also gained support in 1986 from the European Commission for the development of Conformance Testing Services for Wide Area Networks (CTS-WAN), and NPL was a subcontractor to NCC for part of this work. A major US contract for NCC and NPL was soon to follow (see section 6.2). As worldwide interest in conformance testing grew, there was a greater need to maintain liaison with groups abroad; and there was a long-standing coordination arrangement with the networks group at the Harwell Laboratory of the Atomic Energy Authority because the Requirements Board funded communications work at both NPL and Harwell. Altogether, commercial, contractual and liaison matters were taking up an increasing share of the time of the NPL staff involved.

NPL's work on protocol implementation testing was led by Dave Rayner; others contributing included Vince Hathway, John Pavel, Godfrey Cowin, Zeng Hua-Xin, Adrian McKie, Roger Hale, Raymond Henley, Dave Eason, Chris Coles, Stephen Nightingale and Steve Hambly. NCC's involvement was led by Tim Wells, and Ian Davidson and Dermot Dwyer of NCC and Amir Tallaee of BT, on secondment to NPL, also made important contributions.

Selected publications on protocol implementation assessment 1980–87

K A Bartlett and D Rayner. The certification of data communication protocols. *Proc. IEEE Symposium on Trends and Applications: 1980, Computer Network Protocols*, held at the National Bureau of Standards, Washington, 29 May 1980, IEEE, 1980, pp.12–17.

D Rayner (ed.). Protocol implementation assessment: philosophy and architecture. NPL Report DNACS 44/81, April 1981; reprinted in Proc. INWG/NPL 1981 Workshop, see below, vol. 2, pp.55–72. Also reproduced in an abridged form in: *Innovative Telecommunications—Key to the Future*, Proc. National Telecommunications Conf., held in New Orleans, November–December 1981, IEEE, 1981, pp.1423–1427.

D Rayner and R W S Hale (eds). *Protocol Testing—Towards Proof?* Proc. INWG/NPL Workshop, held at NPL on 27–29 May 1981. Vol. 1: Specification and Validation; vol. 2: Testing and Certification. NPL, 1981.

R F L Henley (ed.). Implementation assessment of transport and network services: the Test Responder specification. NPL Report DNACS 46/81, July 1981.

D Rayner (ed.). A system for testing protocol implementations. NPL Report DITC 9/82, August 1982. Also published in a slightly earlier version in *Computer Networks*, 6, December 1982, pp.383–395. Other earlier versions were published (1) in C Sunshine (ed.), *Proc. Second Int. Workshop on Protocol Specification, Verification and Testing*, held in Idyllwild, California, 17–20 May 1982, North-Holland, 1982, pp.539–554; and (2) (under the title Protocol Implementation Assessment) in M B Williams (ed.), *Pathways to the Information Society: Proc. Sixth Int. Conf. on Computer Communications*, held in London, September 1982, North-Holland, 1982, pp.931–936.

D Rayner. Towards an objective understanding of conformance. In: H Rudin and C H West (eds), *Protocol Specification, Testing and Verification III, Proc. IFIP WG 6.1 Third Int. Workshop*, held in Rüschlikon, Switzerland, 31 May–2 June 1983, North Holland, 1983, pp.493–503.

P Oliver (ed.). Implementation assessment of a network service: the Test Responder specification. NPL Report DITC 32/83, September 1983.

P Oliver. Implementation assessment of a network service: the Test Responder exerciser specification. NPL Report DITC 44/84, June 1984.

J R Pavel and D J Dwyer. Some experiences of testing protocol implementations. NPL Report DITC 48/84, September 1984.

H-X Zeng and D Rayner. Gateway testing techniques. NPL Report DITC 49/84, October 1984.

P W Hobson (ed.). Implementation assessment of the OSI Network Service: the Test Definition Language. NPL Report DITC 52/84, December 1984.

J R Pavel. A new approach to the design and construction of protocol testers. NPL Report DITC 54/85, March 1985.

G W Cowin. The Scenario Test Driver for the ISO Network Convergence Protocol over X.25 (1980). NPL Report DITC 55/85, June 1985.

A J W Carmichael, P W Hobson and A A Sweetman (eds). Implementation assessment of the OSI Network Service: the Test Responder Specification. NPL Report DITC 56/85, June 1985.

G W Cowin. Overview of a Test Suite for the ISO Network Convergence Protocol over X.25 (1980). NPL Report DITC 59/85, June 1985.

H-X Zeng and D Rayner. The impact of the ferry concept on protocol testing. In: M Diaz (ed.), *Protocol Specification, Testing and Verification V,*

Proc. IFIP WG 6.1 5th International Workshop, held in Toulouse-Moissac, France, 10–13 June 1985, North-Holland, 1986, pp.519–531.

G W Cowin and S E Hambly. Implementation assessment of a network service: specification of a conformance test suite. NPL Report DITC 67/85, December 1985.

Open Systems Standards

In the late 1970s, applications software used the Transport Service (see p.146) directly, but it was clear that other common requirements ought also to be made the subject of standard protocols to avoid the wastefulness and confusion inevitable if there are many different conventions for expressing the same ideas. To conduct these protocols, extra layers of communications software would be needed between the transport layer and the applications.

This was the position when formal international standards work was started in 1978. The ISO committee developed a model of the communications process under the title of Open Systems Interconnection (OSI) which had seven layers altogether. It was designed to allow the applications software developer to gain independence from the suppliers of the communications hardware and software, and to promote free competition between these suppliers. It defined only what should go on in the communication process to express certain requirements; how this was to be achieved was up to the systems developers. For example, it was not necessary for every implementation to include seven separate identifiable modules of software or hardware: the functions of several layers could be combined in a single software module, or some functions could be omitted entirely if the particular application did not need them. The model thus was a *conceptual* model from which its users could select any logically consistent subset or *profile*. It did not say 'you must do all this'; instead it said 'if you have this need, meet it this way; then your implementation will interwork with others'. The lowest layer was the physical communications medium; each of the higher layers used the service provided by the layer below and provided a 'value-added' service to the layer above, as described on p.146. The principles of this Open Systems architecture are at the heart of the Internet and all modern computer communications.

The standards developed by the ISO committee with the support of its national counterparts covered both the services (provided by one layer to the layer above) and the protocols (rules governing interactions between communicating modules at the same level, achieved by using the lower layers). A massive set of standards was slowly built up, the main one being ISO 7498, the Open Systems Interconnection Basic Reference Model (ref. 77; a less formal account is given in ref. 72). NPL's particular contribution, through the British Standards Institution, to this complex undertaking was chiefly in two areas: file-transfer protocols (FTP), where the group had led the 'Blue Book' FTP Implementors' Group for some years, and the network and transport layers, where because of its early start in the networks field the NPL group had exceptionally long experience.

It soon became clear to its developers that if ISO 7498 was to be used effectively, testing services would be needed to assess products and systems for conformance with the new standards; and that the concepts and methods used in these services themselves had to be standardised if the test results were to be credible and consistent. Accordingly in February 1983 work began in ISO which was to lead to an International Standard on OSI Conformance Testing Methodology and Framework, ISO/IEC 9646 (ref. 78). Thanks to NPL's established lead in this area Dave Rayner was appointed as rapporteur of the international working group concerned and led the development throughout. It proved to be a major undertaking. By 1987 two parts of the standard had reached the Draft Proposal stage, and four more parts were in preparation. The continuation of this work is described in section 6.2.

Besides Keith Bartlett and Dave Rayner, other NPL staff contributing to the development of Open Systems standards in this era included Costas Solomonides, Vince Hathway, and Godfrey Cowin.

Selected publications on aspects of standard protocols other than implementation assessment 1979–86

N V Stenning. Definition and verification of computer network protocols. NPL Report DNACS 15/79, February 1979.

B E Aldous. The NPL implementation of Level 2 of the X.25 interface. NPL Report DNACS 18/79, May 1979.

D Rayner. Designing user interfaces for friendliness. In: D Beech (ed.), *Command Language Directions, Proc. IFIP Working Conference on Command Languages*, Berchtesgaden, 10–14 September 1979, North-Holland, 1980, pp.233–241.

A W Jones and D Rayner. UK network-independent file transfer protocol. *Kommunikation in verteilten Systemen* [Proc. workshop on communication in distributed systems, held in Berlin, 3–4 December 1979], Informatik-Fachberichte 22, Springer-Verlag, 1979, pp.110–120.

M J T Guy (ed.). A network-independent file transfer protocol. Revised by the DCPU FTP Implementors' Group, February 1981. [The 'Blue Book'.]

G W Cowin and D Rayner. Survey of NIFTP implementations. NPL Report DNACS 45/81, April 1981.

R W S Hale. File transfer protocols: comparison and critique. NPL Report DNACS 48/81, July 1981. Reproduced in an updated but reduced version under the same title in M B Williams (ed.), *Pathways to the Information Society: Proc. Sixth Int. Conf. on Computer Communications*, held in London, September 1982, North-Holland, 1982, pp.889–895.

B Cohen, D H Pitt and J C P Woodcock. The importance of time in the specification of OSI protocols: an overview and brief survey of the formalisms. NPL Report DITC 78/86, November 1986.

5.3 Data security

Without appropriate precautions, communication networks are inherently insecure. Messages might be read by unauthorised persons, or worse might be maliciously altered; fraudulent messages might be generated and inserted into the network. From the early days of networks, these possibilities had to be taken seriously for all commercial applications, and for many of them, such as banking, security was paramount. The threats were clear; luckily, it was also clear that the computer systems which sent and received the messages could be used to help overcome the problems. The basic requirement was for messages to be encrypted before they were sent, and decrypted on arrival.

OFCHY CHKMU PCSBU GVEAU FEHQU NSUMB
LMTLR OSLKH AUSLP EJOXH

Codes have a perennial fascination. What does it mean? How can you find out? Can you devise a better method of encryption? If so, how might the cryptanalyst attack it? More philosophically, how is it that meaning can be so totally hidden in such a simple string of characters, and yet be quite intact? When these intellectual challenges are combined with the intricacies of the technology of modern cryptography and the commercial importance outlined above, it is no wonder that Donald Davies decided in 1977 that the Division should start a new programme in this area and that he should lead it personally. As already mentioned, he was able to realise his plans in the following year when he managed to exchange his responsibilities as Superintendent of the Division of Computer Science for freedom to spend time on technical work.

The first task of the new Data Security group (at first in the Computing Technology Unit but soon to move to DNACS) was to familiarise itself with the state of the art in civil applications of computer cryptography. There were two recent important developments. The first was the publication in January 1977 of a Data Encryption Standard (DES) by the US National Bureau of Standards. This algorithm had several notable strengths. First it was fully public. Secondly no one was known to have developed a practical method of breaking it, in spite of an open invitation to do so. Thirdly the encryption and decryption algorithms were closely similar. Fourthly it had the important property that the key in use could not be deduced in practice even when a block of plaintext and its corresponding cyphertext were known (though this would be possible in principle given sufficient resources of computing power). And finally it had the backing of the US Department of Commerce, and later of the standards institutions, which meant that it was likely to be widely used.

The other important recent development, also American, was the invention of *public key cryptosystems*. In these systems a pair of keys is used, one for encryption and one for decryption (the two are logically related). Each participant in the communicating group has a unique pair of keys, one of which (his/her *private key*) must be kept secret while the other (his/her *public key*) must be published to all concerned. Then anyone wishing to send a secure message first encrypts it using the *receiver's* public key; the receiver then decrypts it using his/her private key. The surprising thing is that both algorithms, the public key and the cyphertext can all be public knowledge without anyone being able to read the message except the intended recipient. The feasibility of public key crypto-systems was shown in 1976 by Diffie and Hellman (ref. 38), and a practical system was devised in 1978 by Rivest, Shamir and Adleman (ref. 129).

Public key systems have a further striking and useful property: they can be used to give a message a *digital signature*—a means by which someone receiving a message can be confident that it comes from its purported sender and not from an impersonator. To achieve this the sender first 'encrypts' the message using his/her own private key. The receiver tries to 'decrypt' it using the sender's public key. If this reveals a sensible plaintext the receiver can be sure it came from the purported sender because no one else would have had the private key necessary to scramble it in just this way. Of course anyone else could unscramble the message and come to the same conclusion, so the signing process in itself confers no confidentiality; if signature and confidentiality are both required then the two distinct processes can be applied in tandem.

Having thoroughly understood these and other current developments, the group was in a position to start building its reputation as a UK centre of excellence in civil applications of computer security techniques. Group members compiled annotated bibliographies, listed below, of current papers; they studied methods of managing keys; they identified particular keys which should be avoided with DES because they gave less security than normal; they studied network protocols with security built in; they held a well-attended course on security in data communication at NPL in May 1981 (ref. 35); they made a major contribution to the development of data security standards, providing chairmen for both the national and international committees; and they developed a Message Authenticator Algorithm (MAA), based on the digital signature principle, which later formed the basis of an International Standard (ref. 74). As a result of these activities and involvement in commercial lecturing and publishing (notably a book by Davies and Price, ref. 36), they succeeded in attracting considerable consultancy business. All the major UK clearing banks, for instance, used their services at some time in this period.

In 1982 a consortium was formed by NPL and the British Technology Group with several UK companies to develop the technology and application of active tokens such as 'smart cards'; this work is described separately below. The Data Security group also undertook a joint project with the Software Engineering group in 1984–85 to develop a device for the protection of software; this is described in section 5.5.

Donald Davies led the group until his retirement in 1984, when he was succeeded by Wyn Price; these two formed the successful consultancy team. The other members of the group were Bernard Chorley, Graeme Parkin, Chez Ciechanowicz and Michael Lewis.

Selected publications on data security up to 1987

1. Bibliographies and general accounts

D W Davies and D A Bell. The protection of data by cryptography. NPL Report Com Sci 98, January 1978.

D A Bell and S E Olding. An annotated bibliography of cryptography. NPL Report Com Sci 100, January 1978.

W L Price. A further annotated bibliography of cryptography as applied to data protection in computing. NPL Report CTU 2, March 1979.

D W Davies and W L Price. An annotated bibliography of recent publications on data security and cryptography. NPL Report DNACS 25/80, January 1980.

W L Price. A fourth annotated bibliography of recent publications on data security and cryptography. NPL Report DNACS 33/80, September 1980.

D W Davies and W L Price. Selected papers in cryptography and data security. NPL Report DNACS 38/80, November 1980.

[D W Davies and W L Price.] A course on security in data communication, 21–22 May 1981. NPL, 1981.

W L Price. A fifth annotated bibliography of recent publications on data security and cryptography. NPL Report DITC 4/82, March 1982.

D M Yates. Security in computer-controlled information systems. In: A Malcolm and J Poyser (eds), *Computers and the General Practitioner*, Pergamon Press, 1982, pp.29–35.

W L Price. A sixth annotated bibliography of recent publications on data security and cryptography. NPL Report DITC 35/83, December 1983.

W L Price. The application of encipherment for data security in the public domain. In: P Zorkoczy (ed.), *Oxford Surveys in Information Technology 1*, Oxford University Press, 1984, pp.153–174.

W L Price. Seventh annotated bibliography of recent publications on data security and cryptography. NPL Report DITC 64/85, August 1985.

2. Special topics

D W Davies. New techniques for cryptography in networks. *Proc. Eurocomp 78*, Online, 1978, pp.121–132.

D W Davies, W L Price and G I Parkin. An evaluation of public key cryptosystems. NPL Report CTU 1, March 1979.

D W Davies and W L Price. A protocol for secure communication. NPL Report DNACS 21/79, November 1979.

D W Davies and W L Price. The application of digital signatures based on public key cryptosystems. In: J Salz (ed.), *Computer Communications: Increasing Benefits for Society. Proc. 5th Int. Conf. on Computer Communications*, held in Atlanta, October 1980, North-Holland, 1980, pp.525–530. Reprinted in an extended form as NPL Report DNACS 39/80, December 1980.

D W Davies. Enhancement of Teletex procedures to incorporate encipherment and signatures. NPL Report DNACS 42/81, April 1981.

W L Price and D W Davies. Issues in the design of a key distribution centre. NPL Report DNACS 43/81, April 1981.

B J Chorley and G I Parkin. A revised definition of a secure communication protocol and its implementation. NPL Report DITC 5/82, April 1982.

D W Davies and I K Hirst. Encipherment and signature in Teletex. In: M B Williams (ed.), *Pathways to the Information Society: Proc. Sixth Int. Conf. on Computer Communications*, held in London, September 1982, North-Holland, 1982, pp.401–406.

W L Price. Encryption implementation in a layered network architecture. In: M B Williams (ed.), *Pathways to the Information Society: Proc. Sixth Int. Conf. on Computer Communications*, held in London, September 1982, North-Holland, 1982, pp.883–887.

G I Parkin. Enhancement of the CCITT Teletex recommendations to incorporate encipherment and signatures. NPL Report DITC 11/82, October 1982.

D W Davies and D O Clayden. A message authenticator suitable for a main frame computer. NPL Report DITC 17/83, February 1983.

W L Price. Standards for data security, a status report. *Networks 84, Proc. European Computer Communications Conf.*, held in London, July 1984, Online, 1984, pp.271–282.

D W Davies and W L Price. Digital signatures—an update. *Proc. Seventh Int. Conf. on Computer Communications*, held in Sydney, October 1984, pp.845–849; also produced as NPL Report DITC 51/84, October 1984.

A A Aruliah, G I Parkin and B A Wichmann. A Pascal implementation of the DES Encryption Algorithm including Cipher Block Chaining. NPL Report DITC 61/85, June 1985.

A A Aruliah. A Pascal implementation of the RSA algorithm. NPL Report DITC 66/85, September 1985.

W L Price. Survey of key management for data encipherment. NPL Report DITC 70/86, March 1986.

Tokens and Transactions Control Consortium

In the 1980s, a recommended way of ensuring that an NPL work programme was relevant to the needs of commerce and industry was to establish a *club,* a group of firms willing to pay a subscription to be kept in touch with the results of the work and to give their views on its direction at regular meetings. From the Requirements Board's viewpoint, a flourishing club was an excellent indicator of the health of a project. In practice the clear benefits of establishing a club were offset by some disadvantages: the natural reluctance of commercial rivals to disclose their main research interests to each other, the extra burden of reporting and administrative work thrown on the research team, and the inevitable exclusion of non-members of the club which tended to weaken NPL's status as a public institution and give it a more commercial ethos (as no doubt was intended).

In 1982 a club was established by the British Technology Group, in collaboration with the NPL Data Security group, to develop the technology of machine-readable cards and tokens for the control of access to computer systems and accommodation,

The Albasiny era: 1978–1987

and for the conduct of financial transactions. It was called the Tokens and Transactions Control Consortium (TTCC), and attracted a strong membership of both suppliers and users, including at various times Thorn-EMI, Texas Instruments, Racal Guardata, the Post Office, Plessey, Pitney Bowes, Philips Business Systems, ICL, National Girobank, GEC, Fortronic, Ferranti, British Telecom and the Association for Payment Clearing Services (APACS) on behalf of the banks.

At first the club acted primarily as an information clearing house, with NPL contributing up-to-date information on the state of the art in data security techniques and standards, and the companies explaining their needs and interests. Later, in addition, studies and experimental work were carried out by NPL or subcontractors for the Consortium, and in particular the NPL group developed a prototype token, as described below.

Those contributing to the work of the Consortium on behalf of the British Technology Group were Peter Hawkes and David Clayden (who joined BTG following his retirement from NPL in 1981).

The NPL Intelligent Token

A *token* in this context is a plastic card or other small device containing memory and logic in the form of one or more integrated circuits (chips). Its primary purpose is to help establish the identity of its holder, and it can where appropriate keep an internal record of transactions or personal data. Most schemes, both in the 1980s and at the time of writing, have used tokens the same size as credit cards (although at first they were rather thicker); they are called *smart cards* to distinguish them from the common (and still dominant) magnetic stripe cards, which of course have no internal circuit. The advantages of smart cards

Figure 49. Data security: the prototype NPL Token, January 1988.

over the earlier technology are twofold: their processing power can make them more secure, and they are more difficult to copy; however the rough treatment that holders sometimes give their cards can be tough on the integrated circuits, making the smart card less robust.

One of the weaknesses of both magnetic stripe and conventional smart cards is their vulnerability to bugged terminals. Suppose a smart card is inserted in a point-of-sale terminal. The user will have to type in a personal identification number (PIN). The system compares this with a stored record using information on the card before allowing the transaction. But if the terminal is bugged so that the various interchanges are recorded, impostors can gain enough information to help them repeat the transaction fraudulently if they can steal the card or make one like it. Other types of fraud are possible if the thief can control the display on the machine.

The NPL design had two unique features which made it much more secure than the conventional smart card. First it included its own display and keypad (like a calculator), so avoiding the bugged terminal problem (the PIN, for instance, was not passed to the terminal). Secondly it used digital signatures based on a public key cryptosystem, as described above, to prevent impersonation. To use the token, it was first connected to the terminal. Then the user typed in the PIN on the token's keypad. At the same time the terminal sent the token a random number. The token checked that the PIN was correct and, if so, signed the random number and returned it to the terminal. The terminal checked the signature and if it was correct the terminal could be logically satisfied that the real owner had presented the token. From this point on the details of the interaction would vary with the type of application (whether it was access control, point-of-sale, or whatever).

The disadvantage of the NPL 'super smart card' was that while a production version could be made a good deal more compact than the prototype shown in fig. 49, it could not actually be reduced to credit-card dimensions with current technology because of the display requirement. It might well be of course that the greatly increased security made slight extra bulk worthwhile.

Ten years later smart cards, whether super or otherwise, are not in wide use despite many trials. Their technical superiority is not in doubt, but the change will presumably only be made when the losses from fraud with magnetic stripe cards exceed the cost of changing to a more secure technology. Super smart cards have not gone away.

Publications on personal identity verification and the NPL Token

W L Price. A review of methods of personal identity verification. NPL Report DITC 73/86, July 1986.

B J Chorley and W L Price. An intelligent token for secure transactions. NPL Report DITC 85/87, January 1987.

B J Chorley and W L Price. Design, development and application of an intelligent token. *Computer Communications,* 11(6), December 1988, pp.299–303.

5.4 Multiprocessors

If a large computer costs £100,000 or more, but small ones cost only a few hundred pounds each, it is natural to ask whether the work of the large machine might be done more cheaply by a collaborating group of smaller units. This idea was the main reason for the establishment in the Division of Computer Science in mid-1976 of a group to investigate the design of a *multiprocessor,* a device which behaved to the outside world like a computer but internally shared out tasks amongst several processors working in parallel. Such a system would need both complex systems software, to manage the collaboration between the processors, and novel hardware in the form of a powerful internal communication system to enable programs and data to be moved round fast. In the new NPL project the design work on software was led by Peter Wilkinson and that on hardware by Peter Vaswani.

Multiprocessors were seen as suitable for situations where (1) a computer was dedicated to a single application, and (2) this task was naturally divisible into parts which could proceed in parallel. Scrapbook (see section 4.3) and Edit (section 4.7) were good contemporary examples of the type, and there were many others including transaction processing, plant and process control, and telecommunications. Because real-time applications of this kind are commonly written as a set of communicating processes, they lend themselves well to the multiprocessor architecture, and the control task becomes one of farming out processes to the constituent computers and then managing the interactions between them during execution.

Besides being potentially cheap compared with equivalent conventional machines, multiprocessors were seen as more robust (because the loss of a processor should mean that the performance of the system degrades gracefully instead of crashing), and also more flexible, in the sense that new units could readily be added if demand grew.

The NPL multiprocessor design was a collaborative effort by Wilkinson and Vaswani and their colleagues Mark Dowson, Vic Stenning and Robert Milne. Called Demos, it was based on a communications ring like an endless conveyor belt, carrying a fixed number of fixed-length slots at a fast rate (6.25 MHz with 16 bits in parallel). This ring had to be cheap, modular in construction and reliable. Connected to it were the microcomputers, of which there could in principle be over a hundred.

A computer with data to send had to wait for a free slot to put it into, adding the destination address at the same time. Technically this had some similarities to some designs of local computer networks, but in Demos the computers were organised as one unit with a single task, rather than being autonomous and geographically separate devices of various types with disparate purposes, as in a network. In late 1977 a collaborative project was started with the systems house Scicon Ltd to build a prototype system based on these plans.

After much preliminary thinking about alternative approaches, the Demos software design was based on the use of Concurrent Pascal, a language designed for the development of systems consisting of communicating processes. The idea was that the applications program would be written in exactly the same way as for a conventional computer. If it was run on Demos, the processes would really run in parallel, unlike a conventional system in which the time of the single processor has to be shared between all the current processes to give the effect of parallel running. To set up the system, the Concurrent Pascal program would first be compiled, and the compiler output fed to the main Demos software package, called Sysgen. Sysgen would then interact with the system manager to get details of the available hardware (number of processors and memory sizes) and to allocate modules of software to individual processors; it would then give the small resident executive software in each machine instructions on where to send results from each of its modules.

By 1979 Scicon had won a contract to provide a satellite simulation system for the European Space Technology Centre based on Demos software running on Texas 990 microcomputers; they were also planning a version of Demos using Ada in place of Concurrent Pascal.

The prototype Demos system at NPL consisted of three Ferranti Argus 700F minicomputers linked by the Mark I ring described above. By 1982 a new ring was in experimental use with four Intel 8086 microprocessors. It was eight-bit parallel, with a variable packet size up to 64 bytes and could interconnect up to 256 devices. This Mark II ring was demonstrated at the Open Day in November 1982 (see fig. 50); it was more reliable and much cheaper than the earlier version. Scicon had by then developed a process-control system using Demos software on their own 8086-based multiprocessor DEMOS-86.

At this point work on Demos itself was terminated, but the possibility of using the Mark II ring as the basis for a local network was explored briefly under the heading of Integrated Services Local Networks. The idea was that the ring would remain compact, but would have computers connected to it by long serial, possibly fibreoptic, links. Discussions with a company interested in developing a product based on this plan reached a quite

The Albasiny era: 1978–1987

Figure 50. Multiprocessors: the final ring-port being inserted in a four-processor Demos system, with Peter Wilkinson, Peter Neale and Peter Vaswani, November 1982.

advanced stage but in the end no deal acceptable to all the parties involved could be achieved.

Most of the NPL staff contributing to the Demos development have already been mentioned, but Peter Neale also assisted Peter Vaswani on the design and development of the rings. The Scicon staff most involved were Barry Brinkman, Brian Collins and Brian McBride.

Publications on Demos

P T Neale. Problems in designing a high-speed linear data bus for a multimicroprocessor system. NPL Report Com 89, January 1977.

M Dowson. The Demos multiple processor: technical summary. NPL Report Com 102, April 1978.

M Dowson, P T Wilkinson, B Collins, B McBride and R Milne. The Demos multiple processor. In: P A Samet (ed.), *EURO IFIP 79*, North-Holland, 1979, pp.679–684.

P T Neale. The Demos multicomputer ring: the ring closer. NPL Report DNACS 36/80, October 1980.

P K T Vaswani. The Demos multi-computer project: hardware aspects. NPL Report DITC 36/84, January 1984.

P T Neale. Elastic buffers for digital rings. NPL Report DITC 38/84, January 1984.

In addition to these reports on Demos, Bernard Chorley made a general study of multiprocessor architectures for an MSc thesis, which was reproduced as a divisional report:

B J Chorley. Multiple processor systems. NPL Report Com 99, January 1978.

5.5 Software engineering standards

No one doubts that an aircraft or a bridge should be built and maintained in accordance with sound engineering practice, using staff and tools demonstrably fit for their purpose. The use of the term 'software engineering' implies a belief that just the same considerations apply to the construction and maintenance of computer software. It too is a complex technical product whose failures are costly and potentially dangerous, and so its developers need their own disciplines, tools, standards and codes of practice designed to ensure that programs work efficiently and reliably.

In this spirit a new Programming Language Standards group was established in DNACS in January 1981, built round the talents of Brian Wichmann, Mike Woodger and Roger Scowen. Besides contributing to the production of programming language standards, the aim of the group was to promote their effectiveness, especially through the development of methods of testing compilers. The languages chosen were Pascal, Ada and Prolog; a standard metalanguage for use in defining programming languages was also developed. In 1983 the remit of the group was widened and its name changed to Software Engineering Standards. Two new projects were undertaken: a collaborative project to develop a Pascal program validation system, and a joint venture with the Data Security group to develop a novel technique for preventing software piracy, the Software Protection Device. These projects are described in turn below.

Pascal compiler validation

The programming language Pascal, developed by Niklaus Wirth of Zürich in 1969–70 in the Algol tradition, gradually established itself as one of the most popular languages in general use worldwide, particularly in education and research. Inevitably, variants arose; and because this meant that Pascal programs could no longer always be moved readily from one computer system to another, there was counter-pressure for standardisation. This need was met by a British-led initiative which resulted in an International Standard for Pascal, ISO 7185, in October 1981, published in the form of a British Standard, BS 6192, in February 1982.

In 1979 Brian Wichmann started a collaboration with Arthur Sale of the University of Tasmania aimed at the development of a series of tests for Pascal compilers. The reasoning behind this work was that since software faults are costly and sometimes dangerous, any fault in a compiler would be particularly damaging because it could potentially affect all programs processed by the compiler. What is needed is a *validation suite,* a set of programs for submission to the compiler which is designed to test it thoroughly. Both valid and invalid programs will be included in the suite, because it is as important that a compiler shall reject invalid code—with appropriate diagnostic information to help the programmer find the fault—as it is for valid programs to be compiled correctly. Besides tests based strictly on language standards, it may be useful to include quality checks; for example, the validation suite for Pascal compilers developed by Sale and Wichmann included checks on the accuracy of the trigonometric and other mathematical functions. By 1982 this suite consisted of 553 separate programs, and about 400 copies had been sold worldwide. A conference on Pascal compiler validation was held at NPL in February 1982 and its proceedings (ref. 154) published the following year.

Testing tools such as the Pascal suite can be used in three ways: *first-party testing*, in which the supplier has a copy of the tool and tests his product before copies of it are sold; *second-party testing*, in which the purchaser tests what he has bought before accepting it; and *third-party testing*, in which an experienced, independent and demonstrably competent body carries out the tests for anyone who will pay them to do so. In practice, second-party testing is only feasible for large-scale purchasers. Market forces will determine which of the other two methods is more used; purchasers often prefer third-party testing, which is seen to be unbiased; manufacturers tend to like first-party testing, where the testing is entirely under their control and any problems can be resolved in-house.

The DTI's policy in this area was to promote the quality of UK products by encouraging the establishment of third-party testing laboratories, accredited by NAMAS to establish their competence, and then leave market forces to determine how they developed. In the case of Pascal compilers, this policy led to the establishment of a successful validation service by BSI Quality Assurance Services (BSI-QAS) with technical advice from NPL; the service issued its first two certificates in September 1983.

Brian Wichmann led this work for NPL, with help from Chez Ciechanowicz and collaboration from Arthur Sale as already mentioned; John Charter and John Souter of BSI-QAS established the Pascal Compiler Validation Service.

Publications on Pascal compiler validation

B A Wichmann and A H J Sale. A Pascal processor validation suite. NPL Report CSU 7/80, March 1980.

R S Scowen and Z J Ciechanowicz. Compiler validation—a survey. NPL Report CSU 8/81, December 1980.

B A Wichmann. Latest results from the procedure calling test, Ackermann's function. NPL Report DITC 3/82, March 1982. [Includes reprints of two earlier papers on the same subject.]

B A Wichmann and I D Hill. A pseudo-random number generator. NPL Report DITC 6/82, June 1982.

B A Wichmann. A note on the accuracy of two microprocessors. NPL Report DITC 18/83, February 1983.

B A Wichmann and Z J Ciechanowicz (eds). Pascal compiler validation. John Wiley and Sons, 1983.

Z J Ciechanowicz and B A Wichmann. A readers' guide to Pascal compiler validation reports (amended). NPL Report DITC 24/83, October 1983.

D A Joslin and B A Wichmann. A survey of extensions in Pascal implementations. NPL Report DITC 69/86, January 1986.

R S Smith and B A Wichmann. A survey of restrictions in Pascal implementations. NPL Report DITC 72/86, April 1986.

Pascal program validation

The group's change of name from Programming Language Standards to Software Engineering Standards in 1983 reflected an intention to shift the emphasis from compilers to the whole toolset available to those developing, testing and maintaining software. The first work undertaken with this wider remit was a collaborative project, funded by DTI under the Alvey initiative, to develop a prototype Pascal program validation system (PPPVS). Four other organisations were involved, including ICL and Liverpool University, and work on the two-year project started in October 1984.

The aim was to develop a collection of software quality assessment tools with a common environment to ensure compatibility. Some of the tools were developed as part of the project and some already existed and were adapted for the PPPVS. There were two types of tool in the system, *static* and *dynamic*. A static tool takes the text of the program under test and analyses it. It might for example detect that if a certain path in the program was followed a value would be assigned to a certain variable without its previous value having been used—not necessarily an error, but an oddity worth pointing out to the programmer so that it can be checked. A dynamic tool actually runs the program under test, but in a controlled way so that its behaviour can be monitored. An example of a dynamic tool is the 'Statement Coverage Analyser' which checked that every statement in the program was executed at least once during a testing session. The tools all used a common database to hold the information they generated about the program under test. Once a testing session was complete, the system would produce a summary of its findings for the programmer or quality manager, who could find further detail if required in the database. More details can be found in the reports listed below.

Peter Wilkinson and Brian Wichmann led this work for NPL, with Guy O'Neill and Graeme Parkin.

Publications on Pascal program validation

B A Wichmann et al. A prototype Pascal program validation system. NPL Report DITC 57/85, March 1985.

B A Wichmann. Floating point interval arithmetic for validation. NPL Report DITC 76/86, October 1986.

P T Wilkinson, J A Bouchard, B A Byrne, M A Hennell, P Jackson, G O'Neill, G I Parkin and B A Wichmann. A prototype system for the validation of Pascal programs. NPL Report DITC 86/87, April 1987.

A W Idema. Validation tests for standard Pascal and extended Pascal. NPL Report DITC 108/88, February 1988.

G O'Neill and P T Wilkinson. Modularity in the Pascal Model Compiler. NPL Report DITC 111/88, January 1988.

A R Lawrence. Appraisal of prototype Pascal validation suite. NPL Report DITC 112/88, February 1988.

Ada

In 1975 Brian Wichmann was invited to a meeting in Washington called by the US Department of Defense. They had discovered that 350 programming languages were in use in their department, and not unnaturally felt that the possibility of replacing them with one standard language deserved exploration[2]. There was also a requirement for a language well suited to real-time applications in military equipment. It was clear that the needs were so diverse that none of the 350 would fit the bill, so preliminary requirements for a new language (the 351st!) were drafted. This draft was called Strawman, and it was followed by further drafts (Woodenman, Tinman, Ironman and Steelman) as the requirement became better defined. At the Ironman stage, tenders were invited for the design of a language to meet the requirements. Four designs were selected from those submitted; they were issued anonymously in blue, red, yellow and green covers so that the evaluators would judge them only on the merits of the design. In fact the first three were US-based, and the Green language was a European offering put forward by a CII-Honeywell Bull consortium led by Dr Jean Ichbiah.

At this stage Brian Wichmann became a consultant for the European bidders, advising on the numeric facilities, and he was a member of the small Green team in the final contest on a Washington stage in April 1979 where the representatives of the two remaining contenders, Red and Green, were grilled by 80 invited experts. On 2 May it was announced that the Green language had been successful; it was subsequently christened Ada in commemoration of the pioneer programmer Ada Countess of Lovelace (see box). Mike Woodger was also a consultant to the successful design team, in particular contributing extensively to the Ada Reference Manual (Ichbiah subsequently referred to him as an 'artist of technical writing'). His involvement is recorded in the Woodger Papers (ref. 180, section F).

---

[2] Mike Woodger tells me that 'the method of payment for military contracts made it in the interest of a contractor to include a language and its compiler—that is why there were so many different ones'.

❑ SIDELINE ❑ DETOUR ❑ DIGRESSION ❑ BYWAY ❑ SCENIC ROUTE ❑

The Ada Portrait

The name of the Ada language was chosen to commemorate Ada Countess of Lovelace, who published algorithms while collaborating with Charles Babbage in 1843; on the basis of this work they are regarded as the world's first programmers. This portrait of Ada was painted by Margaret Carpenter in 1835 and exhibited at the Royal Academy in 1836. The portrait was bought by the UK Government in 1953 and sent for display at the British Embassy in Athens. In the 1960s Donald Davies saw a reproduction of the picture, discovered with the help of Roger Meetham that it was in Athens, and persuaded the then Director, Dr J V Dunworth, to ask whether the picture could be moved to NPL in view of Ada's place in the history of computing. The Embassy were agreeable provided a suitable replacement was forthcoming, and the picture was duly hung in the entrance hall of Bushy House in 1968/69. In 1992, however, it was sadly lost to NPL when it was first removed for conservation work and then installed in the main reception room at No. 11 Downing St; as a notoriously reckless and unsuccessful gambler, Ada might smile at her new appointment to the household of the Chancellor of the Exchequer.

Augusta Ada née Byron aged 19, at the time of her marriage to Lord King, later Earl of Lovelace.

A five-day course on Ada was held at NPL in June 1979 to get UK industry off to a good start in the competition for the Ada-related contracts which were bound to follow its adoption. NPL itself was of course well placed to benefit from its early involvement, and subsequent work included contributions to the Ada standardisation process, monitoring DTI contracts on Ada (the results of this work were presented at a conference at NPL in September 1981), and a European contract on compiler validation. Perhaps the most important consequence for NPL was involvement in two further European contracts for work on mathematical software libraries in Ada, on which George Symm led the NPL contribution.

The design of Ada, which was based on that of Pascal, has proved controversial because of its complexity, though this was largely inevitable given the customer's requirements. For the same reason, it has not proved as popular outside the defence field as its proponents had hoped, but it is still an immensely influential language because of the purchasing power of the US military.

Publications on Ada

J D Ichbiah, B A Wichmann et al. Rationale for the design of the Ada programming language. *ACM Sigplan Notices,* 14(6), Part B, June 1979.

B A Wichmann. Ada is green. *Computer Bulletin,* series 2, 21, September 1979, pp.17,21.

R S Scowen. A cross-reference index for the syntax of the programming language Ada. NPL Report CSU 6, December 1979.

M G Cox and S J Hammarling. Evaluation of the language Ada for use in numerical computations. NPL Report DNACS 30/80, July 1980.

J C D Nissen, P Wallis, B A Wichmann et al. Ada-Europe guidelines for the portability of Ada programs. NPL Report DNACS 52/81, November 1981; second edition NPL Report DITC 27/83, July 1983.

J C D Nissen, B A Wichmann et al. Ada-Europe guidelines for Ada compiler specification and selection. NPL Report DITC 10/82, October 1982.

G T Symm, B A Wichmann, J Kok and D T Winter. Guidelines for the design of large modular scientific libraries in Ada. Interim report, NPL Report DITC 14/82, November 1982; second interim report, DITC 28/83, July 1983; final report, DITC 37/84, March 1984.

B A Wichmann. Tutorial material on the real data types in Ada. NPL Report DITC 34/83, January 1984.

P J L Wallis and B A Wichmann. Requirements analysis for Ada compilers. *Comm. ACM*, 27(1), January 1984, pp.37–41.

B A Wichmann. Is Ada too big? A designer answers the critics. *Comm. ACM*, 27(2), February 1984, pp.98–103.

B A Wichmann and J G J Meijerink. Converting to Ada packages. NPL Report DITC 39/84, March 1984.

J Kok and G T Symm. A proposal for standard basic functions in Ada. NPL Report DITC 45/84, June 1984.

G T Symm. Contributions to a numerical library in Ada. NPL Report DITC 98/87, August 1987.

D A Watt, W Findaly and B A Wichmann. *Ada: Language and Methodology*. Prentice-Hall, 1987.

Syntactic metalanguage

Programming languages have to be defined clearly and unambiguously, because programmers need to be able to check that the statements they write are valid, and that they carry the intended meaning. A good example was set by the designers of Algol, who gave a sequence of definitions starting with a basic character set, and defining each subsequent element in the language in terms of other elements already defined. To express these definitions they used a straightforward mathematical-style system of symbols which became known as *Backus–Naur Form* (BNF). Other language designers adopted this basic idea of having a *syntactic metalanguage* in which to express their definitions, but they did so in a variety of ways which could confuse the programmer. Clearly a standard was needed, and Roger Scowen developed a proposal based on BNF which resulted in a new British Standard Syntactic Metalanguage, BS 6154; an identical international standard was published in 1996 as ISO/IEC 14977. Details are given in these two reports:

R S Scowen. An introduction to the standard syntactic metalanguage. NPL Report DNACS 47/81, July 1981.

R S Scowen. An introduction and handbook for the standard syntactic metalanguage. NPL Report DITC 19/83, February 1983.

Prolog standardisation

The programming language Prolog was invented in France in the early 1970s. It works very differently from conventional (algorithmic) computer languages. A Prolog program consists of a collection of statements declaring what entities it is concerned with and what relations hold between them. This program is read by the Prolog processor (a normal algorithmic program) which absorbs and organises the facts and is then able to answer questions about them. Prolog is thus best suited to problems involving substantial bodies of data with complex rules governing their interrelations, such as expert systems, databases, and the analysis of texts in both natural and formal languages.

As the use of Prolog spread, dialects were developed and an international standard became necessary to avoid waste of effort. Roger Scowen played a major part in coordinating UK input to the standardisation process, chairing the BSI committees and ISO working group concerned and making a substantial personal technical contribution as project editor; he also supervised a contract for the development of a validation suite for Prolog processors. The standard was to have a long gestation period, but finally saw the light of day in 1995 as ISO/IEC 13211:1995.

Software protection

Computer software is easy and cheap to copy. If copies are given away or sold illegally, the original suppliers are being cheated out of some revenue, an offence known as *software piracy*. If some way could be found to tailor each legitimate copy of the software so that it would only work in its home environment, any pirate copies would be useless. Such a system would clearly have to cost less than the losses to the suppliers it was designed to prevent.

On this basis several techniques for software protection were developed in the 1980s. Some involved arranging the software so that it would only run if the user gave a password, or if the user could tell the system what word appeared in a random place in a manual (thus showing that he/she had a copy of it). If the computer had a unique serial number which was available to the software, this could be inserted in the software before the sale was completed and subsequently checked each time the software was run. These all helped against casual fraud, but an expert could find and bypass the checking routine, and once this was done pirate copies would work anywhere.

A stronger scheme was to make the working of the program dependent on the presence of a particular piece of hardware, a *Software Protection Device* (SPD). This could either be plugged in to one of the computer's ports or held internally. Of course if the software simply checked for the presence of this device, the check could be bypassed as before; the device must do something logically vital to the correct running of the software.

In 1984–85 Brian Wichmann, Bernard Chorley, Graeme Parkin and Simon Elsom designed (and patented) a device on these lines based on the principle of public key cryptosystems (see p.210). The device consisted of a microprocessor inside a sealed box. The software was held in the main computer as usual, except that part of it was encrypted. This part was passed to the SPD to decrypt and run. Each SPD had its own private key held internally; its public key was available to any supplier wishing to encrypt software for it (see box for more details). An important element in the security of the system was that the device was tamper resistant in the sense that any attempt to open it or otherwise get at its contents resulted in the loss of the private key it contained.

A club of interested companies was formed to support this development, but although technically successful the SPD did not catch on more widely. Probably the reason is that software protection devices offer nothing to the user, or to the computer manufacturer, and involve considerable organisation; the one who benefits is the software supplier. This benefit might be shared with users by reducing prices on protected software, but it is less clear how the computer manufacturer could be persuaded that it was in his interest to include a built-in software protection device (and external devices don't appeal to users). Software piracy is not the first case of a problem for which technology has provided a solution, but where commercial realities have determined that for the time being at least the solution will not be used.

Besides those mentioned above an important contribution to this work was made by Derrick Grover of the British Technology Group.

❑ SIDELINE ❑ DETOUR ❑ DIGRESSION ❑ BYWAY ❑ SCENIC ROUTE ❑

Details of the Software Protection Device

To avoid the need for the supplier to encrypt each copy of the software differently, a two-stage process was used. The supplier coded all copies of the software with the same key, using the DES system (see p.210). Then only this DES key, and the duration of the licence if applicable, were encrypted using the SPD's public key and inserted into the software at the time of sale. When the software was to be run, these two items were passed to the SPD, which decrypted them using its private key. Then the DES-encrypted software was passed to the SPD, which could now decrypt it and run it (providing the licence had not expired), passing the results back to the main system.

This complex but very secure technique meant that each user only needed one SPD, however many items of protected software were to be run; it also allowed back-up copies to be made and enabled fixed-duration licences to be sold.

B J Chorley, G I Parkin, B A Wichmann and S M Elsom (inventors). Software protection device. UK Patent No. 2,163,577, date of application 20 August 1985.

G I Parkin and B A Wichmann. Intelligent modules. In: D Grover (ed.), *The Protection of Computer Software—its Technology and Applications,* Cambridge University Press, 1989, pp.106–118.

5.6 Mathematical software

In 1978 the Numerical Analysis Branch of the newly established DNACS was finding it difficult to persuade the Requirements Board that their work deserved long-term support at the existing level. The Division argued that numerical mathematics was a vital element in most work in science and engineering, and that experience showed that continuing research produced useful results, even though this progress was less visible to those outside the field than advances in, say, computer technology. The Board was not fully convinced. The Division felt this was largely because of the way the Requirements Board system had been established: it was not too surprising that a Computers, Systems and Electronics Board took this line, and if there had been an Applied Mathematics Board, things might have been very different. However, the system was fixed, and the Board's misgivings meant that there was great pressure on the Branch to increase their income if they were to avoid a major reduction in strength. Sustained efforts were made to meet the Board's financial targets, but a cloud of anxiety, defensiveness and some resentment had by now largely replaced the blue skies of confidence and stability which prevailed in the earlier years of Mathematics Division.

The new emphasis on finances meant that relations with the Numerical Algorithms Group (see p.186) had to be put on a more politically correct footing. This group had been established as a collaborative venture between academic institutions (from each according to his ability, to each according to his need), with costs covered by sales. At the time, this seemed like a common-sense approach, and NPL contributed algorithms without charge; but now this was not at all the tune the Division was being told to sing. David Martin, as head of the Branch, had the unenviable task of not only telling NAG that they would be asked to pay for any future contributions from NPL, but also persuading them to pay for a licence to sell copies of NPL's past contributions. He succeeded in this without damaging the Division's good working relations with NAG, and an agreement was signed in December 1982.

But in spite of this and other successful contracts, pressure on NPL to reduce staff numbers eventually meant that the threatened cuts in the Branch were not averted. In accordance with a decision by the Director, its strength was reduced from 26 to 11 between 1978 and 1982, and the Numerical Analysis Branch was abolished as such in 1983, though some of the work continued in a new Mathematical Analysis and Software group. David Martin's post went with the Branch, and he retired in August 1983. The surviving group was led by Maurice Cox.

With staff numbers cut by more than half, the areas of work covered had to be drastically reduced. Linear algebra research virtually ended with the retirement in 1980 of its distinguished pioneer, Jim Wilkinson, and work on optimisation was also wound up in 1981. In the two remaining areas, data approximation and differential equations, a wide variety of short-term application projects were undertaken, of which one or two examples are given below. To complement the short projects, the group needed a longer-term theme, and this was duly identified in 1983 under the heading of Algorithms for Metrology; this work also is described further below. As explained in the Introduction, no mathematical detail on these subjects is given here, and the interested reader is referred to the cited reports.

Data fitting and approximation: examples

It is said that a man once parked his horse and cart outside a pub in Cheshire and went in for a drink; when he emerged both had disappeared down a large hole which had opened up in the ground. If true, this was one of the more dramatic examples of a problem which has plagued the county for many years: subsidence caused by the past practice of pumping brine from underground to extract the salt. Because of the cost of damage to buildings and roads, and the potential danger to the public, surveys are now carried out periodically in areas where brine has been extracted to check the ground levels for any movement that might indicate the onset of subsidence. What the surveyor does is to choose an (irregular) set of points covering the area of interest; typically there are between 500 and 1000 of these. Then, using a theodolite, he measures the difference in height of many adjacent pairs of these points; typically there would be two or three times as many measurements as there are points. Such a survey has two aims: firstly to derive a mean corrected level for each point, and secondly to compare this level with the level of the same point in previous surveys of the same area to detect any change.

From this point on, the problem is one of numerical mathematics: how to determine the mean corrected levels. The observational data are intentionally *over-determined;* that is they will appear to be slightly inconsistent because each observation will have a small error. What is needed is a value for each height which best fits the observed differences. In work carried out in 1978 commissioned by ICI Ltd, Maurice Cox showed that the existing methods for carrying out these calculations could be much improved; he also developed further statistical calculations to help detect the onset of subsidence. The people of Cheshire (and the cars parked outside their pubs) are now just a little safer as a result of his work.

Another area to which numerical analysis makes an unexpected and inconspicuous but vital contribution is the measurement of minute concentrations of particular substances in body fluids. Drug testing for international athletes catches the headlines, and of course there is much routine work of the same kind in hospital and forensic laboratories. The technique concerned is called *radioimmunoassay*. To measure the concentration of a specific substance S in a given sample, the first move is to add to the sample a controlled amount of S in which each molecule has been tagged with a radioactive marker. Then a small quantity of antibodies to substance S is mixed in. When the antibodies have had time to bind with molecules of S, the sample is divided using standard chemical techniques in such a way that the antibodies, together with the molecules of S to which they have bound, are in one part, while the remaining free molecules of S are in the other part. The radioactivity of each part is measured, and the ratio of the two values calculated. Now if say there was no S in the original sample, all the bound S will be radioactive, so the ratio (bound/free) will be as high as it can be; whereas if there were many molecules of S in the original sample, they will provide a good proportion of the bound molecules, and since they are not radioactive the bound/free ratio will be lower. Before any real samples are tested, the process is carried out with a set of artificial samples with known concentrations of S, and a graph drawn of the bound/free ratio against the concentration. When a real sample has been tested, the observed bound/free ratio can then be compared with this curve, and the concentration simply read off.

The numerical technique of course comes in in the 'drawing' of the curve; it is not a curve on paper but a curve represented in a computer, chosen as the best fit with the data which is also consistent with the theory of the chemical process. In an exhaustive series of experiments the method was proved to be more reliable than earlier techniques in which the curve fitting did not make use of the chemical theory, and NPL's method became widely used. The work was carried out by Maurice Cox, Helen Jones (later Dr Anthony), and Enid Long in collaboration with the Middlesex Hospital; later work was commissioned by Amersham International.

Reports on level surveys and radioimmunoassay

M G Cox. The least squares adjustment of errors in level surveys. NPL Report DNACS 9/78, October 1978.

M G Cox, E M R Long and P G Malan. On fitting the general form of a fundamental physical model of radioimmunoassay. NPL Report DNACS 27/80, April 1980.

M G Cox and H M Jones. An automatic algorithm for immunoassay curve calibration using controlled quadratic splines. NPL Report DITC 116/88, April 1988.

Differential equations: example

The offshore oil industry uses both manned and unmanned submersible vehicles for a wide variety of underwater inspection and maintenance tasks. A submersible is usually connected to a surface vessel or an underwater station by an *umbilical*, a flexible cable which may contain power conductors for motors, instrumentation cables, fibre optics, gas or fluid hoses and coaxial cables for closed-circuit television, in addition to the main strength member. As a result, the umbilical may well be so thick that it is affected by underwater currents to an extent which restricts the performance and mobility of the submersible. The Numerical Analysis Branch was commissioned by the Offshore Supplies Office of the Department of Energy to develop a mathematical model of the behaviour and effects of umbilicals so that operators could develop experience in driving submersibles in different current conditions and with various umbilical characteristics.

It was found that the motion of an umbilical could be described by four partial differential equations together with boundary conditions supplied by the equations of motion of the submersible. These equations were solved by a numerical technique developed by Dave Ferriss; the results were demonstrated at the 1982 Open Day and the work is described in these two reports:

D H Ferriss. Numerical determination of the three-dimensional equilibrium configuration of an underwater umbilical subjected to steady hydrodynamic loading. NPL Report DNACS 50/81, October 1981.

D H Ferriss. Numerical determination of the configuration of an underwater umbilical subjected to steady hydrodynamic loading, Part 2: Unsteady aspects. NPL Report DITC 2/82, March 1982.

Algorithms for Metrology

The future work of the Mathematical Software group was greatly influenced by a meeting in 1983 between Peter Clapham, then Superintendent of the Division of Mechanical and Optical Metrology (DMOM) and Maurice Cox of DITC. Peter Clapham made the suggestion that Maurice and his group should look at DMOM's current methods of measuring physical shape to see whether the mathematical aspects of the work could be improved.

Consider for example an engineering component with a surface which is meant to be flat within a stated tolerance. How can its conformity with this requirement be checked? The first stage is for the position of a number of points on the surface to be measured using a *coordinate measuring machine* (CMM); the machine uses a probe, which may be either mechanical or optical, to measure the position of each point. This provides a large quantity of data in the form of sets of coordinates. The remaining question is one of numerical mathematics: is there a plane such that the perpendicular distance from each of these points to the plane is less than the stated tolerance? If so the component has passed the test (though of course it is not an absolute test because there could still be bumps or spikes on the surface in between the selected points).

DMOM's invitation gave the Mathematical Software group an excellent opportunity, of which they took full advantage. It proved to be technically challenging work, well matched to the available skills, and it was politically ideal because it linked the group firmly to NPL's core activity, the science of physical measurement.

When examined in detail, the subject proved to have many facets. First, software for dimensional metrology needed the qualities of numerical stability and modularity, familiar ground in DITC although perhaps not so familiar in DMOM. Secondly the definitions of flatness, roundness and so on underlying the design of the software needed to be unambiguous and widely accepted; if possible they should be national or international standards. Thirdly the software should be thoroughly tested, and the test procedure itself had to be formulated and agreed. And finally a system for packaging and disseminating the software was needed. Clearly the group was embarking on a major new activity.

A consultative meeting was held at NPL in March 1984 attended by 80 representatives from industry; it recommended that BSI should develop standards for the verification of the performance of CMMs, definitions of geometrical form suitable for use in software associated with CMMs, and methods for verifying software provided by CMM manufacturers. A new BSI committee structure was soon established for these purposes, with strong NPL support. The initial NPL work is described in the reports listed below. Software was then developed for the assessment of flatness, circularity, sphericity, cylindricity and conicity; this work was in full swing by 1987 and the resulting reports are listed and later work described in section 6.4. Besides Maurice Cox, those particularly involved in Algorithms for Metrology in its formative years were Gerald Anthony and subsequently Alistair Forbes.

M G Cox and K Jackson. Algorithms and software for engineering metrology: a statement of need. NPL Report MOM 65, June 1983.

G T Anthony and M G Cox. The design and validation of software for dimensional metrology. NPL Report DITC 50/84, October 1984.

Software libraries

Following the successful launch of the Numerical Optimization Software Library (NOSL) mentioned on p.187, it was decided to select two further sets of Fortran routines from the NPL Algorithms Library for package sale, one on data approximation and one on linear algebra. The NPL Data Approximation Subroutine Library (DASL) was launched at a Tutorial Conference on Data Fitting organised by NPL and held in Cambridge in March 1982.

NOSL, DASL, and the NPL Linear Algebra Subroutine Library were all promoted at the 1982 Open Day. Licences to use the libraries were sold through NAG Ltd, and a steady flow of sales was reported in the following years. The libraries proved to be an effective way of disseminating the group's expertise for the benefit of UK industry.

In 1982–84 George Symm led the NPL contribution to a collaborative European project on the design of large scientific software libraries in Ada (see p.224 for references).

M G Cox. Versatile parameter lists for scientific library routines. NPL Report DNACS 16/79, March 1979.

M G Cox. Topic libraries for mathematical computation. NPL Report DITC 30/83, August 1983.

NPL. A brief guide to the NPL Numerical Optimization Software Library. NPL, September 1983.

NPL. A brief guide to the NPL Linear Algebra Subroutine Library. NPL, April 1984.

G T Anthony and M G Cox. The National Physical Laboratory's Data Approximation Subroutine Library. NPL Report DITC 71/86, June 1986.

M G Cox. The NPL Data Approximation Subroutine Library: current and planned facilities. NPL Report DITC 104/87, November 1987.

5.7 Human–computer interaction

By 1977 the advent of small cheap computers had revolutionised the opportunities for computer interaction by non-specialists. Chris Evans's imaginative enthusiasm for the new possibilities, evident in his book *The Mighty Micro* (ref. 49), had led to his first micro-based project, the medical history-taking system MICKIE described in section 4.6. This was followed by MAVIS, an information-handling system and teaching aid for the disabled; MALTA, a flight simulator; and most notably Edutext and Microtext, authoring tools aimed primarily at teachers. All these are described further below. Another good idea, which never got off the ground, was a hand-held device like a personal organiser, called Muppet initially and later rechristened Minnie. The group was thus diversifying and building well on its early success when in 1979 its progress was tragically derailed by Chris's untimely death. He had been the guiding spirit of the work on human–computer interaction from its inception and also had many extramural skills and achievements; a brief appreciation of his unusual talents is given below (p.297). There was no one person who could take his place, and though the work he had initiated continued it remained somewhat fragmented until Nigel Bevan was appointed to head the group in 1984.

MAVIS

MAVIS (Microprocessor-driven Audio/Visual Information System) was a pilot project to investigate how microprocessor-based systems could be used to help disabled people, undertaken in collaboration with the Loughborough University of Technology. It was aimed at two distinct groups: severely handicapped children, who need to be able to play, manipulate toys, do lessons, draw and make music—and without help in these activities can become seriously frustrated; and secondly similarly disabled adults, to help them handle information and control their environment.

The facilities for children included pointer boards (arrays of pictures on the screen from which the child can select one to express a request), Bliss symbols (selected from a sequence of pointer boards, enabling the user to express simple sentences), a music generator (allowing sequences of notes with pitch, loudness and duration to be defined and then played), and an experimental toy robot. For adults there were text management facilities and again pointer boards for environmental control. A range of input devices was available to suit individual disabilities.

Following experiments with an initial prototype based on the Motorola M6800, three copies of an engineered version based on the Zilog Z80 were built by Ferranti Instrumentation Ltd. Each of these machines fitted into a (large) briefcase; a television screen was used for output. They were tested in 1979–80 by a group of disabled students at Banstead Place Assessment Centre, Surrey (see fig. 51), and by a four-year-old girl at the Richard Cloudesley

Figure 50. MAVIS in use at Banstead Place, Surrey, January 1980.

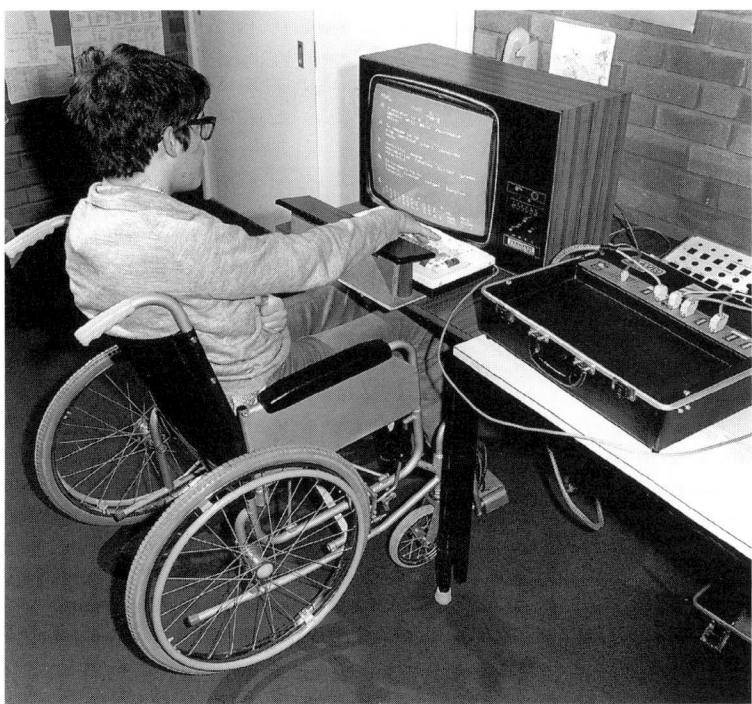

School, Moorgate. These evaluations were successful, but Ferranti eventually decided not to pursue the development for commercial reasons.

The main contributors to MAVIS were the authors of the report listed below; the evaluation work was completed by Julia Charles and Julia Howlett (later Mrs Schofield) after the latter left NPL, with support from BP Ltd.

J Howlett, C R Evans, N Bevan, T J Folkard and R F Penn. MAVIS: a microprocessor driven audio/visual information system for the handicapped. NPL Report DNACS 6/78, September 1978; reprinted in an updated version in *Int. J. Man-Machine Studies,* 14(1), 1981, pp.29–37. See also Julia Schofield's book, ref. 133 pp.45–76.

MALTA

Simulators have a vital part to play in training pilots to fly aircraft. The development of microprocessors meant that their advantages need no longer be restricted to airline and military pilots but could also be extended to those learning to fly light aircraft. On this basis, a simulator was built at NPL in 1979–82 by Tony Day and Peter Carter, with a console provided by an external contractor. Besides allowing practice at take-off, navigation, approach and landing, various wind and cloud conditions could be set by the instructor and emergencies such as engine failure on take-off which are too dangerous to test in real aircraft could be simulated. Great care was taken to model accurately the flight characteristics

Figure 51. MALTA with Ernie Albasiny, August 1984.

of real aircraft. The system, shown in fig. 52, was given the name MALTA (for Microprocessor Aircraft Landing Training Aid). It was shown at the NPL Open Days in 1982 and attracted considerable attention at the Farnborough Air Shows in 1982 and 1984.

Edutext/Microtext

The medical history-taking work and its various spin-offs had shown that computer-based systems could successfully conduct interactive dialogues with untrained users both to elicit information and for training. It was clear that the benefits of this technique would spread much more rapidly if teachers, for example, could be given a software tool with which to construct their own dialogues to suit their particular needs. This was the idea behind the development of Edutext, on which work started in 1978. Based on the script language used on MICKIE (see p.179), it allowed the user to construct what would now be called hypertext, in which it is the reader's response to what is currently on the screen that determines what is seen next. After a session the student or subject's results were summarised for the teacher or manager. Graphs and charts could be included in the script, and commands could be included to control special hardware such as clocks, timers, slide projectors and video recorders (see fig. 53). The underlying aim of Edutext was to allow the teacher/manager to concentrate on concepts relevant to the application rather than

Figure 52. Edutext with Bob Watson, November 1982. Note the BBC Microcomputer in the foreground.

those relating to the computer, and in this respect it echoed Mike Woodger's work on levels of language outlined on p.182. The main target applications were education and training, but the system was also well suited to interviewing and interactive demonstrations. Teachers could exchange training material prepared using Edutext because the scripts could be run on machines of different types provided they had equivalent facilities.

The name Microtext was chosen for the version of Edutext to be marketed commercially. By December 1982 licence agreements had been signed with BBC Publications and Acornsoft Ltd, for use on the BBC Microcomputer, and with two other companies. By 1987 over 6000 systems had been sold.

The work on Edutext and Microtext was led by Nigel Bevan and Bob Watson; others involved included Steve Collins, Dianne Murray, Tony Mansfield, Michael Bangham, Steve Rata and Cathy Thomas.

N Bevan. Is there an optimum speed for presenting text on a VDU? *Int. J. of Man-Machine Studies,* 14(1), 1981, pp.59–76.

N W S Bevan and R S Watson. The design and evaluation of the Microtext authoring system for computer-based training. NPL Report DITC 25/83, June 1983.

N Bevan and R Watson. *Microtext for the BBC Microcomputer.* Acornsoft, 1983.

Speech recognition

The NPL work on speech recognition outlined in section 4.5 differed from the work of other research groups in the same field in that it was aimed at continuous speech, seeking to identify recognisable elements against a noisy background rather than trying to make sense of everything. Another distinction was that at the basic level there was no attempt to identify a sequence of delimited phonemes but rather to detect the presence or absence of features of the speech sound, some of which could occur in parallel, and then compare a whole time segment with the list of vocabulary items expected in the current situation. This enabled a probability to be assigned to each item in the list and a final match was deduced on the basis of syntax.

This approach attracted interest from several electronics companies and systems houses, and in 1981 a Speech Club was established with these companies as members, to help to steer the work and to benefit from its results. The Club was wound up in 1984 when the existing technology had been transferred. Further progress needed a thorough reappraisal of models of speech, and although David Schofield and Brian Pay worked together on this, it was not supported by the Requirements Board, and work on speech ended with Brian Pay's retirement in 1987.

Human–computer interaction

Publications on speech recognition 1978–85

B E Pay and C R Evans. An approach to the automatic recognition of speech. *Int. J. of Man-Machine Studies*, 14(1), 1981, pp.13–27.

M P Cooke. A speech controlled information-retrieval system. NPL Report DITC 15/83, January 1983.

D Schofield and D R Manning. A theoretical model for the Speech Input Device SID3. 1. Filters. NPL Report DITC 20/83, April 1983.

D Schofield and D R Manning. A theoretical model for the Speech Input Device SID3. 2. Correlators. NPL Report DITC 21/83, April 1983.

R E Rengger and D R Manning. A hardware preprocessor for use in speech recognition: Speech Input Device SID3. NPL Report DITC 22/83, May 1983.

D R Manning, B E Pay, R E Rengger and D Schofield. Research on automatic speech recognition at the National Physical Laboratory. NPL Report DITC 31/83, September 1983.

M P Cooke. A computer model of peripheral auditory processing. NPL Report DITC 58/85, May 1985.

D Schofield. Visualisations of speech based on a model of the peripheral auditory system. NPL Report DITC 62/85, July 1985.

Electronic paper

Is the use of keyboard and mouse to create and edit documents unnecessarily complicated? Could the interface to a word processor be made more like pencil and paper, which people find natural and convenient? These were the questions behind a proposal made to the Requirements Board in August 1984. The idea was that the screen should be replaced by *electronic paper*, a thin flat

Figure 53. Electronic paper with Michael Stevens, May 1987.

panel which could be held at any convenient angle. The user could write on it using a light pen, and the panel would show what was written, like ordinary paper; but, like a computer screen, it could also change in response to commands.

Three main modes were proposed, *write, draw* and *edit,* selected by touching a menu in the corner of the panel. In write mode, the user would write using clear cursive script; after a short delay the handwritten words would be replaced by their printed counterparts. In draw mode, similarly, the user would sketch a diagram and its lines would then be replaced by accurately drawn equivalents. In edit mode, a number of simple actions with the pen could be used to edit text; for example, a line through a letter or a word or a paragraph would delete it, text could be moved by putting brackets round it and then marking the new position, and so on. The underlying aim was to design a human–computer interface which matched people's natural forms of expression so well that it needed no manuals and only minimal learning.

These interesting and ambitious plans attracted collaboration from the Central Computer and Telecommunications Agency (CCTA), Nottingham University, Trent Polytechnic and others. Working demonstrations were produced of most of the components of the system, the editing in particular proving to be practical and convenient. Drawing was restricted to boxes and horizontal and vertical lines, and the prototype panel was not as thin as it might be, as the photograph (fig. 54) shows, but the real problem area was predictably the recognition of cursive script. Work was terminated in 1988, but electronic paper may yet prove to have been an idea ahead of its time.

The work was carried out by the Programmable Vision Systems group (it is described here because it clearly has more to do with human–computer interaction than with vision). The chief contributors were Michael Stevens, Peter Pobgee, Hilary Symm and Paul Kenward, and the group was led by Ed Brocklehurst.

Publications on electronic paper

M G Cox and P M Harris. An algorithm for loop detection in cursive script recognition. NPL Report DITC 120/88, July 1988.

M J Stevens. A text editor driven by hand-drawn symbols. NPL Report DITC 124/88, September 1988.

P J Pobgee. A prototype system for interactive input of cursive information. NPL Report DITC 125/88, September 1988.

E R Brocklehurst and M J Stevens. Software modules for Electronic Paper. NPL Report DITC 127/88, October 1988.

E R Brocklehurst, D M Ford and H J Symm. Feature extraction for cursive script recognition. NPL Report DITC 130/88, November 1988.

D M Ford and H J Symm. Segmentation and reduction analysis for cursive script recognition. NPL Report DITC 131/88, November 1988.

E R Brocklehurst and P D Kenward. Preprocessing for cursive script recognition. NPL Report DITC 132/88, November 1988.

E R Brocklehurst. The NPL Electronic Paper project. NPL Report DITC 133/88, November 1988.

P J Pobgee. EPT, a dynamic tutorial for introducing users to Electronic Paper. NPL Report DITC 134/88, November 1988.

5.8 Vision systems

Linear Array Processor

Machines that can interpret a visual scene intelligently are useful in many fields. Examples are the automated inspection of manufactured goods to find defects, and the development of robots which can see. In both these cases the processing of each image will normally have to be complete by the time the next one arrives. In the early 1980s this meant that in practical situations a single microprocessor only had time for a rather crude image analysis. To overcome the problem several groups had developed two-dimensional arrays of processors, one for each element or pixel of the image. These provided a spectacular increase in processing speed but they were expensive and bulky. In 1982 Piers Plummer of the newly established NPL Programmable Vision Systems group proposed a compromise: a row or *linear array* of processors, one for each pixel across the image, say 256 processors in a typical case. The picture was fed to the array a line at a time; the individual processors could recall information from recent lines as well as communicating with their neighbours about the current line. The array was programmed in a high-level language defining the sequence of picture-processing operations required, and a compiler translated this into code for the individual processors.

A typical application for the Linear Array Processor was to watch out for cracks in glassware or metal castings on a production line. Following the successful demonstration of a prototype system at the 1982 Open Day, further development was carried out in collaboration with UWIST, and a marketing licence was signed with British Robotic Systems Ltd. By 1986 about 20 machines were in use in industry and university research departments.

A P N Plummer (inventor). Parallel Digital Signal Processing. UK Patent No. 2 129 545, date of application 2 November 1982.

V F Leavers and J F Boyce. An implementation of the Hough Transform using a Linear Array Processor in conjunction with a PDP/11 microprocessor. NPL Report DITC 74/86, October 1986.

V F Leavers and J F Boyce. Automatic shape parametrisation in machine vision. NPL Report DITC 79/86, November 1986.

Static signature validation

The Verisign system described on p.169 was designed to check *dynamic* signatures, that is records of the signing process which include timing information. After that development was completed the Division was approached by a bank with a different problem—the checking of *static* signatures on cheques. If a cheque book and guarantee card are stolen, the thief may not try to copy the owner's signature when using the cheques. Instead he may replace the specimen signature on the card with the owner's name in his own handwriting, and then he only has to repeat this convincingly on the cheque to complete his fraud. The idea behind the new NPL work was that if certain numeric values dependent on the owner's real signature were calculated and pre-printed on the cheque, a machine could check these against the written signature when the cheque was presented. It should thus be able to detect crude frauds of the type described above, even though a sufficiently skilled forger trying to copy the real signature might still be able to defeat it.

A prototype device using seven selected numeric parameters, with a television camera to capture the image of the cheque, was developed at NPL and described in the 1984 Report (see ref. 99 pp.61–62). It worked well enough for a firm to take over production of a commercial device in which the camera was to be replaced by a cheaper photodiode array. This work was led by Ed Brocklehurst, and others involved included Peter Pobgee, Michael Stevens, Paul Kenward and Hilary Symm.

E R Brocklehurst. Computer methods of signature verification. NPL Report DITC 41/84, May 1984.

Other work on programmable vision systems

Double-exposure speckle interferometry is an optical technique widely used in engineering to measure strain and deformation. As first developed, it was time consuming and dependent on the judgement of a human operator, but in collaborative work with the Division of Mechanical and Optical Metrology first reported in 1982, Peter Pobgee devised a method of automating the measurement of the orientation and spacing of interference fringes which greatly speeded up the process. As in the automatic inspection work described on p.170, the 'camera' was a linear array of 512 photodiodes, and a microcomputer was used for the calculations.

P J Pobgee. Automatic analysis of speckle photographs by microcomputer. NPL Report DITC 47/84, September 1984.

5.9 Telerobotics

Imagine a robot-like device that is remote from you but under your complete personal control. It can see and hear, but only in the sense that a television camera can see or a microphone can hear: it passes on to you the images and sounds, and is not designed to process or act on them autonomously. Likewise it can move itself around, manipulate objects around it, and it can speak—but again only as your agent. Such a device I will call a *proxy*. It will have very limited 'intelligence'—to the extent that microcomputers might well be needed, for example, to control balance when moving—but no intelligence in any deeper sense such as working out for itself how to achieve a goal.

It is intended simply to give you as far as possible a complete sensory impression of being present in the remote location without the delay and expense of getting there; as a bonus the places visited can include some where human travel would be dangerous or impossible.

These paragraphs are the start of a speculative article by the writer, published in 1982 (ref. 183). At the time the idea had no connection with NPL, but in early 1984 the NPL management invited suggestions for new projects to be supported by the General Research Surcharge (a means by which the Director could fund a limited amount of exploratory work by charging a little extra for everything else). Amongst other suggestions, DITC put forward a proposal for preliminary work in the field of *telerobotics:* to survey existing work in the area and to identify any opportunity for an NPL contribution. This proposal was accepted, and work began in March 1984. Those involved were Peter Vaswani, who led the group, Ralph Rengger, Roger Manning and Peter Neale.

Their survey found many examples of existing special-purpose systems in which a robot-like device was controlled by a remote human operator. These were all developed for applications in hostile environments: handling radioactive materials in the nuclear industry, underwater tasks in the oil and gas industries, assembling and servicing space stations in earth orbit, mining, and bomb disposal and other defence and security tasks. The group found that there was a diverse range of research and development opportunities, and identified five areas in particular where progress was currently restricted by the available technology: (1) the means at an operator's disposal for remotely controlling the movements and actions of a robot manipulator; (2) the dexterity of robot grippers and the means of controlling grasping actions; (3) remote viewing systems; (4) sensory feedback systems for force, touch, slip and proximity; and (5) communication systems for remote, untethered robots.

The group chose the first of these five for a preliminary investigation. Conventional mechanisms for operator control involved joysticks, switch boxes or replica arms, and the group decided to investigate the possibility of freehand control, in which the operator's own movements are mirrored by those of the robot. An ideal device was found for this purpose, the 3Space Tracker manufactured by McDonnell Douglas. This allowed the position and orientation of a small object (a cube) to be monitored continuously. In all, six parameters are needed to define the position and orientation of an object in space (three spatial coordinates and three angles of yaw, pitch and roll). The system recorded these six numbers 60 times per second. The group developed a prototype telerobotic system in which the cube was attached to an operator's hand and the output from the tracking equipment was fed to a BBC Microcomputer which translated the stream of data into controls for a robot arm. Closed-circuit television was used to give the operator a view of the work area. This worked well, allowing simple tasks to be performed remotely, and gave the group considerable encouragement that they had found a promising candidate for one element of a telerobotic system.

Before long the group were, inevitably, under pressure to identify a commercial application for their work and a source of funding other than the General Research Surcharge. Conventional (autonomous) robotic devices are of course widely used in manufacturing industry, and it was here that the group identified two requirements where human control of the robot would be useful, and the techniques developed to achieve it would also be relevant to the control of a true telerobotic device. These were first the *training* of a robot by leading it through the required sequence of actions (as opposed to the usual technique of programming it); and secondly the resolution of an unforeseen problem, where the robot has got itself into a situation which it is not programmed to deal with, so that some form of human intervention is required.

The group also identified three partners who agreed in principle to participate in a future project if partial financial support was forthcoming: a robot manufacturer, a company developing remote-handling systems, and the University of Southampton who had considerable relevant experience in the development of manipulators for use by disabled patients. A detailed proposal for a collaborative project was prepared, and funding for the work was being sought from DTI when in August 1986 the project was unexpectedly terminated by NPL management's decision to withdraw; the reason given was that it had been decided that telerobotics was after all not an appropriate area for NPL involvement.

The work of the group is described in their final report:

D R Manning, P T Neale, R E Rengger and P K T Vaswani. Improving the man-machine interface to robotic systems. NPL Report DITC 100/87, September 1987.

5.10 Computing services

On 1 June 1978, over ten years after the short-lived attempt to establish a Central Computer Unit, a second bite was taken at the same cherry. This time it was successful because there was no problem with finding the right leader, and a Computing Services Unit (CSU) was set up under Frank Blake. He reported at first directly to a Deputy Director of the Laboratory, and later, from 1982, to Albasiny, the head of DITC (see fig. 1). These moves had no visible effect on the programme of the Unit, but there was a more far-reaching change in January 1981 when it was decided that research work associated with computing services was a luxury which could no longer be afforded, and Brian Wichmann and Roger Scowen were transferred from CSU to DNACS, shortly to become DITC. David Schofield had already moved from DNAC to the then Com. Sci. on promotion in March 1978, so CSU without its three most innovative software engineers had in future to accept a service role without any research element.

A major revolution in NPL's computing services was brought about by the advent of cheap but powerful personal computers in the early 1980s. Previously, the services had been built on two key resources: the mainframes and other service-providing computers with their software, and the network with its terminals, then mostly visual display units. This central concentration of computing power, inevitable in its day, meant that CSU was in a strong position, with full responsibility for developing and maintaining reliable services and for judging when to change horses as the technology continued its rapid evolution. The first microcomputers, notably the BBC Microcomputer, did not greatly affect this position; they had only basic word-processing facilities and were mainly used in NPL as programmable calculators and in controlling and monitoring experimental work, though they could be connected to the network if required. But the arrival of more powerful personal computers (PCs) in the 1980s meant that their users could take many computing-related decisions independently of CSU, and by 1987 many users had all the computing power they needed on their desks. CSU still had many vital roles: as network and database managers, as a source of documentation, advice and training, as providers of mainframe computing to those who still needed it, and as providers of high-quality printing services; but their total control of computing power had been lost.

Frank Blake retired at the end of 1985 and was succeeded as head of CSU by John Cooper.

Mainframes

By 1979 the two KDF9s, though still working well, were completely out of date as the basis of the computing service of a national laboratory. There had been a long battle to replace them with an appropriate new machine, and this was finally resolved with the delivery in March 1979 of an ICL 2972 mainframe computer. A new computer hall was planned for the south wing of the Charles Babbage Building; until this was ready the machine was temporarily installed in premises rented from ICL at Feltham.

By the end of 1979 it was providing a service based on the VME/B operating system, with remote access for its users at their terminals in Teddington and minicab commuting to Feltham by the CSU operating staff. The two KDF9s were finally closed down on 29 August 1980, by which time the older machine had been in service for 16 years. The new computer hall was opened in October 1981 and the central services, including the 2972, Edit and the Central File Store were moved in one by one. In 1982 the 2972 had 4 Mbytes of fast store and 600 Mbytes of on-line file storage, which are reasonable figures for a personal computer at the time of writing (1996); by 1987 it had been enhanced to 12 Mbytes of main store and 2000 Mbytes of exchangeable disc store.

For a trial period starting in 1982, the machine acted as host for an ICL Distributed Array Processor (DAP), a unit containing 4096 processors which could work in parallel. Use of the DAP could greatly speed up any numerical process which could take advantage of the parallelism, but the experimental service was never widely used either by NPL or external customers, probably because the users judged that the special programming required was only justified for tasks with exceptionally long run times.

The main languages available on the 2972 were Fortran 77, Pascal, Algol 60 and Basic; by 1986 NPL was one of the last strongholds of Algol 60, with over 300 program runs still being made per week, and users were being encouraged to change to Pascal. Applications software on the 2972 included the NAG and NPL libraries (see p.186), the RAPPORT relational database management system, and a comprehensive graphical output system based on the GHOST package developed at the Culham Laboratory.

The computer manager throughout this period was Dickie Bird, assisted by Joyce Brick. Other major contributors to mainframe services were Tony Hillman with John Nappey on systems software, Clive Hall on graphics and databases, and John Cooper assisted by Betty Curtis, Clifford Nott and Shirley Johnson on customer services, especially documentation and training.

Text-handling services

Edit with Pages (see p.190) remained throughout this period as the main document preparation service in NPL, though by 1987 it was starting to meet stiff competition from the powerful word-processing packages available on PCs. Many of the Edit services were available on the 2972 from 1981. A Mailbox facility was added to Edit in 1982, following the example set by Scrapbook ten years earlier. For communication outside NPL, files could be prepared for transmission by Telex (a widely used national and international teleprinter network). By 1982 multifont dot matrix printers were available, and a high-quality printing service

Computing services

(TOPIC) was established; a phototypesetter was added to its resources in June 1983. By 1986 TOPIC was using laser printers, and these soon swept the field because of their excellent print quality combined with graphical capabilities which finally made the old graph plotters obsolete.

The NPL Network

In 1982 a new NPL network was commissioned. It had three packet-switching nodes (GEC 4000 series computers) and all communication links between computers followed the internationally agreed CCITT Recommendation X.25 on the format and use of packets. The new network was phased in gradually, and for some time the old network remained in operation particularly to handle traffic with terminals; there was a gateway between the two. The configuration of the X.25 network in 1987 is shown in fig. 55.

Microcomputers began to replace the old VDUs as terminals on the network, and by 1985 the number of micros on the site justified the production of a special micros edition of *NPL Computing*. By 1987 the total number of terminals had risen to 500.

Dennis Blake retired in October 1983 and was succeeded as network manager by Les Pink.

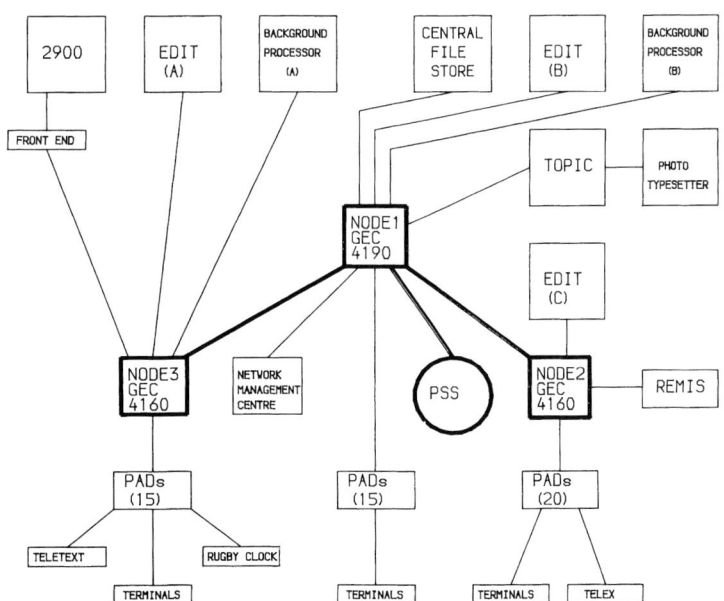

Figure 54. The NPL X.25 Network, May 1987. PAD = packet assembler/disassembler, PSS = Packet SwitchStream (public network).

Publications by CSU in 1978–87

D Schofield, A L Hillman and J L Rodgers. MM/1, a man-machine interface: a contribution towards a standard. NPL Report CSU 2/78, October 1978.

J R A Cooper. NPL Algorithms Library Brief Guide—1979. NPL Report CSU 3/79, January 1979.

B R Heap. A simple algorithm for drawing a curve through a set of points. NPL Report CSU 4/79, December 1979.

R S Scowen. A cross-reference index for the syntax of the programming language Fortran 77. NPL Report CSU 5, December 1979.

R S Scowen. A cross-reference index for the syntax of the programming language Ada. NPL Report CSU 6, December 1979.

Shirley Johnson (ed.). NPL Computing. Issues in this period are 254, 14 June 1978, to 403, 15 April 1987.

NPL Internal Computing Documents. A selection only is listed; dates are those of first issue.
  GHOST 80 User Manual. Doc. G1, March 1986 (replacing an earlier G1, Graphical Output System).
  Curve fitting macros and procedures. Doc. L7, December 1978.
  BBC Micro—computer or terminal. Doc. M1, June 1985.
  MS-DOS Micros on the NPL Network. Doc. M2, February 1987.
  Spooler, PSS and calls to external services. Doc. N2.
  Edit utilities and jobs. Doc. S4, December 1979.
  PostScript Pages on Edit. Doc. W2.
  The TSSD User Manual. Doc. W3.
  NPL Local TSSD Guide. Doc. W4.

6 Agency status and detachment from Government: 1987–1995

6.1 Outline of developments

Tom Blaney was appointed Superintendent of DITC on 27 April 1987. He was an experienced scientist and research manager, having previously been a Branch Head in NPL's Division of Electrical Science, but had no specialist knowledge of information technology. This meant that the emphasis in his approach to his new responsibilities was on the management of the Division and the health of its relations with its customers, rather than on personal initiatives regarding its technical aims and strategy; probably anyone in the post would have had to adopt the same priorities faced with the organisational upheavals which were soon to ensue.

The first gust of the wind of change came in the form of a Government report *Improving Management in Government: the Next Steps* (ref. 82) published in 1988. This was based on a firm political belief that the most effective path to progress was through the pressures of commercial competitiveness. It recommended the metamorphosis of appropriate Government bodies into semi-autonomous agencies; these came to be known as Next Steps Agencies from the title of the report. It was clear that NPL was a candidate for Agency status, and this was duly announced in June 1988.

As a step in this direction the Requirements Board system was immediately abolished. Instead, DTI became the direct customer for most of the work of NPL. The intention was to focus the work programmes more closely on the needs of the DTI Divisions as they perceived them. The move weakened the influence of external bodies, particularly the universities, over what was done at NPL, and emphasised central DTI control; it thus took a step further the process started by the formation of the Boards in the early 1970s. New formal machinery was established to regulate the customer–contractor relationship. The key body was to be the Measurement and Technology Support Individual Programmes Committee (MTSIPC), which was to consist solely of civil servants and have a financial and administrative rather than a technical role. Its task was to ensure that the customer Divisions had followed correct procedures in formulating their requirements, getting sound external advice, planning and costing the programme, obtaining multiple bids where appropriate, planning how the progress of the work was to be monitored and its eventual results assessed, setting up schedules for project management meetings, deciding how frequently reports were to be prepared,

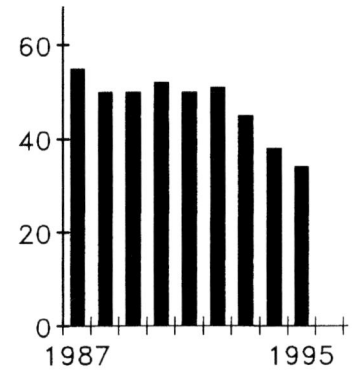

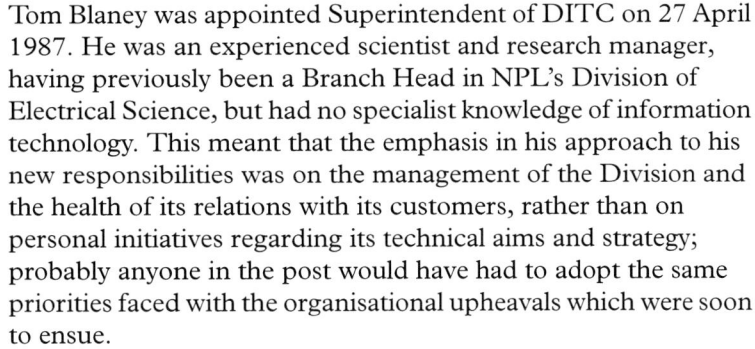

Figure 56. DITC/CISE staff numbers, 1987–95.

Figure 57. Tom Blaney, Donald Davies, Adrian Marks, Ernie Albasiny, Derek Barber and Ted Newman, a gathering of senior staff from different eras, in March 1992.

and so on. The key buzzword of the day was ROAME: Rationale, Objectives, Appraisal, Monitoring and Evaluation. All programmes submitted to the MTSIPC had to have ROAME statements; indeed these were the major part of the case, with technical plans appended. The power of the MTSIPC lay in the fact that its parent body, the Research and Technology Policy Division, and not the customer Divisions, controlled the purse strings of the relevant budget (for larger projects Ministerial approval was also needed). It held its first meeting in June 1989.

Within this framework, research establishments had to compete with private sector companies for work the Government required to be done, besides undertaking non-Government business on a normal commercial basis. There was no presumption that work of some kind would be found by Government, a harder line than that taken under the Requirements Board system where the emphasis was on finding a technical programme that both the Board and the establishment were happy with. Once a programme was agreed, the Department took its interest as customer to such a level of detail that the research group concerned had little flexibility left—again a further step in a process started with the formation of the Requirements Boards 17 years before.

In parallel with the establishment of the MTSIPC and its procedural obstacle course, NPL's progress towards Agency status was continuing. A Framework Document (ref. 122) setting out the extent of the Laboratory's autonomy was negotiated, and NPL duly became an Executive Agency of the Department of Trade and Industry on 3 July 1990. As will be seen from the following sections, the Division did manage to carry out substantial technical work in this period in spite of the extra administrative and commercial activities introduced by the change to Agency status. The Division saw its chief role as giving technical support for the Department's policy of promoting the quality of products and procedures in the IT field. There was a consequent new emphasis on *formal methods,* quasi-mathematical techniques for increasing confidence in the reliability of systems and their fitness for purpose. The other main contribution to quality in IT was in work related to standards, test development and accreditation of test facilities. These areas continued to be given priority when funding could be obtained.

In January 1992 Tom Blaney was appointed Head of the Division of Electrical Science, his former home ground. (The title of Superintendent, which had had an archaic ring for many years, had been quietly dropped in favour of 'Division Head'.) Adrian Marks was appointed Head of DITC in his place on 16 March 1992; an outline of his earlier career in the Ministry of Defence is given on p.301.

Considered as part of a commercial business, the Division looked vulnerable because its emphasis on standards-related work made it too dependent on a single customer, DTI; ironically the specialisation on standards at the expense of wider research and development was of course the result of the Department's own policies in the Requirements Board era. The Division made increased efforts to seek funding outside UK Government sources, but its fears were soon confirmed when the sections in DTI which had previously been its customers were closed down and the budget for IT standards work drastically cut. This happened as a result of the appointment in 1992 of a new Chief Adviser on Science and Technology in DTI, Dr Geoffrey Robinson from IBM, who perhaps unsurprisingly had little liking for interventionist activities in IT such as standards support, and succeeded in eliminating many of them by the time he returned to IBM in 1994. Existing contracts were of course honoured, but as a result of the sweeping cuts in DTI's IT programme DITC's staff numbers were reduced and its work gradually became more fragmented and opportunistic, with more small projects and a further reduction in the scope for longer-term work.

Agency status proved to be only a short stage in the process of detaching NPL from Government. It was announced on 14 April 1994 that the Laboratory was to be put on a GOCO (Government-Owned, Contractor-Operated) basis. Bids were invited for companies to manage NPL; the winners were Serco Group plc. They created a subsidiary company, NPL Management Ltd, which took over the management of the Laboratory on 1 October 1995. The staff became employees of the new company. The terms of the contract obliged the contractors to maintain NPL in its primary role as the centre of the National Measurement System, so that it could be returned to the Department as a going concern at the end of the five-year period of the contract if this was not renewed. This provision made no mention of the information technology activities, whose future therefore depended on the commercial judgement of the company.

One of the first actions of the new management was to change the names of all the constituent parts of NPL. DITC became the Centre for Information Systems Engineering (CISE), and CSU became the Information Technology Support Unit (ITSU). The link between the two was severed. Adrian Marks remained briefly as head of CISE, with the section heads responsible directly to him. David Schofield became responsible for ITSU only, and his Unit was joined with other NPL services under the Director of Finance. CISE lasted only a few weeks as such, because in December 1995 it was decided that the continuing reduction in staff numbers (see fig. 56) made it no longer viable as a Centre in its own right and it was downgraded to become the Information Systems Engineering Branch of the Centre for Mechanical and Optical Technology (CMOT), with whom the Mathematical Software group had for some years had strong links[1]. Adrian Marks was moved within NPL and Dave Rayner was appointed to head the new branch. His prime task was to strengthen its commercial position, because inevitably that alone would determine its future; the more idealistic ethos of scientific research and public service in which Mathematics Division was founded in 1945 was no longer even a distant memory for the staff.

At this point, commercially challenged but somewhat frustrated in the face of the short-sightedness of the current national attitude to technical innovation, we reach the time of writing and therefore the end of this historical account. The technical work in this final period is outlined in the following sections as for previous eras, and a retrospective postscript is given in section 7.

6.2 Protocol standards

Test system development

In 1987 the Protocol Standards group was concentrating on the development of a testing system for the OSI File Transfer Access and Management (FTAM) protocol, which was the subject of two major contracts. In the United States the major computer suppliers had set up a new consortium, the Corporation for Open Systems (COS), to provide them with tools to help in OSI development, and in May 1987 a three-way contract was signed between COS, NPL and the National Computing Centre (NCC) under which NCC and NPL were to supply an FTAM test system

---

[1] However, in 1997, as part of a rationalisation of NPL's structure with a larger number of Centres, CISE was re-established as such.

to COS. This was successfully achieved; the final component of the system was delivered in July 1988. A slightly less advanced version had been delivered to the European Commission in October 1987 under the CTS-WAN contract mentioned on p.206. As a result of these contracts the FTAM test system came into worldwide use; it also formed the basis for the development by COS of their own test system for Message Handling Services (MHS). This work marked the end of NPL's direct involvement in test system production as the technology was judged to have been moved successfully out of the research area.

OSI conformance testing standards

In designing a system for testing protocol implementations, it is clearly sensible to separate the tests from the software which applies them; otherwise the software would be wastefully repetitive and inflexible, and discussion and alteration of the tests would be difficult. Standard suites of tests will be needed, because if every testing centre developed its own, results from different testing organisations would not be compatible. These basic design decisions have several important consequences. First, standard notations are needed in which tests can be defined, in the same way as programming languages are necessary to enable programs to be defined. Secondly, test suites require specifications of their scope and objectives (which became known as *test suite structure and test purposes* documents) to define what they do and how they can be used, again with close analogies in the field of software. Finally, a distinction was drawn between *abstract* test suites, expressed for clarity and precision in human use, and *executable* test suites, expressed in a form which could be input directly to the test system. As these concepts were formulated, they were embodied in the developing international standard for OSI Conformance Testing Methodology and Framework (ISO/IEC 9646) (ref. 78) under the leadership of Dave Rayner of NPL.

NPL made particular technical contributions in three areas: the development of standard test notations (the 'Tree and Tabular Combined Notation' TTCN for abstract test suites and its executable form ETTCN); the development of the test suite structure and test purposes standard for FTAM; and the standardisation of requirements for test laboratories and their clients. Examples of these requirements are the form of protocol implementation conformance statements (PICS) provided by the client to define exactly what has been implemented, the supplementary statement (PIXIT) provided by the client to give all further information needed for testing, and the format of test reports produced by the laboratory. The group also developed and made available many software tools to support test development using TTCN.

Accreditation of IT test laboratories

In the field of physical measurement it had become generally accepted during the 1980s that test laboratories should be accredited by an independent organisation established for the purpose by the national government; without such a scheme, inferior services might arise which would undermine the effectiveness of the standards and public confidence in them. In the UK the National Testing Laboratory Accreditation Scheme (NATLAS) was established at NPL for this purpose in 1980. In 1985 NATLAS merged with the British Calibration Service to form the National Measurement Accreditation Service (NAMAS); in 1995 NAMAS was separated from NPL to form part of the present (1996) UK Accreditation Service (UKAS). Soon after its formation NAMAS extended its scope by starting to accredit testing services in the IT field. Their existing criteria for accreditation needed considerable interpretation to make them applicable in this new area, and Dave Rayner developed the key NAMAS document (ref. 128) expressing this interpretation. He was also instrumental in getting this document, with appropriate changes, accepted first in Europe (ref. 152) and then worldwide (ref. 80); this work and his leadership of the development of ISO/IEC 9646 rank as the two major achievements of the group in this period.

Harmonised IT conformance testing services in Europe

Testing authorities in different countries need to recognise each others' test reports and certificates if repeated testing, which is wasteful and unpopular with both suppliers and their customers, is to be avoided. Accreditation is a necessary first step, but the authorities still need to negotiate a mutual recognition agreement. In 1988 a European Committee on IT Testing and Certification (ECITC) was established to foster harmonisation in this area, for example by providing a framework for mutual recognition agreements. NPL made a major contribution to this work through Dave Rayner's chairmanship of ECITC's OSI Testing Liaison group.

The use of formal description techniques in OSI conformance testing

OSI standards are complex and difficult to state precisely in natural language alone. For this reason the OSI standardisers developed two standard formal description techniques, LOTOS (which proved particularly appropriate for defining the protocols themselves) and Estelle (which proved particularly appropriate for specifying the internal workings of model protocol implementations). NPL developed special expertise in LOTOS, and used this in two projects: first to produce a LOTOS specification of the

OSI Transaction Processing protocol, which was incorporated in the international standard concerned, and secondly to investigate the use of LOTOS in conformance testing. Two such applications were identified: to use the LOTOS specification as an independent check that tests were conducted in conformance with the protocol standard, and secondly to investigate the possibility of deriving tests automatically from the protocol standard. Work in this area continues at the time of writing (1996).

OSI and the Internet

In spite of the large scale international effort devoted to the development of OSI between 1978 and 1995, and active support from governments, particularly in Europe, the resulting standards were not adopted by the IT industry on anything like the scale expected. Instead, industrial development effort in the early 1990s was focused on using the dramatically successful Internet, which had already achieved many of the objectives of the original OSI initiative. This came about principally because, with hindsight, the OSI standards looked over-complex and had taken too long to develop, whereas the rival Internet protocols, derived from those used in the ARPANET, lacked many sophisticated features but were relatively simple and straightforward to implement. But the field is complex, the future is uncertain, many of the concepts and tools developed in an OSI context are applicable more widely, and it would therefore be unfair to characterise the current position as a simple victory of one camp over another. All that can safely be said, with hindsight, is that the development of the OSI standards would probably have benefited from a more commercial ethos and more prototyping to bring home to the standardisers the necessity of keeping things as simple as possible. In the marketplace, timing is of the essence; if standards committees are trying to lead a market but do not take enough account of this fact, their work may be to that extent in vain.

Dave Rayner led the Protocol Standards (later Open Systems) group throughout this period. The other major contributors to the work were Michael Gill, Bronia Szczygiel, Alan Boshier, Godfrey Cowin, Robin Barker, Simon Ashford, Frank Brady and John Bunting.

Selected publications on Open Systems standards 1987–95

F Brady, A G Boshier, D Pitt and B M Szczygiel. One2One—a tool for translating ASN.1 to ACT ONE. In: J Quemada, J Mañas and E Vazquez (eds), *Formal Description Techniques III, Proc. IFIP 3rd Int. Conf. on Formal Description Techniques for Distributed Systems and Communications Protocols, FORTE '90,* held in Madrid, 5–8 November 1990, North-Holland, 1991, pp.539–542. An earlier version was produced as NPL Report DITC 165/90, June 1990.

D Rayner. ISO/IEC 9646 and beyond. In: I Davidson and D M Litwack (eds), *Protocol Test Systems III, Proc. IFIP TC6 3rd Int. Workshop on Protocol Test Systems,* held in McClean, Virginia, 30 October–1 November 1990, North-Holland, 1991, pp.17–27.

D Rayner (ed.). Interpretation of accreditation requirements for IT test laboratories for software and communications testing services. NAMAS NIS 35, November 1990.

S J Ashford and G Cowin. Maintenance of abstract test suites in TTCN: a comparison of three tools. NPL Report DITC 174/91, March 1991.

G Cowin. Experiences in developing a test suite structure and test purposes document for Open Systems. NPL Report DITC 179/91, March 1991.

ISO/IEC [G W Cowin (ed.)]. Information Technology—Open Systems Interconnection—Test suite structure and test purposes for FTAM. ISO/IEC 10170: 1993.

J W Bunting. Verification of sections of the FTAM protocol using Prolog. NPL Report DITC 199/92, April 1992.

ISO/IEC [B M Szczygiel, F Brady and R M Barker (eds)]. LOTOS description of the TP Protocol. Annex H of: Information Technology—Open Systems Interconnection—Distributed Transaction Processing—Part 3: Protocol Specification, ISO/IEC 10026-3: 1992.

ISO/IEC [F Brady (ed.)]. Information Technology—Open Systems Interconnection—Conformance Test Suite for the OSI TP Protocol—Part 1: Test Suite Structure and Test Purposes, ISO/IEC DIS 13650-1, 1993.

S J Ashford. Automatic test case generation using Prolog. NPL Report DITC 215/93, January 1993.

R M Barker and F Brady. The automatic generation of test purposes for the OSI distributed transaction processing protocol. *Proc. 13th IFIP Symposium on Protocol Specification, Testing and Verification,* held in Liège, 25–28 May 1993, E3, pp.1–16.

S J Ashford, J W Bunting and D Rayner. Developers' TTCN: specification, examples and tool descriptions. NPL Report DITC 237/95, September 1995; an earlier version was published as NPL Report DITC 195/92, February 1992.

6.3 Data security

For the first year of this period, while the Requirements Board system lasted, there was no radical redirection in the work of the Data Security group as described in section 5.3. Work on the NPL Token was concluded; contributions to standards-making continued, notably the progress of the Message Authenticator Algorithm towards its later adoption as an International Standard.

The future of the Tokens and Transactions Control Consortium (see p.213) was reviewed in 1988 when the research it had supported on the design and development of the NPL Token was complete. The members of the consortium decided they wanted the awareness service in the field of machine-readable cards and tokens to continue. It was agreed that this service would be run by NPL alone, without the involvement of the British Technology Group, and that in view of this restructuring the association should be renamed; the name chosen was the Advanced Token

Technology Club (ATTC). Like its predecessor, this was a successful club, though it was to prove short-lived.

By 1989 public awareness of the importance of IT security was increasing. There were two related causes for concern: first, the hackers and virus developers, who had shown they could vandalise systems and snoop into other people's business, posing a clear threat of serious damage; and secondly reports of financial fraud based on weaknesses in electronic funds transfer systems. In 1990 the Computer Misuse Act tackled a key aspect of the problem, making it an offence to use a computer for these malicious purposes. The IT Security Section in the Department of Trade and Industry which was involved in the preparation for this legislation became the main customer for the NPL group following the abolition of the Requirements Board system in 1988.

The work they commissioned covered three main topics: support for the development of standards in data security; research and development in methods of testing systems for conformance to standards; and the technical management of the Department's Commercial Computer Security Centre (CCSC). The work done under these headings is described separately below. The ATTC was wound up in 1990 when it became clear that the requirements of the DTI customers were leading the group away from the technology of tokens.

One independent short study deserves mention. In 1992 Fiona Williams and Samantha Green investigated how security techniques could help to make software tamper resistant. The idea was to frustrate certain malpractices, including the dissemination of viruses, by enabling software customers to check that what they were installing or running was uncontaminated. The method used was an application of digital signatures (see p.211). Participating software developers would have to include with their software a tag consisting of a number logically dependent on the whole of the program (using a *hash function*), and would give this tag a digital signature. Then the customer could check the signature and the validity of the hash (using trusted software); if the software had been tampered with, the check would not work. Details are given in the report on software stamping listed below. For practical use, the technique would involve significant organisation, particularly in ensuring wide publicity for the public keys involved (to prevent impersonation), and it would only be adopted if the damage caused by software tampering justified the cost of this organisation. The technique does not deal with software *piracy* (because the signed tag can be copied too), only with tampering—but tampering can be serious for the user: it is easy to imagine a financial package which was clean when it left the supplier being subsequently bugged to benefit a fraudster.

Wyn Price led the group until his retirement in 1990, when he was succeeded by Bernard Chorley. Other members of the group during this period included Richard Lampard, Mike Lai, Bronia

Szczygiel, Fiona Williams, Harold Munster, Roger Manning, Peter Neale, Andrew Harry, Andy Lovering and Stephen Hehir. In 1995, when group boundaries became much more flexible under commercial pressure, Bronia Szczygiel became responsible for managing work involving security expertise.

General publications on data security 1987–95

P K T Vaswani. A classified bibliography on publications relevant to data security in LANs. NPL Report DITC 99/87, September 1987.

W L Price. A state-of-the-art survey of low-cost security in Local Area Networks. NPL Report DITC 113/88, April 1988.

W L Price. Appraisal of security of data handling systems and products: a tutorial and discussion document. NPL Report DITC 141/89, March 1989.

W L Price. Hash functions: a tutorial and status report. NPL Report DITC 151/89, November 1989.

F Williams and S Green. Software stamping. NPL Report DITC 198/92, April 1992.

NPL. NPL Data Security Group Bulletin. Issues 1 (Autumn 1991) to 9 (Summer 1995).

B J Chorley and W L Price. Security assessment and conformance testing. In Lindsay and Price (1991), ref. 84 pp.43–54.

R Lampard. Making IT secure. *Byte UK*, 17(2), 1992, pp.41–52.

Standards in data security: formal methods and strict conformance testing

If product standards are to be useful, suppliers must be able to claim that a certain aspect of a particular product or system conforms to a stated standard. They can only do this safely if they have reliable evidence of conformance. This evidence must be produced by a prescribed assessment procedure, carried out by a body which can be shown to have the necessary competence. This argument applies to data security standards as much as to others, and it was therefore natural in 1988–89 for the Data Security group to propose to their DTI customer that work should be undertaken on techniques for assessing aspects of products and systems for which conformance to security standards was claimed.

It was apparent at once that the approach developed by the Protocols Standards group and described in section 5.2 was not adequate in this field. This is because it was a 'black-box' approach, relying on subjecting the item under test to a wide range of different circumstances and comparing the outcome in each case with the standard. To see why this is insufficient for security testing, suppose that in writing software to process bank account transactions I have inserted a section of program which will add £50,000 to the recorded balance of my account on a certain future date. Random black-box testing will almost certainly not find even this crude fraud because all normal transactions are processed correctly, and the tests are unlikely to hit on the particular date on which I expect to collect my jackpot. Clearly for security testing a stronger approach is needed which assesses the internal logic of the process under test; only this approach will enable the rogue bit of program (called a *logic bomb*) to be found and highlighted for appropriate management action before any damage is done.

The internal logic of a process can only be assessed if there is a specification available defining what it is supposed to do. To ensure that this specification is unambiguous it may be written in a formal (i.e. quasi-mathematical) language. Several such languages were available when the group started this work, including VDM, Z, SDL, LOTOS, Estelle and RAISE, and an early task of the group was therefore to investigate these and assess their suitability for use in the data security field.

There were two threads in this work. First, as regards the use of formal methods in standards, a comparative study was made using the Message Authenticator Algorithm (MAA) as an example. Here VDM was found to be the most appropriate tool; in fact as a direct result of this work weaknesses were identified in the published standard, and a revised version was issued in 1992 (see ref. 74). Secondly, as regards the use of formal methods to provide a basis for security assessments of software, the RAISE language was identified as the most appropriate. However to prove mathematically that a formal specification and a module of software are functionally equivalent is a highly complex and expensive process, and attention turned to less ambitious ways of gaining confidence in the security of products or systems.

The term *strict conformance testing* was coined to describe the process of assessing an implementation of an IT security standard. As first conceived, the concept covered a range of possible techniques: black-box testing as developed for communication protocol implementations (checking that prescribed functions are carried out correctly); extended black-box testing (checking as far as possible that no other functions are carried out); program proving using a formal specification; white-box testing, in which the tester has access to the internal structure of the item under test while it is in operation; detailed examination of the program text without running it, probably using software tools to search for abnormalities; and checking that an appropriate quality system was in use while the software was being constructed. In later use, the term was restricted to the two types of black-box testing only. More detail is given in the reports listed below. The work is still in progress at the time of writing.

Publications on standards and formal methods in data security

D W Davies and D O Clayden. The Message Authenticator Algorithm (MAA) and its implementation. NPL Report DITC 109/88, February 1988.

G I Parkin and G O'Neill. Specification of the MAA Standard in VDM. NPL Report DITC 160/90, February 1990.

Cranfield IT Institute Ltd. Formal description techniques and security standard conformance testing. NPL Report DITC 175/91, March 1991.

Cranfield IT Institute Ltd. Software metrics and security standard conformance testing. NPL Report DITC 176/91, April 1991.

R Lampard. Formal methods in IT security standards: scope for usage. NPL Report DITC 177/91, March 1991.

R Lampard. An appraisal of communicating sequential processes. NPL Report DITC 178/91, March 1991.

R Lampard. Formal description techniques in data security: an evaluation and comparison. NPL Report DITC 182/91, April 1991.

M K F Lai. Using the Modula-2 Standard to verify Modula-2 programs. NPL Report DITC 183/91, June 1991.

M K F Lai. A formal interpretation of the MAA Standard in Z. NPL Report DITC 184/91, June 1991.

R Lampard. Specification of the two-way handshake in VDM. NPL Report DITC 188/91, September 1991.

D R Manning. Software metrics and the conformance testing of data security standards. NPL Report DITC 189/91, September 1991.

D R Manning. The representation of data security standards in SDL. NPL Report DITC 190/91, September 1991.

H Munster. LOTOS specification of the MAA standard, with an evaluation of LOTOS. NPL Report DITC 191/91, September 1991.

G I Parkin and G O'Neill. Specification of the MAA Standard in VDM. In: S Prehn and W J Toetenel (eds), *Proc. VDM '91: Formal Software Development Methods,* Springer-Verlag, October 1991, pp.526–544. This specification is also in ISO 8731-2: 1992, see ref. 74.

A Harry. VDM specification of the MD4 message digest algorithm. NPL Report DITC 204/92, August 1992.

A Harry. The use of formal methods in data security standards. NPL Report DITC 205/92, August 1992.

A Harry. RAISE specification of the MD4 message digest algorithm. NPL Report DITC 206/92, September 1992.

A Harry. State of the art report on the automatic generation of reference implementation and test code from formal specifications. NPL Report DITC 207/92, October 1992.

A Harry. The value of reference implementations and prototyping in a formal design and testing methodology. NPL Report DITC 208/92, October 1992.

A Harry. The application of programming languages to the production of reference implementations. NPL Report DITC 209/92, October 1992.

A Harry. VDM specification of the secure hash algorithm. NPL Report DITC 212/92, December 1992.

R Manning, B Szczygiel and A Harry. Testability of data security standards. NPL Report DITC 217/93, February 1993.

Data Security Group. Standards and conformance testing in data security: results of initial programme of investigation. NPL Report DITC 218/93, March 1993.

R Lampard. The requirements for a methodology to test secure open systems. NPL Report DITC 222/93, September 1993.

A Lovering. Issues in using formal methods for specifying security standards. NPL Report DITC 224/93, October 1993.

A Harry. Z and RAISE: a case study and comparison. NPL Report DITC 230/95, May 1995.

B Szczygiel and R Lampard. A strict conformance test suite for ISO/IEC 9798-4. NPL Report DITC 231/95, May 1995.

Data Security Group. The final progress report on the programme: a new approach to testing of IT security. NPL Report DITC 233/95, June 1995.

B Szczygiel. The results of the new approach consultation exercise. NPL Report DITC 234/95, June 1995.

A S Lovering. Formal methods, structured techniques and security—a unified methodology. NPL Report DITC 235/95, June 1995.

B Szczygiel, R Lampard and R M Barker. The application of quality assurance procedures to security evaluation. NPL Report DITC 236/95, July 1995.

Commercial Computer Security Centre (CCSC)

In 1987 the Department of Trade and Industry established a unit with this title to provide technical advice to UK industry on IT security issues and to stimulate a systematic approach to the assessment of security aspects of civil IT systems. This approach was to be based on the experience and requirements developed by purchasers in the defence field, particularly the US Department of Defense. Because of the defence link the Centre was originally established at the Royal Signals and Radar Establishment at Malvern, but in April 1990 it was moved to NPL, where it was staffed by consultants, with technical management by NPL on behalf of the Department.

The work at Malvern had resulted in seven volumes of proposed criteria and codes of practice which were a major contribution to the state of the art of IT security evaluation. Because the markets for IT products are international, separate criteria in each country would cause problems for suppliers and waste of effort by evaluators. It was therefore important to harmonise national security evaluation criteria, so making a basis for international acceptance of national evaluation results. When the Centre moved to NPL the emphasis of the work had shifted to these international harmonisation issues.

In May 1990 draft harmonised evaluation criteria were published under the name of ITSEC; these were followed by an IT Security Evaluation Manual (ITSEM). The next step was to establish an organisation in the UK to assess and certify evaluations of products and systems carried out by industry using these documents. A UK Certification Body was established at Cheltenham for this purpose in May 1991, including two members of NPL staff, Tim Moore and Jim Alyson, on secondment. NPL staff also acted as lead assessors for NAMAS in the accreditation of the testing laboratories, which were called CLEFS

(Commercial Licensed Evaluation Facilities). The CCSC was closed down when its task was complete in 1993, and at the time of writing (1996) the certification body is in full operation, still with NPL involvement.

Publications on CCSC, ITSEC and ITSEM

D Brewer, B Chorley, R Lampard, M Nash and F Williams. The UK Department of Trade and Industry's Commercial Computer Security Centre. In: Lindsay and Price (1991), ref. 84 pp.15–22.

M Nash, D Brewer, B Chorley, R Lampard and F Williams. Security criteria harmonisation: the Information Technology Security Evaluation Criteria. In: Lindsay and Price (1991), ref. 84 pp.23–34.

R Lampard. Specifying ITSEC functionality classes using the claims language. NPL Report DITC 186/91, August 1991.

R Lampard. Automatic claims derivation from a user's security policy using AI techniques. NPL Report DITC 187/91, September 1991.

R Lampard. The information technology security evaluation manual: a summary of evaluation philosophy. *Proc. 7th European Conference on Information Systems Security, Control and Audit*, Brussels, November 1992.

6.4 Mathematical software

Work in numerical mathematics in this period maintained the pattern established by the end of the previous era, with algorithms for metrology as the main theme and projects in other areas being undertaken as opportunity offered. In addition to the metrology work, three of these secondary projects are outlined below: work on neural networks, on applications of the Boundary Element Method, and on the behaviour of materials.

Four conferences organised in the period deserve particular mention. In July 1987 a major international conference on reliable numerical computation (ref. 23) was held at NPL in memory of Jim Wilkinson who had died the previous year; in July 1988 a conference on the twin topics of Algorithms for Approximation and Scientific Software and Systems, organised jointly with the Royal Military College of Science, was held at Shrivenham; and conferences on Advanced Mathematical Tools in Metrology were held in Turin in October 1993 and in Oxford in September 1995. The last two, supported by European Commission funding, were particularly important for the group, giving them an opportunity to promote understanding of their work in industry and elsewhere, to demonstrate the need for continuing financial support and generally to consolidate their claim to international leadership in the field of algorithms for metrology.

After the sharp cuts in the previous era, staff numbers remained constant at 10 or 11 until 1990; there was then a further slow reduction until the Mathematical Software group was only five strong by September 1995; Maurice Cox, Alistair Forbes, Peter

Harris, Simon Hannaby and Bernard Butler were the survivors. To allow Maurice to spend more time on technical work George Symm headed the group from 1990 until his retirement in 1994. In spite of the overall decline in numbers the group remained strong in the key area of dimensional metrology; it has continued to win contracts and at the time of writing (1996) prospects for some future expansion look good.

Algorithms for metrology

By the start of this period the development of software and standards for dimensional metrology described in section 5.6 had emerged as the main theme of the work of the group. In 1987 existing software for coordinate measuring machines (CMMs) was investigated as part of an intercomparison study commissioned by the CEC's Bureau of Reference (BCR), in which NPL played a leading part. This confirmed that a significant proportion of the commercially available programs for the assessment of simple geometric features could give misleading results. Because CMMs are widely used in inspection and quality control, these failures could lead to the acceptance of faulty components with potentially serious consequences. To improve the situation, a series of studies of particular geometric forms was carried out, led by Maurice Cox and Alistair Forbes, and the results were filtered through the appropriate BSI committee and distilled into a British Standard Guide for the assessment of geometric forms, BS 7172.

When the shape of a mechanical component is measured, apparent departures from nominal form can arise in two ways: first, there may be real defects in the component, which will cause systematic deviations, and secondly the measurement process itself will inevitably involve small errors, both random and systematic. In the late 1980s the least-squares criterion, as defined in BS 7172, was normally used in the assessment. For example, suppose the surface being assessed is meant to be flat. First the positions of a set of points on the surface were measured using a CMM; then a nominal plane surface was chosen so as to minimise the sum of the squares of the distances of the measured points from it. The flatness was defined as the minimum distance apart of two planes parallel to this one and such that all the measured points lay on or between them. This process was well understood and the software was reasonably straightforward to write and fast to run. However there was an alternative definition of the nominal surface: to choose it so that the maximum distance of the measured points from it was minimised (this is known as the Chebyshev criterion). This gave a measure of flatness nearer to the traditional engineering concept of tolerance than the least-squares method, though it was more complex to program and slower to run. In 1990–93 the BCR funded a major project to develop new Chebyshev-based reference software for CMMs, with NPL as the prime contractor. The success of this work led to further contracts, funded partly by BCR and partly by DTI, for work by NPL and industrial collaborators to develop and transfer the technology; one contract for example was concerned with techniques for measuring large artefacts such as helicopter rotor blades where accurate measurements of parts of the object need to be combined to enable the whole to be assessed.

In the 1990s the group put an increasing emphasis on standard methods for testing numerical software; for example, outside the field of dimensional metrology, reference data sets were developed for testing statistical software used by analytical chemists. At the time of writing (1996) Maurice Cox is leading work in ISO on the development of an international standard for testing CMM software, and work is in progress on the establishment of a CMM software testing service at NPL.

Selected publications on algorithms for metrology

A B Forbes. Fitting an ellipse to data. NPL Report DITC 95/87, December 1987.

A B Forbes. Fitting a generalized parabola to data. NPL Report DITC 96/87, September 1987.

A B Forbes. Fitting a circle to radially suppressed data. NPL Report DITC 103/87, December 1987.

M G Cox and H M Jones. An algorithm for least-squares circle fitting to data with specified uncertainty ellipses. NPL Report DITC 118/88, June 1988.

A B Forbes. Least-squares best-fit geometric elements. NPL Report DITC 140/89, April 1989.

A B Forbes. Robust circle and sphere fitting by least squares. NPL Report DITC 153/89, November 1989.

BSI. Assessment of position, size and departure from nominal form of geometric features. BS 7172: 1989.

M G Cox. Mathematical modelling in manufacturing metrology. NPL Report DITC 157/90, February 1990; also published in B J Davies (ed.), *Proc. 28th International MATADOR Conference*, UMIST and MacMillan Education Ltd, 1990, pp.533–539.

E J Griffin, M G Cox et al. Software management guidelines for automated measuring systems. NPL Report DES 99, July 1990.

G T Anthony, H M Anthony, M G Cox and A B Forbes. The parametrization of geometric form. CEC Report EUR 13517 EN, Luxembourg, 1991.

M G Cox. Improving CMM software quality. NPL Report DITC 194/92, January 1992.

M G Cox. Assessing CMM software quality. *Quality Today,* January 1992.

A B Forbes. Position calibration software for the form assessment of complex workpieces. NPL Report DITC 203/92, July 1992.

A B Forbes. Geometric tolerance assessment. NPL Report DITC 210/92, October 1992.

M G Cox and A B Forbes. Strategies for testing form assessment software. NPL Report DITC 211/92, December 1992.

Mathematical Software Group. Chebyshev best-fit geometric elements. NPL Report DITC 221/93, September 1993.

G T Anthony, B P Butler, M G Cox, A B Forbes, S A Hannaby, P M Harris et al. Chebyshev reference software for the evaluation of coordinate measuring machine data. CEC Report EUR 15304 EN, Brussels-Luxembourg, 1993.

G T Anthony, M G Cox and A B Forbes. Correctness of assessment software in coordinate metrology. In: N Ikawa et al. (eds), *International Progress in Precision Engineering: Proc. 7th International Precision Engineering Seminar,* Butterworth-Heinemann, 1993, pp.28–39.

M G Cox and P M Harris. Assessing fundamental geometric form from measured coordinate data. In: A K Kochhar (ed.), *Proc. 30th International MATADOR Conference,* UMIST, Manchester, 1993, pp.655–662.

A B Forbes. Position calibration software for the form assessment of complex workpieces. In: A K Kochhar (ed.), *Proc. 30th International MATADOR Conference,* UMIST, Manchester, 1993, pp.663–670.

P Ciarlini, M G Cox, R Monaco and F Pavese (eds). *Advanced Mathematical Tools in Metrology.* Proc. conf. held in Turin, October 1993, World Scientific, Singapore, 1994. This book includes four NPL papers:
  M G Cox. Survey of numerical methods and metrology applications: discrete processes, pp.1–22.
  B P Butler, A B Forbes and P M Harris. Geometric tolerance assessment problems, pp.95–104.
  M G Cox. A classification of mathematical software for metrology, pp.239–246.
  A B Forbes. Mathematical software for metrology: meeting the needs of the metrologist, pp.247–254.

A B Forbes. Validation of assessment software in dimensional metrology. NPL Report DITC 225/94, February 1994; also published in M J Downs (ed.), *Laser Dimensional Metrology: Recent Advances for Industrial Application,* Proc. SPIE [Soc. of Photo-Optical Instrumentation Engineers], 2088, 1994, pp.27–36.

B P Butler, M G Cox and A B Forbes. The reconstruction of workpiece surfaces from probe centre data. In: R B Fisher (ed.), *Design and Application of Curves and Surfaces,* Clarendon Press, 1994, pp.99–116.

B P Butler, A B Forbes and P M Harris. Algorithms for geometric tolerance assessment. NPL Report DITC 228/94, November 1994.

ISO. Co-ordinate metrology: definitions and applications of the fundamental geometric principles. Part 6: method for testing software for computing Gaussian substitute features in co-ordinate metrology. ISO CD 10360 part 6, 1995.

P Ciarlini, M G Cox, F Pavese and D Richter (eds). *Advanced Mathematical Tools for Metrology II.* Proc. conf. held in Oxford, September 1995, World Scientific, 1996. This book includes three NPL papers:
  M G Cox. Constructing and solving mathematical models of measurement, pp.7–21.
  A B Forbes. Model parametrization, pp.29–47.
  A B Forbes and P M Harris. A comparison of methods used for the calculation of effective area in the calibration of pressure balances, pp.149–160.

Neural networks

A *neural network* consists of a large number of simple computing units which are interconnected by one-way channels and operate in parallel. At each step in a computation, each unit or *node* calculates an output based on the state of its inputs, and this output is passed to the connected nodes to form part of their input in the next step. The algorithm in each node is simple but, crucially, it can vary with time depending on the node's experience. Input is given to the network at a designated set of nodes, and may comprise real numbers or binary patterns; output likewise is produced by a designated set of nodes, which may or may not be the same set as the input nodes. The network is made to do useful work not by programming but by *training;* in other words it is given an input and also told what the output should be, and this process is repeated many times; at each stage the numerical weights incorporated in the algorithm in each node are varied slightly to bring the overall output nearer to its target. Neural networks are so called because their operation appears to model some aspects of the working of the brain.

To investigate the properties of neural networks they can be simulated in a conventional computer; the simulated network will be relatively very slow, but once a useful design has been achieved it can be implemented on parallel hardware if speed is important.

Turing was apparently the first to propose artificial neural networks whose performance could be developed by training (see refs. 140 and 22), and academic interest in both natural and artificial networks became strong in the period 1954–69, led by Uttley, Rosenblatt and others, but it was dampened when it was shown by Minsky and Papert (ref. 91) that one particular type of network had only limited capabilities. Interest was reawakened in the late 1980s when useful work was obtained from networks of other types: they were reported as doing better than conventional systems at a wide range of tasks including scoring loan applications for creditworthiness and detecting explosives in airport luggage (by recognising the 'signatures' of particular substances in the complex gamma-ray emissions produced when the luggage is bombarded with neutrons).

In 1988 a small group was formed in DITC to gain experience in neural nets with the aim of eventually establishing a role for NPL in promoting quality and best practice in the field; the main contributors were Tony Mansfield and Alistair Forbes, with Peter Vaswani also involved for a time at the start. The group was supported from the General Research Surcharge. The initial work established two significant results: first that treating the training phase as a mathematical problem can reduce the time taken and produce a network that gives the correct result for a wider range of input values, and secondly that some well-known mathematical methods can be implemented efficiently using a neural network. Work was also started on methods of assessing the reliability of neural nets, essential if they are ever to undertake some safety-critical tasks to which they appear potentially well-suited, and industrial contacts were established.

Work on neural networks was suspended in early 1993 for lack of funds.

Publications on neural networks

A B Forbes and A J Mansfield. Neural implementation of a method for solving systems of linear algebraic equations. NPL Report DITC 155/89, November 1989.

A J Mansfield. An introduction to neural networks. In: J C Mason and M G Cox (eds), *Scientific Software Systems,* Chapman and Hall, 1990, pp.112–122.

A B Forbes and A J Mansfield. Neural implementation of a method for solving systems of linear equations. *Network 1,* 1990, pp.217–229.

A J Mansfield. Training perceptrons by linear programming. NPL Report DITC 181/91, August 1991.

A J Mansfield. Comparison of perceptron training by linear programming and by the perceptron convergence procedure. *Proc. Int. Joint Conf. on Neural Networks,* Seattle, 1991, pp.II-25-30.

The Boundary Element Method: an example application

Equipment to monitor rates of radioactive decay is important in the nuclear power industry. Typically the key element in the monitoring device is a box in which an electrostatic field is maintained between two or more electrodes; when charged particles produced by the radioactive decay process enter the box, the field is disturbed, and this change can be detected by circuits connected to the electrodes.

In 1989, to improve their detailed understanding of the working of these devices, the Division of Radiation Science and Acoustics at NPL asked the Mathematical Software group to investigate the shape of the undisturbed electrostatic field in a device of this type. In this design there were in effect three electrodes, each maintained at a constant potential; two were areas of the interior surface of the box and the third was a fine wire running through it. In such a situation the electrostatic field takes up a form which is consistent with the potentials of the electrodes and in the space between them is determined by the requirement that the electrostatic potential must satisfy Laplace's equation. The positions and potentials of the electrodes form part of the boundary conditions in the sense defined on p.185, and the mathematical problem is to find the solution of Laplace's equation which is consistent with the boundary conditions.

This provides a typical application for the *Boundary Element Method,* in which the boundary is divided into a number of elements and a set of simultaneous linear algebraic equations is derived for certain values on these elements. These equations are solved by standard methods of linear algebra, and this allows an approximate solution to the governing differential equation to be calculated. The number of boundary elements can be increased to bring the results as near as required to the exact solution; in this case, 104 were sufficient. The results were represented graphically to show how the shape of the field changed with different values of the electrode potentials.

This work was one of many problems involving applications and extensions of numerical methods for the solution of partial differential equations, including the boundary element method, undertaken by George Symm and Simon Hannaby in this period.

Publications on numerical methods for the solution of partial differential equations

S A Hannaby. Finite element mesh generation and isoparametric elements. NPL Report DITC 97/87, August 1987.

S A Hannaby. A comparison of four finite and infinite element techniques. NPL Report DITC 123/88, August 1988.

G T Symm. Computation of the field in a multi-element proportional counter. In: C A Brebbia and N G Zamani (eds), *Boundary Element Techniques: Applications in Engineering*, Proc. 4th Int. Conf. on Boundary Element Technology, held in Windsor, Canada, June 1989, Computational Mechanics Publications, 1989, pp.49–57.

S Jenkins, A W Preece, T E Hodgetts, G T Symm, A G P Warham and R N Clarke. Comparison of three numerical treatments for the open-ended coaxial line sensor. *Electronics Letters*, 26, 1990, pp.234–236.

G T Symm. A problem in magnet design. In: C A Brebbia and A Chaudouet-Miranda (eds), *Boundary Elements in Mechanical and Electrical Engineering*, Computational Mechanics Publications, 1990, pp.431–440.

G S Gipson and G T Symm (eds). Boundary integral equation methods (boundary element methods). *Mathematical and Computer Modelling*, 15(3–5), 1991.

G T Symm. The method of infinite matrices—an alternative to BEM. In: C A Brebbia and G S Gipson (eds), *Boundary Elements XIII*, Computational Mechanics Publications, 1991, pp.825–837.

G T Symm. Design of a cryogenic current comparator. In: C A Brebbia et al. (eds), *Boundary Element Methods XIV*, Vol. 1: Field Problems and Applications. Computational Mechanics Publications, 1992, pp.519–526.

A P Gregory, R N Clarke, T E Hodgetts and G T Symm. RF and microwave dielectric measurements upon layered materials using a reflectometric coaxial sensor. NPL Report DES 125, March 1993.

S A Hannaby. The use and analysis of infinite elements. PhD thesis, City University, London, February 1994.

Behaviour of materials

Chemists use English in a way all their own. A *system* is that part of the universe to which the chemist's attention is currently directed; it may be the contents of a test tube or a pile of slag in a furnace or the atmosphere of Mars. A *phase* is a part of a system which is internally homogeneous. A *species* is a chemical substance (regardless of its state), and a *component* is an aggregate of species acting as a single unit in a chemical interaction. Thus a system consisting of distinct volumes of water, ice and water vapour is a three-phase single component system.

When engineers choose materials, they need to know in advance how they will behave in stated conditions. For example, a lamp may be made of silica glass with tungsten electrodes and molybdenum seals, and contain a cocktail of gases chosen to achieve the required colour and intensity of light. How will this system behave chemically under stated conditions of temperature and pressure? To answer such questions, physical chemists discover the behaviour of simple systems by experiment and record the results in a data bank; then the properties of more complex systems can be predicted using data selected from the bank and the known laws of physical chemistry. The most important of these laws in this context states that a system will change in such a way that a quantity known as the Gibbs energy decreases, and will reach equilibrium when the Gibbs energy is at a minimum. If the conditions are changed, for example the temperature is increased, further changes will in general occur until the Gibbs energy is again at a minimum.

The Gibbs energy is a mathematical function of (1) numerical data relating to each species present and its state, (2) temperature, and (3) pressure in the case of gaseous phases. Determining how a system will behave therefore becomes a matter of minimising this function, a process of numerical optimisation in the sense described on p.186. For very simple systems this process is straightforward, but practical systems may contain 100 species, 20 components and 50 phases and in such cases the use of mathematical software is essential.

In 1983 Susan Hodson of the Mathematical Software group began a fruitful collaboration with Tom Barry of the Metallurgical Thermochemistry Section in the then Division of Materials Applications (later the Division of Materials Metrology). Her role was to develop the mathematical software module (called Multiphase) of what became MTDATA, an NPL product comprising software and data for the calculation of phase equilibria. MTDATA is used to predict the behaviour of complex multicomponent systems when experimental data are available only for subsystems. It is an interactive system with graphical output which will run on desktop computers, and it has been a considerable success story, with its own user group and a steadily expanding clientele; its development, and Susan Hodson's involvement, continue at the time of writing.

Publications on MTDATA

A T Dinsdale, S M Hodson, T I Barry and J R Taylor. Computations using MTDATA of metal-matte-slag-gas equilibria. *27th Annual Conf. of Metallurgists*, CIM, Montreal, 1988, 11, p.59.

R H Davies, S M Hodson et al. MTDATA—the NPL databank for metallurgical thermochemistry. In: F H Hayes (ed.), *User Aspects of Phase Diagrams*, proc. int. conf. held at Petten, 25–27 June 1990, Institute of Metals, 1990, pp.140–152.

T I Barry, S M Hodson et al. MTDATA handbook: documentation for the NPL metallurgical and thermochemical databank. NPL, 1989.

6.5 Software engineering

Brian Wichmann's work on compiler validation and on the Ada language in 1975–87, described in section 5.5, brought him an international standing which made him the chief asset of the Software Engineering group in the following years. In this period his main contributions were in the fields of standards for computer arithmetic, safety-critical software, and software testing, often with particular reference to Ada. In parallel with this work the group developed a general expertise in the use of formal methods. These topics are considered briefly in turn below. In addition, Roger Scowen continued his work on the international standardisation of Prolog (see p.225).

Brian Wichmann headed the group in the early years of this period. To give him more time for technical work, Roger Scowen took over as head in 1991–92, and Nick North in 1992–95. The other main contributors were Peter Wilkinson until his departure in 1988, Tony Mansfield, Graeme Parkin, Guy O'Neill, Paul Kenward, Steve Austin and David Barfoot.

Quality and standards in computer arithmetic

As discussed in section 3.9, most numbers cannot be held exactly in a computer. This means that the designers of the basic arithmetic processes such as division, subtraction, and testing for zero, whether in hardware or software, are faced with difficulties. For example, if 0.7 and 1.4 are not held exactly, as would be the case with most ways of representing them, the result of dividing 0.7 by 1.4 and then subtracting 0.5 will probably not be exactly zero, though it will be very close to it; this in turn will mean that if the result is straightforwardly tested to see if it is zero the answer will be 'no'. The only general solution to this problem is to test, not that the result is zero, but that its magnitude is less than some very small number; then results will look sensible. However, problems could still arise if, for example, compiler writers or language standards adopted different practices in this area, because a correct program might then give different results depending on which system was in use, clearly an unsatisfactory state of affairs.

There are many other issues lurking in the small print of the computer arithmetic manual. For example, what happens if you take the largest integer that the system in use can represent and add one to it? What happens if you try to divide by zero? All computer systems deal systematically with these matters under the heading of overflow; the point is that in 1987 there were still many different conventions in use, leading to a risk of malfunction, and therefore expense and possible danger, when software modules were altered or used in a new context.

A software package for testing computer arithmetic facilities was presented at the NPL Open Days in 1987. Known as FPV (Floating Point Validation) and available in both Fortran 77 and Pascal, it had been developed by the Numerical Algorithms Group (NAG) Ltd in collaboration with NPL, and formed the basis for a subsequent testing service run by NAG. It could check for many possible defects, but its status was weakened by the fact that at that time there were no agreed international standards against which the behaviour of the system under test could be compared.

In late 1987 Brian Wichmann circulated preliminary proposals for a new standard to meet this need. After the long gestation period usual in such cases, these proposals eventually led to the Language Independent Arithmetic Standard (ref. 79), of which Part 1 was published in 1994, a considerable step forward based very largely on Brian's original initiative.

B A Wichmann. Getting the correct answers. NPL Report DITC 167/90, June 1990.
B A Wichmann. The language compatible arithmetic standard and Ada. NPL Report DITC 173/91, February 1991.
B A Wichmann. Microprocessor design faults. *Microprocessors and Microsystems,* 17(7), 1993, pp.399–401.

Safety-critical software

When the Ada language was published, it attracted some criticism from influential independent experts on the grounds that (1) it was too complex, (2) this complexity made it difficult for a programmer to be sure that the program correctly represented his intentions, and (3) this uncertainty made the language inherently dangerous in applications where human safety was involved. The resulting controversy drew attention to the special need for those developing safety-critical software to have tools and codes of practice available to ensure that the risks of software errors were minimised. Brian Wichmann made recommendations in this area and his reports are listed below.

In 1995 the Ada language was revised by the International Organization for Standardization with funding from the US Department of Defense. Brian Wichmann was again involved, this time taking responsibility for an annex on the special requirements of high-integrity systems (usually those where safety or security depends on their correct operation).

Publications on safety-critical software

B A Wichmann. Insecurities in the Ada programming language. NPL Report DITC 137/89, January 1989; an interim version was published as DITC 122/88, August 1988.
G O'Neill and B A Wichmann. A contribution to the debate on safety-critical software. NPL Report DITC 126/88, September 1988.

B A Wichmann. Requirements for programming languages in safety and security software standards. *Computer Standards and Interfaces,* 14, 1992, pp.433–441.

B A Wichmann (ed.). *Software in Safety-Related Systems.* Wiley, 1992.

B A Wichmann. A development model for safety-critical software. In: B A Wichmann (ed.), *Software in Safety-Related Systems,* Wiley, 1992, pp.209–223.

B A Wichmann. High-level languages without a compiler? Ada UK Yearbook, 1992, pp.228–231.

B A Wichmann and J McHugh. Ada 9X safety and security annex. In: W J Taylor (ed.), *Ada in Transition,* IOS Press, 1992, pp.46–55.

B A Wichmann. Are Booleans safe? ACM Ada Letters, May/June 1993, pp.88–90.

B A Wichmann. Programming critical systems: the Ada 9X solution. *Computer Bulletin,* 5(5), October 1993, pp.15–16.

B A Wichmann. Producing critical systems: the Ada 9X solution. In: F Redmill and T Anderson (eds), *Technology and Assessment of Safety-Critical Systems,* Springer-Verlag, 1994, pp.194–203.

B A Wichmann. Agreeing the safety and security annex. In: C Loftus (ed.), *Ada Yearbook 1994,* IOS Press, 1994, pp.141–146.

B A Wichmann. A review of a safety-critical software standard. NPL, June 1994.

B A Wichmann. Why is it difficult producing safety critical software? *Ingenuity* [ICL's technical journal], 10(1), May 1995, pp.96–104.

Other work on Ada

It is not always appreciated that a product can conform to a standard and yet be quite unsatisfactory in performance. For example, a compiler may produce correct object code but do so unreasonably slowly, or the object code it produces may be formally correct but itself run too slowly, or the diagnostic messages produced by the compiler when it detects errors in its input may be difficult to understand. In 1987–88 the Ministry of Defence launched an Ada Evaluation Service, run for them by BSI-QAS, to assess compiler quality in this sense; it was separate from the existing Ada Validation Service, whose task was to assess conformance with the published standard. Brian Wichmann chaired an international group reviewing the evaluation service to ensure that it was as useful as possible to users of Ada outside the defence community.

The group also took part in the review process for the Portable Common Tools Environment (PCTE), a European initiative to enable a set of Ada (or C) software engineering tools to be used on a range of host systems.

Brian Wichmann contributed to several other Ada projects and initiatives, including the Ada 9X revision mentioned above which started in 1989 and Low-Ada (a proposed intermediate language for use in the validation of Ada programs); further details are given in the reports listed below.

B A Wichmann. Low-Ada: an Ada validation tool. NPL Report DITC 144/89, August 1989.

S Witchalls. An Ada evaluation report for the Verdix Corp.—VADS version 5.5 release H compiler. NPL Report DITC 145/89, July 1989.

B A Wichmann. Exponentiate in Ada. NPL Report DITC 146/89, September 1989.

B Jansen. Storage allocation in Ada. NPL Report DITC 156/90, February 1990.

P D Kenward and B A Wichmann. Approved Ada uniformity issues. NPL Report DITC 172/91, January 1991.

B A Wichmann. Why Ada is for you. In: M Woodman (ed.), *Programming Language Choice: Practice and Experience,* Thomson Computer Press, 1996, pp.125–133.

Testing compilers with generated programs

The test suite for Pascal compilers described in section 5.5 consisted of programs written by human programmers in the normal way. But for some purposes it would be useful to generate test programs automatically using a software tool developed for the purpose. This is because the tests could then be made much more severe: they could include complex multiply-nested structures which would be too time consuming and error prone to write in the normal way but which conform to the standard and therefore should be compiled correctly. This idea was explored first in the context of Pascal, using software developed for the purpose called the Pascal Program Generator. In 1990 work started in collaboration with BSI-QAS to develop a similar tool for Ada, a much bigger task undertaken by Steve Austin and Rhys Wilkins with guidance from Brian Wichmann. The Ada Program Test Generator was completed successfully in 1991, and the idea was later extended to other languages including Haskell and Chill.

B A Wichmann and M Davies. Experience with a compiler testing tool [the Pascal Program Generator]. NPL Report DITC 138/89, March 1989.

S M Austin, D R Wilkins and B A Wichmann. An Ada program test generator. *Proc. Conf. Tri-Ada'91,* held in San Jose, October 1991, ACM, 1991.

Formal methods

Formal methods have already been mentioned in the context of OSI conformance testing (p.252) and data security (p.256), where they are particularly useful; but they can also be applied in the design and assessment of any other system which is meant to work in a certain way but which is complicated enough for it not to be obvious that it can be relied on to do so. Railway signalling is a good example. There will be many possible combinations of settings of points and signals; some of these are safe and some are unsafe. If the criteria for classifying a particular combination as safe or unsafe can be expressed formally (that is, using a mathematical-style notation), this formalisation will be a valuable tool. It could be used for example as the basis for a watchdog system, to ring alarm bells if a human controller attempted to set up an unsafe combination; or if the signals are computer controlled, it could be used to help in designing the software and checking it before installation.

As computer systems became more complex, and started to be used in situations such as financial transaction processing and spacecraft control where failure was expensive or life threatening, it became clear that formal methods, though no panacea, offered a powerful technique for reducing the risk of malfunction, and so formed a vital item in the software engineer's toolbox. The software engineering group, in particular Graeme Parkin, established an expertise in the more important available techniques, notably the Vienna Development Method (VDM), so-called because it was derived from work at IBM Vienna. The group contributed to the establishment of an international standard for VDM, and actively promoted its adoption, for example by developing and distributing software tools to help in its use. Their work on the Message Authenticator Algorithm standard, described above (p.257) under the heading of Data Security, provides a good example of the benefits of using VDM.

In 1992 Graeme Parkin and Steve Austin carried out a survey of industry and higher education which sought to establish what formal methods were in use, what were their perceived benefits and limitations, and what barriers to their wider adoption were felt to exist. The results were published in March 1993 (see list below). They showed that the most widely used methods were VDM and Z, and that their commonest uses were in specification and proof, with refinement (the process of moving in stages from a formal specification to an executable program) third. The perceived benefits included the clarification of requirements, the early removal of errors (late removal is much more expensive), and the possibility of proving properties of the system under construction. The perceived limitations included the fact that clients could not read a formal specification, and the inability of formal methods to express important system characteristics such as its usability, performance and maintainability. The survey attracted considerable interest.

Work on formal methods continues at the time of writing (1996).

Publications on formal methods

G O'Neill. Rapid prototyping of formal specifications using Miranda. NPL Report DITC 150/89, November 1989.

N D North. An implementation of sets and maps as Miranda abstract data types. NPL Report DITC 162/90, February 1990.

P Mukherjee and V Stavridou. The formal specification of safety requirements for the storage of explosives. NPL Report DITC 185/91, August 1991.

Z Jabry and S Austin. An experiment in VDM to SQL translation. NPL Report DITC 193/91, November 1991.

G O'Neill. Automatic translation of VDM specifications into standard ML programs. NPL Report DITC 196/92, February 1992.

S M Austin and G I Parkin. Formal methods: a survey. NPL, March 1993.

G I Parkin and B A Wichmann. Conformity clause for VDM-SL. In: J C P Woodcock and P G Larsen (eds), *Industrial Strength Formal Methods Europe FME '93, Proc. 1st Int. Symposium on Formal Methods*, held in Odense, Denmark, April 1993, Springer-Verlag, 1993, pp.501–520.

P Mukherjee and B A Wichmann. STV [Single Transferable Vote]: a case study of the use of VDM. NPL Report DITC 219/93, May 1993.

P Mukherjee and B A Wichmann. Formal specification of the STV algorithm. In: M G Hinchey and J P Bowen (eds), *Applications of Formal Methods*, Prentice-Hall, 1995, pp.73-96.

G I Parkin. Survey of formal methods in software engineering. *Software Reliability and Metrics Club Newsletter*, September 1993.

G I Parkin. Vienna Development Method Specification Language (VDM-SL). *Computer Standards and Interfaces*, 16, September 1994, pp.527–530.

G I Parkin and S M Austin. Overview: survey of formal methods in industry. *Proc. IFIP TC6/WG6.1 6th Int. Conf. on Formal Description Techniques*, North-Holland, 1994.

A Harry. *Formal Methods Fact File: VDM and Z*. John Wiley and Sons, 1996.

Publications on the use of formal methods in Open Systems standards and in data security are included in the lists on pp.253 and 258 respectively.

6.6 Parallel processing

In a conventional computer, elementary actions are carried out sequentially by a single processor. For many tasks this requirement for strictly sequential operation is unnecessary: some parts of the task could in principle be carried out in parallel, and if this could be done in practice, using extra processors, time would be saved. As the technology developed, this option of having several processors working in parallel became more attractive for three reasons: processors became cheaper, memory became faster (thus amplifying the bottleneck effect of a single processor), and the complexities of organising a task so that it could be shared out became better understood. Three main flavours of *parallel processors* emerged. The first is known as SIMD (single instruction, multiple data). In this type at each step a central controller issues the same instruction to all the processors and they all carry it out on their own data. This is useful in many common numerical tasks such as forming vector products; the ICL DAP attached to NPL's 2900 mainframe in 1982 (see p.244) had an SIMD architecture. The second type is known as MIMD-DM (multiple instructions, multiple data, distributed memory); in this type each processor is given its own section of program which it carries out independently using its own memory. The Demos system developed in DITC in 1976–82 (see pp.216–218) was an early version of the MIMD-DM type. The third type, MIMD-SM (SM = shared memory), is similar except that the independent processors use memory in common, with a strictly enforced protocol to ensure that the shared memory is used in an orderly way.

In 1988 the Division saw an opportunity to encourage quality and fitness for purpose in this field by developing benchmarks for parallel processors, sets of standard tasks which could be given to such systems to allow their performance to be compared. Early work was supported by DTI, and from 1992 to 1995 the group took part in a collaborative project PEPS (Performance Evaluation of Parallel Systems) funded by the European Commission under the Esprit programme.

As originally planned, PEPS had four main strands: *characterisation* (to derive mathematical expressions for the performance of a parallel system in terms of parameters describing its architecture and the intended application); *modelling* (using simulation to predict the properties of a planned parallel system or the effects of proposed changes in an existing system); *monitoring* (using software tools to provide information on a system in use); and *benchmarks* (to allow the performance of different systems to be compared). NPL's main contribution was to be in the benchmarks area.

Unfortunately for the NPL group, the ambitious benchmark plans proved to be politically impracticable: many benchmarks had already been developed and it was eventually decided that another 'standard' set was unlikely to be accepted as such. In the meantime related US-based work had progressed on a more pragmatic basis. NPL's work on benchmarks was terminated in 1994, and the Laboratory's main role in PEPS was changed. The new task had two threads: first, the establishment of a set of *test cases*, examples of real programs, both scientific and commercial, which could be used to validate the tools and techniques developed in the project, and secondly the development of a methodology giving guidance on how the tools and techniques could best be used in combination. This work was completed in 1996.

The work on parallel processing was carried out by Trevor Chambers, Michael Stevens, Hilary Symm and Peter Pobgee; the group was led by Ed Brocklehurst until his retirement in 1994 and then by Tony Mansfield.

Publications on parallel processing

E R Brocklehurst and P J Pobgee. Parallel processing, a glossary of terms. NPL Report DITC 164/90, May 1990, with an update in report DITC 170/90, November 1990.

E R Brocklehurst, M J Stevens and H J Symm. A comparison of some parallel Fortran dialects. NPL Report DITC 180/91, April 1991.

E R Brocklehurst. Survey of benchmarks. NPL Report DITC 192/91, November 1991.

E R Brocklehurst, M J Stevens and H J Symm. A finite element benchmark for parallel processors. NPL Report DITC 197/92, April 1992.

T H E Chambers, M J Stevens and H J Symm. A neural network benchmark for parallel processors. NPL Report DITC 201/92, July 1992.

T H E Chambers (ed.). *Parallel Processors: Benchmarking and Assessment.* Proc. of an NPL/BCS conference held at NPL, March 1992.

PEPS Bulletin: the Bulletin of the Performance Evaluation of Parallel Systems Project. Issue 1, May 1993, to Issue 6, May 1996; produced for the PEPS project by NPL.

T Chambers and C Lazou. Innovations in parallel benchmarking. *Performance Evaluation of Parallel Systems: PEPS '93*, proc. conf. held at Warwick Univ., November 1993, pp.1–10.

A Mansfield. SOSIP and the PEPS benchmarking methodology. In *PEPS '93* as above, pp.11–16.

6.7 Human–computer interaction

In 1987 it was becoming economically feasible for computers to store and process a wide range of structured audiovisual material, not just the familiar text and graphics. The term *multimedia* was coming into use to describe the new capability. The NPL Human–Computer Interaction group had established a major project aimed at developing, demonstrating and evaluating new types of interface for the widening range of interactive systems. It was a collaborative project with Aberdeen University and others, supported by DTI under the Alvey programme, with the title 'An Intelligent Interface for Integrated Knowledge-Based Systems' (IIIKBS). NPL's contribution was in the design of interfaces which would automatically tailor themselves to suit the individual user, so-called *adaptive interfaces;* more detail is given below. When this project was completed in 1989 the group was able to concentrate on the second aspect of its programme, the establishment of a centre of excellence in methods of measuring the *usability* of interactive systems, offering a service whose clients could get quantitative comparisons of different interface designs; the group's long experience of such designs since its foundation in 1969 meant it was particularly well placed for this role. At the same time the practice of interface design had matured to the point where national and international standardisation was starting to be considered, and here too the group's wide experience enabled it to make a leading contribution. The main areas of work in this period were therefore adaptive interfaces, usability measurement, and standards in HCI, and these are now considered briefly in turn.

Adaptive interfaces

Human speakers and writers understand instinctively that simply knowing their subject matter and being able to express it are not enough to achieve effective communication: they also need to know who their audience is so that they can set the content, pace and style of their presentation appropriately. A doctor explaining a diagnosis, for example, will try to take into account the patient's age, attitude, intelligence and level of background knowledge, and if these are misjudged time will be wasted, misunderstandings may arise, and the level of the patient's satisfaction with the doctor is likely to drop. The analogy is clear: if computer systems were able to take into account some facts about the individual user, corresponding benefits should accrue: time would be saved, the risk of misunderstanding would be reduced, and the level of the user's satisfaction with the system would rise.

On this basis, the idea explored by the NPL HCI group in their contribution to the IIIKBS project mentioned above was that a knowledge-based system should where possible have access to a 'profile' of each user, so that it could provide different interfaces and interaction sequences both for different users and for the same user over time as behaviour changed or familiarity with the system was gained. If standards could be developed and adopted, a user could carry details of his or her personal profile in a smart card or diskette for use with many interactive systems. A user profile could include test scores, age, sex, educational level, keyboard and mouse skills, database navigation behaviour, learning style, personality type, and problem-solving ability. The system would not only adapt its behaviour to this profile but would monitor the interaction and modify its model of the user accordingly.

This work was led by Dianne Murray. It was successfully completed in 1989 with demonstrations of a prototype system.

Publications on adaptive interfaces

C J H Fowler and D M Murray. Gender and cognitive style differences at the human-computer interface. NPL Report DITC 90/87, June 1987; also published in H J Bullinger et al. (eds), *Proc. INTERACT 87, Second IFIP Conf. on Human-Computer Interaction,* held in Stuttgart, Elsevier, 1987.

D Benyon, P Innocent and D M Murray. System adaptivity and the modelling of stereotypes. NPL Report DITC 91/87, June 1987; also published in *Proc. INTERACT 87* as above.

D M Murray. Embedded user models. *Proc. INTERACT 87* as above.

D M Murray. A survey of user cognitive modelling. NPL Report DITC 92/87, May 1988.

D Benyon, S Milan and D Murray. Modelling users' cognitive abilities in an adaptive system. NPL Report DITC 115/88, March 1988; also published in J Rasmussen and P Zunde (eds), *Proc. 5th Symposium EFISS,* held at Riso National Laboratory, Denmark, November 1987, Plenum, 1987.

D Benyon and Dianne Murray. Experience with adaptive interfaces. *Computer Journal*, 31(5), 1988, pp.465–473; reprinted in *Human Computer Interaction*, Cambridge University Press, 1988.

D M Murray. Building a user modelling shell. In: P Zunde (ed.), *Proc. 6th Symposium EFISS*, held in Atlanta October 1988, Plenum, 1988.

Usability

Users of computer systems want to be able to achieve their goals accurately and quickly, with a minimum of physical and mental strain. That they should be able to do so is clearly a matter of economic importance as well as job satisfaction. In other words, usability matters. The usability of a computer system may appear at first sight to be a slippery subjective quality, but the work of the NPL group in this period showed how it could be quantified, giving a basis for objective comparisons between different products or different ways of achieving the same results.

The usability of a product has been defined as the extent to which it can be used to achieve specified goals with effectiveness, efficiency and satisfaction in a specified context of use (ISO 9241-11, ref. 76). Clearly a basic requirement in measuring it is the ability to observe interactive sessions scientifically: systematic records will be needed of what the user does when, and with what result. Only then will there be any basis for objective evaluation and comparison. Accordingly a usability laboratory was constructed by the group in 1987 (see fig. 58). It provided a controlled environment in which a subject could carry out an

Figure 58. The usability laboratory with Rosemary Bowden, Ralph Rengger and Cathy Thomas, and Steve Austin as the subject, April 1993.

appointed interactive task with minimum distraction, equipped with one-way glass, closed-circuit television and other monitoring equipment so that a full record of the proceedings could be captured for later analysis. This successful facility was designed by Ralph Rengger.

In 1990 Nigel Bevan was responsible for a proposal by NPL and six international partners for a collaborative project on methods of measuring usability which was approved by the EC for funding under the Esprit programme. This project became known as MUSiC (at first this stood for Metrics for Usability Standards in Computing, but this was changed later to the more appropriate Measuring Usability of Systems in Context). It was completed in 1994 and was a marked success for all concerned, resulting in a coherent set of tools and techniques for assessing interactive systems which attracted wide interest and many customers for NPL's usability services. These included British Gas plc, London Electricity, the National Westminster Bank, the Woolwich Building Society, Argos, ICL, Thames Water, the Inland Revenue and many more. Some clients were helped to set up their own usability laboratories. An NPL Usability Forum was established to spread understanding of the new tools and techniques. These services continue to flourish at the time of writing; in 1995 the first application of the techniques to interactive shopping was reported, and approval has been given for an EC-supported project to establish a group of European Usability Support Centres led by NPL.

The HCI group was led by Nigel Bevan throughout this period; other members of the group included Bob Watson, Ralph Rengger, Miles Macleod, Dianne Murray, Michael Bangham, Cathy Thomas, Rosemary Bowden, Steve Collins, David Barfoot, Ian Curson, Johnny Maissel and G-K Wong.

Selected publications on usability

S Howard and D M Murray. An outline of techniques for evaluating the human-computer interface. In: P Zunde (ed.), *Proc. 4th Symposium EFISS,* held in Atlanta October 1986, Plenum Press, 1986.

S Howard and D M Murray. A taxonomy of evaluation techniques for HCI. In: H J Bullinger et al. (eds), *Proc. INTERACT 87, Second IFIP Conf. on Human-Computer Interaction,* held in Stuttgart, September 1987, Elsevier, 1987.

C Thomas and S Milan. Input devices for tasks using interactive video. NPL Report DITC 87/87, April 1987. Also published under the title 'Which input device should be used with interactive video?' in *Proc. INTERACT 87* as above.

R E Rengger and M C R Turner. Employing usability engineering concepts in the evaluation of a CBT/IV workstation. NPL Report DITC 117/88, May 1988.

R E Rengger. Exploring experimentally derived usability metrics by a laboratory evaluation of Electronic Paper. NPL Report DITC 119/88, July 1988.

C Harding and R Rengger. The first steps towards a Usability Problem Description Language. NPL Report DITC 154/89, November 1989.

G E Pretor-Pinney and R E Rengger. Criteria for device selection: a comparison between a mouse and a touchscreen as an input device for interactive video. NPL Report DITC 158/90, February 1990.

J D Maissel. Development of a methodology for icon evaluation. NPL Report DITC 159/90, January 1990.

R E Rengger. A preliminary design for a methodology for Experimentally Measuring Usability—EMU. NPL Report DITC 163/90, April 1990.

F de Souza and N Bevan. The use of guidelines in menu interface design. In: D Diaper et al. (eds), *Human Computer Interaction: Proc. INTERACT '90, 3rd IFIP Int. Conf. on HCI*, held in Cambridge, UK, 27–31 August 1990, North-Holland, 1990, pp.435–440.

F L de Souza, J B Long and N Bevan. Types of error and difficulty in using human-factors guidelines: the case of interface menu design. In: E J Lovesey (ed.), *Contemporary Ergonomics 1990, Proc. Ergonomics Soc. 1990 Ann. Conf.*, held in Leeds, 3–6 April 1990, Taylor and Francis, 1990, pp.340–346.

G-K Wong and R Rengger. The validity of questionnaires designed to measure user-satisfaction of computer systems. NPL Report DITC 169/90, October 1990.

N Bevan, J Kirakowski and J Maissel. What is usability? In: H J Bullinger (ed.), *Proc. 4th Int. Conf. on Human Computer Interaction*, held in Stuttgart, September 1991, Elsevier.

R Rengger. Indicators of usability based on performance. In: H J Bullinger (ed.), *Proc. 4th Int. Conf. on Human Computer Interaction*, held in Stuttgart, September 1991, Elsevier.

R Rengger. Measuring system usability. *Proc. 8th Int. Conf. on Systems Engineering ICSE '91*, held in Coventry, September 1991, Coventry Polytechnic, 1991, pp.713–720.

M Macleod. An introduction to usability evaluation. NPL Report DITC 202/92, June 1992.

R Bowden and J Kirakowski. The stability and utility of the ESPRIT Project MUSiC performance-based indicators of usability and tools: an evaluation of the usability of the NPL iSDX telephone system. NPL Report DITC 213/92, December 1992.

M Macleod and N Bevan. MUSiC video analysis and context tools for usability measurement. *Human Factors in Computing Systems, Proc. INTERCHI '93*, held in Amsterdam, 24–29 April 1993, ACM, 1993, p.55.

M Corbett, M Macleod and M Kelly. Quantitative usability evaluation: the ESPRIT MUSiC project. *Proc. HCI Int. '93 Conference*, Florida, USA, August 1993.

M Macleod and R Rengger. The development of DRUM, a software tool for video-assisted usability evaluation. *People and Computers VIII*, Proc. HCI'93 Conf., held in Loughborough, UK, September 1993, Cambridge University Press, 1993.

N Bevan and M Macleod. Usability assessment and measurement. In: M Kelly (ed.), *The Management and Measurement of Software Quality*, Ashgate Technical/Gower Press, 1994.

N Bevan and M Macleod. Usability measurement in context. *Behaviour and Information Technology*, 13(1/2), 1994, pp.132–145.

M Macleod. Usability: practical methods for testing and improvement. *Proc. Norwegian Computer Soc. Software '94 Conference*, Sandvika, Norway, 1–4 Feb 1994.

W P M Mayles, A J Neal, S Heisig, M Macleod and R Rengger. The application of MUSiC methods to assessment of usability of treatment planning software. In: A R Hounsell, J M Wilkinson and P C Williams (eds), *Proc. 11th Conf. on Use of Computers in Radiation Therapy,* held in Manchester, 20–24 March 1994, pp.166–167.

M Macleod. Usability in context: improving quality of use. In: G Bradley and H W Hendricks (eds), *Human Factors in Organizational Design and Management IV,* Proc. Int. Ergonomics Assoc. 4th Int. Symposium on Human Factors in Organizational Design and Management, held in Stockholm, 29 May–1 June 1994, Elsevier/North-Holland, 1994.

R Bowden, C Thomas and N Bevan (eds). Usability context analysis: a practical guide. Version 4, NPL, June 1995.

R Bowden and I Curson. The MUSiC Performance Measurement Handbook. Version 3, NPL, 1995.

N Bevan. Usability is quality of use. In: Y Anzai and K Ogawa (eds), *Proc. 6th Int. Conf. on Human Computer Interaction,* Elsevier, July 1995.

N Bevan. Measuring usability as quality of use. *J. of Software Quality,* 4, 1995, pp.115–130.

M Macleod. Performance measurement and ecological validity. In: P Jordan (ed.), *Usability Evaluation in Industry,* Taylor and Francis, 1996.

Human–computer interaction standards

Throughout this period the HCI group took a leading part in the development of international standards in their field. The aim of these standards is not to restrict the inventiveness of interface designers, but to offer guidance on quality in interface design distilled from user experience of interactive systems. The chief contributions were Nigel Bevan's chairmanship of the ISO/IEC Working Group on User System Interfaces and Symbols and his editorship of the international standards on Guidance on Usability (ref. 76); software product evaluation (ISO/IEC 14598-1, not yet published); and software quality characteristics (ref. 75).

N Bevan and K Holdaway. User system interaction standards. *Computer Communications,* 12(2), 1989, pp.97–102.

K Holdaway and N Bevan. User needs for user system interaction standards. In: C D Evans, B L Meek and R S Walker (eds), *User Needs in Information Technology Standards,* Butterworth-Heinemann, 1993, pp.231–241.

J Brooke, N Bevan, F Brigham, S Harker and D Youmans. Usability statements and standardisation: work in progress in ISO. In: D Diaper et al. (eds), *Human Computer Interaction: Proc. INTERACT '90, 3rd IFIP Int. Conf. on HCI,* held in Cambridge, UK, 27–31 August 1990, North-Holland, 1990, pp.357–361.

N Bevan. Enforcement of HCI? *Computer Bulletin,* May 1991.

N Bevan. Standards relevant to European Directives for display terminals. In: H J Bullinger (ed.), *Proc. 4th Int. Conf. on Human Computer Interaction,* held in Stuttgart, September 1991, Elsevier.

ISO. Ergonomic requirements for office work with visual display terminals (VDTs): Part 11, Guidance on Usability. DIS 9241 Part 11, March 1995.

N Bevan. Human-computer interaction standards. In: Y Anzai and K Ogawa (eds), *Proc. 6th Int. Conf. on Human Computer Interaction,* Elsevier, July 1995.

6.8 Computing services

The dominant technical developments in this nine-year period were a rapid increase in the memory size and processing speed of personal computers, together with the establishment of the worldwide Internet. In most cases the desktop computer could now handle all its user's demands for word processing, the development of new programs and the use of established software. This meant that the role of the NPL mainframe computer also changed: from being primarily a processing resource it became a data-handling resource, holding backup copies, software libraries and shared databases. By the end of 1995 the use of the Internet was growing explosively, both as a means of accessing remote data and as a basis for electronic mail, which by then was in universal use by the technical and scientific community, both academic and commercial.

John Cooper remained head of CSU until his retirement in March 1993. David Schofield then took over responsibility for CSU in addition to his duties as deputy head of DITC. When the management of NPL was taken over by contractors in October 1995, CSU was renamed the Information Technology Services Unit (ITSU). David Schofield became head of ITSU, responsible to the Director of Finance, and the connection of the Unit with CISE (previously DITC) was severed.

Central services

In 1989 the ICL 2900 series mainframe computer with its associated DAP was replaced by a Digital Equipment Corporation VAX 6330 three-processor system running under the VMS operating system. The new machine was delivered in February (at first as a 6320, but before acceptance this proved insufficiently powerful), and the transfer of work was completed in September. The machine had 64 Mbytes of main memory and 6.25 gigabytes of disc storage. Besides the increase in capacity, it was much less expensive to run than its predecessor, support costs being about 75 per cent down.

Software available on the VAX included the ORACLE database system, the powerful mathematical package Matlab, PAFEC finite element software and the REDUCE algebraic manipulator, in addition to the familiar languages Fortran 77, Pascal, C, Basic and Ada, and the NAG Library.

In 1987 Edit was still going strong, with over 500 users; indeed it was still being enhanced occasionally, for example the ability to send messages directly by fax was added in 1989. However its long reign was eventually terminated by the rapid spread of personal computers with word-processing facilities and by the obsolescence of its hardware. Edit and the Central File Store were closed down on 28 February 1992. The Pages text formatting system which was the original main facility of Edit lived on; a VAX version was available from July 1989.

Dickie Bird was computer manager until his retirement in 1993; other staff helping to provide the central computing services in this period included Tony Hillman, Clive Hall, Martin Kiff, George Tondryk, Norman Waters, Steve Wilson, Shirley Johnson (editor of *NPL Computing* 1975–95), Mike Parsons, Raj Patel and Lynn Stygall.

Distributed services: personal computers and networks

The accelerating rise in the popularity of personal computers was initially viewed with some mistrust in some quarters in CSU because of its perceived implications for the future of mainframes on which CSU services had traditionally been based. Whatever doubts there might be, the PC was clearly here to stay, and 1987 saw two key events in its establishment at NPL: the first edition of CSU Document M2, *MS-DOS Micros on the NPL Network*, and the first of many training sessions on the use of PCs. In-house standards for basic software were needed to ensure compatibility; the recommended system for general use in 1988 was SMART, which offered word processing, spreadsheet, database and graphics in an integrated package. A small but very useful item of software called CFSinstall, developed by Martin Kiff, was made available in February 1989: once installed on your PC, it would on request install other software from the Central File Store over the network. A less welcome innovation in 1989 was the first warning in *NPL Computing* about the danger of viruses. WordPerfect replaced SMART as the recommended word-processing package for use in NPL in February 1991.

Early electronic mail systems, including those in Scrapbook and Edit at NPL, each provided a service to a closed community of accredited users; these users might be geographically quite widespread if the right network connections existed, but there was no traffic between one mail system and another. For example, in November 1985 *NPL Computing* drew its readers' attention to two such services to which connections could be established through the NPL network: Alvey Mail for those participating in the Alvey programme of DTI-funded research and development; and a national commercial service, Telecom Gold. The international community soon adopted the now-familiar e-mail addressing convention (fred@somewhere.else), and in January 1989 the breakthrough was announced to NPL users: in future the Edit mailbox would accept and forward outgoing messages so addressed, and would also accept incoming messages for NPL users. The VAX-based version of this service was announced in March 1990.

The increase in network traffic as the use of database systems and e-mail spread meant that plans had to be prepared for a replacement for the existing X.25 network. These plans were based on a fibreoptic ring using the FDDI (Fibre Distributed Data Interface) standard, with Ethernet local area networks connected to it. Its installation is in progress at the time of writing (early 1996), and there is a gateway to the old X.25 network so that the changeover causes minimum disruption to the users.

Les Pink managed the NPL Network until his retirement in June 1995, when his responsibilities were taken over by Adrian Smith. Martin Kiff masterminded e-mail, Internet and World Wide Web matters; the NPL Web site which he initiated can be found at http://www.npl.co.uk.

Publications by CSU 1987–95

Shirley Johnson (ed.). *NPL Computing.* Issues in this period are 404, 13 May 1987, to 519, December 1995 (the final issue).
CSU. NPL Internal Computing Documents. In addition to new editions of many earlier documents, the following new documents were issued:
Software Guide. Doc A4, November 1988.
NPL utility programs for micros. Doc M3, February 1988.

7 Retrospective postscript

This short final section is opinion rather than history. It aims to pick out the key achievements in the work outlined in the foregoing pages, and to consider briefly what lessons can be learnt.

The key achievements of NPL's fifty years of work in computing I believe to be:

- Turing's plans for ACE, outlined in section 2.3. These were ahead of all other computer plans in the world at the time.

- The Pilot ACE computer, described in section 2.4—one of the world's first computers in the modern sense. This was a major *engineering* achievement, based on Turing's paper plans but quite distinct from them. Although its architecture proved not to be on the evolutionary mainstream, the early date of the machine combined with the use made of it ensured that it was very influential.

- Wilkinson's work on error analysis, outlined in section 3.9. This enabled a wide range of calculations by computer to be carried out reliably for the first time.

- Davies's invention of packet-switching and designs for data communication networks (section 4.2). These were a cornerstone of the development which led to the Internet and the whole current headlong evolution of systems using computers and communications in tandem.

Also deserving mention are:

- the computing service based on Pilot ACE, the first external computing service in the world;

- the first NPL Network, again an engineering achievement in its own right, distinct from the theoretical work which preceded it, and the world's first general-purpose local-area network;

- Scrapbook, with its pioneering combination of word processing, electronic mail and hypertext, including hypertext in which the links cross a network;

- methods of testing systems, or aspects of systems, for conformance with standards, especially in the areas of communication protocols, compilers and data security.

Besides these major achievements, and the many other contributions included in the history, there was an important hidden benefit derived from NPL's position as a Government establishment: it could provide regular transfusions of technical literacy into the administrative Civil Service whose task it was to advise Ministers and carry out their policies. This benefit is often overlooked, either because it is not recognised or because it is difficult or impossible to quantify; but it is very real. Two examples from the text come to mind. First, the course on computers in 1957 mentioned in section 2.6; how much was it worth for the UK to have a future joint head of the Home Civil Service who had a basic understanding of the capabilities of computers? Secondly the scheme for providing BBC Microcomputers for schools (see section 5.1), which transformed the level of computer literacy in a whole generation of British children, and to which the NPL-derived expertise of Donald Bell made a signal contribution.

The history also provides an opportunity to judge what methods of managing research have given the best results.

First on terminology. Broad distinctions can be drawn between *pure science*, in which knowledge is pursued for its own sake; *applied science* in which lines of scientific enquiry are selected because they appear relevant to the attainment of some practical goal; *technology*, in which the knowledge gained by science is used to develop new artefacts and techniques; and *industry*, which uses technology (and other vital ingredients such as organisation and finance) to make profits[1]. Directly or indirectly, these profits fuel the whole process. The profits also fuel improvements in the standard of living. Since these improvements are popular with voters, democratic governments in the developed world have usually felt justified in spending taxpayers' money to support science and technology.

It was in this spirit that NPL, and later DSIR, were established early in the twentieth century to carry out work in applied science and technology aimed chiefly at UK civil needs, particularly in industry. Care was taken to interfere as little as possible with the competitive process, which meant in practice that either a piece of work was fully funded, usually by one firm, or the results were available to all. The size and budget of the Laboratory were determined by Government on the basis of the previous year's figures; the work programme was determined by the Director and his senior staff, subject to the control of an active Executive Committee of eminent persons; and the taxpayer paid the bill.

This was still the pattern of NPL work in 1945, at the start of the period covered in this book, but over the subsequent fifty years there was an accelerating process of change involving three overlapping stages. First, control of the work programme was shifted from the Laboratory to central Government appointees. Second, each year's budget was determined more on the perceived

---

[1] The loop is closed in an interesting way, because the artefacts produced by technology and industry are themselves part of the physical world and as such their properties may be the subject of scientific enquiry and analysis.

need for the work and less on what happened in the previous year; and finally, in a major political change, the criteria for determining the work programme became overtly commercial, with the Government as merely an important customer. This last change has been particularly far reaching in the IT field, in which the vast extent of private investment makes Governments feel there is now little need for public funds to be spent. Over the period of fifty years, NPL's ethos has been transformed: commercial competitiveness has changed from being seen as inappropriate to being the dominant criterion for measuring success.

In some respects the changes have been beneficial. There is much more pressure to ensure that the work is needed, and so less risk of public money being wasted. There is more awareness of costs, and many petty restrictions and outdated practices have been abolished. But professional expertise has been devalued and overshadowed by business and management skills as the predominant required qualities in senior staff. Financial considerations now pervade, instead of simply imposing necessary constraints. And one feature of critical importance has been seriously damaged in the process of change: the level of opportunity for individual technical creativity. The lesson of history is that the major technical advances have derived from talented individuals given a fair degree of freedom, with small supporting teams, and not from either big collaborative projects, with their attendant overload of schedules, meetings, finance, bids, milestones, reports and general hassle, or from small short-term commercial contracts.

Information technology is surely only at the beginning of its era, so the need for long-term work has not gone away, in spite of the development of a great international IT industry. Somewhere there is a Donald Davies, a Jim Wilkinson or even an Alan Turing of the future. History shows it is in the national interest to support them. Would they flourish under the present system? If not, what should be done about it?

Annex A: People

This section aims to give a brief outline of the careers of the major players in this saga, with apologies to the many others who made important contributions but who must be omitted if the list is to be kept within reasonable bounds. Three names are outstanding: those of Alan Turing, Jim Wilkinson, and Donald Davies, all as it happens Fellows of the Royal Society, and they are given slightly fuller treatment.

E L (Ernie) Albasiny

MA FIMA, b.9.12.31.
Appt. NPL as TSO in Maths 12.7.54; joined High-speed Computing Section; SO 30.3.55; numerical solution of parabolic partial differential equations; SSO 1.1.59; transf. to Theoretical Physics group to work on molecular wave functions 1959. In 1963–64 visiting lecturer, University of Wisconsin. PSO 1.6.65; Applied Maths group: structural elasticity (cooling towers). Prom. SPSO 3.11.69 and appt. head of Numerical and Mathematical Analysis Branch DNAM. Prom. DCSO and appt. Supt. DNAC 27.11.72, DNACS June 1978 and DITC Dec. 1981; ret. 31.5.87.

Gerald G Alway

MA, b.6.2.27.
Appt. NPL as TAEO in Maths 18.8.47; worked on Test Assembly; SO 1.6.48; seconded to Electronics Section for Pilot ACE development, including multiplier design; SSO 1.1.54; mathematical software; PSO 1.1.60. Transf. Auto 17.3.65; programming research; DEMOCRAT; transf. CCU on formation Nov. 1967; network software. Died 11.7.70; obit. *NPL News* 243, July 1970, p.18.

Annex A: People

Derek L A Barber

BSc(Eng) CEng FIEE MBCS MRTS [Memb. Roy. Television Soc.], b.9.11.29.
General Post Office 31.12.45–31.8.54.
Appt. NPL as SO in CME 1.9.54; data-handling equipment for control systems; SSO 1.4.58; PSO 1.1.63; British Standard Interface; head of newly formed Data Communications group 1966. Prom. SPSO 3.3.69 and appt. branch head responsible for groups in data communications, information systems and Palantype transcription. Seconded to EURATOM 1.5.73 and appt. Director of COST Project 11 (the European Informatics Network). Transf. DTI HQ (Electronics Applications Div.) 14.4.80; support for microelectronics projects in industry. Res. 31.12.80; appt. Logica UK Ltd as Principal Consultant. Seconded back to DTI as Director Infrastructure and Communications in Alvey Project, July 1983–Oct. 1985; ret. from Logica May 1990 and formed consultancy Tonsor Systems.

Keith A Bartlett

b.6.5.33.
Appt. RRE Malvern as Apprentice 31.8.50; AEO 31.8.55 (RAF 23.9.55–22.9.58).
Appt. NPL 22.10.62 as Act EO in Auto; ACE maintenance; EO 1.6.63; data communications 1967; hardware design and development for NPL Network; SSO 1.6.69; network interconnection (EPSS); PSO 1.6.73; standard protocols; head Data Communication Protocols Unit 1.10.78. Transf. DTI HQ (Electronics Applications Div.) on prom. to SPSO 1.6.81; microprocessor applications support; transf. to IT Div. as head of IT Standards Unit 1982; transf. Alvey Directorate as Director Infrastructure and Communications 1985; appt. Director Networking in Information Engineering Directorate with personal prom. to G5 1988; ret. 1991.

Donald A Bell

BSc PhD CEng FIMechE MIEE FBCS, b.28.5.41.
Appt. NPL as TSO in Auto 3.10.66; pattern recognition; SO 21.11.68; PL-516; SSO 1.6.69; PSO 1.6.72; automatic inspection; data security. Transf. to HQ (CSE4c) 16.1.78; BBC computers in schools; G6, G5 in HQ. Prom. G3 and appt. Director National Engineering Laboratory 1983; res. 1990. Visiting Prof. Univ. of Strathclyde from 1986, head of R & D Strathclyde Institute 1990–91, technical director Marchland Consulting Ltd from 1991.

Annex A: People

Nigel W S Bevan

BSc PhD MBCS, b.18.7.46.
Programmer and technical manager, BOAC (later British Airways) 1968–72.
Appt. NPL as HSO in DNACS 1.9.78; human–computer interaction; SSO 1.2.80; PhD 1983; Microtext; PSO 1.6.84; head of Human–Computer Interaction group from 1984. Seconded to Alvey Directorate 1985 and transf. to HQ as Tech. Asst to Chief Engineer & Scientist 7.7.86; returned to NPL 4.2.87. Usability assessment and measurement; technical co-ordinator of ESPRIT MUSiC project; international standards for user interfaces; editor of ISO guidelines on usability (ref. 76) and standards on software product evaluation and software quality characteristics (ref. 75).

N F (Dickie) Bird

BSc MBCS, b.29.10.33.
Appt. NPL as T. Ass. (Sci.) in Maths 18.10.54; mathematical programming for DEUCE and later ACE; AEO 1.4.56; EO 1.1.63; programming for Theoretical Physics Section 1964. KDF9 Computer Manager 1967; SEO 23.6.69; assim. to SSO 1.1.71. Transf. CSU on formation 1.6.78; manager of ICL 2972; TPSO 6.11.80; PSO 1.6.82; manager of VAX systems and other CSU computers. Ret. 31.10.93.

Dennis V Blake

BSc CEng FIEE FBCS MInstMC, b.25.10.23.
Admiralty Signals Establishment July 1943–48; radar systems.
Appt. NPL 5.1.48 as AEO in Control Mechanisms Section, Metrology Div.; SO 11.2.49; SSO 1.1.52; electronic simulator. PSO 1.1.57; organised 1958 symposium on Mechanisation of Thought Processes and edited its proceedings (ref. 109). Transf. from CME to Applied Physics Div. Sep. 1959; scheduling (school timetables); reliability. Transf. to Ship Division 1.1.63; head of instrumentation section; data collection and processing for ship and propeller model tests; NPL Standard Interface; British Standard Interface and other BSI work. Transf. to DNAC 21.8.72; NPL Network. Transf. to CSU on formation 1.6.78; ret. 31.10.83. Died 21.3.1984; obit. *NPL Bulletin* 70, April 1984, pp.8–9.

Frank M Blake

Grad IEE, b.16.1.28.
Royal Navy 1945–48; Decca 1948–54, navigation systems and radar. Appt. NPL as TAEO in CME 3.8.54; Pilot ACE maintenance; EO 2.6.55; ACE design and development; SO 1.3.58; SSO 1.1.60. Seconded to GPO as PSO on staff of HM Treasury Technical Support Unit 1.10.62; software appraisal for Govt depts.

Returned to NPL 1.10.64 as PSO in Auto; head of programming research group and chairman ACTP software technical committee. Transf. to CCU on formation Nov. 1967. Seconded to NATO Division of Scientific Affairs, Brussels as consultant on software engineering 1.7.69.

Returned to NPL as PSO in Com Sci 1.5.71; computer performance evaluation; commercial exploitation of Division's work. Transf. to DoI (Research Requirements Div.) 1.4.74 on prom. to SPSO and appt. as Exec. Offr CSERB. Transf. back to NPL 2.8.76 and appt. head Computing Branch DNAC; head of CSU on formation 1.6.78. Ret. 31.12.85.

T G (Tom) Blaney

BSc PhD, b.3.9.41.
Case Institute of Technology, Cleveland, Ohio 1967–69; electronic properties of metals and alloys.
Appt. NPL as TSSO in Elec. Sci. 9.6.69; SSO 31.7.69; submillimetre-wavelength radiation; Josephson devices and their applications; laser frequency metrology; PSO 1.6.74; IEE Gyr and Landis Commemorative Prize 1979; SPSO 18.5.81; establishment of NPL programme for measurement standards in fibre optics; DTI support for the optoelectronics industry. Prom. G5 and appt. Supt. DITC 27.4.87; appt. Head Div. of Electrical Science 24.1.92.

E R (Ed) Brocklehurst

BSc, b.7.11.43.
Appt. NPL as TSO in Maths 1.9.66; linear and integer programming; SO 12.2.68; SSO 1.6.71; PSO 1.6.75. Head of Programmable Vision Systems Group from 1980; electronic paper; parallel processing. Ret. 30.3.94.

Bernard J Chorley

MTech, b.21.5.50.
Appt. NPL as TSA in Metrology Div. 3.9.68; laser-based force measuring equipment; assim. TASO 1.1.71. Transf. Com Sci 17.1.72; SO 26.3.73; dynamic signature recognition (Verisign); MTech 1978; HSO 1.5.78; data security from 1980; SSO 1.2.83; software protection device; smart cards and tokens; G7 1.6.86; head of Data Security group in DITC from 1990; testing of secure systems; applications of formal methods in this area; Lead Assessor for NAMAS; Divisional Quality Manager 1995.

David O Clayden

CEng MIEE, b.15.11.22.
EMI Ltd Dec. 1939–Sep. 1947; radar with Blumlein and Newman; television.
   Appt. NPL as AEO in Electronics Section 22.9.47; Pilot ACE development; EO 1.1.51; SO 22.8.51; SSO 1.1.54; ACE design; PSO 1.1.56. Pattern recognition; ACTP (chairman of hardware technical committee); data security. Ret. officially 6.5.81 but continued association with NPL through work for DTI on microelectronics (consultant on the 'Microtrain' which carried demonstrations round industrial centres), and for the British Technology Group on cryptography and on personal identification systems.

Charles W Clenshaw

DSc CMath FIMA, b.15.3.26.
Appt. NPL 22.10.45 as Temp. Asst. III in Maths; AEO 23.4.47; SO 22.11.51; approximation theory; SSO 1.1.56; applications of Chebyshev polynomials in numerical analysis; PSO 1.1.60; prom. SPSO 3.7.61 and appt. head of numerical methods group; contributor to *Modern Computing Methods* (ref. 107); work on optimisation started in his group 1965. Res. 30.9.69; appt. Prof. of Mathematics, Univ. of Lancaster. Ret. 31.7.85.

M B (Max) Clowes

Maxwell Bernard Clowes BSc PhD, b.31.1.34.
Appt. NPL as TSO in CME 19.5.59; pattern recognition; SRF 2.5.60; TSSO 2.5.63. Res. 30.9.63.

Papers published in 1967 and 1969 give his affiliation as MRC Psycholinguistics Research Unit, University of Oxford and Division of Computing Research, CSIRO, Canberra respectively.

Appt. Senior Research Fellow, Laboratory of Experimental Psychology, Univ. of Sussex 1969; Prof. of Artificial Intelligence in School of Social Sciences 1974; res. December 1980.

Died 28.4.81; brief obit. *The Bulletin*, Univ. of Sussex, 12.5.81.

F M Colebrook

Francis Morley Colebrook OBE BSc, b.15.3.1893.
Served in First World War; Mentioned in Dispatches.
Appt. NPL 4.7.21 as JA in Electricity Dept; worked on radio; A2 1.4.24; A1 1.4.28; SO1 1.4.33; transf. to Radio Dept on formation 1933; SO 1.1.35; SSO 1.4.36; PSO 1.4.42; SPSO 1.1.46. Many publications on radio topics, including *Basic Mathematics for Radio Students*, second edition, Iliffe, 1949. Appt. Head Electronics Section, responsible for Pilot ACE development March 1948; appt. head of newly formed CME Div. 10.6.54 but never took up post as he was seriously ill. Died 21.6.54; obit. *NPL News* 51, July 1954, p.16.

John R A Cooper

ARCS BSc DIC PhD, b.29.7.35.
Appt. NPL as Vacation Student in Maths 1956.
Re-appt. as TSO in Maths 1.10.58; Theoretical Physics Section: molecular structure calculations using DEUCE and ACE; SO 15.10.58; SSO 20.8.63; solid-state calculations using KDF9; PSO 1.6.71. Transf. to Computing Section: numerical algorithms and computer user documentation. Transf. CSU on formation 1.6.78; Computing Applications and Information Section; prom. acting G6 as Acting Head CSU 6.1.86, both substantive from 28.1.88. Ret. 30.3.93.

Maurice G Cox

BSc PhD FIMA CMath, b.8.10.40.
General Electric Co, Rugby, 1963–67.
Appt. NPL as SSO in Maths Div. 1.1.68; data approximation; fitting curves and surfaces to numerical data; splines; PSO 1.6.71; PhD 22.10.75; radioimmunoassay; subsidence prediction; Data Approximation Subroutine Library launched 1982; SPSO (IM) 1.7.83; head of Mathematical Software group, DITC, 1983–1990 and 1994 on; edited proc. of Wilkinson memorial conference held at NPL in July 1987 (ref. 23), and six other international conferences; geometric-form assessment; generalised immunoassay systems; terrain following; structured linear systems; coordinate metrology; numerical software validation; Visiting Prof. in Computational Mathematics, Kingston Univ. from 1992; author of over 100 papers on approximation, linear algebra, metrology and related topics.

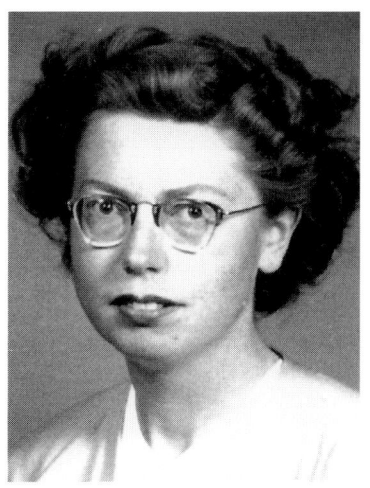

Betty Curtis

BSc MSc, b.16.5.26.
Appt. NPL as TAEO in Maths 1.11.47; programming for Test Assembly (making her one of the first professional programmers in the world to write for a modern stored-program computer); AEO 7.9.48; programming for Pilot ACE; EO 1.1.53; programming for ACE and KDF9; SEO 1.6.66; provision of software and computing information for NPL users; assim. SSO 1.1.71; ret. from CSU 29.5.86.

C G Darwin

Sir Charles Galton Darwin KBE MC MA ScD FRS b.19.12.1887. Grandson of *the* Charles Darwin; read Maths at Cambridge; lecturer in Mathematical Physics Manchester Univ. 1910–14; attached to Royal Engineers and to Royal Flying Corps 1914–18; lecturer in Maths, Cambridge 1919–22; Prof. Nat. Philosophy Edinburgh 1923–36; Master, Christ's College Cambridge 1936–38.

Appt. Director NPL 1.12.38. On loan to Ministry of Supply from 15.3.41; seconded to Washington as first director of the British office set up to improve Anglo-American scientific war co-operation; returned from loan 10.2.42. With Hartree, one of the prime movers in the establishment of Mathematics Div. NPL. Ret. 31.8.49. Died 31.12.62.

Memoir: G P Thomson. Charles Galton Darwin. *Biographical Memoirs of Fellows of the Royal Society,* 9, 1963, pp.69–85.

Donald W Davies

Donald Watts Davies CBE BSc ARCS DistFBCS FRS, b.7.6.24. BSc in Physics (1943) and in Maths (1947), both with first-class honours from Imperial College London; awarded Lubbock Memorial Prize as the leading mathematician of his year in London University (1947); in between the two degrees he worked at Birmingham University and at ICI Billingham on atomic research as an assistant to Dr Klaus Fuchs.

Appt. NPL as TSO in Maths 1.9.47; briefly assistant to Turing; worked on Test Assembly; SO 1.6.48; seconded to Electronics Section to work on Pilot ACE development; SSO 1.7.50; use of Pilot ACE for road traffic simulation; PSO 1.1.54; Commonwealth Fund Fellowship in USA 1954–55. Transf. to CME Div. April 1955; ACE development; SPSO 12.1.60; initiated and contributed to work on machine translation and cryotrons; acting DCSO and acting Supt Autonomics Div. 1.9.62–15.6.63 while Dr Uttley was away; technical manager of Advanced Computer Techniques Project (ACTP). Transf. briefly to MinTech HQ 31.12.65.

Returned to NPL 1.8.66 on prom. DCSO and appt. Supt Autonomics Div.; data communications; pioneer of packet-switching; John Player Award of the British Computer Society 1974; Distinguished Fellow BCS 1975. Transf. to be Head Computing Technology Unit NPL 1.6.78; data security, in particular public key cryptography; regraded as Individual Merit DCSO 1.7.79 and CTU merged into DNACS. Consultancy to banks etc.; CBE 1983; Vice-President (Technical) British Computer Society 1983; an influential author (refs 28–36 and 63). Ret. from NPL 30.6.84; elected FRS 1987; Visiting Prof. in Computer Science Dept, Royal Holloway and Bedford New College 1987 on; Hon. DSc Salford 1989; continued consultancy work on data security.

Recommending him for the Commonwealth Fund Fellowship in 1954, Colebrook wrote: 'D W Davies is one of the most brilliant young men I have ever met; outstanding not only in intellectual power but also in the range of his scientific, technical and general knowledge. He is equally unusual in his ability to apply this knowledge to mechanical and electrical design and even to the actual construction of complex equipment. He is, for example, one of the very small number of persons who could draw up a complete "logical" design of an electronic computer, realise this design in actual circuitry, assemble it himself (with a high probability that it would work as designed) and then programme it and use it for the solution of computational problems.' As will be seen from the summary above, this breadth of both interest and ability remained a feature of his later distinguished career. His attraction to intellectual challenges and puzzles is clear also in his private interests, which over the years have included: (1) the design and construction of two noughts-and-crosses machines, which in the days before home computers were considerable attractions at the annual NPL children's parties (see also his paper on the theory of chess and noughts and crosses, *Science News,* 16(40), 1950); (2) historic cryptographic machines, particularly the German machines of the Second World War; (3) computing history, as mentioned in section 4.1; see also his article Charles Babbage 1792–1871, *NPL News* 214, Feb. 1968, pp.6–8; and (4) mathematical recreations (see two articles in *NPL News,* one on the theory of games, no. 320, Dec. 1976, p.11, and one on 'packing a circular suitcase', no. 327, July 1977, p.7).

Annex A: People

Paul Dean

CB BSc PhD CPhys CMath FIMA FInstP, b.23.1.33.
Appt. NPL as SSO in Maths 7.10.57; Theoretical Physics group; vibrations of disordered atomic lattices; structure and spectra of glasses; PSO 1.1.63; SPSO (Personal) 1.7.67; appt. Head CCU for six months in 1967–68. Prom. DCSO 2.9.69 and appt. Supt Div. of Quantum Metrology; prom. CSO 2.12.74 and appt. Deputy Director (B) NPL; transf. to DoI HQ 1.10.76 and prom. Under Secretary in charge of R & D Contracts Div. and Space and Air Research Div.

Appt. Director NPL 1.10.77; CB 1981; reduced scale of mathematical work in NPL 1981–82; prime mover in the establishment of EUROMET and of the National Testing Laboratory Accreditation Scheme (NATLAS), the principal forerunner of the present (1996) UKAS. Ret. 31.3.90.

C R (Chris) Evans

Christopher Riche Evans BA PhD, b.29.5.31
Appt. NPL 30.9.63 to 'temp. S class post' in Auto; stabilised retinal images; SRF 15.6.65; PRF 20.2.67; man–machine interaction for untrained users, especially in medical history-taking (MICKIE); PSO 21.2.72; use of computers to help the disabled (MAVIS); hand-held interactive devices. Died 10.10.79.

Chris Evans, a psychologist by training, was a charismatic character with an enthusiastic interest in both people and computers and an infectious optimism about their joint future. He had a talent for communication both in speech and in writing, and was a prolific author, lecturer and television presenter, always busy with several simultaneous extramural projects in addition to his official work. He enjoyed combining his unconventional image with his position as a civil servant; for example, visitors to his NPL office could choose to sit in an old dentist's chair, and might see a tame rat (left over from the biology work) peeping at them from a shelf. His two best known books are *Cults of Unreason* (ref. 47), a study of irrational religious cults and why some people are attracted to them, and *The Mighty Micro* (ref. 49), which opened many people's eyes to the prospects which the advent of cheap computers was unfolding in the late 1970s. Amongst the television series he presented were one on the Mighty Micro and one on alleged paranormal events, which he investigated with a characteristic combination of enthusiasm and professional detachment, at the same time keeping the entertainment level high. Other interests were dreams (refs 41, 42, 44), and computing history, where he wrote a popular book published posthumously (ref. 50) and conducted a unique series of recorded interviews with computing pioneers, published on tape by the Science Museum (ref. 48). He was also a founder member and secretary of the Brain Research Association, and a qualified pilot. His energy, enthusiasm and gift for exposition inspired many others, both at NPL and outside; his group included a stream of students and Guest Workers. He found a surprising use for the many brochures, handouts and reports he received which ended up in the wastepaper basket: each week he sent the accumulated pile to the novelist J G Ballard, who was a personal friend and who welcomed the insight they gave into developments in computing. (I am grateful to Mr Ballard for confirming this story.) Arthur C Clarke described *The Mighty Micro* as 'just about the most entertaining and mind-expanding book I've ever read'—a remarkable endorsement of Chris's powers as a prophet of the computer age. Obits. *Int. J. Man-Machine Studies,* 14(1), January 1981 (memorial issue), pp.3–11; and (by E L Albasiny) in *NPL News,* 344, Winter 1979, pp.23–24.

E C Fieller

Edgar Charles Fieller MA, b.21.6.07.
Boots Ltd (statistician) 1934–42; appt. Ministry of Aircraft Production as TSSO 1.4.42; operations research, Fighter Command; TPSO 1.4.44; PSO 1.1.46.
Appt. NPL as PSO in Maths 1.2.46; head of Mathematical Statistics Section; SPSO 1.5.47; in charge of Maths Div. following Womersley's departure Sep. 1950–Feb. 1951. Transf. to Ministry of Supply 31.3.52. Died 1.12.60.

Leslie Fox

MA DPhil DSc Hon.FIMA, b.30.9.18.
Admiralty Computing Service July 1943–Oct. 1945; relaxation methods. Appt. NPL as SO in Maths 1.10.45; SSO 2.10.46; PSO 1.1.49; SPSO 1.4.52; differential equations, linear algebra, approximation theory, integral equations; production of mathematical tables. DSc 1956; visiting lecturer in USA (on leave from NPL) 20.9.56–18.6.57.

Res. from NPL 30.9.57 to become the first Director of the Oxford University Computing Laboratory; Prof. of Numerical Analysis at Oxford and Fellow of Balliol College 1963; visiting professorships at California (Berkeley), Illinois, Ljubljana and the Open University; author or co-author of eight books and 86 papers on numerical analysis. Ret. Sep. 1983; the Institute of Mathematics and its Applications (IMA) held a symposium at the Royal Society: 'The Contributions of L. Fox to Numerical Analysis'.

Died 1.8.92; obit. *The Times* 2.9.92, which includes a description of him as 'one of the world leaders in the remarkable explosion in numerical analysis that took place during and after the second world war'.

Annex A: People

Stanley Gill

MA PhD, b.26.3.26.
Appt. NPL as TAEO in Maths 17.6.46; ACE plans; AEO 15.7.47; Test Assembly.

Res. 30.6.48; research student at Cambridge working on EDSAC; differential equations; returned to NPL for two one-month appointments working on Pilot ACE development 23.8.48 and 1.7.49.

Research Fellow, St John's College, Cambridge 1952–55; Visiting Prof., University of Illinois; Ferranti Ltd 1955–63; ICT Ltd 1963–64 and part-time Prof. of Automatic Data Processing, Manchester; Prof. of Computing Science, Imperial College London 1964–70; Pres. British Computer Society 1967–68; Senior Consultant PA International Management Consultants Ltd. Died 5.4.75; obit. *The Times* 9.4.75.

W L (Bill) Gleed

b.17.11.15.
Various jobs 1935–46 including Electrician 1 (Sgt) RAF 1940–45; English Electric Co from ?1946; member of the EE team at NPL assisting with Pilot ACE development 1949.

Appt. NPL as T Ass (Sci) in Electronics Section 26.9.49, continuing with Pilot ACE development; T Snr Ass (Sci) 1.1.51; became expert in magnetic coating of drums; ACE development; TEO 1.1.55; EO 6.12.55; cryotrons 1959–66. Transf. to HQ 16.10.67. Subsequently transf. to MoD (?) and ret. c.1975. Died 17.9.86.

His innovative practical skills (and a memorable irrepressible cheerfulness) made him a vital contributor to the early development of computers at NPL; a tribute by Donald Davies appeared in *NPL Bulletin*, 100, Oct. 1986, p.15.

E T (Charles) Goodwin

Eric Thomson Goodwin CBE MA PhD CMath FIMA, b.30.7.13.
Read Mathematics at Cambridge; outstanding undergraduate and post-graduate career including Rayleigh Prize 1936; Lecturer, Sheffield University 1937–39; Cambridge Maths. Lab. (Ministry of Supply Ordnance Board External Ballistics Dept) 5.9.39–7.6.43; Admiralty Signals Establishment Witley as TEO 7.6.43–1.1.45 (radar); on loan to HM Nautical Almanac Office Bath as TSEO in Admiralty Computing Service 1.1.45–Sep. 1945.

Appt. NPL 16.9.45 as TSSO in Maths.; PSO 1.1.46; head of General Computing Section; rare double prom. to DCSO and appt. Supt. Maths. Div. 9.2.51; major contributor to *Modern Computing Methods* (ref. 107) 1957–61; one of the prime movers in the establishment of the Institute of Mathematics and its Applications in 1964 and Vice-President 1967; acting head CCU 1968–71 in addition to remaining Supt DNAM; Supt DNAC 1971. Prom. CSO (B) and appt. Deputy Director (C) NPL 13.12.71, responsible for Engineering Sciences group of Divs including Com Sci and DNAC. Ret. 31.12.74 and CBE; an appreciation written by J H Wilkinson appears in *NPL News* 297, Jan. 1975, pp.10–14.

Annex A: People

P H (Percy) Hammond

Percival Hudson Hammond BSc, b.13.8.24.
Admiralty Signals Establishment 1944–46, Durham University 1947–48. Appt. RRE Malvern as SO 1949; later SSO and PSO. Worked on circuit design, servomechanism dynamics, human factors in control systems, and missile guidance.

Appt. NPL as PSO in CME 2.3.59 on transfer from RRE; head of Adaptive Control group in Auto Div. (see section 3.3); SPSO 1.5.61. Transfer to Warren Spring Laboratory 31.3.68; head of Control Engineering Div.

Prom. DCSO and appt. Head of Computer Aided Design Centre, Cambridge, November 1980; responsible for taking Centre into private ownership; ret. July 1983.

Visiting Prof. in Dept of Electrical and Electronic Engineering, Queen Mary College, London, 1968–80.

Hon. Prof. in Dept of Electrical and Electronic Engineering, Swansea University College, 1987 on.

J G (Geoff) Hayes

MA FRSS FIMA, b.27.11.23.
Ministry of Supply as EO 18.9.44–21.9.47.

Appt. NPL as SO in Maths. 22.9.47; statistics section, staying at NPL when the rest of the section transferred to Ministry of Supply in 1951; SSO 1.1.53; PSO 1.1.60; data approximation: ship fairing; curve and surface fitting; SPSO (IM) 1.7.78. Ret. 30.11.83.

Harry D Huskey

MA PhD FIEEE FBCS, b.19.1.16.
Instructor in Mathematics, Univ. of Pennsylvania, 1943–46; worked on ENIAC at Moore School of Electrical Engineering, 1945–46.

Temp. Appt in Maths Div. NPL 4.1.47 for one year; led work on ACE Test Assembly (see section 2.3). Joined National Bureau of Standards on return to US 1948; SWAC; Bendix G-15 (see section 2.4). Moved to Univ. of California at Berkeley 1954 as Prof. Math. and Elect. Eng.; President ACM 1960–62; transf. Santa Cruz campus 1967; Prof. of Computer and Information Science; ret. 1986.

Details of his early work are given in his *Annals of the History of Computing* paper, ref. 68.

Adrian J Marks

BSc MSc, b.22.6.54.
Appt. Senior Lecturer in Computing Science, Royal Military College of Science, Shrivenham 1980; Principal Lecturer 1983. Transf. to Royal Armaments R & D Estab., Chertsey as G7 1984; robotics. Prom. G6 1985 and appt. to MoD central staff; IT strategy; appt. Assistant Dir. Science (Air) MoD 1989; operational research team management. Prom. G5 and appt. NPL as Head DITC 16.3.92; transf. to Centre for Ionising Radiation and Acoustics as Dir., December 1995.

David W Martin

MA DPhil FIMA, b.22.5.30.
Massachusetts Institute of Technology 1954–56; meteorology.
   Appt. NPL as TSO in Maths 22.5.56; applied maths including heat flow and ship resistance; SSO 1.8.57; contributor to *Modern Computing Methods* 1961; PSO 1.1.63; deformation and vibration of elastic structures (cooling towers, multistorey buildings, lifting gear), equations of fluid flow; first chairman Computer Users' Panel 1967; particular interest in problems of technology transfer in mathematical services. Prom. SPSO 2.4.73 and appt. head of Numerical and Mathematical Analysis Branch, DNAC; collaboration with Numerical Algorithms Group Ltd (NAG), University Consortium for Industrial Numerical Analysis (UCINA) and Engineering Sciences Data Unit; member of NAG Council and Executive, UCINA Steering Committee and editorial board of the International Journal of Numerical Methods in Engineering. Ret. 31.8.83 (cuts in the effort devoted to mathematics had led to the abolition of his post).

John McDaniel

BSc SM, b.27.7.31.
MIT 1956–58. Appt. NPL as TSSO in CME 5.8.58; clerical mechanisation (production control); SSO Jan. 1959; machine translation from July 1959; head of group from 1960; PSO 1.6.63; head of Information Systems group from 1967; res. 31.8.68 to work on mechanised information systems for Pergamon Press. Returned to Civil Service 30.7.72 as PSO in the Central Computer and Telecommunications Agency of HM Treasury, Technical Services Division; G6 1976; ret. 27.7.91.

A Roger Meetham

MA DPhil DSc FRMetS, b.1.1.10.
Building Research Station: temp. appt 1.5.35, pioneering survey of urban atmospheric pollution, SO 1.4.39; to DSIR HQ 17.1.40, on loan to Ministry of Home Security 1.5.41 (work on smoke screens), on loan to NPL 1.12.41, back to HQ 1.1.42. Fuel Research Station 1.4.45, prom. PSO 1.1.46, DSc 1947, founder editor of the journal *Weather*, left 14.10.49.

Appt. NPL 15.10.49 as PSO in Physics Div.; continued work on atmospheric pollution; cryogenics and calorimetry; transf. App. Phys. Div. on formation 1958. Transf. to CME Div. Sept. 1959; assistance to Supt especially re new building; information retrieval; graph theory. Books include *Atmospheric Pollution: its Origins and Prevention*, Pergamon Press, first published 1952, third edition 1964 (this work 'proved to be of great value in the debates which led to the Clean Air Act of 1956'); *Basic Physics*, Pergamon Press, 1957; *The Depth of Cold*, English Universities Press, 1967; *Information Retrieval*, Aldus Books, 1969; and the *Encyclopaedia of Linguistics, Information and Control*, ref. 89. Ret. 15.4.70; Open University tutor in Physics; died 8.4.93. Obits. *The Queen's College* [Oxford] *Record*, Dec. 1994, p.16; and *Quart. J. Roy. Meteorological Soc.*, 120(520), Oct. 1994, p.1698.

J G L (Jack) Michel

OBE MSc AIA [Assoc. Inst. Actuaries] CMath FIMA, b.16.7.16.
Actuary with Prudential Assurance Co 1935–41; Ministry of Supply 1941–45, working on the Manchester University differential analyser under Prof. Hartree.

Temp. Appt NPL 1.1.46, Maths Div.; remained at Manchester working on the DA which had been hired for NPL's use; SSO 1.9.46; came to NPL with the machine in November 1948; overall responsibility for the new NPL 20-integrator DA, including design, development contract supervision, installation and use; PSO 1.1.50. Prom. SPSO 1.12.57 and appt. Head of Applied Mathematics and Theoretical Physics Branch; Head of Computing Branch DNAC, incorporating the former CCU, April 1971; OBE June 1976; ret. 31.7.76 but re-employed as SSO 1.8.76; final ret. 31.8.77.

G F (Geoff) Miller

BA FIMA, b.21.4.26.
RAF Oct. 1945–March 1948.
Appt. NPL as TSO in Maths 1.10.51; SO 19.10.51; SSO 1.1.55; PSO 1.1.59; SPSO (PM) 1.7.66. Undertook a wide range of problems in numerical and applied mathematics including particularly differential and integral equations, quadrature, and the provision of algorithms for mathematical functions, especially Bessel functions. Application areas of his work included analysis of elastic waves, flow of oil in pipelines, polymer manufacture, wave scattering, analysis of blood flow, aircraft noise measurement and analysis of experimental spectra. Ret. 30.4.86; re-employed as short-term part-time SPSO in Div. of Electrical Science 18.5.87–17.3.88.

E A (Ted) Newman

Edward Arthur Newman BSc CEng MIEE MInstP FBCS, b.27.4.18. Research physicist EMI Ltd 1941–47; worked with Blumlein; radar and television.

Appt. NPL 4.9.47 as SO in Electronics Section, Radio Division; ACE plans; key contributor to electronic design of Pilot ACE; SSO 8.9.48; PSO 1.1.51; SPSO (Org) 1.11.55; clerical mechanisation; officer-in-charge CME 1.6.56–31.12.56.

Transf. to Applied Physics Div. 1.9.59 as deputy to Supt; school timetables, teaching machines, reliability. Transf. back to Auto 12.8.63; visual pattern recognition and speech recognition; ACTP. Ret. 31.12.77; Visiting Prof., Dept of Computer Science, Westfield College, 1978. Died 7.8.93; obits. (1) *The Times* 17.8.93 p.17; (2) (by D W Davies) *IEEE Annals of the History of Computing,* 17(1), 1995, pp.64–66.

In addition to his energy, enthusiasm and technical ability, Ted Newman will be remembered for a special quality, a combination of friendly outspokenness, impishness and irreverent originality which made him a most stimulating colleague. His contributions to a discussion were perceptive, sometimes maverick or even outrageous, but often contained a new and valuable insight. This led, for example, to his being in demand to start off discussion at lectures, where he could be relied on to stimulate debate and argument. This ability to provoke action by others meant that his real contribution to a project was often greater than a conventional record will show.

Annex A: People

Frank W J Olver

BSc MSc DSc, b.15.12.24.
HM Nautical Almanac Office Bath as TEO in Admiralty Computing Service 16.10.44–Sep. 1945.

Appt. NPL as TJSO in Maths Div. 16.9.45; numerical analysis; SO 2.10.46; MSc 17.7.48; SSO 1.1.52; head of Desk Machine Computation Section 1954; PSO 1.1.56; temporary appt to US National Bureau of Standards (NBS) from Sep. 1957 to Dec. 1958 on leave from NPL; prom. SPSO 17.12.58 and appt. Head of Numerical Methods Branch; DSc 25.1.61. Research topics included polynomial equations, ordinary differential equations, approximation theory, error analysis, computation of special functions in mathematical physics, and the asymptotic solution of differential equations.

Res. 30.6.61 to take up appt as mathematician at NBS; appt. Research Prof. Univ. of Maryland 25.8.69, continuing to work for NBS part-time until 3.11.86; published *Asymptotics and Special Functions*, Academic Press, 1974; ret. 30.6.92 and appt. Prof. Emeritus.

C F (Fred) Osborne

CEng MIMechE MIEE, b.15.4.20.
Admiralty draughtsman and mechanical design engineer 21.1.35–20.4.47, including apprenticeship at Royal Naval Dockyards in Malta and Chatham and service with the Admiralty delegation in Washington.

Appt. NPL 21.1.47 as EO in Engineering Div.; electronic means of calibrating mechanical testing equipment; transf. Electronics Section 1948; chief mechanical designer for both Pilot ACE and ACE, notably the delay lines and drums on both machines; SEO 1.4.56. Prom. CEO 30.8.62 and appt. Head of West Design Office and West Workshop; assimilated to PSO 1.1.71; Head of Technical Services for NPL 1976; ret. 31.12.77.

L J (Lew) Page

Lewis James Page BSc GradIEE, b.3.7.22.
Ministry of Supply Aug. 1942–Nov. 1948; DSIR (Food Research) Dec. 1948–Feb. 1952.

Appt. NPL as EO in Electronics Section 4.2.52; Pilot ACE completion and ACE development; SSO 1.1.58; PSO 1.1.61; cryotrons (reliability and photolithography); ACTP project leader from 1966.
Died 2.1.70; obit. *NPL News* 237, Jan. 1970, p.21.

Seymour A Papert

BA PhD, b.1.3.28.
Univ. of Witwatersrand (maths) 1945–52; Cambridge (maths) 1954–56; Univ. of Paris 1956–57; Univ. of Geneva (child development) 1957–59.

Appt. NPL as SRF 1.9.59 (Fulbright Fellowship); learning and pattern recognition in the brain; TSSO 1.10.61; res. 31.10.61.

Returned to Univ. of Geneva as asst lecturer in cybernetics 1962–63. MIT from 1963, at first as research associate in electronic engineering; Prof. of Applied Math. and co-director Artificial Intelligence Lab. from 1967; neural nets (co-author with M Minsky of book *Perceptrons*, MIT Press, 1968); artificial intelligence. Prof. of Education from 1974; pioneer of computer education; Logo computer language for children; published *Mindstorms: Children, Computers and Powerful Ideas*, Basic Books, 1980; appt. Lego Prof. of Learning Research; published *The Children's Machine*, Basic Books, 1992; *The Connected Family*, Longstreet Press, 1996.

John R Parks

PhD CEng MIEE, b.1.2.32.
EMI Research Labs, Hayes 1948–51.

Appt. NPL as T Ass (Sci) in Electronics Section 1.10.51; member of ACE Pilot Model team; AEO c. Oct. 1953; National Service c. Dec. 1953–Dec. 1955; DEUCE maintenance; design and installation of DEUCE magnetic tape system; EO 1.1.59; founder member of Pattern Recognition group in Auto; SO 1.2.63; SSO 1.6.64; development of practical character recognition systems; head of Pattern Recognition group 1966–74; PhD March 1967; PSO 1.6.67; awarded IEE A F Bulgin Premium 1968; Visiting Prof. University of Pisa 1969; automatic inspection and machine tool monitoring; signature validation; image enhancement.

Transf. to Computers, Systems and Electronics Div. DoI 3.11.74; Advanced Instrumentation Project; transf. to Electronics Applications (LA) Div. on formation 1977; prom. SPSO Oct. 1978; Microelectronics Applications Project; seconded to Quest Automation Ltd March 1980 as Technical Manager in charge of research company; returned to LA Div. 1982; CAD Scheme; Joint Opto-Electronic Research Scheme; Visiting Prof. UWIST 1983; seconded Thorn-EMI Ltd 1984 as head of Cognitive Systems Dept; ret. from Civil Service December 1985; consultant in vision systems, robotics and personal identification techniques.

Annex A: People

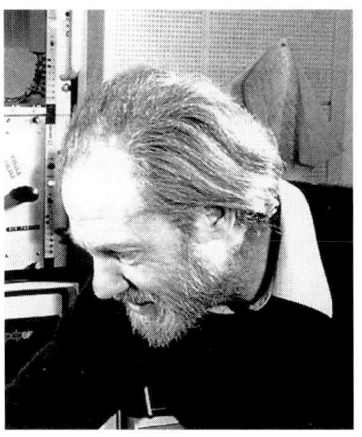

Brian E Pay

b.18.5.31.
Appt. NPL as Workshop Boy 5.4.48; National Service in the Royal Navy c. Nov. 1949–Nov. 1951; then Improver in Metrology Div.; transf. to Light Div. c. March 1952; Apprentice Mechanic (still in Light Div.) c. June 1952; transf. to Metrology Drawing Office as Apprentice c. Jan. 1953; transf. to Electronics Section as Mechanic c. June 1953; T Ass (Sci) c. Nov. 1953; Ass (Sci) c. Jan. 1954 (now in Central Drawing Office); transf. CME c. Dec. 1954; AEO 1.4.56; West Design Office; EO 1.1.61; speech recognition from 1961; SEO 1.2.70; assim. SSO 1.1.71; Head of Speech Rec. Section. Ret. 30.9.87.

Wyn L Price

BEng PhD DSc CEng FIEE FBCS, b.9.6.30.
Appt. NPL as TSO in CME Division 4.10.54; worked on DEUCE and ACE magnetic tape systems; SSO 4.1.61; machine translation 1961–67; PSO 1.6.68; Palantype transcription 1967–70; data network simulation 1970–79; data security 1979 on; Head of Data Security group from 1984. DSc June 1986. Personal promotion to G6 21.1.88; ret. 8.6.90.

David Rayner

BSc PhD, b.2.3.51.
Appt. NPL as HSO in Com. Sci. 1.10.75; job control languages; standard protocols, especially for file transfer; SSO 1.2.77; pioneer in methods of testing protocol implementations for conformance to standards; PSO 1.6.80 and Head of Protocol Standards (later Open Systems) group; collaboration with other organisations to promote harmonised protocol testing services; rapporteur for OSI conformance testing for the International Standards Organisation, leading to the major seven-part standard ISO/IEC 9646 (ref. 78); personal promotion to G6 1.7.86; prime mover in the development of criteria for the accreditation of testing laboratories in software and computer communications; principal author of the key UK document in this area, NAMAS NIS 35 (1990), and of its European successor (ref. 152); convenor of the ISO/IEC group producing international guidelines (ref. 80) based on them; major contributor to the European Committee on IT Testing and Certification (ECITC); chairman of the European Workshop on Open Systems (EWOS) expert group on conformance testing; a lead assessor for NAMAS, later UKAS, on OSI and data security. Appt. Head of Information Systems Engineering Branch, CMOT, Jan. 1996.

Malcolm G Robinson

BA, b.14.1.48.
Appt. NPL 7.7.69 as TSO in Com. Sci.; Information Systems group; SHREWD; principal software designer of Scrapbook; HSO 1.6.72. Res. 30.11.73 to join an insurance company. Died 4.7.82.

Roger A Scantlebury

BSc MInstP, b.9.8.36.
Appt. NPL as TAEO in CME 1.9.55; AEO Dec. 55; DEUCE maintenance. Transf. App. Phys. Div. 1.10.59; teaching machines; SO 11.9.61; transf. back to Auto c. 1963; cryotrons: reliability and photolithography; SSO 22.7.64; founder member of Data Communications group 1966; key contributor to establishment of first NPL network; head of group March 1969; PSO 1.6.69; interconnection of networks, particularly UK/NPL participation in the European Informatics Network. Res. 31.3.77; joined Logica Ltd.

David Schofield

BA DPhil (chemistry); b.24.11.36.
Res. Assoc. Cornell Univ. (chemistry and aerospace) 1961–62.
Appt. NPL as JRF in Aero 3.1.63; high temperature chemistry and hypersonic aerodynamics; SSO 31.8.64; seconded to CCU for 6 months in 1967. PSO 1.6.69 and transf. to Div. of Quantum Metrology; high temperature standards. Transf. to Computing Branch DNAC May 1971; head of systems software development, Edit. Prom. SPSO 1.3.78 and transf. Com. Sci. as Branch Head; responsible for groups in human–computer interaction, speech recognition and software engineering. Deputy Head DITC 1.4.92–30.9.95 and in addition Head CSU from 1.4.93; Head IT Support Unit from 1.10.95.

Annex A: People

Roger S Scowen

BA, b.20.3.40.
Appt. NPL as JRF in Auto 8.2.65; programming research, Babel. Transf. to CCU on formation Nov. 1967; TSSO 8.2.68, SSO 12.5.71; SOAP, WATER; PSO 1.6.74. Seconded to IBM UK for 1 year 25.1.76; economic modelling. Transf. to CSU on formation 1.6.78; programming language syntax, compiler validation. Transf. to DNACS, later DITC, 5.1.81; syntactic metalanguage, Prolog standardisation; Head of Software Engineering group 1991–92; ret. 30.3.94.

C M (Costas) Solomonides

BSc MSc DPhil, b.27.12.43.
Research Associate in Experimental Particle Physics, SERC Rutherford Laboratory and Westfield College, Univ. of London 1969–74.
    Appt. NPL as SSO in Com. Sci. 1.10.74; simulation of data networks; PSO 1.6.77; network protocols and standards. Res. 31.5.80.
    Scicon Ltd, Manager Telecommunication Consultancy Section 1980–83; PA Consulting Group, Manager of Business Development 1983–87; Professor of Information Technology, IT Institute, Univ. of Salford 1988–93; Chief Executive, Professional Services, Cyprus Development Bank, Nicosia, Cyprus 1993–95.

Peter R Stuart

CPhys BSc PhD FInstP, b.20.7.30.
Appt. NPL as SSO in CME 29.9.58; head of Cryotrons group (see section 3.8); PSO 1.1.62. Transf. to Inorganic Materials Unit 1.9.66 and to Div. of Inorganic and Metallic Structure 1.9.67; thin-film physics and scanning electron microscopy; transf. to Div. of Mechanical and Optical Metrology 10.2.75; X-ray optics; head of sections responsible for measurement standards for pressure, vacuum, viscosity and hardness. Ret. 31.7.92.

George T Symm

BSc PhD FIMA, b.11.1.39.
Appt. NPL as TSO in Maths 1.1.63; integral equations; visiting Research Assoc. Brown Univ., USA 1965; SSO 27.4.66; boundary element methods (BEM) for the solution of problems involving partial differential equations, and their application in electrostatics, elastostatics, etc.; PSO 1.6.72; author of many papers and an influential book (ref. 81) on BEM: numerical aspects of the Ada language and the design of numerical software libraries in Ada; Visiting Research Fellow, Brunel Univ. 1974; Visiting Prof., City Univ. from 1987; head of Mathematical Software Group DITC from 1990. Ret. 30.3.94.

Adam J M Szanser

BSc PhD FIL FRAS, b.12.10.08.
Polish Army Signals Corps 1931–46, reaching rank of Major; Polish Resettlement Corps (British Army) 1946–48; HM Statistics Office 1949–61; Fellow of Institute of Linguists 1960.

Appt. NPL as EO in Auto 3.7.61; machine translation; A/SSO 1.1.63; SSO 3.7.65; appt. Fellow of the Royal Astronomical Society 1966 (private interest). 1967 Palantype transcription (error correction); PSO 1.6.68; PhD 1969; moved to MMI group c. 1971, continued work on error correction. Ret. 1.6.71, becoming disestablished HSO; final ret. 31.3.73. Died 15.6.78.

H A Thomas

Horace Augustus Thomas BSc DSc MIEE, b.1.3.01.
Appt. NPL as JA in Electricity Dept 1.10.22; worked on radio; A2 1.4.27; A1 1.10.30; SO1 1.4.33; transf. to Radio Dept on formation 1933; SO 1.1.35; DSc 1936; SSO 1.5.45; PSO 1.10.45; Electronics Section 1947; responsible for ACE development from about March 1947 to about Feb. 1948; industrial applications of electronics. Res. 28.2.49, and joined the Research Dept of Unilever Ltd. Died 6.4.73.

Annex A: People

R H (Dick) Tizard

Richard Henry Tizard MA CEng FIEE FBCS MInstMC, b.25.6.17. Appt. to Dir. Sci. Res. Air Ministry, Farnborough, as JSO Sep. 1939; transf. to Dir. Sci. Res. Admiralty as TEO March 1942; res. Jan. 1946 to take up graduate apprenticeship at British Thomson-Houston Co Ltd, Rugby, Feb. 1946–April 1947.

Appt. NPL as SSO in Control Mechanisms Section, Metrology Div. 12.5.47; automatic speed control for ship tank carriage; analogue computer for simulation of control systems; PSO 1.1.50. Seconded to Vickers-Armstrongs, Weybridge for 6 months in 1950 to design the autopilot for Dr Barnes Wallis's first swing-wing aircraft. Appt. head of CM Section Dec. 1950; design of data handling equipment. Transf. CME Div. on formation 10.6.54; prom. SPSO 22.6.54 and appt. Officer-in-Charge CME following Colebrook's death; prom. DCSO and appt. Supt. CME 1.11.55. Res. 31.5.56 and appt. to a two-year Fellowship at London School of Economics to work on applications of control theory to economics; 1958–60 industrial consultant. Elected a Founder Fellow of Churchill College, Cambridge, 1960; Tutor and Director of Studies in Engineering, Senior Tutor 1964–75, Admissions Tutor 1964–80, Retired Fellow from Oct. 1984, continuing part-time teaching and other College activities.

(In addition to these more notable achievements, he is particularly remembered in NPL legend for having come to work on a horse following a bet with his superior officer; the details of the bet are recorded for posterity in *NPL News* 19, Nov. 1951, pp.3–4.)

A M Turing

Alan Mathison Turing OBE MA PhD FRS, b.23.6.12.
Major scholarship to King's College, Cambridge 1931; Maths Tripos Part II Distinction 1934; Fellow of King's College March 1935; Smith's Prize (for a mathematical essay) 1936; *Computable Numbers* paper (ref. 137) published 1937; Princeton Univ. from 1936, PhD 1938; returned to Cambridge 1938; appt. Government Code and Cypher School, Bletchley Park Sep. 1939; cryptanalysis; ('Temporary Senior Administrative Officer, Foreign Office, Sept. 1939–August 1945' in NPL's records). His main achievements before joining NPL are outlined in section 2.2.

Appt. NPL as TSSO in Maths. 1.10.45; PSO 1.1.46; produced plans for a computer to be called the ACE (ref. 138), which made him a world leader in computer design; OBE 1946; further logical design and program development; SPSO 1.1.47; returned to Cambridge on leave from NPL Oct. 1947 (NPL's personnel records show that he was put on to half pay 'from 1.10.47 to 30.9.48 while at Cambridge'); *Intelligent Machinery* paper (ref. 140) 1948; left 31.5.48. His work at NPL is described in section 2.3.

He was then appointed as Reader (and Deputy Director of the Computing Laboratory) at the University of Manchester. He contributed to the design of the instruction code for the Mark I computer (the successor to the prototype already working when he arrived). He also wrote a programming manual for the Mark I, but did not take part in its logical design. Instead he returned to machine intelligence: if machines in time developed so far that they might reasonably be described as thinking, what criteria could be applied to determine when this point had been reached? His paper on this subject, *Computing Machinery and Intelligence* (ref. 142), published in 1950, has since caught the public imagination because he proposes in it what is now called the *Turing Test:* that a computer can reasonably be considered as thinking if its responses to questioning over a communication channel cannot be distinguished from those of a person. He was elected a Fellow of the Royal Society in 1951, by which time his mind was running on a new topic, a fundamental question in biology: how is it that patterned variations can appear in originally homogeneous tissue as it develops? In 1952 he published a highly original paper on this subject (*The Chemical Basis of Morphogenesis,* ref. 143), which remained little noticed by biologists over the next 20 years, but has since been recognised as a major contribution well ahead of its time. He died on 7 June 1954, almost certainly by suicide.

He is the subject of a most thorough biography by Andrew Hodges (ref. 66). This has largely superseded both his mother's biography (ref. 145) and the main contemporary obituary by M H A Newman (Alan Mathison Turing 1912–1954, *Biographical Memoirs of Fellows of the Royal Society,* 1, 1955, pp.253–263), both of which omit his wartime work because it was still secret and with hindsight can be seen as lacking balance in other respects. A short obituary by E T Goodwin appears in *NPL News* 50, June 1954, pp.22–23 (it gives the date of Turing's death incorrectly).

Julian R Ullmann

MA PhD, b.21.6.36.
Appt. NPL as TSO in CME 17.8.59; pattern recognition theory; JRF 14.2.62; left at end of fellowship 28.2.65.

Senior Research Fellow at Post Office Research Station, Dollis Hill 1965–68.

Re-appt. NPL as TSSO in Auto 22.8.68; continued work on pattern recognition theory; TPSO 1.6.70; PSO 1.6.72; published book on pattern recognition techniques (ref. 146) 1973.

Res. 17.11.75 to take up appt as Prof. of Computer Science at Sheffield Univ.; Head of Dept from Oct. 1980. Appt. Prof. of Computer Science Univ. of London 26.3.86; Head of Dept of Computer Science, Royal Holloway and Bedford New College, March 1986–30.8.89; Head of Dept of Computer Science, King's College London from 1.11.89. Author of three textbooks on computer science.

Annex A: People

A M (Pete) Uttley

Albert Maurel Uttley BSc PhD AFRAeS, b.14.8.06.
Maths Kings College London BSc 1926, Teacher's Diploma 1927; teaching 1927–34. BSc Psychology 1936, PhD Psychology 1940.

Ministry of Aircraft Production, later Ministry of Supply (Telecommunications Research Establishment, Malvern): TSO 1.1.41; TSSO 1.10.43; design of radar trainers for aircrew; TPSO 1.4.45; PSO 1.1.46; electronics for automatic guidance of astronomical telescopes; SPSO 1.1.47; Fellow of Institute of Navigation 1950; Simms Gold Medal RAeS 1950 (for a paper on navigational systems and instrument aids); DCSO 1.1.51; AFRAeS 1951.

Led team developing TREAC computer 1946–53 (see Campbell-Kelly ref. 16 p.129); also worked on problems of control involving a human operator, on learning machines and on visual pattern recognition.

Transf. NPL as DCSO and appt. Supt CME Div. 1.1.57; see section 3.1 for an outline of his approach to this task. Fellow at Center for Advanced Study of Behavioral Sciences, Stanford University (unpaid leave from NPL) 3.9.62–14.6.63, working on mathematical models of neuron interaction. Pres. Biological Engineering Soc. 1963. Ret. from NPL 31.7.66.

Research Professor in Experimental Psychology Laboratory, University of Sussex 1966–73; published book on the nervous system in 1979 (ref. 148). Died 13.9.85.

Peter K T Vaswani

BSc PhD, b.29.3.34.
Appt. NPL as TSSO in Auto 9.5.60; information retrieval; SSO 1.4.66; PSO 1.6.69; man–machine interaction 1969–75; multiprocessor systems design 1976–83; telerobotics 1984–86; neural networks. Transf. from DITC to National Measurement Accreditation Service (NAMAS) 21.8.89; accreditation services in IT and electronics. Ret. 31.3.94; continued NAMAS (later UKAS) work as consultant.

Tom Vickers

MA FIMA FBCS, b.28.7.19.
Ordnance Board (Ministry of Supply), working at Mathematical Laboratory, Cambridge 24.2.41–30.4.43; EO, Armaments Research Dept, Fort Halstead 1.5.43–30.4.46.

Temp. Appt. NPL Maths. Div. 1.5.46; manager of computing service using Pilot ACE, the first external computer service in the world; SEO Jan. 1955; Head of General Computing group responsible for NPL computing services using DEUCE, ACE, and later KDF9, and including programming, desk machines and punched card sections; CEO 1.4.60; PSO 1.6.65; ret. 31.12.77. Wide interest in computer education, for example assisting in the development of CNAA syllabuses in computing and acting as external examiner. Book Review Editor for the British Computer Society and an active contributor to their work on education, publications, membership and professional development.

Brenda Webber (later Mrs James)

b.17.3.37.
Appt. NPL as Temp. Ass. (Sci.) in Maths 14.9.53; computing services, on Pilot ACE from 1954; Ass. (Sci.) 6.1.56; DEUCE service; AEO 10.3.61; day-to-day management of ACE service; management of KDF9 service from the delivery of the first machine in 1964; EO 1.6.65; part-time from 3.7.67; res. 31.3.69.

Brian A Wichmann

BSc DPhil FBCS, b.2.4.39.
Appt. NPL as TSO in Auto 1.10.64; software research: modular operating systems; pattern recognition; SSO 7.6.66; transf. to CCU on formation Nov. 1967; design of PL-516 language; PSO 1.6.69; Algol compilation and assessment; computer performance measurement (benchmarks); SPSO (IM) 1.7.77; transf. CSU on formation 1.6.78; transf. to DNACS 5.1.81; Pascal validation suite; design of numerical facilities in Ada; founding chairman of Ada-Europe; software protection devices; prom. G5 (IM) 1.7.90; language-independent standards for arithmetic operations; software for safety-critical systems; Visiting Professor Open University 1993. Author of nearly 200 publications on software engineering topics, including four books (refs. 151, 153–155). His private interests include tiling patterns; see for instance his paper 'An encyclopaedia of tiling patterns' *Mathematical Gazette,* 78(483), November 1994, pp.265–273.

Annex A: People

J H (Jim) Wilkinson

James Hardy Wilkinson MA ScD DTech DSc FRS HonFIMA DistFBCS, b.27.9.19.

Sir Joseph Williamson's Mathematical School, Rochester; major scholarship to Trinity College, Cambridge at the age of 16; Pemberton Prize, Trinity College, as the most outstanding freshman in any subject 1937; Maths Tripos Part II 1st 1938; Part III Distinction and Mathison Prize as the most outstanding third-year man in any subject 1939. Ordnance Board (Ministry of Supply), working at Mathematical Laboratory, Cambridge 1.1.40–1943; Armaments Research Dept, Fort Halstead 1943–30.4.46; ballistics, thermodynamics of explosives.

Temp. Appt NPL 1.5.46 in Maths Div.; half-time assistant to Turing on ACE plans, half-time numerical analysis in desk machine section; SSO 14.11.46; Test Assembly; led ACE group in Maths Div. after Turing's departure to Cambridge 1.10.47; seconded to Electronics Section for Pilot ACE development 1948; PSO 1.1.51; world-class leader in numerical methods based on the availability of computers; SPSO (Personal) 1.7.54; linear algebra, error analysis; DCSO (Personal) 1.7.62. Prolific output including two particularly influential books, refs 166 and 167; ScD (Cambridge) 1963; Visiting Prof. Univ. of Michigan, Ann Arbor most summers 1957–73 and at Stanford Univ. 1961, 1967, 1969 and 1977–84; in a published list (*Computer Journal*, 11, 1968, pp.116–117) of the most-cited papers in computing he led with three in the top 25; FRS 1969; one of the prime movers in the establishment of the Numerical Algorithms Group in 1970; ACM A M Turing Award 1970; Soc. for Industrial and Applied Maths J von Neumann Award 1970; Distinguished Fellow British Computer Soc. 1973; Foreign Honorary Member, American Academy of Arts and Sciences 1974; very rare prom. to CSO (IM) 1.7.74; Hon. Fellowship Inst. of Maths and its Applications 1977; other awards and honorary degrees. Ret. 24.1.80. Published a first-hand account (ref. 171) of the early years of computing at NPL 1980. Died 5.10.86; obit. *The Times* 9.10.86. A memorial conference (proceedings ref. 23) was held at NPL in July 1987. Memoirs include:

(1) E L Albasiny. Dr James Hardy Wilkinson FRS 1919–1986. *Utilitas Mathematica*, 31, 1987, pp.7–12.
(2) L Fox. James Hardy Wilkinson. *Biographical Memoirs of Fellows of the Royal Society*, 33, 1987, pp.669–708.
(3) G Golub. Prologue: reflections on Jim Wilkinson. In: Cox and Hammarling ref. 23, pp.1–5.
(4) E T Goodwin. Dr James Hardy Wilkinson FRS FIMA. *Bull. Inst. Mathematics and its Applications*, 23, 1987, pp.76–77.
(5) B N Parlett. The contribution of J H Wilkinson to numerical analysis. In: S G Nash (ed.), *A History of Scientific Computing*, Addison-Wesley, 1990, pp.17–30.

Peter T Wilkinson

BSc PhD, b.27.7.39.
Appt. NPL as JRF in Auto 1.8.66; programming research; SSO 21.5.68; data communications network software design; PSO 1.6.71; multiprocessor systems; Pascal program validation. Prom. G6 and transf. IT Div. DTI 24.6.88; software quality improvement schemes, particularly TickIT. Seconded to British Computer Society as Technical Director 1.2.94.

W (Willie) Wilson

Walter Wilson MBE BSc, b.12.8.09.
Appt. NPL as Junior Observer in Engineering Dept 17.9.28; assim. Assistant III 1.4.33; BSc in Physics and Pure Maths 1936; strain-measuring systems; transf. to Electricity (Electrical Standards) Dept 19.4.37; projects included radio frequency test work, dielectric heating, and the development of a camera with a tuning-fork shutter to photograph projectiles in flight; Assistant II by 1.4.44; Assistant I 1.4.45; SEO 1.1.46; MBE 10.1.46; transf. from Electricity to Radio Div. 18.8.47; Electronics Section; Pilot ACE development. Transf. from CME to App. Phys. c. Oct. 1959; CEO 1.6.61. Ret. and re-employed as disestablished SSA 13.8.69; disest. SA 11.5.70; assim. ASO 1.1.71; part-time ASO 1.6.72. Final ret. 30.3.73. Died 17.3.86. Known affectionately to all as Big Willie and much respected for his innovative versatility and encyclopaedic knowledge of electronic components.

J R Womersley

John Ronald Womersley BSc ARCS DIC, b.20.6.07.
Cotton Industry Research Association 1930–37; collaborated with Hartree on the development and application of the Manchester differential analyser; 'Research Dept Woolwich Ballistics Branch' 1937–42; Ministry of Supply 1942: SSO 10.11.42; Assistant Director 24.4.44.

Appt. NPL as first Supt Mathematics Div. (no grade recorded) 1.4.45, during visit to USA February–May 1945; DCSO 1.1.46. Successfully established the Division; resigned 23.9.50.

He then joined the British Tabulating Machine Co., where a commercial version of the Birkbeck College APE(X)C computer was subsequently developed under the acronym HEC. In 1956 this was successfully marketed as the BTM 1201, but Womersley, being as an obituarist noted of a restless disposition, had by then left BTM, and he worked successively on a Medical Research Council project on arterial blood flow and on mathematical work for the US Air Force at Wright Field, Ohio before his untimely death on 7 March 1958 at the age of 50.

Obituaries: (1) by F Smithies, *The Times*, 19.3.58, p.13; (2) also by F Smithies, *J. Lond. Math. Soc.*, 34, 1959, pp.370–372; (3) by C G Darwin, *Nature*, 181, 3 May 1958, p.1240, reprinted in *NPL News* 96, April 1958, pp.14–16.

For further details of his work at BTM, see Hendry ref. 64 pp.73, 105, 153, 204 and Lavington ref. 83 pp.63–64.

Annex A: People

Michael Woodger

BSc, b.28.3.23.
Ministry of Supply 1.7.43–8.9.45; part-time demonstrator University College London 1.10.45.

Temp. appt. NPL 20.5.46, Maths Div; assistant to Alan Turing; SO 23.6.47; worked on Test Assembly and (on secondment to Electronics Section) on Pilot ACE development; matrix routines for General Interpretive Program; SSO 1.1.52; PSO 1.1.57; Algol design (joint author of the ALGOL 60 Report, ref. 94); founder member and *de facto* secretary of IFIP WG 2.1 on Algol from 23.3.62. Transf. Auto 17.3.65; programming research; a major contributor to IFIP WG 2.3 on programming methodology, and its chairman 1969–76 and 1979–86; levels of language; databases; Ada design. Ret. 31.3.83. Continued work on Ada with Alsys, France, 1.4.83–31.5.91; Ada 9X 15.7.92–31.7.94. Collected documents throughout his career, particularly papers relating to the early NPL computers and to Algol and Ada; by the time of his retirement these formed a unique archive which was deposited in the Science Museum (see ref. 180). His two papers on Pilot ACE and ACE (refs 176 and 178) are an important part of the primary historical record of those machines.

E P H (Pat) Woodroffe

BSc, b.18.5.24.
Electronic Transmission Equipment Ltd (Philips group) 1944–49; broadcast and marine transmitters and radar detection equipment. Appt. NPL as TAEO in Physics Div. 1.6.49; ultrasonics; AEO 27.2.50; EO 1.1.53. Transf. CME 1955; ACE development; data-handling equipment for adaptive control systems; SEO 1.1.63; NPL network hardware design and development; assimilated SSO 1.1.71. Res. 31.5.78; later worked for Ceedata Ltd and (from 1982) for Racal Radar.

Michael A Wright

BSc, b.10.6.24.
Appt. NPL as temp. JSO in Electricity Div. 1.8.44; ship degaussing etc.; SO 18.4.47. Transf. to Radio Div. 18.8.47; Electronics Section; Pilot ACE development (delay lines); SSO 1.1.54; mechanisation of clerical procedures 1954–59.

Res. 30.11.59 to join National Research Development Corporation; support for computer development projects including ATLAS, and studies of applications in traffic control, shipbuilding and medicine. Re-employed in MinTech 1.10.65; reappointed NPL as PSO in Com. Sci. 10.8.70; ACTP (chairman of software technical committee). Transf. to DTI Computers Systems and Electronics Div. 2.4.79; secretary of Computers and Communications Committee of EARB; worked on STARTS and Alvey; ret. 1983.

David M Yates

MA PhD FBCS, b.29.11.34.
Royal Navy (meteorology) 1956–59; Leo Computers Ltd 1959–62. Appt. NPL as TSO in Auto 5.3.62; machine translation; SSO 8.11.62; information systems, SHREWD 1967; PSO 1.6.68; Head of Information Systems group 1968; Scrapbook. Act. SPSO 1.5.73; SPSO 23.7.76 and appt. Branch Head responsible for groups in protocol standards, data security, and later mathematical software; act. Supt briefly in 1985 and 1986. Ret. 30.3.92.

Annex B: Patents

This is a list of UK patents which are related (in one or two cases only indirectly related) to computing at NPL. The list is in Patent Number order. The dates given are those of application (not of final filing or publication).

E A Newman and H A Thomas. Measurement or control of physical quantities. 666,581, 14.2.49.

E A Newman and H A Thomas. Measurement or control of physical quantities. 666,582, 14.2.49.

E A Newman and D O Clayden. Improvements in thermionic valve circuits. 676,911, 23.3.50.

E A Newman. Electronic pulse output circuits for thermionic valves. 679,862, 14.1.50.

D W Davies. Improvements in or relating to devices for producing mechanical displacements. 682,998, 16.8.50.

A M Turing. Acoustic delay lines. 694,679, 30.3.51.

E A Newman. Electrical pulse shaping circuits. 698,950, 23.11.50.

E A Newman and D O Clayden. Digital computing engines [half adder]. 700,007, 22.12.49.

D W Davies. Electrical pulse generators. 702,401, 19.3.51.

J H Wilkinson. Improvements in or related to digital computers [Pilot ACE multiplier] 717,114, 4.1.50.

E A Newman and D O Clayden. Improvements in or relating to electronic storage devices. [note by DOC: ACE Pilot Model circulation]. 717,115, 14.1.50.

E A Newman, D W Davies and R F Braybrook. Improvements in or relating to tree type electrical circuits [note by DOC: ACE Pilot Model tree]. 717,118, 28.2.50.

D W Davies. Electrical pulse generating circuits. 717,138, 26.11.51.

D W Davies and M Woodger. Improvements in or relating to electronic digital computing engines [note by DOC: control of Turing's ACE]. 718,894, 4.5.50.

A M Turing, D W Davies and M Woodger. Improvements in or relating to electronic digital computing engines [note by DOC: control of Turing's ACE]. 718,895, 4.5.50.

D W Davies. Electronic digital computing engines [note by DOC: ACE Pilot Model adder]. 718,901, 21.4.51.

E A Newman, D W Davies and D O Clayden. Electrical digital computing engines [note by DOC: ACE Pilot Model control]. 719,066, 2.6.51.

D W Davies. Thermionic valve circuits. 724,013, 6.6.52.

M A Wright. Electrical pulse circuits [note by DOC: one-shot trigger]. 728,283, 19.3.51.

G M Davis. Electrical digital computing engines. 731,733, 11.1.53 [NPL property under terms of agreement with English Electric].

E A Newman, D W Davies and D O Clayden. Apparatus for recording electrical digit signals [note by DOC: Magnetic Drums]. 732,221, 22.11.50.

D O Clayden. Electrical multivibrator circuits. 732,310, 8.11.51.

D O Clayden. Electronic digital computers. 732,311, 22.11.50.

D W Davies. Electrical pulse counting circuits. 734,013, 23.4.52.

E A Newman. Electrical gate circuits. 741,883, 14.3.53.

Annex B: Patents

E A Newman and D O Clayden. Electronic digital computers [note by DOC: Drum store control]. 741,950, 11.2.53.

E A Newman and D O Clayden. Electrical signal storage apparatus [note by DOC: DEUCE and ACE drum transfer system]. 743,416, 4.2.53.

D O Clayden. Electronic devices for producing mechanical displacements. 745,496, 27.11.53.

D O Clayden. Electrical binary-digital pulse signalling systems. 748,771, 20.4.53.

D O Clayden. Control arrangements for electronic digital computers [note by DOC: A trigger for each source and destination as on ACE]. 757,356, 4.12.53.

M A Wright. Electrical signal storage systems. 760,967, 12.2.54.

L J Page and W L Gleed. Magnetic recording surfaces. 766,823 27.4.54.

D O Clayden. Electrical pulse synchronising systems. 767,095, 4.5.53.

D O Clayden, R T Clayden, E A Newman and G M Davis. Dividers for electrical digital computing engines. 777,839, 19.5.54.

E A Newman and D O Clayden. Electrical control systems. 786,489, 2.7.54.

E A Newman and M A Wright. Electronic digital computers. 792,707, 22.10.54.

D W Davies. Digital information storage devices. 797,912, 21.3.56.

D W Davies and D O Clayden. Electrical digital computing engines. 799,078, 5.3.56.

D O Clayden, R T Clayden, E A Newman and G M Davis. Electrical digital computing engines. 799,900, 27.3.56.

E A Newman and D O Clayden. Electrical digital computing engines. 802,175, 5.3.56.

E A Newman. Electrical signal storage systems. 806,782, 30.3.54.

W T Bane, R H Tizard and M P Atkinson. Electrical counting and scaling devices. 811,065, 1.5.56.

W T Bane, D L A Barber and M P Atkinson. Means for determining the sense of movement of a moving member. 815,336, 15.5.56.

D O Clayden and L J Page. Electrical pulse circuits. 821,679, 16.4.57.

D W Davies and L J Page. Electrical pulse circuits. 825,244, 18.6.57.

R H Tizard. Improvements in and relating to control systems. 828,191, 29.11.54.

D W Davies. Means for reading magnetic recording. 850,963, 7.3.56.

G Russell and A M Uttley. Improvements in or relating to automatic control systems. 852,639, 5.7.56.

G Russell and A M Uttley. Voltage generating and voltage comparison circuits. 852,640, 5.7.56.

C F Osborne and L J Page. Improvements in or relating to electromagnetic devices for producing mechanical displacements. 853,388, 11.9.57.

D O Clayden. Electrical digital computing engines. 861,190, 22.8.57.

P H Hammond and A M Uttley. Improvements in or relating to automatic control systems. 862,322, 28.1.57.

D O Clayden. Improvements in or relating to devices for producing mechanical displacements. 862,590, 25.10.57.

J B Stringer. Electrical digital computing engines. 866,214, 13.8.57.

C H Davis and J. B Stringer. Improvements in or relating to electrical calculating devices. 866,215, 13.8.57.

E R Dymott and R G Chalmers. Improvements in and relating to the production of scales photographically. 897,297, 10.10.57.

A M Andrew. Improvements in or relating to apparatus for the electrical storage of quantitative information. 904,752, 29.3.60.

E A Newman and J B Stringer. Electrical digital computing engines. 907,381, 18.8.58.

D L A Barber and J M Burch. Means for counting electrical pulses. 921,368, 24.6.60.

D L A Barber. Improvements in or relating to multivibrator circuit arrangements. 929,064, 6.3.61 and 4.8.61.

D L A Barber and M P Atkinson. Improvements in and relating to the measurements of displacements. 932,471, 26.6.58 and 23.4.59.

D L A Barber and M P Atkinson. Improvements in and relating to the measurements of displacements. 953,050, 26.5.59.

D L A Barber. Improvements in and relating to electrical counting apparatus. 954,699, 19.7.60.

E A Newman, R A Scantlebury and M Longden. Improvements in or relating to instruction devices. 968,601, 4.5.61.

M B Clowes and J R Parks. Improvements in or relating to character recognition systems and arrangements. 981,431, 20.5.60 and 21.12.60.

M B Clowes and J R Parks. Improved two-dimensional potentiometer and arrangements for use therewith. 982,008, 6.1.61.

A M Uttley. Improvements in or relating to fluid measuring apparatus. 982,547, 12.5.60.

D L A Barber. Improvements in and relating to measuring equipment. 989,514, 5.10.62.

D L A Barber. Improvements in apparatus for the measurement of torsion and the like. 991,782, 20.5.60.

E A Newman, D V Blake and J S Appleby. Improvements in or relating to frequency analysers. 1,002,032, 5.5.61.

D L A Barber. Improvements in or relating to electrical noise generating arrangements. 1,019,062, 8.5.61 and 11.8.61.

M B Clowes. Improvements in or relating to character recognition systems and arrangements. 1,025,172, 5.1.62.

D L A Barber. Method of analysing fluid mixtures. 1,040,046, 26.3.62.

J R Parks. Improvements in or relating to electronic systems and arrangements for recognising printed characters. 1,040,294 1.5.62.

J R Parks. Improvements in or relating to character recognition systems and arrangements. 1,054,929, 7.12.62.

M Longden, L J Page and R A Scantlebury. Electrical relay devices. 1,071,067, 13.8.63.

P H Hammond. Measuring composition of liquid mixtures. 1,073,461, 27.1.64.

E A Newman. Improvements in or relating to machine recognition of speech. 1,101,721, 31.1.64.

E A Newman. Improvements in or relating to logic circuits. 1,101,722, 31.1.64.

E A Newman. Improvements in or relating to correlation circuits. 1,101,723, 31.1.64.

J R Parks and C H Davis. Improvements in or relating to electronic systems and arrangements for recognising printed or written characters. 1,107,713, 13.4.64.

M B Clowes, J R Parks and D O Clayden. Improvements in or relating to character recognition systems and apparatus. 1,116,711, 29.11.63.

D L A Barber, C F Osborne and E S Trickett. Coding apparatus. 1,154,456, 8.9.66.

J R Parks. Improvements in or relating to electronic systems and apparatus for recognising printed characters. 1,170,234, 12.11.65.

[J R Parks and R E Rengger]. Improvements in or relating to a system and apparatus for improving the contrast of analogue density patterns such as printed characters. 1,173,281, 15.9.65.

Annex B: Patents

J R Parks and R E Rengger. Improvements in or relating to the reading of projected trace errors. 1,216,674, 31.5.67.

C R Evans and D J Drage. Apparatus for simulating perceptual phenomena [the artificial retina]. 1,263,078, 30.4.68.

J R Parks, C H Davis and G O Plumb. Improvements in or relating to apparatus for character recognition [multifont character recognition system]. 1 280 155, 25.6.68.

K A Bartlett and R A Scantlebury. Control apparatus for units which become ready for operation at irregular times. 1 294 326, 21.5.69.

J R Ullmann. Improvements in or relating to apparatus for effecting recognition of patterns such as written or printed characters. 1 296 701, 20.6.69.

P J Pobgee. Graphical input apparatus for electrical apparatus [CHIT (1)]. 1 310 683, 6.8.69.

J R Parks. Improvements in or relating to apparatus for effecting autocorrelation of an electric signal waveform. 1 318 341, 2.6.69.

E A Newman, B E Pay and D R Manning. Single frequency identification for speech recognition. 1 337 385.

B E Pay. Improvements in apparatus for speech recognition. 1 346 302, 7.5.70.

C R Evans and P B Whittle. Improvements in or relating to the operation of keyboard machines ['yes/no/?' mask for teletype keyboard]. 1 359 657, 1.9.70.

[J R Parks and G Cowin.] Improvements in or relating to pattern recognition systems and apparatus. 1 431 438, 11.9.72.

J R Parks, P J Pobgee and J P Yardley. Apparatus for recognising handwriting [Verisign]. 1 480 066, 6.7.73.

D A Bell, B J Chorley, J R Parks and R L Wanek. Improvements in or relating to the automatic inspection of machined parts. 1 504 537, 12.6.75.

J R Ullmann. Improvements in or relating to the machine recognition of patterns. 1 523 272, 5.6.74.

J L Rodgers and D Schofield. Improvements in or relating to computer stores [clothesline store]. 1 525 045, 11.2.76.

P J Pobgee. Improvements in graphical input apparatus for electrical equipment [CHIT (2)]. 1 559 173, 21.10.75.

P J Pobgee. Improvements in graphical input apparatus for electrical equipment [CHIT (3)]. 1 597 374, 9.3.77.

P J Pobgee. Improvements in graphical input apparatus for electrical equipment [(CHIT (4)]. 1 597 375, 9.3.77.

D C Barnes and J M Howlett. Improvements in or relating to apparatus for Braille character embossing [attachment for line printer]. 2 021 047, 3.5.79.

R S Scowen and J L Rodgers. Computer store arrangements [incorporating a check that values are used before being reassigned]. 2 030 739, 29.9.78.

R E Rengger and D R Manning. Improvements in or relating to speech recognition systems. 2 091 466, 4.12.81.

E P H Woodroffe. Generation of boundaries on raster display [signal generator for MALTA]. 2 091 979, 26.1.82.

D A Bell. Apparatus and methods for making payments electronically. 2 102 606, 17.6.82.

A P N Plummer. Parallel digital signal processing [linear array processor]. 2 129 545, 2.11.82.

B J Chorley, G I Parkin, B A Wichmann and S M Elsom. Software protection device. 2 163 577, 20.8.85.

Acronyms and abbreviations

A1	Assistant 1
A2	Assistant 2
ACE	Automatic Computing Engine
ACTP	Advanced Computer Techniques Project
AEO	Assistant Experimental Officer (later merged into SO)
ASO	Assistant Scientific Officer
Ass. (Sci.)	Assistant (Scientific), later renamed Scientific Assistant
ATTC	Advanced Token Technology Club
Auto	Autonomics Division, NPL (1960–68)
BCR	Bureau Communautaire de Référence
BCS	British Computer Society
BSI	British Standards Institution
BSI-QAS	British Standards Institution Quality Assurance Services
CCSC	Commercial Computer Security Centre
CCU	Central Computer Unit, NPL (1967–71)
CEO	Chief Experimental Officer (later merged into Grade 7)
CFM	Computer Field Maintenance Ltd
CISE	Centre for Information Systems Engineering, NPL (1995 and 1997 on)
CME	Control Mechanisms and Electronics Division, NPL (1954–60)
CMM	Coordinate Measuring Machine
CMOT	Centre for Mechanical and Optical Technology, NPL (1995 on)
Com. Sci.	Division of Computer Science, NPL (1968–78)
CPP	Computer Policy Panel
CRT	Cathode ray tube
CSERB	Computers, Systems and Electronics Requirements Board
CSO	Chief Scientific Officer (later merged into Grades 3 and 4)
CSU	Computing Services Unit, NPL (1978–95)
CTU	Computing Technology Unit, NPL (1978–80)
CUP	Computer Users' Panel
DA	Differential Analyser
DAP	Distributed Array Processor
DASL	Data Approximation Subroutine Library
DCPU	Data Communications Protocols Unit
DCSO	Deputy Chief Scientific Officer (later merged into Grade 5)
DHP	Data Handling Panel
DITC	Division of Information Technology and Computing, NPL (1981–95)
DNAC	Division of Numerical Analysis and Computing, NPL (1971–78)
DNACS	Division of Numerical Analysis and Computer Science, NPL (1978–81)
DNAM	Division of Numerical and Applied Mathematics, NPL (1967–71)
DoI	Department of Industry
DSIR	Department of Scientific and Industrial Research (1918–65)
DTI	Department of Trade and Industry
EARB	Electronics and Avionics Requirements Board
EIN	European Informatics Network
EO	Experimental Officer (later merged into HSO)
FBCS	Fellow of the British Computer Society

Acronyms and abbreviations

FIMA	Fellow of the Institute of Mathematics and its Applications
GPO	General Post Office
HCI	Human–computer interaction
HMSO	Her Majesty's Stationery Office
HSO	Higher Scientific Officer
ICCC	International Conference on Computer Communication
IEC	International Electrotechnical Commission
IEE	Institution of Electrical Engineers
IFIP	International Federation for Information Processing
IM	Individual Merit
ISE	Information Systems Engineering Branch of CMOT, NPL (from December 1995)
ISO	International Organization for Standardization
IT	Information Technology
ITSU	Information Technology Support Unit, NPL (from October 1995)
JA	Junior Assistant
JRF	Junior Research Fellow
Maths	Mathematics Division, NPL (1945–67)
MCI	Man–computer interaction (now called HCI)
MinTech	Ministry of Technology
MMI	Man–machine interaction (now called HCI)
MT	Machine translation
NAG	Numerical Algorithms Group Ltd
NAMAS	National Measurement Accreditation Service (merged into UKAS in 1995)
NAO	Nautical Almanac Office
NCC	National Computing Centre
NEL	National Engineering Laboratory
NOSL	Numerical Optimization Software Library
NPL	National Physical Laboratory
OSI	Open Systems Interconnection
PC	Personal Computer
PM	Personal Merit
PRF	Principal Research Fellow
PSO	Principal Scientific Officer (later merged into Grade 7)
RRDE	Radar Research and Development Establishment, Malvern
RRE	Royal Radar Establishment, Malvern
SA	Scientific Assistant (later renamed ASO)
SEO	Senior Experimental Officer (later merged into SSO)
SO	Scientific Officer
SPSO	Senior Principal Scientific Officer (later merged into Grade 6)
SRF	Senior Research Fellow
SSA	Senior Scientific Assistant (later merged into SO)
SSO	Senior Scientific Officer
TAEO	Temporary Assistant Experimental Officer
TASO	Temporary Assistant Scientific Officer

TEO	Temporary Experimental Officer
TPSO	Temporary Principal Scientific Officer
TRE	Telecommunications Research Establishment, Malvern
TRON	Electronics Section, NPL (1947–54)
TSA	Temporary Scientific Assistant
TSO	Temporary Scientific Officer
TSSO	Temporary Senior Scientific Officer
TTCC	Tokens and Transactions Control Consortium
UKAS	United Kingdom Accreditation Service
VDU	Visual Display Unit

Illustrations

Except as otherwise noted here, all the illustrations are Crown Copyright, and are reproduced by permission of the Controller of HMSO. For Crown Copyright photographs, NPL Photographic Section's reference number is given after the title in the list below. I am grateful to the following for permission to reproduce other photographs: the Hulton Getty Collection for figure 3; Brenda James for figures 6 and 16; the British Computer Society for supplying the picture of Stanley Gill on p.299 and the Southern Daily Echo, Southampton, for permission to reproduce it; and Harry Huskey and Costas Solomonides for the pictures of themselves on pp.300 and 308 respectively. The picture of Alan Turing on p.310 is reproduced by courtesy of the National Portrait Gallery, London. Diagrams prepared by the author, which form part of the text for copyright purposes, are marked (A).

1 Organisational history of computing at NPL (A), p.9.
2 Simplified diagram of Pilot ACE, p.34.
3 Members of the Pilot ACE team at the press demonstration, November 1950. Left to right: E A Newman, F M Colebrook, J H Wilkinson, D W Davies (Central Press Photos Ltd no. 33991), p.36.
4 Pilot ACE installed in Mathematics Division, March 1952 (CS 2364), p.37.
– The Paris Model, 1951 (CS 1117), p.38.
5 The ACE family of computers (A), p.41.
6 NPL's DEUCE in about 1956, with Brenda Webber, p.45.
7 Two integrators on the Manchester Differential Analyser (undated, but taken before the move from Manchester) (CS 10592B), p.47.
8 NPL's second Differential Analyser: an operator following an input curve, August 1954 (CS 5356), p.48.
9 NPL's second Differential Analyser, Building 21, August 1954 (CS 5326), p.49.
10 The Electronic Simulator, September 1954 (CS 5431), p.53.
11 Growth in the Uttley era: CME/Auto staff numbers 1957–66 (A), p.57.
12 The new Autonomics Building, January 1965 (CS 16781), p.59.
13 Staff of Autonomics Division, November 1964 (CS 16741), p.61.
14 ACE under construction, May 1957, with (l. to r.) Frank Blake, Lew Page and Bill Gleed (CS 10319), p.68.
15 ACE, July 1959 (CS 12839), p.70.

Illustrations

16 An informal picture of ACE in about 1963, p.71.

17 Adaptive control: the distillation column (CS 16625), p.74.

18 Adaptive control: Ferranti Hermes computer (CS 18253), p.75.

19 Pattern recognition: John Parks with the 'Breadboard' Cyclops prototype, May 1964 (CS 16491), p.82.

20 Pattern recognition: Cyclops 1 with Roger Manning, June 1968 (CS 18313/8), p.82.

21 Visual perception: an initial after-image and later fragmented versions of it, p.86.

22 Visual perception: equipment for studying after-images with P Stilliard as the subject, November 1964 (CS 16720), p.86.

23 Learning systems: the NPL tortoise, November 1958 (CS 12192), p.92.

24 Learning systems: the 'Hungarian machine (Tortoise)', November 1958 (CS 12194), p.92.

25 Machine translation: example of unedited results, p.98.

26 Cryotrons: a vacuum evaporation unit with the bell-jar raised, April 1964 (CS 16479), p.105.

27 A cryotron selection tree and dummy store, September 1964 (CS 16655), p.106.

28 NPL central computers (A), p.114.

29 The KDF9 computer, August 1964, with (l. to r.) Joyce Dickerson, Brenda Webber and Monica Trumble (CS 16628C), p.114.

30 Staff numbers in Auto/Com. Sci., 1966–77 (A), p.117.

31 The NPL site in 1970, p.126.

32 The planned NPL Network, showing its connection to the proposed high-level national network, p.130.

33 The NPL Network, February 1972, p.133.

34 The Mark II NPL Network, p.134.

35 The NPL node computer of the European Informatics Network, 1977, with Roger Scantlebury, Derek Barber, and Donald Davies (CS/C 1435/5), p.142.

36 Teletext in Europe via the NPL Network and European Informatics Network, July 1976 (C 1349), p.143.

37 Sgt Colliar of the Thames Valley Police using SHREWD, December 1970 (CS 19439), p.151.

38 One of the Division's CTL Modular One installations, with Vince Hathway and Angela Stephens, October 1971 (CS 19922), p.153.

39 Section of a Palantype paper band with its English transcription, p.160.

40 The Palantype machine modified for computer input (CS 19524), p.161.

41 Sample of output from the experimental Palantype transcription system, p.163.

Illustrations

42 Pattern recognition: John Parks using CHIT connected to the Honeywell DDP-516 computer, 1971 (CS 19924), p.166.

43 Verisign and Datapad with Celia Searle, July 1974 (CS 20925), p.169.

44 Speech recognition: Brian Pay using a PDP-8 computer, October 1971 (CS 19920), p.173.

45 'Tell me, does the pain ever wake you in the early hours of the morning?' Peggy Anderson, July 1971 (CS/C 436/11), p.177.

46 Record of medical history-taking session, September 1970, p.178.

47 MICKIE, the Medical Interviewing Computer, September 1978 (CS 22610/5), p.179.

48 DNACS/DITC staff numbers 1978–87 (A), p.199.

49 Data security: the NPL Token, January 1988 (C 5581), p.214.

50 Demos: Peter Wilkinson, Peter Neale and Peter Vaswani, November 1982 (CS 23939/5), p.218.

– Augusta Ada, later Countess of Lovelace, by Margaret Carpenter (CS 21793), p.223.

51 MAVIS in use at Banstead Place, Surrey, January 1980 (CS 23069/6), p.233.

52 MALTA with Ernie Albasiny, August 1984 (CS/C 3717/11), p.234.

53 Edutext with Bob Watson, November 1982 (CS 23938/6), p.235.

54 Electronic paper with Michael Stevens, May 1987 (CS/C 5011/17), p.237.

55 The X.25 Network, 1987, p.245.

56 DITC/CISE staff numbers 1987–95 (A), p.247.

57 Tom Blaney, Donald Davies, Adrian Marks, Ernie Albasiny, Derek Barber and Ted Newman, March 1992 (C 7418/7), p.248.

58 The usability laboratory with Rosemary Bowden, Ralph Rengger, Cathy Thomas, and Steve Austin as the subject, April 1993 (C 7816/4), p.277.

References and bibliography

1. E L Albasiny. Report on the history of Mathematics Division, NPL, unpublished draft.
2. ALPAC. Language and machines: computers in translation and linguistics. A report by the Automatic Language Processing Advisory Committee [ALPAC], Div. of Behavioural Science, National Academy of Sciences, National Research Council, Washington DC, 1966.
3. Anon. Mathematics at the National Physical Laboratory. *Nature*, 155, 1945, p.431.
4. Anon. An Automatic Computing Engine for the National Physical Laboratory. *Nature*, 158, 1946, p.827.
5. Anon. The Automatic Computing Engine. Military College of Science, Shrivenham, 1947. ['This account is based on a series of informal talks given by Dr A M Turing and Mr Wilkinson of the Mathematics Division of the National Physical Laboratory.' There is a copy in the Woodger Papers, ref. 180, box M15; a note by Woodger in the same box quotes G C Tootill as saying that the author was Tommy Marshall.]
6. Anon. Calculating machines. *Nature*, 161, 1948, pp.712–713.
7. Anon. Automatic computing equipment at the N.P.L. *Engineering*, 171, 5 January 1951, pp.6–8; reprinted in a shortened version under the title 'Automatic computation at the National Physical Laboratory' in B V Bowden (ed.), *Faster than Thought*, Pitman, 1953, pp.135–139.
8. Anon. Keeping the computer flag flying. *Nature*, 234, 1971, pp.240–241.
9. K Baker. *The Turbulent Years: My Life in Politics*. Faber, 1993.
10. P Baran. On distributed communications networks. *IEEE Trans. on Communications Systems*, CS-12, 1, March 1964, pp.1–9.
11. K A Bartlett, R A Scantlebury and P T Wilkinson. A note on reliable full-duplex transmission over half-duplex links. *Comm. ACM*, 12(5), May 1969, pp.260–261.
12. C G Bell and A Newall. *Computer Structures: Readings and Examples*. McGraw-Hill, 1971.
13. F M Blake, D O Clayden, D W Davies, L J Page and J B Stringer. Some features of the ACE computer. *Data Processing & Automatic Computing Machines*, Proceedings of a Conference held at Weapons Research Establishment, Salisbury, South Australia, June 3rd–8th 1957, Australian Defence Scientific Service Dept. of Supply, Session II, pp.224–1 to 224–29.
14. V Bush. As we may think. *The Atlantic Monthly*, 176, 1945, pp.101–108.
15. M Campbell-Kelly. Programming the Pilot ACE: early programming activity at the National Physical Laboratory. *Annals of the History of Computing*, 3(2), April 1981, pp.133–162.
16. M Campbell-Kelly. The development of computer programming in Britain (1945 to 1955). *Annals of the History of Computing*, 4(2), April 1982, pp.121–139.
17. M Campbell-Kelly. Data communications at the National Physical Laboratory (1965–1975). *Annals of the History of Computing*, 9(3/4), 1988, pp.221–247; previously published as Research Report 82, Dept of Computer Science, Univ. of Warwick, August 1986. [The earlier version includes a fuller bibliography.]
18. B E Carpenter and R W Doran. The other Turing machine. *Computer Journal*, 20(3), 1977, pp.269–279.

19 B E Carpenter and R W Doran (eds). *A M Turing's ACE Report of 1946 and Other Papers.* MIT Press and Tomash Publishers, 1986.

20 CCITT. Recommendation X.25: interface between packet-mode data terminal equipment (DTE) and data circuit terminating equipment (DCE). First appeared in CCITT Orange Book, Vol. VIII, Fascicle VIII.2, CCITT, Geneva, 1977; there were subsequent enhancements.

21 D O Clayden, L J Page and C F Osborne. The magnetic storage drum on the ACE Pilot Model. *Proc. IEE,* 103, part B, supplement no. 3, 1956, pp.509–514.

22 B J Copeland and D Proudfoot. On Alan Turing's anticipation of connectionism. *Synthese,* 108, 1996, pp.361–377.

23 M G Cox and S Hammarling (eds). *Reliable Numerical Computation.* Oxford Scientific Publications, Clarendon Press, 1990.

24 P A Crisman (ed.). *The Compatible Time-sharing System: a Programmer's Guide.* Second edition, MIT Press, 1965.

25 M Croarken. *Early Scientific Computing in Britain.* Clarendon Press, 1990.

26 C G Darwin. Establishment of a mathematical department. NPL Executive Committee paper E.832. Undated; not later than October 1943.

27 C G Darwin (chairman). Report of interdepartmental technical committee on a proposed central mathematical station. Dated 3 April 1944; presented to DSIR Advisory Council 10 May 1944 (Public Record Office ref. DSIR 1/10); discussed by NPL Executive Committee as paper E.845 16 May 1944.

28 D W Davies. The organization of a Russian-English stem dictionary on magnetic tape. *Journal of Language and Speech,* 3(4), 1960, pp.193–222.

29 D W Davies. *Digital Techniques.* Blackie, 1963.

30 D W Davies. Proposal for the development of a national communication service for on-line data processing. 8 pp. typescript, dated 15 December 1965.

31 D W Davies. Proposal for a digital communication network. NPL, June 1966 [distributed widely but not formally published].

32 D W Davies, K A Bartlett, R A Scantlebury and P T Wilkinson. A digital communication network for computers giving rapid response at remote terminals. *Proc. ACM Symposium on Operating System Principles,* Gatlinburg, USA, 1967.

33 D W Davies and D L A Barber. *Communication Networks for Computers.* John Wiley and Sons, 1973. [Also translated into Russian, Hungarian, Polish and Romanian.]

34 D W Davies, D L A Barber, W L Price and C M Solomonides. *Computer Networks and their Protocols.* John Wiley and Sons, 1979. [Also translated into Russian, Hungarian, Romanian and Japanese.]

35 [D W Davies and W L Price]. A course on security in data communication, 21–22 May 1981. NPL, 1981.

36 D W Davies and W L Price. *Security for Computer Networks.* John Wiley and Sons, first edition 1984, second edition 1989. [Also translated into Japanese.]

37 G M Davis. An introduction to programme construction for the Pilot Model of the ACE. Report No. NJ3 y1, The English Electric Co Ltd, 15 October 1952.

38 W Diffie and M E Hellman. New directions in cryptography. *IEEE Trans. on Information Theory,* IT-22, 6, 1976, pp.644–654.

39 M Dowson, P T Wilkinson, B Collins, B McBride and R Milne. The Demos multiple processor. In: P A Samet (ed.), *EURO IFIP 79,* North-Holland, 1979, pp.679–684.

References and bibliography

40 DSIR. Advisory Council minutes. Public Record Office ref. DSIR 1/10.
41 C R Evans and E A Newman. Dreaming: an analogy with computers. *New Scientist*, 24(419), 26 November 1964, pp.577–579.
42 C R Evans and E A Newman. Human dream processes as analogous to computer program clearance. *Nature*, 206, p.534.
43 C R Evans and A D J Robertson (eds). *Brain Physiology and Psychology: Key Papers*. Butterworths, 1966.
44 C R Evans. The stuff of dreams. *New Scientist*, 34(545), 18 May 1967, pp.409–410.
45 C R Evans and A D J Robertson (eds). *Cybernetics: Key Papers*. Butterworths, 1968.
46 C R Evans and T B Mulholland (eds). *Attention in Neurophysiology: An International Conference*. Butterworths, London, 1969. [Proceedings of a conference held at NPL in October 1967.]
47 C R Evans. *Cults of Unreason*. Harrap, 1973.
48 [C R Evans (compiler).] *Pioneers of Computing*. Science Museum, London, undated. [A series of 20 audio cassette tapes of interviews with computer pioneers, recorded in the late 1970s.]
    Those interviewed were: D W Davies (tape no. 1), K Zuse (2), J P Eckert (3), J W Forrester (4), T Kilburn (5), J M M Pinkerton (6), F C Williams (7), J W Mauchly (8), A D Booth (9), J H Wilkinson (10), A W Burks (11), S M Ulam (12), H D Huskey (13), R J Slutz (14), M H A Newman (15), T H Flowers (16), A W M Coombs (17), C C Hurd (18), G M Hopper (19), and A Porter (20).
    [Interviews were also held with J V Atanasoff, G Brown, H H Goldstine, I J Good, H L Hazen, D Michie, H Ross, H Schreyer, H Simmons, G R Stibitz, M V Wilkes and M Woodger. Taped records of these 12 unpublished interviews are held by the Science Museum.]
49 C R Evans. *The Mighty Micro: the Impact of the Micro-chip Revolution*. Victor Gollancz, 1979; updated edition, Coronet Books, 1980.
50 C R Evans. *The Making of the Micro: a History of the Computer*. Gollancz, 1981.
51 E A Feigenbaum and J Feldman (eds). *Computers and Thought*. McGraw-Hill, 1963.
52 L Fox. Early numerical analysis in the United Kingdom. In: S G Nash (ed.), *A History of Scientific Computing*, Addison-Wesley, 1990, pp.280–300.
53 Lord Fulton [chairman of committee]. *The Civil Service*. Cmnd. 3638, HMSO, 1968.
54 P Gill and W Murray (eds). *Numerical Methods for Constrained Optimization*. Proceedings of a conference held at NPL, January 1974. Academic Press, 1974.
55 S Gill. Second progress report on the Automatic Computing Engine. Mathematics Division, NPL, DSIR, June 1949.
56 E T Goodwin. The uses of the ACE computor [sic]. *J. Roy. Aero. Soc.*, 59, 1955, pp.279–281.
57 E T Goodwin et al. Maths Division: 10th anniversary. *NPL News*, 64 [numbered in binary as 1000000], August 1955. [This issue includes several informal articles, mostly unsigned, giving personal reminiscences of the first ten years of Mathematics Division.]
58 E T Goodwin. Twenty-one today. *NPL News*, 192, April 1966, pp.4–5; reprinted in 'The National Physical Laboratory 1900–1970', NPL, 1970 [an anthology of NPL News articles produced for the 70th anniversary of the establishment of the Laboratory].

References and bibliography

59 A C D Haley. DEUCE: a high-speed general-purpose computer. *Proc. IEE*, 103, part B, supplement no. 2, 1956, pp.165–173.

60 Lord Halsbury. Ten years of computer development. *Computer Journal*, 1(4), 1959, pp.153–159.

61 A Harry. *Formal Methods Fact File: VDM and Z*. John Wiley and Sons, 1996.

62 D R Hartree. Differential analyser. *Permanent Records of Research and Development*, Monograph No. 17–502, Ministry of Supply, January 1949.

63 P L Hawkes, D W Davies and W L Price. *Integrated Circuit Cards, Tags and Tokens: New Technology and Applications*. BSP Professional Books, 1990.

64 J Hendry. *Innovating for Failure: Government Policy and the Early British Computer Industry*. MIT Press, 1989.

65 A L Hillman and D Schofield. EDIT—an interactive network service; design and implementation. *Software Practice and Experience*, 7, 1977, pp.595–611.

66 A Hodges. *Alan Turing: The Enigma*. Burnett Books Ltd and Hutchinson, 1983; reprinted Unwin 1985; reprinted with a new preface, Vintage, 1992.

67 [H D Huskey]. Untitled report to J R Womersley on the state of computer developments worldwide. Undated, but almost certainly written in March 1947. 11pp., typescript. In the Woodger Papers, ref. 180, folder M12, which also includes a note by Woodger giving evidence for the date. Reproduced in ref. 68 pp.356–359.

68 H D Huskey. From ACE to the G-15. *Annals of the History of Computing*, 6(4), October 1984, pp.350–371.

69 IEE. Convention on Digital-Computer Techniques. *Proc. IEE*, 103, Part B, Supplements 1–3, 1956. There are eight papers by members of NPL staff:

G G Alway. The use of the Pilot ACE for testing a new design of proton synchrotron, pp.12–15.

D W Davies. Sorting of data on an electronic computer, pp.87–93.

E A Newman and M A Wright. The use of a computer for payroll work, p.94.

E A Newman and M A Wright. An automatic floating-address machine, pp.134–137.

E L Albasiny. The solution of non-linear heat conduction problems on the Pilot ACE, pp.158–162.

E A Newman and D O Clayden. The ACE, p.279.

D W Davies. Introduction to session on 'computer input and output, including analogue-digital conversion', pp.425–426.

D O Clayden, L J Page and C F Osborne. The magnetic storage drum on the ACE Pilot Model, pp.509–514.

70 IEE/NPL. *Conference on Pattern Recognition*, held at NPL, 29–31 July 1968. Conference Publication No. 42, IEE, 1968.

71 IEE/NPL. *Man–Computer Interaction*. Proceedings of a conference held at NPL, 2–4 September 1970. Conference Publication No. 68, IEE, 1970.

72 IEEE. Open Systems Interconnection (OSI)—new international standards architecture and protocols for distributed information systems. *Proc. IEEE*, 71(12) [special issue on OSI], December 1983.

73 Institute of Physics. *Machine Perception of Patterns and Pictures*. Proceedings of a conference organised by the IoP in collaboration with NPL and the IEE, held at NPL, 12–14 April 1972. IoP Conference Series No. 13, 1972. There are five papers by members of NPL staff:

J R Ullmann. Correspondence in character recognition, pp.34–44.

A M Day, J R Parks and P J Pobgee. On-line written input to computers, pp.233–240.

E A Newman. The theoretical structure of pattern, pp.285–293.

D W Davies. Measurement of the topology of a picture from samples taken on a regular array, pp.303–310.

A J Szanser. Elastic matching in automatic pattern recognition, pp.328–333.

74 ISO. ISO 8731-2: Banking—approved algorithms for message authentication. Part 2: Message Authenticator Algorithm. ISO, 1987; revised edition 1992.

75 ISO. ISO 9126-1: Information technology—software product evaluation—quality characteristics and guidelines for their use. ISO, 1991.

76 ISO. ISO DIS 9241-11: Ergonomic requirements for office work with visual display terminals (VDTs). Part 11: Guidance on Usability. ISO, March 1995.

77 ISO/IEC. ISO/IEC 7498: Information technology—Open Systems Interconnection—Basic Reference Model. ISO/IEC, first edition 1984, second edition [with minor change to title] 1995.

78 ISO/IEC. ISO/IEC 9646: Information technology—Open Systems Interconnection—Conformance testing methodology and framework.
   Part 1: General concepts, 1994.
   Part 2: Abstract test suite specification, 1994.
   Part 3: The Tree and Tabular Combined Notation (TTCN), 1992; second edition in preparation.
   Part 4: Test realization, 1994.
   Part 5: Requirements on test laboratories and clients for the conformance assessment process, 1994.
   Part 6: Protocol profile test specification, 1994.
   Part 7: Implementation conformance statements, 1995.

79 ISO/IEC. ISO/IEC 10967-1: Information technology—language independent arithmetic—integer and floating point arithmetic. ISO, 1994.

80 ISO/IEC. Information technology—interpretation of accreditation requirements in ISO/IEC Guide 25—for information technology and telecommunications testing laboratories for software and protocol testing services. ISO/IEC TR 13233, 1995.

81 M A Jaswon and G T Symm. *Integral Equation Methods in Potential Theory and Elastostatics.* Academic Press, 1977, reprinted 1984. [Also translated into Japanese.]

82 Kate Jenkins, Karen Caines and A Jackson. Improving management in Government: the next steps. Report to the Prime Minister. Efficiency Unit, HMSO, 1988.

83 S Lavington. *Early British Computers.* Manchester University Press, 1980.

84 D T Lindsay and W L Price (eds). *Information Security: Creating Confidence in Information Processing.* Proc. IFIP TC-11 7th Int. Conf. on Information Security (IFIP/Sec'91), held in Brighton, May 1991, North-Holland, 1991.

85 R Malik. In the beginning—early days with ACE. *Data Systems,* March 1969, pp.56–59, 82.

86 D R Manning, B E Pay, R E Rengger and D Schofield. Research on automatic speech recognition at the National Physical Laboratory. NPL Report DITC 31/83, September 1983.

87 J McDaniel, A M Day, W L Price, A J M Szanser, S Whelan and D M Yates. Translation of Russian scientific texts into English by computer—a final report. NPL Report Auto 35, July 1967.

References and bibliography

88 A R Meetham. *Information Retrieval.* Aldus Books, 1969.
89 A R Meetham and R A Hudson (eds). *Encyclopaedia of Linguistics, Information and Control.* Pergamon Press, 1969.
90 N Metropolis, J Howlett and Gian-Carlo Rota (eds). *A History of Computing in the Twentieth Century.* Academic Press, 1980.
91 M Minsky and S A Papert. *Perceptrons: an Introduction to Computational Geometry.* MIT Press, 1969.
92 G Mounin. *La Machine à Traduire: Histoire des Problèmes Linguistiques.* Mouton, 1964.
93 W Murray (ed.). *Numerical Methods for Unconstrained Optimization.* Proceedings of a conference held at NPL, January 1971, Academic Press, 1972.
94 P Naur (ed.) et al. Revised report on the algorithmic language ALGOL 60. *Comm. ACM,* 6(1), January 1963, pp.1–17 and *Computer Journal,* 5, January 1963, pp.349–367 [original version in *Comm. ACM,* 3(5), May 1960, pp.299–314].
95 E A Newman. The Pilot Model of the A. C. E. *Manchester University Computer Inaugural Conference,* July 1951, pp.24–25.
96 E A Newman, D O Clayden and M A Wright. The mercury-delay-line storage system of the ACE Pilot Model electronic computer. *Proc. IEE* 100 part II, 76, August 1953, pp.445–452.
97 E A Newman and M A Wright. An automatic floating-address machine. *Proc. IEE* 103 Part B Supplement No. 1, 1956, pp.134–137.
98 NPL. National Physical Laboratory: Minutes of the Executive Committee. Annual volumes for the years 1899 to 1963 inclusive, unpublished.
99 NPL. National Physical Laboratory Annual Reports. There have been three series, plus one individual report for 1984.
  The first series starts from the foundation of the Laboratory in 1900; its later volumes are as follows:
    1940–45 (one volume, published in 1952)
    1946–67 (one volume per year)
    1968–69 (one volume)
  Extracts, without illustrations, were produced as Divisional Annual Report booklets.
  The computing-related publications in the second series are two triennial reports:
    Engineering Sciences Group Research 1971. Volume 1: Computer Science, Numerical Analysis and Computing [stated in preface to cover 1969–71 inclusive].
    Engineering Sciences Group Research 1972–4. Volume 1: Computer Science, Numerical Analysis and Computing.
    There are other volumes covering other aspects of the Laboratory's work.
  No NPL Annual Reports were produced for 1975–83 inclusive, but in 1984 there was a detailed report:
    National Physical Laboratory: a report on current work. NPL, 1984.
  Third series (less detailed):
    1984–89 (one volume per year).
    1990/91–1994/95 Annual Report and Accounts (one per financial year).
100 NPL. Automatic Computing Engine. Administration Division file AD 74/01, held in the Public Record Office, ref. DSIR 10/385.
101 NPL. ACE (Test Assembly). In NPL file CME 27/03, typescript, 15 pp. + 4 pp. blueprints; undated, c. 1948.
102 NPL. *NPL News.* Published monthly from May 1950 (no. 1) to June 1978 (no. 338) inclusive, then quarterly from Autumn 1978 (no. 339)

to Winter 1983 (no. 360), and irregularly thereafter. Note that the issues for October and November 1964, and the supplement to the November 1964 issue, were numbered incorrectly. From July 1978 the in-house role of *NPL News* was taken over by *NPL Bulletin*, ref. 121 below.

103 NPL (Mathematics Division). Proposals for full-scale A.C.E. In NPL file CME 27/03, typescript, 3pp., 10 August 1953.

104 NPL. *Automatic Digital Computation*. Proceedings of a symposium held at NPL on 25–28 March 1953. HMSO, 1954. There are nine papers by members of NPL staff:
    J H Wilkinson. The Pilot ACE, pp.5–14.
    G G Alway. Optimum coding, pp.65–69.
    D W Davies. Input and output, pp.102–116.
    D O Clayden. Echelon storage systems, pp.117–120.
    J H Wilkinson. Linear algebra on the Pilot ACE, pp.129–136.
    L Fox and H H Robertson. The numerical solution of ordinary differential equations, pp.137–147.
    E T Goodwin. Mathematical tables, pp.155–160.
    M A Wright. Mercury delay line storage, pp.195–199.
    E A Newman. Preventive or curative maintenance, pp.235–238.

105 NPL. *A Description of the Work of the National Physical Laboratory*. DSIR, 1955.

106 NPL. *Wage Accounting by Electronic Computer: Report No. 1 of the Interdepartmental Study Group on the Application of Computer Techniques to Clerical Work*. DSIR, HMSO, 1956.

107 NPL. *Modern Computing Methods*. Notes on Applied Science No. 16, HMSO, 1957; second edition completely revised 1961.

108 NPL. ACE News. Issue no. 1 (4 May 1959) to issue no. 18 (November 1963).

109 NPL. *Mechanisation of Thought Processes: Proceedings of a Symposium held at the National Physical Laboratory on 24th, 25th, 26th and 27th November 1958*. 2 vols, HMSO, 1959.

110 NPL. ACE Programming Manual. Mathematics Division, NPL, ref. Ma/48, 1 November 1959 with later additions [a ring binder].

111 NPL. *The New Autonomics Laboratory of the National Physical Laboratory*. NPL, Ministry of Technology, 1965 [a booklet prepared for the opening of Building 93 on 5 April 1965].

112 NPL. *1961 International Conference on Machine Translation of Languages and Applied Language Analysis: Proceedings of the Conference held at the National Physical Laboratory, Teddington, Middlesex, on 5th, 6th, 7th and 8th September* [1961]. 2 vols, HMSO, 1962.

113 NPL. *NPL Computing* [a newsletter about NPL's central computing services produced by CCU, later DNAC Computing Branch, later CSU; the first issue is dated 12 January 1968. Historical notes are included in issue 200 (27 September 1974) and in issue 500 (8 July 1992, pp.9–12)].

114 NPL. Open Day handouts for 1968, 1972, 1976, 1982, and 1987. Sets for 1976 and 1987 were produced in booklet form in the years of issue; the remainder survive as file copies only.

115 NPL. Division of Computer Science Progress Report July 1969–February 1971. NPL Report Com Sci 48, April 1971. [An earlier version of the text of the Division's contribution to the NPL report for 1969–71, see ref. 99].

116 NPL. Engineering Sciences Group Research 1971. Volume 1: *Computer Science, Numerical Analysis and Computing*. HMSO, 1972. [Covers 1969–71; see ref. 99 for related reports.]

References and bibliography

117 NPL. Division of Computer Science Progress Report 1972–73. NPL Report COM 74, April 1974. [An earlier version of the text of the Division's contribution to the NPL report for 1972–74, see ref. 99.]

118 NPL. Engineering Sciences Group Research 1972–4. Volume 1: *Computer Science, Numerical Analysis and Computing.* HMSO, 1975. [See ref. 99 for related reports.]

119 NPL. NPL Computing Divisions 1976 [a bound collection of handouts at an Open Day].

120 NPL. Computing and Numerical Analysis at the National Physical Laboratory, June 1977.

121 NPL. *NPL Bulletin.* Published monthly from July 1978 (no. 1) to March 1992 (no. 165) inclusive and fortnightly thereafter; see also *NPL News* ref. 102 above.

122 NPL. National Physical Laboratory Executive Agency 1990: Policy and Resources Framework. NPL, 1990.

123 B E Pay and C R Evans. An approach to the automatic recognition of speech. *International Journal of Man-Machine Studies*, 14, 1981, pp.13–27.

124 W L Price. Palantype transcription by computer—a final report. NPL Report Com Sci 45, February 1971.

125 W L Price. Data network simulation: experiments at the National Physical Laboratory 1968–76. *Computer Networks*, 1(4), May 1977, pp.199–210; reprinted in W W Chu (ed.), *Advances in Computer Communications and Networking*, Artech House, 1979, pp.291–308.

126 E Pyatt. *The National Physical Laboratory: a History.* Adam Hilger Ltd, 1983; reprinted Mauve Publications Ltd, Teddington, 1993; title on spine of reprinted edition is 'History of the National Physical Laboratory'.

127 B Randell. On Alan Turing and the origins of digital computers. In: B Meltzer and D Michie (eds), *Machine Intelligence 7,* Edinburgh University Press, 1972, pp.3–20.

128 D Rayner (ed.). Interpretation of accreditation requirements for IT test laboratories for software and communications testing services. NAMAS document NIS 35, November 1990.

129 R L Rivest, A Shamir and L Adleman. A method of obtaining digital signatures and public-key cryptosystems. *Comm. ACM*, 21(2), 1978, pp.120–126.

130 M G Robinson and D M Yates. The Scrapbook information system. *The Information Scientist*, December 1973, pp.135–143.

131 Lord Rothschild. The organisation and management of government R. & D. *A Framework for Government Research and Development*, Cmnd. 4814, HMSO, 1971.

132 R A Scantlebury and P T Wilkinson. The National Physical Laboratory Data Communication Network. NPL Report Com 85, December 1976.

133 Julia M Schofield. *Microcomputer-based Aids for the Disabled.* In series: British Computer Society monographs in informatics, P A Samet (ed.), Heyden & Son Ltd on behalf of the British Computer Society, 1981.

134 N Stern. The BINAC: a case study in the history of technology. *Annals of the History of Computing*, 1(1), July 1979, pp.9–20.

135 H A Thomas. A plan for the design, development and production of the 'ACE'. Radio Division, NPL, 12 April 1947 (typescript, 10 pp.). [There is a copy in the Public Record Office, ref. DSIR 10/385, and another in the Woodger Papers, ref. 180, folder M12.]

136 Sir Burke Trend [chairman]. [Report of the] *Committee of Enquiry into the Organisation of Civil Science.* Cmnd. 2171, HMSO, October 1963.

137 A M Turing. On computable numbers, with an application to the Entscheidungsproblem. *Proc. London Mathematical Society,* series 2, 42, 1937, pp.230–265, with a correction note in vol. 43, 1937, p.544–546. Both the original paper and the correction are reprinted in R Goodman (ed.), *Annual Review in Automatic Programming,* 1, Pergamon, 1960, pp.230–267.

138 A M Turing. Proposals for development in the Mathematics Division of an Automatic Computing Engine (ACE). Report to the NPL Executive Committee E.882, presented 19 March 1946. Reprinted twice, first under the title 'A M Turing's original proposal for the development of an electronic computer. Reprinted with a foreword by D W Davies' as NPL Report Com Sci 57, April 1972; and secondly in Carpenter and Doran (1986) ref. 19 above, pp.20–105.

139 A M Turing. Lecture to the London Mathematical Society on 20 February 1947. In Carpenter and Doran (1986) ref. 19 above, pp.106–124.

140 A M Turing. Intelligent machinery. 1948. [22 pp., typescript, submitted to NPL as a report on period of sabbatical leave at Cambridge.] Reprinted in Evans and Robertson (1968), ref. 45 above, pp.27–52, and in B Meltzer and D Michie (eds), *Machine Intelligence 5,* Edinburgh University Press, 1969, pp.3–23. [There is a significant error in the second reprint, p.6: the date 8 August 1947, referring to a working machine in Manchester, reads 8/7/48 in the original].

141 A M Turing. Rounding-off errors in matrix processes. *Quart. J. of Mechanics and Applied Mathematics,* 1, 1948, pp.287–308.

142 A M Turing. Computing machinery and intelligence. *Mind,* 59, 1950, pp.433–460. Reprints include: Feigenbaum and Feldman (1963), ref. 51 above, pp.11–35; Evans and Robertson (1966), ref. 43 above, pp.213–240; and D R Hofstadter and D C Dennett, *The Mind's I,* Basic Books and Harvester, 1981, pp.53–67.

143 A M Turing. The chemical basis of morphogenesis. *Phil. Trans. Roy. Soc. Lond. Series B,* 237, 1952, pp.37–72.

144 A M Turing. *Collected Works.*
   Vol. 1. Mechanical intelligence. D C Ince (ed.), Elsevier, 1992.
   Vol. 2. Pure mathematics. J L Britton (ed.), Elsevier, 1992.
   Vol. 3. Morphogenesis. P T Saunders (ed.), Elsevier, 1992.
   Vol. 4. Mathematical logic. R O Gandy and C E M Yates (eds) (in preparation).

145 Sara Turing. *Alan M Turing.* W Heffer & Sons Ltd, 1959.

146 J R Ullmann. *Pattern Recognition Techniques.* Butterworths, 1973.

147 A M Uttley. A visit to the United States and Canada in 1959. NPL, DSIR, August 1959.

148 A M Uttley. *Information Transmission in the Nervous System.* Academic Press, 1979.

149 P K T Vaswani and J B Cameron. The National Physical Laboratory experiments in statistical word associations and their use in document indexing and retrieval. NPL Report Com Sci 42, April 1970.

150 J von Neumann. First draft of a report on the EDVAC. Moore School of Electrical Engineering, University of Pennsylvania, 30 June 1945. Reprinted in B Randell (ed.), *The Origins of Digital Computers,* third edition, Springer-Verlag, 1982, pp.383–392.

151 D A Watt, W Findaly and B A Wichmann. *Ada: Language and Methodology.* Prentice-Hall, 1987.

152 WELAC/ECITC. Interpretation of accreditation requirements in ISO/IEC Guide 25 and EN 45001: guidance for information technology and telecommunications testing laboratories for software

and communications testing services. European Laboratory Accreditation Publication ELA-G5, WELAC/ECITC, October 1993.
153 B A Wichmann. *ALGOL 60 Compilation and Assessment.* Academic Press, 1973.
154 B A Wichmann and Z J Ciechanowicz (eds). *Pascal Compiler Validation.* John Wiley & Sons, 1983.
155 B A Wichmann (ed.). *Software in Safety-related Systems.* John Wiley & Sons, 1992.
156 J H Wilkinson. The automatic computing engine at the National Physical Laboratory. In: D R Hartree et al., A discussion on computing machines, *Proc. Roy. Soc. Lond. Series A,* 195, 1948, pp.285–286.
157 J H Wilkinson. Progress report on the Automatic Computing Engine. NPL Report ref. MA/17/1024, April 1948.
158 J H Wilkinson. Coding on automatic digital computing machines. *Report of a Conference on High Speed Automatic Calculating-machines, University Mathematical Laboratory, Cambridge, 22–25 June 1949.* Issued by the Laboratory with the co-operation of the Ministry of Supply, January 1950, pp.28–35.
159 J H Wilkinson. Report on the pilot model of the Automatic Computing Engine. Part II: The logical design of the pilot model. Mathematics Division and Electronics Section, NPL, September 1951.
160 J H Wilkinson. Programming and coding for the pilot model of the ACE. NPL Report Maths 22, 1951; there is a 3 pp. appendix dated 1 March 1954. [There are copies of both these scarce documents in the Woodger Papers, ref. 180 below, folder N30.]
161 J H Wilkinson. The Pilot ACE. In: *Automatic Digital Computation.* Proceedings of a symposium held at NPL, 25–28 March 1953, HMSO, 1954, pp.5–14. Reprinted in C G Bell and A Newall, *Computer Structures: Readings and Examples,* McGraw-Hill, 1971, pp.193–199.
162 J H Wilkinson. Electronic computing machines and their uses. *J. of Scientific Instruments,* 32, November 1955, pp.409–415.
163 J H Wilkinson. An assessment of the system of optimum coding used on the pilot Automatic Computing Engine at the National Physical Laboratory. *Phil. Trans. Roy. Soc. Lond. Series A,* 248, 1956, pp.253–281.
164 J H Wilkinson. British progress in digital computer design. *Automation Progress,* January 1957, pp.5–9, 36.
165 J H Wilkinson and D W Davies. The Automatic Computing Engine at the National Physical Laboratory. *Nature,* 183, 1959, pp.22–23.
166 J H Wilkinson. *Rounding Errors in Algebraic Processes. Notes on Applied Science No. 32,* HMSO, 1963.
167 J H Wilkinson. *The Algebraic Eigenvalue Problem.* Oxford University Press, 1965.
168 J H Wilkinson. Some comments from a numerical analyst. *JACM,* 18(2), April 1971, pp.137–147.
169 J H Wilkinson and C Reinsch (eds). *Handbook for Automatic Computation. Volume 2: Linear Algebra.* Springer-Verlag, 1971.
170 J H Wilkinson. The Pilot ACE at the National Physical Laboratory. *The Radio and Electronic Engineer,* 45(7), July 1975, pp.336–340.
171 J H Wilkinson. Turing's work at the National Physical Laboratory and the construction of Pilot ACE, DEUCE and ACE. In: N Metropolis, J Howlett and Gian-Carlo Rota (eds), *A History of Computing in the Twentieth Century,* Academic Press, 1980, pp.101–114 [a modified version of ref. 170 above].
172 M R Williams. *A History of Computing Technology.* Prentice-Hall, 1985.

References and bibliography

173 J R Womersley. Proposed Mathematics Division. Presentation to the NPL Executive Committee 19 December 1944, reported in the minutes of the meeting.

174 J R Womersley. 'ACE' machine project. Memorandum to the NPL Executive Committee E.881, dated 13 February 1946, presented 19 March.

175 [J R Womersley.] ACE project—origin and early history. Typescript, 1p., dated 26 November 1946, Public Record Office ref. DSIR 10/385.

176 M Woodger. Automatic Computing Engine of the National Physical Laboratory. *Nature,* 167, 1951, p.270.

177 M Woodger. A comparison of one and three address codes. *Manchester University Computer Inaugural Conference,* July 1951, pp.19–23.

178 M Woodger. The history and present use of digital computers at the National Physical Laboratory. *Process Control and Automation,* November 1958, pp.438–443. Reprinted in Carpenter and Doran (1986) ref. 19 above, pp.125–140.

179 M Woodger. In the beginning . . . *Computer Weekly,* 17 April 1969, pp.8–9.

180 M Woodger (collector and part author). The Woodger Papers. Held in the Science Museum Library, South Kensington, ref. ARCH: NPL. This is a world-class collection of original documents relating particularly to the early history of computing at NPL (1945–60) and to the development of programming languages, notably Algol. The following items are particularly important:
   ACE miscellaneous, 1946–49, folder M11
   History, primary documents, 1945–78, folder M15
   ACE development, 1946–54, folder N30
   Algol, folders in L series

181 D M Yates and W Russell. On-line data retrieval for a local police intelligence unit. *Police Research Bulletin,* 16, October 1970, pp.4–12.

182 D M Yates. NPL's role in computing standards work. *Language Implementation Validation: Proceedings of a Two-day Workshop held at NCC, Manchester, 12–13 September 1979,* NCC, 1980, pp.173–176.

183 D M Yates. Flights of fancy by proxy. *New Scientist,* 95(1324), 23 September 1982, pp.840–842. Reprinted in *Science Digest,* 91(5), May 1983, pp.30–34, and elsewhere.

Index

Abies Informatics, 179
Accreditation of IT test laboratories, 252
ACE, early plans for, 19–31, 285
    full-scale, 41, 57, 63, 66–72, 84, 90, 94–103, 107–115
    Pilot, 28, 30, 31–46, 49, 50, 52, 66, 113, 114, 123, 285
ACTP, 62, 63, 66, 104, 117, 120, 125, 189, 199, 292, 293, 296, 303, 304, 317
Ada, 217, 219, 222–224, 232, 268–271, 281, 309, 313, 316
Adaptive control, 57, 58, 72–80, 89, 117, 300, 316
Adaptive interfaces, 276
Admiralty, 12, 18, 50, 291, 299, 300, 304, 310
Admiralty Computing Service, 12, 13, 18, 298, 299, 304
Advanced Computer Techniques Project, *see* ACTP
Advanced Token Technology Club, 255
AERE Harwell, 141, 206
After-images, 86–88
Agency status, 247–249
Albasiny, E L (Ernie), 8, 112, 124, 184, 199, 234, 243, 248, 289
Aldous, Brian E, 60, 135
Algol, 70, 111, 113, 114, 118, 124, 186–197, 224, 244, 313, 316, 334
Algorithms for metrology, 228, 230, 261
Allam, Derek S, 60, 107
Alway, Gerald G, 28, 30, 66, 124, 125, 289
Andrew, Dr A M, 73, 92
Anthony, Gerald T, 231
Anthony, Dr Helen M, 229
Applied Physics Division, 63, 172, 291, 303, 307
Architects, 119, 182
Arithmetic, computer standards in, 268
ARPANET, 130, 139
Ashford, Simon J, 253
ATTC, 255
Aughtie, Dr F, 27, 30
Austin, S M (Steve), 268, 271, 277
Autocorrelation, 81
Automatic inspection, 170, 240, 290, 305
Autonomics Division, 9, 58, 61, 117

Babbage Building (hut), 48, 49, 59, 126
    see also Charles Babbage Building
Babel, 125, 187, 192–195, 308
Baker, Derek S, 60, 71, 102, 150, 152
Baker, Kenneth, MP, 201

Ballard, J G, 297
Bangham, Michael J, 236, 278
Banks, 81, 211, 214
Barber, Derek L A, 10, 52, 60, 74–77, 118, 128, 135, 139–144, 203, 248, 290
Barker, Robin M, 10, 253
Bartlett, Keith A, 10, 60, 71, 128, 132, 135, 140, 145, 146, 203–204, 209, 290
BBC Microcomputer, 157, 201, 235, 236, 242, 243, 286
Bell, Dr Donald A, 10, 134, 166, 171, 196, 201, 286, 290
Benchmarks, 195, 274
Bendix G-15, 40–43, 300
Bevan, Michael J, 10, 157
Bevan, Dr Nigel W S, 10, 179, 232, 236, 278, 280, 291
Biology, 58, 85, 117, 118, 311
Bird, N F (Dickie), 10, 189, 244, 282, 291
Blake, Dennis V, 52, 63, 64, 76, 189, 245, 291
Blake, Frank M, 10, 52, 60, 66, 68, 72, 119, 124, 126, 199, 243, 292
Blaney, Dr T G (Tom), 247–249, 292
Bletchley Park, 16, 17, 19, 120, 310
Blumlein, H D, 26, 293, 303
Bombas and bombes, 16
Bowden, Rosemary G, 277, 278
Braille, 84
Breathing, 89
Brick, Joyce, 115, 244
Briggs, Paul A N, 60, 78
British Standard Interface, 76, 128, 132, 134, 168, 173, 189, 290, 291
British Steel Corporation, 118
Brocklehurst, E R (Ed), 186, 238, 240, 274, 292
Brown, Alan F, 27, 39, 60
Bunce, W D (Bill), 10
Burns, Prof. B de L, 60, 90
Burton, Alan J, 185
Bushy House, 9, 37, 49, 126, 223
Byrne, B J (Tim), 39, 60

Cameron, John B, 102
Campbell-Kelly, Dr Martin, 10, 33, 45
Carter, Peter E, 60, 71, 135, 140, 164, 234
Cashin, Dr Peter M, 158
CCSC, 255, 259
CCU, 9, 125, 183, 187, 194, 242
CEDAR, 182
Central Computer Unit, 9, 125, 183, 187, 194, 242

341

Index

Central file store, 134, 135, 191, 196, 245, 281
CFM, 135, 188
Chambers, Trevor H E, 274
Charles Babbage Building (B.93), 59, 117, 126, 187, 243
Chebyshev polynomials, 108–110, 293
CHIT, 166, 167
Chorley, Bernard J, 10, 170, 171, 212, 218, 226, 255, 293
Ciechanowicz, Dr Z J (Chez), 212, 220
CISE, 9, 250
Clapham, Dr Peter B, 10, 230
Clayden, David O, 10, 26, 31, 32, 52, 60, 67, 72, 81, 83, 126, 128, 214, 293
Clayden, Ronald T, 35, 43
Clenshaw, Charles W, 108–110, 186, 293
Clerical mechanisation, 54, 57, 301, 303, 317
Clothesline store, 193
Clowes, Dr M B (Max), 81, 83, 87, 294
CME Division, 8, 9, 52, 55, 57, 63
CMOT, 126, 250
Colebrook, F Morley, 27, 30, 36, 52, 67, 294, 296
Coloured Book protocols, 204
Commercial Computer Security Centre, 255, 259
Computable numbers, 15
   paper on, by Turing, 15, 17, 18, 20, 310, 337
Computer Analysts and Programmers Ltd (CAP), 134, 135
Computer Field Maintenance Ltd, 135, 188
Computer Science, Division of, 9, 117, 124, 199
Computer Users' Panel, 188, 301
Computers:
   ACE, 41, 57, 63, 66–72, 84, 90, 94–103, 107–115
   BBC Micro, 157, 201, 235, 236, 242, 243, 286
   Bendix G-15, 40–43, 300
   BINAC, 35
   DDP 516, 132, 166, 171, 196
   DEC VAX, 114, 281, 282
   DEUCE, 9, 38, 39, 41, 44–46, 50, 52, 54, 63, 80, 107, 112–115
   EDSAC, 35, 120, 299
   EDVAC, 14, 18, 19, 23
   Elliott 4120, 66, 125
   EMI Electronic Business Machine, 41, 43
   Hermes, 75, 76, 89, 115
   ICL 1900, 149
   ICL 2900, 114, 243, 281
   KDF9, 66, 72, 76, 102, 112–115, 133, 136, 147, 162, 163, 186–192, 243, 244
   Manchester Prototype Mark I, 35
   Modular One, 133, 153, 156
   MOSAIC, 26, 40, 41
   Packard-Bell PB 250, 40, 41, 43
   Paris Model, 38, 40, 41
   PDP-11, 189, 191
   PDP-8, 173, 187
   Pilot ACE, 28, 30, 31–46, 49, 50, 52, 66, 113, 114, 123, 285
   SEAC, 35, 43
   Whirlwind, 36
Computers, Systems and Electronics Requirements Board, 121, 184, 202, 292
Computing services, 8, 9
   in 1945–56, 37, 45, 50
   in 1957–66, 113–115
   in 1966–78, 183, 187–197
   in 1978–87, 242–246
   in 1987–95, 281–283
Computing Services Unit, 9, 199, 243, 250, 281
Computing, Software and Communications Committee, 202
Computing Technology Unit, 9, 124, 199, 210
Conclave, 157
Conditional probability, 73, 78, 91, 92
Conferences:
   on Attention in Neurophysiology (1967), 118, 331
   on Automatic Digital Computation (1953), 50, 335
   on Machine Perception of Patterns and Pictures (1972), 118, 332
   on Machine Translation (1961), 60, 95, 335
   on Man–Computer Interaction (1970), 118, 176, 332
   on Mechanisation of Thought Processes (1958), 58, 94, 335
   on Pascal Compiler Validation (1982), 220
   on Pattern Recognition (1968), 118, 332
   on Reliable Numerical Computation (1987), 260, 295, 314
Conformance testing, 209, 251–253, 256–259, 285, 306
   see also Pascal compiler validation, Protocol implementation assessment
Control Mechanisms and Electronics Division, 8, 9, 52, 55, 57, 63
Cooper, Dr John R A, 10, 112, 186, 243, 244, 281, 294
Corby, Carol A, 102, 135
Corporation for Open Systems (COS), 250
COST, 141
Cowin, Godfrey W, 138, 206, 209, 253
Cox, Prof. Maurice G, 10, 186, 228–230, 260, 262, 295
Croarken, Dr Mary, 10, 14
Cromer House, 9, 18, 49, 126
Cryotrons, 58, 62, 66, 103–107
CSERB, 121, 184, 202, 292
CSU, 9, 199, 243, 250, 281

CTU, 9, 124, 199, 210
CUP, 188, 301
Curtis, A R (Joe), 108
Curtis, Betty, 38, 189, 244, 295
Cyclades network, 143
Cyclops 1, 82
Cyclops 2, 83, 165
Cyclops 3, 165, 166

DAP, 244, 273, 281
DART, 188
Darwin, Sir Charles, 13, 24, 28, 295, 315
DASL, 231
Data Approximation Subroutine Library, 231
Data communications, 77, 117, 126–147
Data Communications Protocols Unit, 203–204
Data handling, 52, 75–77, 79, 290, 310, 316
Data Handling Panel, 188
Data security, 120, 199, 202, 210–216, 219, 254–260
Datapad, 168, 169
Davies, Alan T, 60, 135, 159
Davies, Donald W, 10, 16, 28, 30, 36, 42, 52, 58, 60–63, 67, 72, 81, 94, 103, 117, 118, 120, 123, 124, 127–132, 136, 139, 141, 142, 148, 175, 199, 202, 210, 212, 223, 248, 285, 296, 331
Davis, C H (Bob), 60, 72, 83
Davis, George M, 35, 40, 45
Dawes, N W (Nick), 140, 192
Day, A M (Tony), 60, 95, 164, 234
DCPU, 203–204
Dean, Dr Paul, 112, 183, 297
Delay line store, mercury,
  in Turing era, 20, 23, 27
  on ACE, 67–71
  on DEUCE, 44
  on MOSAIC, 41
  on Pilot ACE, 31–35, 37, 39
DEMOCRAT, 66, 289
Demos, 216–218, 274
Dennis, Dr Keith, 10, 186
DEUCE, 9, 38, 39, 41, 44–46, 50, 52, 54, 63, 80, 107, 112–115
Dewis, Dr Ian G, 140
DHP, 188
Dickerson, Joyce, later Mrs Brick, 45, 114, 115
Differential analyser, 14, 18, 46, 47–49, 51, 107, 302, 315
Digital signatures, 211, 255
DISGOL, 181
DISPAC, 181
Distillation column, 73–77, 79
Distributed array processor, 244, 273, 281
DITC, 9, 202, 250

DNAC, 9, 183, 199
DNACS, 9, 124, 199
DNAM, 9, 183
Dowson, Mark, 157, 158, 216
Dreams, 87, 297
Drum, on ACE, 68–70, 72, 95
  on Bendix G-15, 43
  on DEUCE, 45
  on EMI Electronic Business Machine, 44
  on Pilot ACE, 31, 32, 38, 52
DSIR, 11, 61
Duncan, Fraser G, 124, 125
Dutch students, 119
Dymott, E R (Eddie), 60, 78, 152

EARB, 202
Eason, D C (Dave), 158, 206
Edit, 190–192, 216, 244, 245, 281, 307
EDSAC, 35, 120, 299
Edutext, 232, 235–236
EDVAC, 14, 18, 19, 23
Edwards, Gwen, later Mrs Peters, 45, 185
EIN, 118, 128, 139, 141–144, 157, 159, 290, 307
Eldon, 187–191
Electronic mail, 154, 156, 158, 191, 244, 281, 282
Electronic paper, 237–239, 292
Electronic simulator, 51, 53, 291
Electronics and Avionics Requirements Board, 202
Electronics Section, 9, 27, 52, 52, 67
Elliott 4120, 66, 125
Elliott, J Rosemary, later Mrs Lewis, 60, 83
Ellis, K, 84
English Electric Co Ltd, 35, 38, 40, 41, 43, 44, 45, 52, 319
ENIAC, 14, 17, 24, 300
Enigma, 16, 17, 120
EPSS, 131, 140–143, 290
Ermintrude, 172
European Informatics Network, 118, 128, 139, 141–144, 157, 159, 290, 307
Evans, Dr C R (Chris), 60, 85–87, 174–181, 232, 297
Experimental Packet Switched Service, 131, 140–143, 290

Fact retrieval, 147
Ferriss, D H (Dave), 230
Fieller, E C, 28, 49, 298
Fincham, Dr W F (Bill), 60, 89
Floor tiles, 10, 59
Flowers, T H, 26, 42, 120, 331
Fog index, 193
Forbes, Alistair B, 231, 261, 264

343

Index

Formal methods, 249, 252, 256, 271
Fortran, 111, 187–192, 231, 244, 269, 281
Fox, Dr Leslie, 12, 18, 67, 110, 298
Fulton report, 120, 331

General Research Surcharge, 241, 242, 264
Gill, Michael H, 253
Gill, Dr Philip E, 186
Gill, Prof. Stanley, 28, 39, 130, 299
GIPSY, 181
Gleed, W L (Bill), 39, 60, 68, 72, 107, 299
Godfrey, K R, 78
Good, Dr I J, 120, 331
Goodwin, Dr E T (Charles), 12, 18, 46, 49, 67, 107, 110, 183, 184, 199, 299
Goodwin, Jackie, 10
Graph theory, 101
Graphics software, 181, 189, 244

Hall, Clive, 10, 190, 244, 282
Hambly, S E (Steve), 158, 206
Hammond, P H (Percy), 10, 57, 60, 73, 74, 77, 118, 300
Harry, Andrew, 256
Hartree, Prof. D R, 7, 13, 24, 42, 48, 50, 295, 302, 315
Harvard University, 58, 94, 95, 161
Harwell, 141, 206
Hathway, V (Vince), 140, 153, 158, 206, 209
Hawtree, Valerie, later Mrs Block, 60, 102
Hayes, J G (Geoff), 12, 46, 112, 186, 300
Healey, Roger, 136
Heap, Dr Brian R, 189
Hermes, 75, 76, 89, 115
Hill, Dr J S, 60, 107
Hillman, A L (Tony), 187, 189, 192, 244, 282
Hodges, Dr Andrew, 10, 17, 20, 27, 120, 311
Hodson, Susan M, 10, 108, 186, 267
Home Office, 148, 152
Howlett, Julia M, later Dr Julia Schofield, 234
Hsu Kung-Shih, 102
Human–computer interaction, 232–239, 275–280, 291; *see also* Man–machine interaction
Huskey, Prof. Harry D, 24, 28, 42, 43, 300, 331
Hypertext, 155, 158, 191, 235, 285

ICL 1900, 149
ICL 2900, 114, 243, 281
Information retrieval, 58, 69, 100–103, 117, 302, 312
Information systems, 117, 147–160, 301, 317
Information Systems Engineering,
  branch of CMOT, 250, 306
  Centre for, 8, 9, 250

Information Technology and Computing, Division of, 9, 202, 250
Information Technology Support Unit, 9, 250, 281
Information utilities, 147
Inorganic Materials Unit, 106
Inter-Bank Research Organisation, 167, 170
Internet, 126, 130, 148, 208, 253, 281, 283, 285

Jenkinson, Celia, 60, 99
  and see Searle, Mrs Celia
Johnson, Shirley, 244, 283

KDF9, 66, 72, 76, 102, 112–115, 133, 136, 147, 162, 163, 186–192, 243, 244
KDF9 Weekly, 115, 188
Kenward, Paul D, 238, 240, 268
Kiff, Martin G, 282, 283

Lampard, Richard, 255
Larcombe, Sylvia, 60, 152
Laws, John, 135, 144
Leitch, Iain A M, 135
Levels of language, 176, 182, 236, 316
Linear algebra, 184, 185, 228, 295, 298, 314
Linear algebra subroutine library, 232
Linear array processor, 239
Lockett, Dr F John, 185
Logica Ltd, 137, 142, 290, 307
Long, Enid M R, 229
Longden, Maureen, later Mrs Vaswani, 60, 65, 66, 106, 107
LOTOS, 252, 257
Lovelace, Lady Ada, 223

Machine translation, 58, 60, 69, 93–100, 117, 148, 161, 296, 301, 306, 309, 317
Macleod, Miles, 278
Magnetic ink characters, 81
MALTA, 232, 234
Man–machine interaction, 117, 119, 125, 175–183, 297, 312
  see also Human–computer interaction
Manning, D Roger, 60, 83, 175, 241, 256
Mansfield, Dr A J (Tony), 10, 236, 264, 268, 274
Marks, Adrian J, 10, 248–250, 301
Martin, Dr David W, 110, 112, 184, 186, 188, 228, 301
Mathematical software, 184–187, 227–232, 260–267
Mathematics Division, 9, 11–51, 58, 71, 107–115, 126, 183, 199, 227
MAVIS, 232–234, 297
McDaniel, John, 60, 95, 148, 301
McKie, Adrian A, 206

Medical history taking, 177–181, 232, 235, 297
Medical Research Council, 89, 119, 315
Meetham, Dr A Roger, 60, 100, 118, 223, 302
Michel, J G L (Jack), 8, 10, 12, 18, 49, 110, 112, 184, 189, 302
MICKIE, 179–181, 232, 235, 297
Microtext, 232, 235–236, 291
Milepost Business Systems, 157
Miller, G F (Geoff), 108, 110, 185, 303
Ministry of Supply, 12, 18, 25, 41, 46, 48
Ministry of Technology, 60, 117, 123
Modern Computing Methods, 110, 293, 299, 301, 335
Modular One, 133, 153, 156
MOSAIC, 26, 40, 41
MTDATA, 267
Multimedia, 275
Multiprocessors, 216–218, 312, 315
Murray, Dianne M, 236, 276, 278
Murray, Dr Walter, 186
MUSiC, 278, 291

NAG, 186, 190, 227, 232, 244, 269, 281, 301, 314
NAMAS, 252
National Computing Centre, 187, 205, 250
National Measurement Accreditation Service, 252
National Physical Laboratory, foundation of, 11
National Research Development Corporation, 167, 170, 317
Nautical Almanac Office, 12, 14, 299, 304
Neale, Peter T, 218, 241, 256
Network, NPL, 131–136, 188, 245, 282
Network interconnection, 139
Network job control, 147
Neural networks, 29, 90–93, 260, 263–265
Neurophysiology, 90, 118
Newman, Andrew M R, 157, 158
Newman, E A (Ted), 26, 31, 36, 52, 54, 55, 60, 63–66, 67, 83, 87, 118, 172, 175, 178, 248, 303
Next Steps, 247
North, N D (Nick), 268
Northampton Polytechnic, 52
NOSL, 187, 231
Nott, Clifford W, 70, 189, 244
Noughts and crosses machine, 296
NPL Algorithms Library, 186, 231, 244, 245
NPL Annual Reports, 9, 123, 334
NPL Bulletin, 336
NPL Computing, 115, 188, 245, 246, 282, 335
NPL Management Ltd, 10, 249
NPL News, 9, 334
NPL Standard Interface, 76, 80, 102, 115, 128, 161, 291

Numerical Algorithms Group, 186, 190, 227, 232, 244, 269, 281, 301, 314
Numerical Analysis and Computer Science, Division of, 9, 124, 199
Numerical Analysis and Computing, Division of, 9, 183, 199
Numerical and Applied Mathematics, Division of, 9, 183
Numerical Optimization Software Library, 187, 231
Nye, P W (Pat), 60, 84

Olding, S E (Sue), later Mrs Chorley, 158, 170, 171
Olver, Dr Frank W J, 12, 18, 110, 304
O'Neill, Guy, 221, 268
Open Days, 60, 119, 200, 201
Open Systems Interconnection, 203–209, 250–254, 306
Optimisation, 184, 186, 228, 267
Optophone, 84
Osborn, J S (Joe), 39, 60, 107
Osborne, C F (Fred), 32, 39, 57, 60, 72, 304
Osborne, Mrs R S (Sue), 10
OSI, 203–209, 250–254, 306

Packet-switching, 128–131
  in NPL network, 131–136
  in network simulation, 136–139
  in interconnected networks, 139–144
Page, L J (Lew), 39, 52, 60, 62, 68, 72, 106, 107, 126, 304
Pages, 190, 191, 244, 281
Palantype, 117, 160–165, 306, 309
Palgol, 191
Papert, Dr Seymour A, 85, 92, 100, 264, 305
Parallel processing, 273–275, 292
Paris Model, 38, 40, 41
Parkin, Graeme I, 10, 212, 221, 226, 268, 272
Parks, Dr John R, 10, 52, 58, 81–83, 166, 167, 170–172, 305
Pascal, 217, 219–223, 244, 269, 281, 313, 315
  compiler validation, 219–221, 271
  program validation, 221
Patents, 319–322
Pattern perception, 85, 118
Pattern recognition, 58, 80–85, 117, 125, 165–175, 196
Pavel, John R, 206
Pay, Brian E, 60, 173–175, 236, 306
PCs, 244, 282
Peekaboo system, 100
PEPS, 274
Peters, Gwen, 115
Photographic Section NPL, 10, 326

Index

Picken, Susan M, 108
  and see Hodson, Mrs Susan M
Pilot ACE, 28, 30, 31–46, 49, 50, 52, 66, 113, 114, 123, 285
Pink, L A (Les), 60, 71, 128, 135, 140, 245, 283
PL-516, 134, 166, 194, 196, 290, 313
Plumb, G O (Gerry), 60, 75, 166, 179
Plummer, Dr A Piers, 239
Pobgee, Peter J, 60, 72, 83, 168, 170, 179, 238, 240, 274
Police, 148–152
POST, 114
Priban, Dr Ian P, 60, 89
Price, Margaret, 115
Price, Dr Wyn L, 10, 52, 60, 72, 95, 136–138, 145, 161, 164, 212, 255, 306
Programmable vision systems, 238, 239–240, 292
Programming courses for schools, 118
Programming research, 66, 118, 124, 125, 176, 181
Prolog, 219, 225, 268, 308
PROMPT, 115
Protocol, alternating bit, 145
Protocol implementation assessment, 205–208
Protocol standards, 203–209, 250–254, 306
Protocols, 145–146
Psychology, 58, 85
Public key cryptosystems, 210, 215, 226
Punched cards, 18, 22, 35, 44, 46, 50, 69, 70, 94, 97, 101, 113, 115
Pyatt, E C (Ted), 10

Quest Automation Ltd, 168, 170, 305

Radio Division, 9, 26, 27, 30, 52
Radioimmunoassay, 229
Rayner, Dr D (Dave), 10, 147, 205–209, 250–254, 306
Reading aids for the blind, 84
Real Time Club, 130
Reason, Roger J, 60, 102, 152
Rees, Neville W, 78
Reliability of computers, 65
Rengger, Ralph E, 60, 83, 84, 175, 241, 277, 278
Requirements Boards, 121–123, 155, 170, 172, 184, 199, 201, 202, 227, 247, 248
Retinal images, 86
Robertson, A D J, 60, 90
Robinson, Malcolm G, 150, 152, 158, 307
Rothschild report, 121–123, 336
Russell, W (Willy), 152
Russian, 93–100

Safety-critical software, 269
SCANAFORM, 171
Scantlebury, Roger A, 52, 60, 63, 64, 106, 107, 128, 130–136, 142–146, 178, 203, 307
Schofield, Dr David, 10, 118, 189, 190, 192, 193, 236, 243, 250, 281, 307
School timetables, 63
Schools programming courses, 118
Science Museum, 9, 10, 39, 48, 297, 316, 339
Scientific and Industrial Research, Department of, 11, 61
Scowen, Roger S, 66, 124, 125, 184, 189, 192, 194, 195, 219, 225, 243, 268, 308
Scrapbook, 119, 133, 144, 152–158, 191, 244, 282, 285, 307, 317
Searle, Celia, later Mrs Kirkby, 10, 99, 152, 158, 164, 169
Serco Group plc, 249
Sexton, John H, 124, 125, 176, 181, 182
Ship fairing, 112, 300
SHREWD, 148–152, 307, 317
SID, 174, 237
Signatures,
  computer verification of, 167–170, 239, 293, 305
  digital, 211, 215, 255
Simulation, 53, 128, 136–139, 296, 306, 308, 310
Smart cards, 214, 276
Smith, Adrian C K, 283
Smith, Dr G K, 90
SNIPE, 192
SOAP, 192, 308
Software engineering, 182, 219–227, 268–273, 292, 308, 313
Software protection device, 219, 225–227, 293, 313
Solomonides, Dr C M (Costas), 138, 209, 308
Speech recognition, 62, 172–175, 236, 303, 306, 307
St Dunstan's, 84
Stephens, Angela M, 153, 179
Stevens, Michael J, 10, 158, 237, 238, 240, 274
Stoddart, Dr Colin T H, 60, 107
Stringer, John B, 72
Stuart, Dr Peter R, 10, 60, 104, 107, 308
Symm, Dr George T, 10, 185, 223, 232, 261, 266, 309
Symm, Hilary J, 185, 238, 240, 274
Syntactic metalanguage, 224, 308
Szanser, Dr Adam J M, 60, 95, 164, 309
Szczygiel, Bronia M, 253, 256

Teaching machines, 64, 65, 178
Teddington Hall, 9, 18, 28, 49, 126
Telerobotics, 240–242
Teletext, 143, 158, 164

Test assembly, 25, 28, 30, 31, 40, 41, 289, 295, 296, 299, 300, 314, 316
Thomas, Cathy M, 236, 277, 278
Thomas, Dr H A, 26–30, 309
Tizard, R H (Dick), 52, 55, 63, 67, 310
Tokens and Transactions Control Consortium, 213, 254
Tondryk, George T, 192, 282
Tootill, G C (Geoff), 141, 329
TOPIC, 245
Tortoise, Hungarian, 91, 92
    NPL, 91, 92
Trade and Industry, Department of, 121, 248, 255, 259
Trend Report, 61, 336
Triad Computing Systems Ltd, 157, 171
TRON, 9, 27
TTCC, 213, 254
Turing, Dr Alan M, 10, 15–33, 38, 40–43, 46, 50, 93, 120, 182, 285, 296, 310, 314, 316
Turney, Margaret, 99

UK Accreditation Service (UKAS), 252
Ullmann, Dr Julian R, 60, 83, 118, 166, 311
Usability, 275–280
Uttley, Dr A M, 42, 50, 57, 58, 60, 62, 63, 73, 74, 80, 85, 91–93, 100, 117, 119, 124, 312

Vaswani, Dr Peter K T, 10, 60, 100, 216, 218, 241, 264, 312
VAX, 113, 281, 282
VDM, 257, 272
Verisign, 169–170, 239, 293
Vickers, Tom, 10, 12, 37, 45, 71, 113, 189, 313
Viewdata, 159
Vision systems, 239–240

Wage accounting, 54
Wallard, Dr Andrew J, 10

Walsh, Carol A, 60, 102, 135, 140, 144
    and see Corby, Mrs Carol A
Wanek, R (Bob), 171, 172
Warren Spring Laboratory, 77, 300
WATER, 192, 193, 308
Watson, R S (Bob) 10, 60, 170, 235, 236, 278
Webber, Brenda, later Mrs James, 45, 71, 114, 115, 313
Wells, Dr T D (Tim), 205
Whelan, S (Steve), 60, 95, 164
Whittle, Peter B, 179
Wichmann, Dr Brian A, 10, 60, 118, 125, 134, 166, 184, 189–192, 194–197, 219–227, 243, 268–273, 313
Wilkes, Prof. M V, 24, 35, 36, 50, 120, 331
Wilkinson, Dr J H (Jim), 12, 24, 25, 27–37, 50, 67, 109, 110, 184–186, 228, 260, 285, 314, 331
Wilkinson, Keith, 60, 128, 135, 144, 152
Wilkinson, Dr Peter T, 10, 124, 125, 128, 132, 135–137, 145, 196, 216, 218, 221, 268, 315
Williams, Prof. F C, 24, 35, 36, 50, 54, 331
Williams, Fiona J, 10, 255, 256
Wilson, Jackie, 179
Wilson, W (Willie), 27, 35, 52, 315
Womersley, J R, 11–14, 18, 19, 22–30, 49, 315, 332
Woodger, M (Mike), 10, 12, 24, 30–31, 38, 39, 66, 70, 111, 124, 159, 176, 182, 219, 222, 236, 316, 329, 331, 332
Woodroffe, E P H (Pat), 52, 60, 72, 78, 128, 135, 189, 316
World Wide Web, 155, 283
Wright, Michael A, 10, 27, 39, 52–54, 126, 317

X.25, 145, 245
Xionics Ltd, 157

Yardley, Dr John P, 171, 175
Yates, Dr David M, 60, 95, 118, 148, 152, 158, 317

Zeng Hua-Xin, Dr, 206